The structure of bus

The structure of business

Martin W Buckley

PITMAN PUBLISHING
128 Long Acre, London WC2E 9AN

© Longman Group UK Ltd 1985

First published in Great Britain 1985
Reprinted 1986, 1987

British Library Cataloguing in Publication Data

Buckley, Martin W.
  The structure of business
  1. Business enterprises
  I. Title
  338.7'024658 HD2731

ISBN 0-273-02593-7

Produced by Longman Singapore Publishers Pte Ltd.
Printed in Singapore.

Contents

Series foreword

I am more than pleased to note that the increasing popularity of the secretarial examinations of the London Chamber of Commerce and Industry, Commercial Education Scheme, has led to a publisher feeling justified in launching a series of books specifically designed to meet our syllabus requirements.

In 1956 the Commercial Education Scheme introduced a comprehensive and progressive scheme of secretarial qualifications which now range from the Secretarial Studies Certificates, through the Private Secretary's Certificate, to the high levels of the Private Secretary's Diploma. The standards were set high, but were a realistic interpretation of the demands by employers of their employees at different points in their careers. The success of this policy is seen in the increasing numbers of candidates from centres in the UK and overseas and with the very considerable public recognition by Press, Radio and Television when the Secretary of the Year Award is announced on the basis of the candidate achieving the best all-round success in the Private Secretary's Diploma.

May I wish all potential students every success, and hope that they and their teachers will find considerable help in this book.

R. W. Cattell, MA, FESB, MBIM
Director of the Commercial Education Scheme
London Chamber of Commerce and Industry.

Preface

The aim of the book is to provide an adequate text for those students studying 'Structure of Business' as part of the series of examinations leading to the London Chamber of Commerce Private Secretary's Certificate. Its success must be judged primarily by how well it meets that purpose. The book may also be of value to students studying for awards of other examining bodies where integration of material from a wide range of business subjects is required – for example Business and Technician Education Council (BTEC) national awards.

However, a word of warning is in order. No textbook can ever tell the students all they need to know. Furthermore, textbooks rapidly become dated. The good student will draw upon a variety of other sources – not least their own experiences – but also the comments of their teachers and publications such as *The Times, Financial Times, Guardian* and *The Economist*. The author has also found HM Treasury *Economic Progress Reports*, Lloyds Bank *Economic Bulletins*, and the various bank reviews a valuable source of additional information.

In writing this book I have drawn upon many years of teaching experience. I owe a debt of gratitude to many of my colleagues at Huddersfield Polytechnic who, often unwittingly, have influenced my thoughts and ideas. Thanks must also go to Christine and Jackie who so painstakingly deciphered and typed my notes, and the London Chamber of Commerce and Industry for permission to use past questions from the 'Structure of Business' examination paper. But most of all I wish to thank my wife and boys for the patience with which they have borne 'the pangs of authorship'. Without their help this book would still have been a figment of the author's imagination.

Martin W. Buckley
March 1984

Acknowledgements

We are grateful to the following for permission to reproduce copyright material:

The Controller of Her Majesty's Stationery Office for our Fig. 2.1 "Option A network – A commercial Railway". From the Serpell Report "Railway Finances".

Setting the scene

Part I

The mixed economy
Chapter 1

All economies, regardless of the stage of their development, or their political complexion, have to answer three fundamental questions:

1. What commodities should be produced? Remember the resources available within any economy are limited and therefore the decision to produce one commodity means that others will not be produced.

2. How will these goods and services be provided? We have to decide who will produce these goods, and what methods of production should be used.

3. How will we distribute these goods among the population? Various groups within the community will all make competing claims for consideration. How much should we give to consumers, business or government?

Economic systems

The questions asked above can be answered in different ways. One way is to allow the community, through the State, to make these decisions. Such systems are often termed 'planned' or 'command' economies. The USSR is often used as an example of this system. Alternatively, we can create a system where decisions are taken by the individual rather than the State. The State plays a passive role, interfering with private decisions as little as possible. Community interest is best served, it is said, by individuals following their own interests. The United States is cited as the economy nearest to this system. Such systems are variously referred to as capitalist *laissez-faire* or free enterprise.

Free enterprise system

The first distinguishing feature of this system is the private ownership of capital. Any of us can purchase whatever tools of production, equipment, buildings, or stock needed to carry on business, or for other private purposes. We can amass and dispose of these assets just as we like so as to maximise our own interests.

Secondly, free enterprise emphasises freedom of choice or entrepreneurship. By freedom of choice we mean you are free to choose your own job and to decide what goods and services you should buy. Businesses or enterprises have a similar freedom. They may buy whatever resources they wish, use them however they want to, enter those markets which they believe to be the most profitable, and generally organise their affairs as they think best.

Yet another important characteristic of free enterprise is competition. Firms compete with one another for our business; moreover, having obtained it they cannot even then be sure of it for the future. Firms have to ensure that they provide goods and services that the consumer likes at prices that are competitive, and if they do not they will very quickly go out of business!

Lastly, capitalism's controlling mechanism is the 'market', and as traditionally the Government plays a passive role – not interfering – we can say the 'free market'. It is in the free market – in which businesses and individuals buy and sell goods and services – that prices are determined.

The price system

The price system is the means by which the three basic questions we asked at the beginning of this chapter are answered under free enterprise. The price system works by allocating a value to all goods and services available within that society. In essence we are asking ourselves how much are we willing to pay for land, labour, capital, raw materials or the goods and services produced with them. If more of product X is wanted, the price of this commodity tends to rise – a green-light situation for businessmen indicating that they can earn high profits here. Similarly, when the demand for product X falls, prices fall – a red-light situation for businessmen. They will quickly seek other production possibilities which will yield a better return on their investment. By this means the decisions of business are brought into line with the decisions of consumers.

Let us look at how the price system answers our three basic questions. What goods and services this society will produce is determined by the importance consumers attach to individual products. The higher they value the product, the more they are willing to pay, and as we have seen, producers will move in accordance with these wishes.

How will these goods and services be produced? Remember we are looking at a competitive market, where efficiency is rewarded by sales and profits, and inefficiency by losses and eventual bankruptcy. Firms seek to produce at the least cost possible; they will seek out the best available combination of raw materials, technology and labour. It may be possible to vary the raw material input – in many cases a wooden spoon may be just as useful as a plastic spoon. Moreover, labour and technology may be interchangeable. Consider the position of the typist and the word processor. The higher the cost of an input the more sparingly it will be used and the greater the search for a substitute.

Finally, the question of how these goods should be distributed among the population is determined by the income the individual has available. The greater his income the more the consumer is able to buy. But that income is dependent upon what resources he owns and how effectively he uses them. The resources may be physical – ownership of land or plant and equipment will yield an income. Others will obtain an income by selling their labour to someone else. The amount they will receive will depend on intelligence, training, work effort, and often just a bit of luck.

The effects of the free enterprise system are difficult to quantify. Individuals have the freedom of how to use their resources, both as businessmen and consumers, but because of inequalities in the power which individuals have this may be used to the detriment of the consumer or the employee. We may be sold inferior goods and have little right of redress; we may be asked to work in unsafe conditions with the alternative being to lose our jobs. Yet again, the atmosphere and rivers may be polluted by effluent from factories. Where these inequalities of power, income and wealth are extreme, it is impossible to argue that the satisfaction of society has been maximised.

Resources are used to produce those goods and services for which there is the greatest demand, but arguably this may be against the best interests of society as a whole. Demand for pornographic material or guns may be great, but it is difficult to argue that the supplying of these demands is in the best interests of society. Additionally, the free enterprise system does not ensure that certain essential services, for example police, fire brigades and hospitals that are required by society, are provided adequately.

Market forces ensure that it is the most efficient users of resources who survive, that is, those who obtain the most cost-effective labour, the cheapest raw materials, and those who find the most efficient production methods. Yet competition may mean that the size of the operating unit is not the most efficient, and financial savings could be made by increasing the size of the firm.

Lastly, while it is possible for the economy to run itself with the minimum of government interference, it is then impossible to guarantee full employment and stable prices or economic growth.

Central planning

Central planning was a concept developed and extended by Marx. Horrified by the social injustice and degradation of the worker caused by the nineteenth-century British factory system, he argued that the only remedy was control by the State. Such a system was called a command economy, because there was a lack of choice. The State owned the country's resources, it owned and operated industry. The individual was subservient to the State which took decisions in what it perceived to be the best interest of the whole community. The State rather than the consumer was sovereign, and decided what and how to produce the goods and services, and moreover, who should receive these goods and services.

So the centrally planned economy seeks to avoid the worst excesses of the free enterprise system. The market imperfections of the free enterprise system certainly do not exist. Inherited wealth does not create economic power. Nor do high levels of unemployment exist. But the system does have its problems. Such economies claim to maximise the welfare of the people more than free enterprise, but the State may make entirely different judgements on what the consumers want to what the consumers themselves may choose. Thus in the 1930s several million people in Russia starved to death because of a State decision to transfer resources from agriculture to business in order to build up the country's industrial base.

Nor must the difficulties of planning a whole country be underestimated. A vast amount of information on a whole multitude of issues must be collected, collated, and analysed. Inevitably, there are delays before the information is filtered to the officials responsible for making a decision. Moreover, these decisions may be taken by officials who are far removed from the 'problem', have little real knowledge of the 'problem', and do not have to pay for their errors of judgement.

The mixed economy

We have discussed two extreme economic systems, but no country fits nicely into the patterns described so far. In the United States, most often used as the example of free enterprise, the Government has intervened in the economy to protect the employee and the consumer, to control business and regulate the level of economic activity. Conversely, in the USSR features of the market system exist. Farmers are allowed to sell a part of their produce for profit in local markets. People are free to choose their own occupation. Consumers are given freedom of choice as to what goods and services to buy from those which are available.

All economies are, in fact, a mixture of both the free enterprise and the planned systems. Yet, as we have seen the mixture can vary, moreover, it may vary within an individual economy over a period of time. Thus in the United Kingdom (UK) central planning assumes more importance when we have a Socialist rather than a Conservative government in power. Again the UK was, during the Second World War, one of the most highly planned economies ever seen.

The UK and France are often cited as examples of the mixed economy. While many of the decisions relating to what goods and services should be produced, how they should be produced and who should receive them are decentralised (i.e. left to the market) the State does intervene in many ways.

1. Public goods and services – the price mechanism is unable to supply certain goods and services satisfactorily. Examples would include defence, the fire service, law courts, and prisons, though the list is very much longer. These cannot be provided on a private basis because an individual could refuse to pay the provider of the service and yet still benefit from that service. These services, then, provide benefits which are indivisible and are shared by everyone. Thus the State takes over the provision of these services and finances them out of taxation.

2. Merit goods – but the State goes further and may very well finance services out of taxation which could be, and are, provided by the market system in other countries. For example, in the United States the Health Service is financed and run by private organisations. In the UK we have a state-run National Health Service. Education is provided by the State in the UK and many other countries, yet it is possible to provide education through the market system. Consider the British public school system (which are actually private schools financed by the parents of the pupils attending those schools).

What is not certain is that if left to the market sufficient of these services will be provided. Moreover, there is a benefit to society from having a healthy, well-educated workforce or a good system of roads and motorways.

3. Transfer payments – not only does the Government raise money through taxes but it redistributes some of this to different groups of people. Money raised through taxes on income or expenditure may be used to help people who are unemployed, pensioners, or those with large families. Other possibilities would be to give grants encouraging firms to invest, or helping a firm in financial difficulties. To the extent that rich people will buy different goods and services to poor people, and that individual companies will make different investment decisions, transfers of this kind distort the market.

4. Subsidised goods – nationalised industries sell their services on the open market. Some are successful and make a profit (British Gas Corporation made a profit in 1980 of £710 m., while the British

National Oil Corporation (BNOC) made £309 m., and British Telecom
£181 m.) others are not so fortunate. British Steel made a loss of
£665 m. in 1980, British Leyland £387 m., and the National Coal Board
£186 m., losses which of course the taxpayer has to make good. These
amounts paid by the taxpayer are really a subsidy to the industry
allowing it to sell its product at a price less than cost. The reasons why
this should be allowed are so complex and so important that the next
section is devoted entirely to a consideration of state enterprise.

State enterprise

When talking of state enterprise it is simple to think just of the large
nationalised industries (or public corporations as they are called in the
UK). Yet they number many more as Table 1.1 indicates. A list of
nationalised industries in other Western European countries would
reveal distinct similarities. For different reasons and in a variety of
ways many countries have taken over large parts of the energy,
transport, and communication industries.

Table 1.1   British state industries

Profit-makers	Loss-makers
British Gas	British Steel
British National Oil Corporation	British Leyland Limited
British Telecom*	National Coal Board
Bank of England	British Airways
Airports Authority*	Atomic Energy
Cable and Wireless*	British Rail
Post and National Giro	National Water Council
Central Electricity Generating Board	British Shipbuilders
National Research and Development	National Enterprise Board
Corporation	National Bus Company
Docks Board*	National Freight Company*
Crown Agents	
Waterways Board	

*Since returned to private ownership.

The debate over public ownership occurs for both economic and
political reasons. In the UK nationalisation is associated with the
Labour Party's desire to create a more socialist society. Conservative
politicians, conversely, would seek to avoid further nationalisation or
even roll back the frontiers.

The reasons for nationalisation

1. We have already noted that there may be goods and services which
would not be produced if the decision was left to the forces of the

market. The cost of providing electricity for people in remote districts is such that it could not and would not be provided commercially. Many of the commuter services around London are uneconomic. Social justice may be the reason why governments are anxious to provide the service. Alternatively, practical considerations such as the consequent reduction in road congestion, road accidents, and even pollution may decide the issue.

Many nationalised industries are capital intensive, accounting for approximately 20 per cent of the total investment in Britain during 1975. It is doubtful whether these industries, if in private hands, could raise the necessary finance for development. Moreover, the profitability of these industries may be insufficient to attract the necessary investment. Consider the falling demand for rail services, the competition and over-capacity in the steel or shipbuilding industries. Without government aid these industries would not provide the goods and services required. Nationalisation ensures that the benefits of the Government's investment accrue to society as a whole, rather than to private shareholders. Similar arguments are used where the Government steps in to bail out firms in financial difficulties. In recent years the Government has taken major shareholdings in both British Leyland and British Petroleum in return for providing much-needed financial assistance.

2. Strategic arguments may also lead to nationalisation. Energy, transport, and communications are needed to fight a war successfully, or merely to ensure unimpeded economic growth. Doubts about the ability of the private sector, especially if controlled from abroad, to guarantee these services will result in, at a minimum, state interference if not outright nationalisation.

3. In later chapters we will see that governments have a number of economic objectives, such as maintaining stable prices or high and stable levels of economic activity. The attainment of these objectives may be found more easy by a government which has increased its control over large sectors of the economy as a result of nationalisation. Thus when the State finds that private businessmen are not investing sufficient funds to maintain high levels of employment and economic activity they may try to make good the deficiency by increasing their own investment expenditure in the nationalised industries. Or perhaps the Government wishes to reduce the current level of pay settlements – how better to do it than by ensuring the public sector workers receive only what the Government believes to be desirable? Yet again poorer regions and isolated communities may be helped by the Government deciding to maintain the uneconomic operations of nationalised industries in those areas.

4. Nationalisation can also permit economies of scale to be realised. Competition between private gas companies would result in a multiplicity of distribution systems. A unified system for gas or electricity supply throughout the whole country would require just one distribution system resulting in lower prices to the consumer. The integration of the steel industry's activities so that they are all carried out on the same site will again result in savings – savings in terms of heat and transport. Nationalisation also permits the use of larger, more efficient production units, or perhaps even administration units. Of course it is not necessary to nationalise the gas or electricity industry to obtain these advantages of size, they could be achieved just as effectively by a private organisation. The argument against leaving the industry in private hands would be that it was a monopoly – capable of holding the consumer to ransom, and charging high prices so as to make large profits.

Nationalisation may be defended on other grounds as well as those listed above. It allows the Government to lead by example, to encourage research and development and better labour relations, it can ease the problems of a declining industry. Again, foreign control of basic industries may be unacceptable to developing countries because decisions relating to those industries are taken outside the country and not necessarily in that country's best interests.

Yet public enterprise is not without drawbacks. Nationalisation is seen as resulting in a restriction of consumer choice. This arises out of its monopoly position in the industry. However, this need not necessarily be so. In Britain private and public airlines, steel-makers and bus companies exist alongside one another.

The existence of a private sector alongside a public sector goes some way towards damping the criticism that nationalised industries are not faced with competition – remember competition is admired because it provides an incentive to operate efficiently and make the best use of the available resources. Competition also exists between industries, gas competes with coal, electricity and oil, as does rail with road transport.

Yet the incentive to compete may not be so great as in private industry. A firm that fails to make a profit will ultimately be dissolved. The nationalised industry is under no such threat. It is able to rely on handouts from the taxpayer to subsidise its loss-making operations.

Inefficiency is also sometimes thought to creep into state enterprise for other reasons. Many are very large-scale organisations serving millions of consumers spread over a wide area. There are obvious problems in administering such units. Communication may be slow or inefficient; co-ordination of activities takes time and money, while public accountability often results in excessive control mechanisms.

The relationship with government may also cause inefficiency. Government objectives may conflict with those of the industry, important investment decisions may be deferred, or uneconomic operations in an area of high unemployment be retained. Perhaps the real criticism here should be levelled, not at the industry, but at the Government.

Privatisation

Since May 1979 a major aim of the Conservative Government has been to reduce the size of the public sector. The return of assets and activities to the public sector plays an important part in this policy. The Government believes that exposure to competition can dramatically improve the efficiency with which these activities are undertaken. The process of privatisation has been achieved by:

1. *The sale of shares on the Stock Exchange, e.g. British Aerospace, Cable and Wireless, Amersham International, Britoil, British Telecom.*

2. *Sales to management/employees, e.g. the National Freight Company.*

3. *Sales of physical assets, e.g. land owned by New Towns Development Corporations, and Regional Water Boards.*
4. *Joint ventures, e.g. GKN and British Steel, have a subsidiary called Allied Steel and Wire Limited, British Rail have merged their hovercraft services with those of Hover Lloyd and formed a new company Hover Speed.*

5. *Contracting out of public services, e.g. refuse disposal in Southend and Peterborough is now undertaken by private firms rather than by the local authority. The Government is encouraging the development of private hospitals and the contracting out of catering and laundry services within the National Health Service to private firms.*

6. *The abolition of statutory monopolies, e.g. the Post Office with those of gas and electricity services also being planned.*

Summary

We are unlikely to reach any firm conclusion about the superiority of one system over another. While the argument is conducted in the language of the economist, at heart the dispute is political. It is about the role of the State within an economy and the freedom of the individual. If you believe that a high degree of equality is required within society you should be willing to sacrifice some of the economic advantages of free enterprise to this ideal. Equally, advocates of free enterprise have to suffer the problems and limitations of the market.

In the UK we believe that the mixed economy with its particular blend of private and public enterprise is right for us. A large measure of individual freedom exists, but within a framework of checks and balances instituted by the State. However, this blend was not always right for us, nor would it be correct to assume that it is best for others. In particular, developing countries may benefit from a higher degree of central planning than exists in the UK, for they may have neither the political processes nor the economic framework (adequate communication and transportation) necessary for free enterprise to be successful.

Examination questions

1. Explain how economic wants are satisfied and scarce resources allocated under:
   (a) a system of free enterprise;
   (b) a command (centrally planned) economy.

2. What do you understand by the term 'free enterprise' or 'capitalism'? What is the role of the price mechanism in a free enterprise economy?

3. In what ways does the State intervene in a mixed economy and for what reasons?

4. Using examples drawn from your own country explain why state ownership has occurred.

5. By reference to your own country outline the extent to which the Government is involved in the economy through public enterprise undertakings.   *(PSC 1979, 1981)*

6. What do you understand by 'the economic problem'? How do different countries/economic systems attempt to resolve it?

The structure of business: I

Chapter 2

The private sector

Within a mixed economy there are numerous organisations that have been created to satisfy our demands for goods and services. In this chapter we will be looking at the objectives and structures of these organisations.

Table 2.1 shows that such organisations exist in both the public and private sector. Within the private sector, the organisation may take one of several forms, for example, sole trader, partnership, or company. The public sector's commercial activities, e.g. (gas, electricity, coal, rail) are normally undertaken by 'public corporations'. Other state activities – the provision of education, defence, aid to industry, or local services, to name but a few, are provided by central or local government administrative units. These administrative units are the subject of separate chapters.

Table 2.1   Public and private sector organisations

Organisations		
Private sector	**Public sector**	
Business units	**Business units**	**Administrative units**
Sole trader	Public corporations	Central government
Partnership		Local government
Limited companies		
Public		
Private		
Co-operatives		
Mixed enterprise		

Firms in the private sector are owned by individuals or groups of individuals. Often these individuals work for, and rely on, the firm for their living. Yet even if the owners do not work for that firm the profits generated by its activities may still make up a substantial part of their income. Thus we can say that the most fundamental objective of the firm in the private sector is to produce a profit for its owners. An economist would go further – he would argue that the firm will try to maximise profits. For many firms, especially those in a competitive industry, this would undoubtedly be true, but for some, other objectives will rank as high as (perhaps even higher than) profitability. Examples could include being a market leader, sales maximisation, or ensuring the stability of the firm.

Let us now consider each of these business units in turn.

The sole trader (sole proprietorship)

The simplest form of business unit is the sole trader. This is a person who sets up his own business organisation. Characteristically he:

(a) provides the capital to run the business (though he may borrow from banks or relatives);

(b) works in the business by himself, though he may very well have other paid assistance;

(c) makes his own decisions – though he would be wise to seek advice from the numerous organisations set up to help small businesses;

(d) bears the risks of loss or receives the profits of his business.

The formal procedures required to set up as a sole trader are minimal. Having obtained premises and purchased whatever equipment is necessary, he may begin trading. Being his own boss, upon making a decision, he is able to implement that decision immediately – far more quickly than any other organisation, and thus adjust to change in market conditions rapidly. Relationships with customers and employees are usually good. The customer is personally known to the proprietor, and his orders are highly valued. The employee works alongside the owner and sees the importance of his own work in the organisation.

Often though, the small trader works long hours with few holidays. Ill-health is a constant worry. More importantly, should his business fail, he alone is liable for its debts. Creditors may seize not only business assets to recoup their debts but also his personal possessions such as house and car. This is termed 'unlimited liability'.

Despite the problems, sole traders are still the most numerous form of business. It is the method by which many businesses start. Sole traders are most common in those areas where the amount of capital required is small, and the customers expect a personal service.

Partnership

Should our sole trader wish to expand he may have to raise finance outside his immediate family. Permanent, or long-term finance is often difficult to obtain. The most usual source of finance for a sole trader – the commercial bank – is only willing to lend for shorter periods of time. The answer for most sole traders is to take a partner. The business thereupon is known as a partnership. This is defined by the Partnership Act 1890 as 'the relationship which subsists between persons carrying on a business in common with a view to profit'. Normally the membership of the partnership is restricted to twenty, though accountants and solicitors are not bound by this.

The business now has the advantage of extra capital available which can be used to expand the business activities. Additional help is now available, releasing our sole trader from the problem of long hours, no holidays, and illness. With the extra help there is the possibility of specialisation, one partner buying, the other selling, so that the sole trader is no longer a jack of all trades, but can become more proficient at one part of the business. In other ways the partnership is the same as the sole trader – the partners provide the finance, make the decisions, and normally work in the business. Good personal relationships still exist with customers and employees. Legal formalities are few and the degree of privacy high.

The major drawback of such businesses like that of the sole trader is unlimited liability. In fact, in some ways, the situation is worse. Partners are not only responsible for their own actions, they are responsible for the actions of their partners. Thus the foolish or untimely act of your co-partner may not only ruin the business but also deprive you of your personal possessions. Other potential difficulties may arise in obtaining the agreement of your co-partners on some issue. If this is not forthcoming it may very well result in the dissolution of the partnership. In fact, death, insanity, and bankruptcy, as well as disagreement, will result in the termination of the partnership agreement. To maintain the business as a going concern the continuing partner has the difficult task of finding money to buy out the other partners at short notice. Often to avoid these financial difficulties upon the death of a partner, each partner will insure the life of the other partner. In the event of this partner's death the partnership then receives a capital sum from the life assurance company which is used to pay off the family of the deceased partner. The surviving partner then becomes the sole owner of the firm.

A variation upon an ordinary partnership as described above is the limited partnership. In this organisation there is a partner whose liability is limited to the amount of money that he has invested in the firm. Should the firm go bankrupt the creditors cannot touch his personal (as opposed to business) assets. In return for this privilege the limited partner undertakes not to take part in the management of business. He may inspect the firm's financial records and tender advice to the partners involved in the day-to-day running of the business, but should he at any time involve himself in its management or administration he will lose his 'limited' status and become an ordinary partner. The Partnership Act 1907 requires at least one ordinary partner in any partnership business. Thus there is always at least one partner who is fully liable for the debts of the business.

Partnership is a form of organisation which is used by many small businesses. It is always the common form of organisation for professional people such as accountants, lawyers, doctors and dentists.

The limited liability company

One major problem of both sole traders and partnerships as forms of business organisations was the lack of capital to finance expansion. Yet there are many people who have small amounts of money which they may be willing to invest in industry. The overriding consideration of these people is the safety of their personal fortunes. During the Industrial Revolution in nineteenth-century Britain many were the stories of once-rich families being reduced to poverty by the partnership principle of unlimited liability. It is not surprising there was an unwillingness to invest in industry or commerce.

The answer was provided by the 'joint-stock' company which allowed people to invest their money without unlimited liability or involvement in the management of business. The earliest examples were the East India or the Hudson's Bay Company created by Royal Charter. Parliament later granted limited liability to companies concerned with transport – canals and railways. But the procedure was cumbersome and costly, and eventually in 1855 Parliament enacted the first Companies Act. This gave general protection for shareholders who invested in a company which was registered as having limited liability.

The businessman who wishes to convert his firm into a company does so by submitting certain documents to the Registrar of Companies. (The advantages and disadvantages of partnerships and limited companies as forms of business organisation are shown in Table 2.2.). The documents are examined, and if they comply with the requirements of the Companies Act the formation of the company will be registered. The major documents required by the Registrar are listed below.

1. The Memorandum of Association
This document gives basic information of interest to shareholders and other people who may deal with the proposed company. It contains six clauses:

(a) The name clause.   The name by which the company chooses to be known. If liability is to be limited this must be followed by the word 'Limited' where the company is private and by 'Public Limited Company' (normally abbreviated to PLC) in the case of a public company. As a matter of law, this name must be displayed outside all the company's places of business and used in all its correspondence. It is the name in which the company sues or is sued.

(b) The registered office clause.   This indicates whether the company is registered in England, Wales, or Scotland and its address. This is necessary to ensure that important documents do reach the company and its officers.

(c) The limited liability clause.   Where the promoters wish the company to have the benefit of limited liability they must state this fact (it is possible to form unlimited companies by the omission of this clause, moreover an ordinary partnership that exceeds twenty partners will automatically become an unlimited company and be judged by company law).

   This clause is notice to all who deal with the company that in the event of it failing, it is only the assets of the company that are available for the payment of the creditors' debts.

(d) The capital clause.   The amount of share capital which the company can raise must be stated (the nominal capital) together with the value of the shares it is to be divided into, say £1, 50p, or 25p (nominal value). The word 'nominal' is used to indicate that this is the value of the capital quoted in the company's accounts. However, the price people are willing to pay for each share will depend upon the company's profits and prospects. Investors may be prepared to pay £1 for each 10p share in a prosperous company, but only 10p for a £1 share in a badly run, loss-making business.

(e) The 'objects' clause.   This clause indicates the purposes for which the company was formed, e.g. machine-tool engineering, retailing bakery, stockbroking, etc. By the *ultra vires* doctrine should a company enter into a contract beyond its powers that contract is of no effect: it is as though it had never been entered into. The justification for this clause is that it protects shareholders from directors and managers changing the scope of the company's future activities. Nowadays though, the protection given is largely illusory because the clause is phrased so widely that companies are only rarely prevented from entering into different kinds of business activity.

   Section 9(i) of the European Communities Act of 1972 changes the position for an innocent co-contractor by allowing him to enforce the *ultra vires* agreement against the company. In such a situation the company may require that any loss made by it should be made good by the directors who first entered into that illegal contract.

Table 2.2 The choice of business unit – A comparison between partnerships and limited companies

Partnerships	Limited companies
Formalities	
Formation by agreeement, oral or written No special formalities – little or no expense	Registration of documents as laid down by Companies Act. Procedure complex and often costly
No public documents to file Financial results not open to public inspection	Documents available to public, include Memorandum and Articles of Association as well as annual accounts
Dissolution normally by agreement of partners. Few formalities	Winding up by procedure laid down in Companies Act on agreement of members or creditors
Agreement of co-partners to be obtained before transferring interest to new partner (NB: difficulties in calculating value of share partnership)	Shares freely transferable (private companies may put restrictions on this). No problems over valuation where there is a Stock Exchange quotation
Personality and liability	
The partnership is not recognised as a separate legal person – it can only sue or be sued through the partners Property must be vested in names of partners	Recognised as having an existence separate from that of its members. It can sue or be sued, purchase land, or raise money in its own name
Normally partners have unlimited liability (NB: exception of limited partner). All assets, business and personal may be seized to satisfy creditors' claims	Where the company includes the word 'limited' in its name the shareholder's liability is limited to his invested capital. Personal assets are not at risk
Membership	
Normally 2–20 (NB: exceptions, e.g. accountants/solicitors may have more, a banking partnership limited to 10)	Any number in excess of 2 (NB: private companies may limit the number of shareholders)
Power to contract	
Fixed by Partnership Agreement, but can be altered by agreement (express, or implied from course of dealing)	Laid down in Memorandum and Articles of Association. These can only be altered by procedure in Companies Acts.

Table 2.2—Cont.

Partnerships	Limited companies
Control	
General partners have the authority to act as agent of the firm. The contracts entered into bind his co-partners (a limited partner will lose his special status if he acts for the firm)	Shareholders vest power to manage firm in the directors. Directors must act in accordance with Memorandum and Articles – otherwise liable to the company for their actions
The organisation has the ability to react quickly to changed circumstances	Changes in policy are made after consultation between managers, directors, and (sometimes) shareholders
Partners may specialise in different areas of business. But often deficient in financial or marketing skills	Specialist managers employed. Non-executive director of wide business experience may be appointed to the board
Finance	
Normally available from family, friends, and bank. Traditionally, partnerships limited to those areas where little capital is needed, e.g. retailing, building, catering, and the professions	May pool the resources of large numbers of small investors. Has greater ability to borrow from other sources
Lack of finance often prevents growth and the benefits of increased size are not obtained	Growth not retarded by lack of finance and economies of scale may be realised (NB: there may also be diseconomies of scale!)
Relationships	
Close links can be maintained between the firm, its suppliers and customers. Similarly morale, motivation, and employee/employer relationships often better	Sheer numbers of suppliers, customers, and employees may preclude same relationships developing
Taxation	
Partners pay income tax on profits	Company pay corporation tax on all profits (including retained earnings). Shareholders pay income tax on their dividends

(f) The association clause.   This is a declaration made by those signing it that they wish to form a company and will accept the shares allocated to their names.

2. The Articles of Association

This document refers to the internal constitution of the company. It gives information on such issues as the rights of the shareholders, the powers of directors, and the holding of meetings. While it is possible to draw up your own set of internal regulations, this is not necessary because the Companies Act 1948, Table A, Schedule 1, provides a specimen set of articles. These articles are eminently fair to all interests and will automatically apply should no other Articles of Association be registered.

3. Statements required by the Registrar

The Registrar of Companies also requires a statement of nominal capital (a tax is payable on this – £0.50 per cent), a list of directors, their addresses, together with a statement indicating their willingness to act as directors and also a declaration that the Companies Acts have been complied with.

Should the Registrar of Companies be satisfied with the documents presented to him, he will issue a certificate of incorporation, making the business a separate legal entity with a life quite separate from that of its shareholders. At this stage a private company may commence business and enter into any contract allowed by its 'objects' clause. There is, however, a further requirement before a public limited company can start business – it must obtain a trading certificate.

The trading certificate is again issued by the Registrar of Companies on receipt of documents indicating that the company has the necessary financial stability to start business. Where the company is raising capital by issuing shares to the public the company must submit a prospectus (i.e. the document inviting the public to buy shares in the business) to the Registrar and statements that the minimum capital necessary to run the business has been subscribed (this is as stated in the prospectus) and that directors have paid for their shares.

Where the promoters and directors can raise sufficient finance without appealing to the public, a statement in lieu of a prospectus (containing much the same information as the prospectus) will be submitted to the Registrar in addition to the statements mentioned above.

Prior to 1980 the distinction between a public and private company was enshrined in the 1947 Companies Act. This defined a private company as one having a membership of between two and fifty members (excluding past employees), restricting the right to transfer shares, and prohibiting the company inviting the general public to subscribe for shares. A public company was defined as one having a membership of seven or over, and not having any of the restrictions mentioned above. The Companies Act of 1980 redefined a public company – now more correctly referred to as a public limited company – as one which has an authorised capital of at least £50,000 and having at least two members.

Private companies are then defined as any companies which do not conform to the requirements of a public limited company. The prohibition on private companies inviting the general public to subscribe for shares was re-enacted, but the restrictions on transfer of shares and membership no longer apply. However, for the 762,000 private companies existing at the time of the Act there is no requirement that they change their articles and it is suggested that these restrictions will continue to apply.

The principle of limited liability has encouraged the development of extremely large firms, experiencing problems entirely different from those experienced by sole traders and partnerships. Ownership of large public limited companies is in the hands of perhaps thousands of shareholders. Obviously all these shareholders cannot be involved in the running of the firm, and in practice policy decisions are made by a board of directors and put into effect by salaried managers. There is, it is said, a divorce between ownership and control.

In principle there should be few problems arising out of the difference between ownership and control of the company. Control of the company lies in the hands of those owning shares in that company. Exercise of that control arises from meetings which the directors have to call for the shareholders to sanction their actions. Thus at the annual general meeting (AGM) which is held after the publication of the company's annual financial results, shareholders will scrutinise the performance of the company and the policy of the directors and vote upon the appointment of directors and the payment of dividends. Extraordinary general meetings and special general meetings will also be held periodically at the request of the shareholders or directors in order to discuss and vote upon urgent issues.

But to control the activities of directors is rather more difficult in practice. We have already noted that it is impossible for shareholders to take part in the running of the company (even if they wanted to). The very diffused nature of shareholdings also makes it impossible for the shareholders to act together and put pressure on the directors. Company meetings are held during working hours, often far away from where the investors live and work. It is not surprising that these meetings are normally poorly attended. The absence of a majority of shareholders from the meetings means that effective control of the company can be exercised with very much less than 51 per cent of the votes. Indeed the directors' own shareholdings may be sufficient to secure control of the company.

Perhaps the only group which could successfully challenge the power of directors would be the institutional shareholders. Pension funds, insurance companies, unit and investment trusts are big business.

Together these institutions account for nearly two-thirds of all purchases of ordinary shares. The size of the institutions and the importance of their holdings would in many cases give them the authority to demand a director on the board to represent their interests. Yet traditionally they have indicated their unwillingness to interfere in or become involved with the running of a company. Recently though, the institutional investor has seemed more willing to intervene in company affairs. In particular, where severance payments to ex-directors have been high, the decision of the board has been challenged. Take, for example, the Post Office Pension Fund which challenged in the courts, the 'golden handshake' of £650,000 offered by Associated Communications Corporation to its former Managing Director.

The divorce of ownership from control in a public limited company would not be so worrying if the objectives of shareholders and directors were the same, but often they are not.

The objectives of the investor are threefold. He wishes to ensure:

1. *Safety of capital* – that the value of his investment does not diminish through poor policy decisions or unforeseen changes in the market or technology.

2. *A good return on his investment* – many shareholders measure the success of the company by the size of the dividend cheque received annually. A consistently high dividend convinces them of the soundness of their investment. Yet a high dividend payment is not always possible. In Britain 60 per cent of all moneys needed for expansion come from retained profits. (But assuming the expansion is successful, investors will see the return through enhanced values of the shares on the Stock Exchange, and higher profits in later years.)

3. *Marketability* – it is no good your capital being safe and earning a high rate of return if the shares cannot readily be converted into cash.

Yet boards of directors and salaried managers may take a wider view to that of the investor, and although accepting the importance of profit as an objective believe that the following are just as important.

1. *Security* – the maximising of profits may bring risks which are unacceptable to the director (or salaried manager). His job depends on the continued existence of the company. From his point of view it is far better to under-achieve and to survive.

2. *Status and prestige* – directors may wish to be identified with a large company, a household name, or a market leader. One way this might be realised is by greater sales. Yet these extra sales may be unprofitable to the company because it has gone beyond the point of most efficient operation. Directors may also insist on

prestigious offices, or investment in projects which have a low profitability but give the company a high public profile.

3. *Power* – increased sales not only bring security but they also bring greater power. The director controls a larger organisation, more people are responsible to him. His power in the industry is also increased as competition from competitors becomes more muted.

The degree of incompatibility between the motives of the shareholder and director will obviously vary from company to company. Where directors have substantial shareholdings, the incompatibility is at a minimum, but where the board consists largely of executive directors drawn from the ranks of salaried managers, differences in objectives are likely to exist.

The board of directors

Overall control of the company is vested in the board of directors. Directors are appointed by the shareholders and therefore the shareholders can be said to have ceded control of the company to them. Whereas the function of the shareholders is to provide the finance necessary for the smooth running of the firm and to bear the risk of failure or success of the company, directors are responsible primarily for determining policy. Their function is to survey the environment within which their company works and to identify the threats and opportunities available to the company in future years. On this analysis is based the company's future strategy. Whatever the strategy it cannot be implemented without people, and consequently directors are vitally interested in (and responsible for) ensuring that the essential positions within the company, the senior staff, are filled by people of the highest calibre, and that the morale of the workforce generally is as high as possible. Finally, while the success of the directors' strategy or policy is measured by the financial results of the company, directors will also be concerned to see that the company has adequate reserves of cash (or near-cash items, e.g. finished goods or debtors) and that stringent controls on expenditure are maintained.

In exercising their duties, directors are sometimes likened to trustees because (by law) they owe duties of good faith and care to the company. In particular they must ensure that they use their power properly for the benefit of all shareholders, and that they avoid situations where there is a conflict between the company and their personal interest. Consequently, a director must disclose any financial interest he has in a contract entered into by the company.

A director is also required to exercise a reasonable standard of care in the course of his duties. What is a reasonable standard of care is variable depending upon the degree of, or particular, expertise of the director. Thus an executive director with accounting qualifications and responsibility for the financial function within a firm would be expected to exercise a far higher degree of skill in money matters than other directors.

The board of directors is headed by a chairman. He is the titular head of the company, responsible for the control of the directors' meetings and representing the company's interests in external affairs. It is normally, but not always, a part-time position, given to a man of wide business experience, capable of taking a more detached view of the company's activities than other directors.

The position of chairman is sometimes amalgamated with that of managing director; however, this is not to be recommended. The managing director is normally a full-time appointment, responsible to the board for the implementation of board policy and the daily running of the firm. Other directors may be full-time or part-time, executive or non-executive. Full-time directors tend to have executive responsibilities within that company, for example the production director will be head of the production function within the organisation. He takes part not only in deciding policy (as a director) but also seeing that it is implemented properly throughout the company. Part-time directors seldom have an executive function and are appointed because of their proven ability with other companies. They meet infrequently at board meetings and often have directorships with other companies at the same time.

Large companies also often employ part-time or non-executive directors. Important public figures – Members of Parliament or individuals associated with consumer interests may be appointed to lend respectability or trustworthiness to the company. Equally importantly these individuals may represent the company's interests outside the organisation.

Many more non-executive directors are appointed to the Board of Directors because of their skills and wide experience in company affairs. Being uninvolved in the day-to-day running of the business such directors are expected to contribute a broader, more independent view of any situation.

Some companies have also experimented with worker directors. Quite apart from giving Board deliberations wider views and greater breadth of experience the aim has also been to improve employer/employee relationships through (1) better communication with the workforce and (2) worker involvement in decision making at the highest levels. Union attitudes to 'worker directors' have varied. The Steel Unions have accepted seats on the group boards of British Steel Corporation whilst the Railway Unions rejected a similar offer of seats on the Board of British Rail. Generally, though the union movement's response has been unfavourable, with many of its leaders arguing that acceptance of directorships may be seen by the rank and file as a sell-out to the company. The position of the union official as a worker director certainly involves a conflict of interest in that he has to acquiesce to Board decisions which are against his members' interests.

Co-operatives

Consumer co-operatives
The Co-operative Wholesale Society (CWS) and the Co-operative
Retail Society (CRS) evolved during the nineteenth century. Their
objective was to eradicate the conflict of interest between the supplier
(who wished to sell at a high price) and the consumer (wanting to buy
at a low price). The members of the co-operatives are the consumers
who purchase its goods. They have the right to elect the management
committee which runs the business and share the profits made from its
operations. The 'shareholders' have only one vote each (regardless of
their investment in the society) which prevents sectional interests
gaining control and using it to their advantage.

In Britain the CRS consists of members of the CWS. It is from this
source that the CRS obtains its stock. The CWS provides the CRS with
the benefits of bulk buying which the societies could not hope to
achieve.

The CRS has experienced increasing competition from supermarkets
since the Second World War and its share of the market has been
decreasing. This can be attributed to lack of business expertise on the
part of its management committee and its salaried staff, together with
an inability to provide the necessary finance for expansion.

In the UK the Co-operative Bank, the Co-operative Insurance
Society, and the Nationwide Building Society are also examples of co-
operatives operating in the field of commerce. Abroad, farmers' co-
operatives for the purchasing of feed, fertilisers, and seed and the
marketing of animals and farm produce have also proved popular.

Worker co-operatives
Worker co-ownership in industry arose out of earlier attempts at
industrial democracy and worker participation. These co-operatives
take the form of a company which is limited by shares in which
workers have some degree of control over the policy and running of the
firm, they bear the risks of failure and reap the benefits of success.

Worker co-operatives, sometimes called producer co-operatives
flourish outside the UK. There is, for example, the very successful
Mondragon experiment in northern Spain. In the UK worker co-
operatives are not so popular. They have failed to find managers of the
right calibre, while capital finance has often been beyond the resources
of the worker-members. In virtually all cases, successful worker co-
operatives have started life as some other form of enterprise.

The means by which co-operatives have developed are various. The
initiative of Ernest Bader (see below) who gave his own firm to his
workforce and founded the Industrial Common Ownership Movement
is important. There are now over a dozen other firms run on similar
lines to Scott Bader Company Limited. Other businesses have been
sold to the workforce – Landsman Co-ownership (which produces

caravans) and the National Freight Corporation (privatised by the present Conservative Government) are examples of this. Within the shoe and textile industry there are still a number of producer co-operatives, throwbacks to those that were first developed in the latter part of the nineteenth century.

The most important development in common ownership recently though, has been those worker co-operatives created out of the remains of failed companies. The Meriden Motor Cycle Co-operative is one such scheme. Faced with the dole queue in times of rising unemployment the workers determined to band together and prevent the job losses by continuing the failed Triumph Motor Cycle business themselves. Because private sources are unwilling to accept the risk, finance for such ventures has inevitably been given by the Government directly, or indirectly, through the Manpower Services Commission. Aid has also been given under the auspices of the Industrial Common Ownership Act 1976 and the Co-operative Development Agency.

Scott Bader Company Limited

Ernest Bader started the firm of Scott Bader in 1920. It was the sole agent for a Swiss manufacturer of celluloid. Other products were added later, and by 1951 the company was a leading manufacturer of polyester resins, while also producing many other chemical products. It was a medium-sized business employing 161 people, a successful company which had made both Bader and his family prosperous. Yet Bader never forgot that this success and prosperity was achieved not by himself alone, but by the efforts of all the other workers in the business. Since its inception an employee profit-sharing scheme had existed, but in 1951 Bader decided to vest the ownership of his firm in the Scott Bader Commonwealth – which would be owned and controlled by the employees of Scott Bader Company Limited.

A constitution which governed not only the distribution of rights and powers within the organisation but also limited its freedom of action was agreed among the members as follows:

1. *The size of the organisation should not grow beyond 350 persons, 'so that every person can embrace it in his mind and imagination'. Alternatively, if the size of the firm did increase beyond that limit separate units organised on the lines of the Commonwealth should be set up.*

2. *Remuneration for work should not vary beyond a range of 1:7.*

3. *Members of the Commonwealth are partners, not employees, and although they may leave the firm at any time, they cannot be dismissed by their co-partners other than for gross personal misconduct.*

4. *The Board of Scott Bader Company Limited is fully accountable to the Commonwealth, which has the power to approve their appointment and determine their remuneration.*

5. *At least 60 per cent of the net profits shall be retained in the firm for taxation and self-finance. Up to 40 per cent of the net profits will be taken by the Commonwealth, half to be paid to those working within the company, and half to be given to charitable purposes outside the organisation.*

6. *None of the Scott Bader products shall be sold to customers who are known to use them for 'war-related' purposes.*

Public corporations

The essential feature of a public corporation is that the assets of an industry have been taken over by the State so that the industry is owned, managed, and controlled by the community. Public corporations, also known as nationalised industries, are only part of the public sector; as we have already seen, however, they are an important part. They employ 8 per cent of the working population and account for 11 per cent of the country's output.

Whereas the main objectives of a private firm are to provide goods and services which are demanded by society and thereby to survive, make a profit, and grow, the objectives of the public corporation are more complex. While public corporations are nationalised so as to ensure that certain goods and services were provided efficiently, it does at the same time have to pursue non-commercial goals.

Consider the case of British Rail. Efficiency may require the closing of several lines or the curtailing of the timetable, but economic and social effects upon that region may be devastating (see Fig. 2.1). Both the British Steel Corporation and the National Coal Board have faced similar decisions. Yet again the cost of supplying gas, water, or electricity to outlying districts may be far higher than the consumer could possibly afford to pay. But what would be the effects of depriving the community of these essential services?

On purely commercial grounds none of these services would be provided and yet, of course they are, on the insistence of the Government. The Government sees public corporations as a legitimate means of pursuing its wider economic and social objectives. Thus we may find that the Government in an attempt to lower the level of economic activity in the country may put off investment plans in public corporations. To protect the balance of payments, or help an 'infant' industry the Government may order public corporations to purchase British goods. In an attempt to reduce the level of inflation the

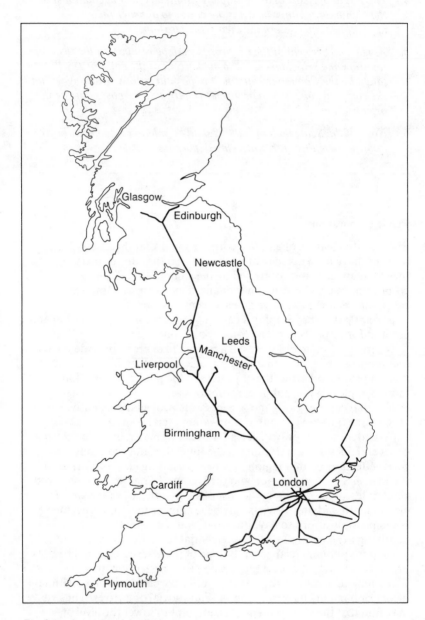

Fig. 2.1 A commercial railway.

Government may insist that nationalised industries make lower pay awards than those in the private sector, or hold the prices of their goods and services steady in spite of rising costs.

In all the above examples the Government has decided that the commercial gain accruing to the public corporation is outweighed by the public gain from a conflicting course of action. As these are political decisions it is then difficult to evaluate the performance of a public corporation solely in commercial terms. Rather, it should be judged having regard to the degree of government interference.

The degree of government interference in the running of the public corporations has, in the past, exacerbated the relationships between the two parties. The Government's response was to publish a White Paper, *Nationalised Industries* in 1978, which tried to clarify the position. It recommended:

1. That ministers should have the power to give specific directions to nationalised industries, where the national interest was affected.

2. Financial targets should be decided by corporations individually for a period of three to five years, and would to a great extent, determine the prices they charge.

3. Targets laid down will reflect:

    (a) the earning power of existing assets;

    (b) the required rate of return of 5 per cent on new investments;

    (c) marketing prospects for the industry;

    (d) the scope for improved productivity;
         but having regard for the social objectives of that industry.

The structure of public corporations
A public corporation has a distinct legal personality which arises from the Act which nationalised it. It can enter into contracts in its own name and be sued on these agreements.

The capital of the public corporation is owned by the Government and traditionally it is to the Government that the public corporations turn for extra finance. This has taken the form of subsidies out of general taxation to finance deficits on operations, borrowing for investment purposes, together with government subsidies and grants.

A public corporation is supervised by a government minister, who, as we have already seen, is able to give general directions to the industry regarding matters of public interest. The government minister is also empowered to appoint the members of the corporation's board.

In general terms the board is responsible for the day-to-day running of the corporation business, but the detailed powers of each board can be found in the Act of Nationalisation. It is the duty of the board to remain within these powers.

Control of the public corporations lies initially in the hands of a government minister who is responsible to Parliament. His role is twofold: first to represent and defend the views of the corporation in Parliament, and secondly to explain his own dealings with the board. Any MP may question him, but he is only expected to answer questions on policy matters, and certainly not on the day-to-day administration of the board's affairs. Greater accountability to Parliament is achieved through debates upon public corporations which follow the publication of their financial results. Investigations and reports from the All-Party Select Committee on Nationalised Industries are also available to MPs, as are the 'efficiency reports' on nationalised industries commissioned by the Government and prepared by the Monopolies and Mergers Commission.

Acts of nationalisation have recognised the need to make public corporations directly responsible to members of the public by the creation of Consumers' Councils. These councils normally have the right to be advised of any plans affecting customers, they may themselves give advice to the board on these plans, and protest legitimate consumer complaints. Councils also have the right to make representations to the appropriate government minister. In practice the effectiveness of this form of control is doubted. Members of the councils are appointed by the minister, and may not adequately reflect the interests of the consumer. Additionally, lack of finance and staff prevents councils from conducting their work effectively.

Mixed enterprise

The concept of mixed enterprise, or shared public and private ownership is not new. It involves an organisation operating within the private sector and governed by company law in which the State has a financial interest as a shareholder. The number of such enterprises increased considerably during the 1970s through state help to 'lame-duck' companies, e.g. British Leyland, the activities of the then NEB (National Enterprise Board), and the present Government's policy of privatisation.

The NEB, which was established in 1975, is the major vehicle by which the Government takes a stake in private industry. Its present guidelines require it to assist:

(a) firms exploiting or developing advanced technology;

(b) private undertakings in assisted areas;

(c) small firms generally.

This investment is to be undertaken wherever possible, in conjunction with private enterprise, and in any event the shareholding is to be disposed of as soon as is practicable.

The NEB's involvement in 'advanced technology firms' has prompted its merger with the National Research Development Council (created to promote the development and exploitation of new technology). At present the two are operating in partnership as the British Technology Group.

Examination questions

1. Three of your friends, Tom, Dick, and Harry, have decided to set up in business as computer consultants. Initially, Tom and Dick will keep their existing jobs and work for the firm on a part-time basis. Harry, however, will work full-time for the new firm from the start. All three are providing the firm with £2,000 in capital. In addition Tom's wife is lending the firm an extra £1,000, but is not going to take part in the running of the business. All three of them have come to you for advice on what type of business organisation to form, and what, if any, other arrangements should be made.

2. What advantages are to be gained by a sole proprietor who decides to convert his enterprise into a partnership? Are there any consequent disadvantages? *(PSC 1980)*

3. Outline the composition and functions of the board of directors within the public joint-stock company. *(PSC 1979)*

4. Explain and distinguish four of the following forms of business unit:

   (a) private limited company;

   (b) limited partnership;

   (c) co-operative retail society;

   (d) public joint-stock company;

   (e) sole proprietorship. *(PSC 1977)*

5. Outline the major differences between the public joint-stock company and the public corporation. Refer in your answer to the pattern of organisation and control and to the financial structure.

6. In relation to the public joint-stock company explain 'divorce between ownership and control'. Refer in your answer to the role of a shareholder in such a company. *(PSC 1979)*

7. How is a public joint-stock company formed? What are its main features? *(PSC 1976)*

8. You are the sole proprietor of a hotel. Examine the factors you would take into account when deciding whether to convert this business unit into:

   (a) a partnership;

   (b) a public limited company.

9. What is the difference between a Co-operative Retail Society and a public limited company?

10. Explain the term 'public ownership'. Give an outline of its pattern within your own country. *(PSC 1981)*

11. Outline the major arguments for and against nationalisation. Examine the major problems nationalised industries have to deal with in the UK.

12. Choosing one major public corporation, outline the reasons for its creation and explain its present structure.

The structure of business: II

Chapter 3

In Chapter 2 we noted a great diversity in the form of business organisation a firm could adopt. This diversity is also reflected in the industry they belong to, the labour and technology they use, or even their size. In this chapter it is this last aspect – size – which we wish to consider in some detail. With the development of modern industrial economies we have seen a growth in the size of business units and the development of multinational corporations. Yet the small firm sector still plays an important part in advanced economies. So how important is size to the businessman and the economy, and what problems result from increasing the scale of business operations (or for that matter remaining small)?

The small firm sector

Definitions of what is a small firm are arbitrary. The Confederation of British Industry (CBI) suggested any business with a turnover of less than £1m., but in the same year (1967) the Government adopted a figure of £50,000. Again, when the CBI suggest that any firm employing under 200 people should be defined as small, other bodies were suggesting figures as low as 10 employees. Perhaps the most authoritative definition of the small firm comes from the Bolton Committee's report on small firms (*Report of the Committee of Enquiry on Small Firms,* Chairman J. Bolton) which was issued in 1971. A small firm, it said, was generally one which employed less than 200 people and having three additional characteristics:

1. A relatively small share of its market.

2. Owners who worked and took a personal interest in the business.

3. Not part of another (larger) organisation.

This was modified for certain sectors, for example construction – twenty-five employees or less, retailing – turnover of £50,000 or less, catering – all establishments except 'chains' or 'multiples'.

Table 3.1 Role of small firms within the UK economy

Definition	Selected sectors	% Small firms within sector by:		
		Output	Employees	No. of firms
200 employees or less, turnover £50,000 or less	Manufacturing	16	20	94
Turnover £50,000 or less	Retailing	32	49	96
25 employees or less	Building and construction	27	33	92
All establishments except chains	Catering	73	75	96
	All sectors	21	31	93

Source: Bolton Report, 1977 (Cmnd. 4811).

As Table 3.1 shows, by any measure small firms play a significant role within the UK economy. The Bolton Committee went further, arguing that their existence was vital to the dynamism of the economy. It pointed to a number of important economic and social functions. These were as follows:

1. They perform tasks for which large-scale industry is ill suited – for example where there is only a small market or where the products do not lend themselves to mass-production techniques.

2. They are often more efficient than large firms, having lower overhead costs.

3. They can adjust to changed market conditions more rapidly than their larger counterparts.

4. Many are selling a combination of product and personal services.

5. They are an important source of innovation in product, processes, and services.

6. They provide jobs for people whose personality ill suits them for work in large impersonal organisations.

7. The sector is a valuable training-ground for 'all-round' managers, expertise acquired is often attractive to and may very well be drawn on by larger firms.

8. They are a source of competition, and thereby stimulate efficiency throughout the industry.

9. They are the traditional breeding-ground for new industries, and the seed-bed from which new large firms grow to challenge the established leaders of industry.

The committee believed, and it has been accepted by successive governments, that should the small firm sector decline below a critical point it would not be able to carry out adequately its role in relation to competition and innovation. It concluded 'we can think of no substitute for the dynamic influence of new firms in preventing the ossification of the economy' (Bolton Report, para. 19.6), and suggested that 'we should regard the decline of the small firm sector past the point of economic viability as so great an evil that energetic discrimination to avert it would be justified' (para 8.16).

Since that time (1971) the decline in the size of the small firm sector in the UK has continued. It is estimated that between 28 and 29 per cent of all employees are now employed in this sector. Moreover, the sector is less important in the UK than in most other industrial societies – 66 per cent of all employees in Japan, 50 per cent in France, and 38 per cent in the United States have jobs in the small firm sector. The reasons for the decline are many, certainly the current recession will have caused many small business failures. (Yet paradoxically it is the recession with its shake-out of labour in larger firms, and redundancy payments which is causing renewed interest in self-employment and, by definition, the small firm sector.) Other problems which face the small firm include:

1. *Financial* – small firms often lack the security, business experience, and profit record to interest potential lenders. Ignorance of sources of finance other than banks and hire-purchase companies frequently compound the problem.

2. *Lack of managerial experience* – many small firms have little knowledge of specialist management techniques such as budgetary control, stock control, market research, and purchasing, nor are they able to afford the services of firms offering such expertise.

3. *Government policy* – monetary and fiscal policy have often had a greater impact on small firms. For example anti-inflation policy, with its tax increases and control of bank and hire-purchase lending impeded development of small firms far more than large firms who were often able to find alternative sources of finance. Yet another aspect of government operations which caused disquiet was the volume of information different departments required from business. The larger firm was commonly able to absorb this extra work, the small firm with its 'kitchen table' administrative unit was not. Finally, certain aspects of the tax regime, highly progressive rates of income tax and corporation tax, along with capital gains and capital transfer tax have proved substantial disincentives to effort.

The depth of the current recession and the continued industrial decline of the UK has created new interest in the small firm sector. The Government sees the sector as playing a vital role in the regeneration of the economy. The focal point for government aid is a separate division within the Department of Industry – the Small Firms Service – which provides an information and advisory service for small businesses. A large number of other government measures (over 100 in 1984) which are designed to aid the sector have also been introduced.

Three areas though have been singled out as requiring special attention. Firstly, the Government has tried to encourage the movement of finance into the small firm sector. For example, the Business Start-up Scheme is designed to encourage outside investors (i.e. other than the owners of the firm) to invest risk (equity) capital, by allowing the investor tax relief on the investment at his highest rate of tax. Another measure, the Loan Guarantee Scheme, is intended to save those worthwhile projects which might fail through lack of bank finance. Government loan guarantees are available to the banker should the borrower pay a 3 per cent premium to the Department of Industry. High-risk capital has also been made available through the British Technology Group and venture capital schemes.

Secondly, the Government has created a more favourable tax regime by reducing the higher levels of income tax, creating a reduced rate of corporation tax for small firms (40 per cent instead of 52 per cent), introducing thresholds below which firms do not have to register for VAT, and generally making it easier to pass businesses on to the next generation intact by changes in capital transfer tax.

Lastly, steps have been taken to reduce the burden of 'oppressive' legislation on the small firm sector. Companies Acts have reduced the financial information required from these firms. Legislation such as the Employment Act (1980) exempts small firms from many of the requirements relating to industrial tribunals and unfair dismissal. Finally, attempts are being made to reduce the administrative burdens caused by the requests of government for statistical information.

Large-scale industry

Throughout the twentieth century we have seen a continuing trend of firms increasing both in size and complexity. Let us consider size first. In 1910 the largest 100 companies share of total manufacturing output was 15 per cent, today it is over 40 per cent. Equally the concentration of sales among the five largest businesses in each industry has risen dramatically. In the cement, fertiliser, and tobacco industries the five largest firms account for 90 per cent of all sales; chemicals, brewing, and vehicles over 60 per cent, while the average for British industry as a whole is 47 per cent.

Business has also become increasingly complex. Firstly, many large firms operate numerous establishments – an establishment being a separate plant or factory. The top fifty firms in the UK operate on average fifty establishments each. Secondly, the establishments operated are not even likely to be in the same industry. More and more firms are becoming multi-product. Thus the Imperial Group, which is by no means unique, has establishments operating in: brewing, canning, crisp manufacture, farming, frozen foods, packaging and paper production, plastics, printing, timber, and hotels.

The method of growth

The business achieves an increase in size in one of two ways, internal expansion or amalgamation. Internal expansion as a means of increasing size is often slow. The firm relies very much on its own resources – ploughed-back profits and whatever other money it can raise from banks and other financial institutions (often difficult to obtain and costly).

Amalgamation of business activities is by far the more popular method of growth. It has accounted for well over half the increase in UK concentration of industry since 1950. It yields an instant increase in size and power (but in the longer term may experience significant organisational diseconomies). A merger occurs where two (there is no reason in practice why it should only be two – the merger of Plessey, English Electric, and International Computers and Tabulators created International Computers Limited, or ICL as it is more commonly known) companies agree to combine their resources issuing shares in the new company for those in the existing firms. A take-over on the other hand is not the result of an agreement between the two parties, but where one company offers to purchase the shares of another (normally reluctant) company and obtains a controlling interest through the open market.

Traditional economic theory would have us believe that the reason for this growth in size of business unit was economies of scale. That is, the idea that unit costs of production fall as the scale of operations increases. These economies fall into five broad categories – technical, marketing, financial, managerial, and risk-bearing.

Technical economies

1. Economies of increased dimensions.　A doubling of cubic capacity or volume can be achieved with a 59 per cent increase in material, hence its alternative name 'the six and ten rule'. The principle applies to tankers, factory/warehouse space, pipes, etc.

2. Economies of linked processes. If processes are integrated in one plant, savings in production time and transportation costs occur. Similarly, integration of processes in iron- and steel-making may result in a saving of over 20 per cent on fuel costs.

3. Economies of gearing. In large-scale operations there can be full utilisation of all equipment. For example if we have three linked processes with a machine capacity of $X = 200$ units per day, $Y = 300$ units, and $Z = 400$ units, a minimum production level of 1,200 units per day (or some multiple thereof) is required to keep all machines working throughout the day.

4. Economies of long production runs. Where heavy fixed costs are incurred, as in car production, the greater the number of units produced the smaller the fixed cost per unit (it is estimated that in oil refining an 800 per cent increase in throughput from 0.5 million to 4 million tons reduces the unit cost by 56 per cent).

Marketing economies

1. Economies of purchase. The large-scale purchaser of raw materials or components can often obtain benefits (e.g. credit terms, discounts, and prompt delivery) that will not be granted to smaller buyers. The greater these costs are as a percentage of total costs the more valuable the saving.

2. Economies of selling and advertising. Better utilisation of the sales force occurs through promoting a whole range of products rather than just one. Moreover, the reputation of one popular product may sell the rest of the range. Costly, but cost effective (because the expense is shared between so many units of production) advertising on television may be used.

Financial economies
The larger organisation is able to find capital more easily – certain sources of capital are not available to smaller firms. It can provide fixed assets as security for the loan and a profit record which can be used to assess risk. These factors may also result in finance being obtained more cheaply by large firms.

Potential diseconomies of large-scale organisations
Most of the diseconomies will occur as a result of the organisation structure becoming exceedingly complex. Co-ordination of activities becomes more difficult as greater numbers of people are involved (especially where, as is often the case, they are employed in different

geographical locations). As the command chain lengthens it becomes increasingly difficult to control the various parts of the organisation. This allows under-utilisation of management and waste to creep in. A lengthening of the command will also cause delays in communication to occur. This slows the decision-making process and reduces the firm's ability to adapt quickly to changed circumstances. Motivation often suffers in large organisations, they are accused of being impersonal. Employees lose their identity and become alienated from the firm. Moreover, the 'bureaucracy' may prevent employee initiative and innovation.

Managerial economies

1. Size allows specialisation of management – which in the same way that division of labour encourages greater production, enables managers to become more proficient in their work and deal with a greater volume of work.

2. Large firms are able to afford highly expensive specialists. They are also more likely to attract them with good working conditions, prospects of advancement, and fringe benefits.

Risk-bearing economies

1. Diversification. Greater security can be achieved by not being reliant upon one product, market, customer, or supplier.

2. Research. Today the cost of research and development is so high that only the large and powerful can afford it (or the possibility of loss should the investment fail).

Improvements in efficiency are the most often quoted motive for business expansion. But often such statements hide other motives which may not be so praiseworthy or in the public interest. These alternative motives include:

1. Market dominance. This has obvious advantages. It gives the possessor a degree of security. The firm through its monopoly or dominant position can control prices in the industry, often allowing high profits to be made. Lack of competition means there is no incentive for the firm to improve its product or service, profits are more than adequate and it may decide to opt for a quiet life. For the same reasons there is little reason for such a firm to invest heavily in research and development of future products. This motive is probably far stronger than many businessmen would have us believe. It could account, equally as well as economies of scale, for the large number of horizontal mergers and take-overs in the UK.

2. Defensive. Business may feel vulnerable for many reasons. The growth of other firms in the same sector may reduce its own power, perhaps even threaten its long-term independence or survival. A declining market will encourage growth by merger or take-over activity to reduce competition and the possibility of a price war. Alternatively, the increased size may give the business greater strength to survive a price war.

Defensive motives may also be paramount where powerful interests exist among the firm's suppliers or customers, and the additional size is needed to bargain with them on equal terms. Yet again, a merger can be used to guarantee sources of raw materials, to secure markets, or to spread risks.

3. Financial. Such motives exist where the existing management of a business is not utilising assets to the best effect (e.g. large unutilised cash resources) or where the market value of the shares does not reflect the underlying value of the assets (possibly because of recent losses, e.g. Dunlop). In these circumstances conglomerates such as Hanson Trust or Lonrho will take over the 'failing' business and by injecting new management, rationalising production, cutting unprofitable products, and reducing overheads seek to make better use of its resources.

The direction of growth

It is useful to distinguish three kinds of business amalgamation. They are referred to as horizontal, vertical, and conglomerate integration.

Horizontal integration of activities occurs where firms producing the same kinds of products or services come together. Recent examples include: Habitat – Mothercare; MFI Furniture Group – Status Discount; C. and J. Clark – K Shoes.

Horizontal integration provides considerable scope for economies of scale. It is also used to increase market share, eliminate competition, or fight off a bid from another company. This has been the most common form of amalgamation in the UK.

Vertical integration involves bringing together under common ownership different stages in the production process. It may take the form of a firm acquiring ownership of a supplier of raw materials (termed 'vertical backward integration') or forward integration where a firm secures its production outlets (e.g. Singer Sewing Machine shops). Common aims of vertical integration are to secure supplies of raw materials or output for finished goods and to obtain economies of linked processes. Vertical mergers account for less than 5 per cent of the values of all mergers.

Lateral integration is said to occur when there is little relationship between either products or processes of the separate firms. Firms having such a diversity of interests are often termed 'conglomerates'. The motives for diversification of interests are many. The reasons most commonly quoted include, the need to:

(a) get out of a product reaching the end of its life cycle;

(b) get out of a market which is highly competitive;

(c) utilise management skills more efficiently;

(d) make a capital gain on the break-up and sale of the firm's assets.

The Imperial Group, which has been mentioned previously, is an ideal example of a company which has diversified into many unrelated activities.

---

4. Managerial. The divorce of ownership from control in modern business has created a class of professional managers to whom profit may not be the prime objective. The status and power of the professional manager comes not from maximum profitability but from the size of the organisation that he controls.

Multinational corporations

A multinational corporation is a business which undertakes planning, financing, production, marketing, and research and development upon an international basis. These activities will be performed in many countries, with management, for the most part, being drawn from the host countries. Ownership is not necessarily dominated by the parent country, and the shares may be traded on Stock Exchanges in several countries.

The multinational corporation is not a particularly new form of business enterprise, though its rapid growth is certainly a twentieth-century phenomenon. Examples of multinational corporations date back to the seventeenth century and the establishment of the Hudson's Bay and East India Companies by British traders. Today the majority of multinationals have their origins in the United States, the UK, Japan, and West Germany.

The importance of multinationals can be gauged in a number of ways. First, as early as 1968 international manufacture had overtaken international trade, with the output of overseas subsidiaries of multinationals exceeding the global value of exports. Secondly, the world's largest 100 economic units are split roughly 60:40 between countries and companies. No company comes near the very big countries like the United States or the Soviet Union, but few realise that General Motors has sales nearly 70 per cent larger than South Africa's Gross National Product (GNP), 60 per cent bigger than Nigeria's, or 10 times greater than Ireland's! Similarly, there are well over a dozen firms including: General Motors; Exxon; Shell; British Petroleum; IBM; Unilever; Philips; Mobil; National Iranian Oil; General Electric; Chrysler; Standard Oil; who have a turnover in excess of either Malaysia's or Hong Kong's GNP. It is estimated that by the turn of the century some 200 multinationals will produce over half of world output.

Several reasons have been put forward for the remarkable growth of multinationals. First, the relaxation of exchange controls allowing more easy transfer of capital between countries has obviously been of paramount importance. Secondly, improvements in communications such as telephones, telex, and air travel have reduced the difficulties in controlling the operations of overseas' subsidiaries. Thirdly, the growth in the popularity of management by objectives has reduced the need for day-to-day control by the parent organisation. Finally, manufacture in overseas countries is seen as a way of avoiding many of those countries' import tariffs and restrictions.

Reaction to the growth of multinationals has been mixed. While they confer obvious benefits on those countries within which they operate, the relationships between state and company have often been strained. The benefits can be summarised as follows:

The balance of payments

1. The development of new manufacturing capacity by the multinational will cause an inflow of foreign currencies into the host country.

2. Imports may be reduced as goods which were not previously produced in the host country are now available to satisfy local demand.

3. Exports may be increased by the multinational's overseas sales efforts.

Competition

Competition within the host country is stimulated, with beneficial effects upon prices, efficiency, and innovation. The import of better management and production techniques by the multinational will force domestic producers to improve their own standards of efficiency in order to survive. In addition their heavy investment into the research and development of new products and processes again forces local firms to reappraise their efforts in these areas.

Increased production
This results in a higher level of employment (often in areas of high unemployment) and a higher GNP and standard of living.

But as we have already noted, the growth of multinationals has been viewed with concern by many host countries – both industrialised and developing. The concern stems from the sheer size and financial strength of many multinationals. This concern is hardly surprising when we remember that the GNP of some host countries, especially among the developing nations, will be considerably less than the turnover of many of the multinationals operating within their territory. The feeling of concern has led to the seizure of multinational assets in several countries and stringent control upon their operations in many others.

Basically, the problem is that host countries believe that decisions taken to further the interests of the multinational (often based in some foreign country) will have significant and detrimental effects upon their economy. Consider the case of Chrysler UK. In 1975 the American parent of Chrysler UK announced the decision to close down its British operation (a decision which was later reversed) and to supply the British market (and a large Iranian contract for cars), from its production units on the Continent. The potential impact upon the balance of payments was thus twofold – a reduction in exports and an increase in imports. Equally worrying was the impact upon employment, especially as many of the jobs at risk were in Scotland where little alternative work was available. Considerable pressure was put upon the British Government and eventually an agreement was hammered out whereby Chrysler UK would be kept open in return for a government rescue package of £162m. in public money and loan guarantees.

The Chrysler case illustrates two points. Firstly, decisions upon where to produce, and to which subsidiary export markets should be given will obviously affect the host country's level of employment, balance of payments, and its inhabitants' standards of living. Secondly, it is not only developing countries which are open to pressure from multinational corporations. Benefits, which would not have been available to other companies, were clearly on offer here because of the impact its restructured operations would have had upon the British economy.

Multinationals are often thought to contribute significantly to international monetary crises. It is logical for them to protect the value of their reserves against currency fluctuations. They will therefore move their (often sizeable) reserves between countries as currencies appreciate and depreciate. Let us take the example of an American multinational with subsidiaries in the UK and Japan. Should the sterling exchange rate depreciate while at the same time the yen is appreciating, our multinational may very well decide to transfer its sterling reserves to Japan. But in doing so it creates an even greater pressure on the sterling exchange rate. Sterling may very well depreciate further, even in situations where there is no underlying imbalance between sterling and other exchange rates.

Finally, multinationals are also able to adjust their affairs so that profits are taken or declared in those countries where the tax system is most advantageous. The UK Monopolies Commission severely criticised the Swiss drug multinational Roche for inflating the prices of raw materials British subsidiaries purchased from its Swiss parent. The effect was to reduce the difference between what was claimed to be the cost price and the selling price, causing low profits to be declared in the UK. The inflated prices of raw materials charged by the Swiss greatly increased the profits made overseas in countries where profits were not so highly taxed.

Competition policy

Competition is admired for its beneficial influence on prices, efficiency, and innovation. The element of competition means that no firm is able to control market prices and thereby increase profits. It is only through a policy of competitive pricing that a firm can expect to gain sufficient orders to survive. Firms in their desire to increase profitability will seek to improve the efficiency with which the product is produced. They will also be searching for those new and improved product designs which will give them a competitive advantage in the longer term.

The role of competition policy is to ensure that viable competition exists in all sectors of British industry. It has taken the form of machinery to investigate monopolies, mergers, anti-competitive and restrictive trade practices, together with power to control those situations which are seen as being against the public interest.

Monopolies and mergers

The Fair Trading Act 1973 gives the Secretary of State for Trade and Industry or the Director General of Fair Trading the power to refer to the Monopolies and Mergers Commission any situation where over 25 per cent of the supply of a product or service is under the control of one person, or two or more people acting together. The legislation extends to local as well as national monopoly situations and also to the investigation of public sector monopolies. Where a monopoly is found to operate against the public interest the commission's recommendations may be enforced through statutory orders or by the Director General obtaining undertakings from the firm(s) concerned to comply with those recommendations.

Where a merger is proposed and will result in the combined parties controlling over 25 per cent of any market, or where the combined assets are in excess of £15m. it may be referred to the Monopolies and Mergers Commission by the Secretary of State. Should the commission find the proposed merger to be against the public interest the Secretary of State can prevent it taking place.

Competition policy in the Common Market

The European Economic Community (EEC) competition law applies to practices which may affect trade between member states. It takes precedence over national law. The commission's powers to regulate anti-competitive behaviour fall broadly into three categories:

1. *Under the Treaty of Rome, Articles 92–94, member states are forbidden to give aid to industry or firms which could distort competition. Excluded from this general prohibition are items such as aid to disaster areas, depressed regions, and new economic activity. Member states are required to give (but do not always comply) the commission details of any aid planned so that its legality can be determined.*

2. *Article 85 bans restrictive practices which limit output, determine prices, allocate markets, and limit investment.*

3. *Article 86 bans 'abuse of a dominant position'. A dominant position exists where a large firm is able to use its strength to impose unfair terms on suppliers, retailers, competitors, or consumers. An abuse occurs where the dominant firm does, in fact, act in this way. Large firms found guilty of an infringement of Articles 85 or 86 will be subject to heavy fines. The maximum is 10 per cent of annual sales affected by the abuse.*

Anti-competitive practices

Restrictive trade practices
These exist where one or more parties accept limitations on their ability to make decisions regarding prices, output, or conditions of sale. By the Restrictive Trade Practices Act 1976 such agreements have to be registered with the Director General of Fair Trading. Non-compliance with these requirements renders the parties liable to prosecution. All agreements registered with the Director General will be referred to the Restrictive Practices Court whose function it is to decide whether the agreement is in the public interest. The onus of proof is placed upon the parties wishing to rely on the agreement who

must show that it has one or more of the following beneficial effects:

- the agreement is necessary to protect consumers from physical injury;
- the removal of the agreement would rob consumers of some substantial advantage;
- the agreement was necessary to counter the action of another group restricting competition;
- without the agreement fair terms could not be negotiated with a monopolist;
- without the agreement serious and persistent unemployment would occur;
- the removal of the agreement would cause loss of export earnings;
- the agreement was necessary to maintain other agreements which the court had already declared to be in the public interest.

Cartels

Individual firms may achieve greater control over their market not only through mergers and takeovers. A similar effect may be achieved through agreements with other firms, concerning shares of the market, agreed selling areas, information sharing or price fixing agreements. Firms involved in such arrangements are said to have formed a 'cartel'. The most well known cartel of modern times is undoubtedly Organisation for Petroleum Exporting Countries (OPEC).

The majority of cartel arrangements lay down production or sales quotas for each firm and the prices at which the product or service will be provided. For example, OPEC's charter states, 'members shall study and formulate a system to ensure the stabilisation of prices by, among other means, the regulation of production'. Further agreements on the distribution of profits, methods of preventing newcomers entering the industry, and penalties for non-compliance with the cartel arrangements may also be made. Interlocking directorates, that is the practice of directors in one firm becoming non-executive directors on the Boards of one or more of their rivals may sometimes be used to 'police' the agreement.

For a cartel arrangement to be successful three conditions are necessary. First, the members need to control the supply (or a substantial part of it) of the product. It is the reduction of supply by members which precipitates the price increase. Secondly, cartel members must be able to agree policy and co-ordinate their actions accordingly. Should members avoid their obligations under the agreement the cartel will quickly disintegrate. Finally demand for the product must be fairly insensitive to changes in price. Where substitute products exist cartel members will not be able to raise prices much without loss of demand.

Cartel arrangements allow firms to charge higher prices and make greater profits than when trading independently and competitively with one another. For precisely these reasons legislation now exists in both America and Europe which makes such agreements illegal. In many developing countries though similar legislation has not been passed.

Examples of cartels may still be found in both America and Europe. Until recently the International Air Transport Association (IATA) regulated the prices airlines could charge – this was with the agreement of both European and American Governments. Then in 1982 the United States withdrew from the IATA agreement with the result that today air fares (per mile) in America are one third cheaper than those in Europe. Put another way 'deregulation' as the Americans call it – or competition – meant that in 1984 it cost roughly the same to fly from London to Madrid as it did from London to New York. In Europe IATA continues to exist because no European Government is prepared to let its flag-flying airline go into liquidation – and most governments doubt the ability of their airline to survive competition!

In addition to proving that beneficial effects do arise from the agreement the court must also satisfy itself that those beneficial effects outweigh any detrimental aspects its implementation might cause. Thus in 1959 the court held that although the Cotton Yarn Spinners Agreement had the effect of mitigating local unemployment, prices would be higher than in a free market and declared the agreement void. In practice the vast majority of agreements have been found to be against the public interest. (One interesting side-effect resulting from the court's almost overwhelming rejection of collusion was the increase in merger activity during the 1960s and 1970s.)

Resale Price Maintenance (RPM)
This was the policy of manufacturers to specify prices at which their product should be sold (together with penalties for non-compliance). The procedure for dealing with such agreements is very similar to that for restrictive trade practice, embodying a general prohibition and a number of 'escape' clauses as follows:
- abolition would result in public health being endangered;
- abolition would result in a substantial reduction in retail outlets;
- abolition would result in a general increase in prices;
- abolition would result in a reduction in after-sales service;
- abolition would result in a substantial reduction in quality or variety of goods available.

This legislation which was first introduced in 1956 and was amended by the Resale Prices Act 1964 has been exceptionally successful. Fixed prices for a manufacturer's products have almost entirely disappeared.

Anti-competitive practices

These comprise any business practices which could distort or restrict competition in the production, sale, or purchase of goods and services in the UK. Examples would include a manufacturer refusing to sell his product to a 'cut-price' store, or tying the sale of one product to another. Under the Competition Act 1980, the Director General of Fair Trading may investigate such practices, and where necessary refer them to the Monopolies and Mergers Commission for consideration. Where the practice is found to be operating against the public interest the Director General may accept an undertaking from the firm concerned or the Secretary of State may enforce compliance through statutory orders.

Examination questions

1. In view of the benefits of large-scale organisation why do small firms continue to exist?

2. Outline the major difficulties facing small firms. In what ways has the Government helped small firms overcome these difficulties?

3. 'The bigger the better.' How far do you agree with this view regarding the size of business units.

4. Explain the motives of the firm which expands its activities by:

    (a) horizontal integration;

    (b) vertical integration;

    (c) lateral integration.

5. Why do governments seek to encourage competition? Give examples of government measures which may be introduced to encourage competition.

6. Is there a case for your government taking more effective measures to limit the activities of multinational corporations with your country?

The organisation, its environment and social responsibility

Chapter 4

The environment of business

Organisations do not exist in a vacuum. They are part of society – a society which provides the resources and accepts the output of the firm. It is society which provides the opportunities for organisations and yet also places limitations on their freedom of action. This is the environment of business.

Until recently the importance of the environment was not recognised. It was thought that a successful organisation was one which had efficient work practices and organisational structure together with a caring attitude for its workforce. Now, it is undoubtedly true that a firm's chances of survival are enhanced by these factors, but it is wrong to believe that a boundary can be drawn between the firm and its environment. The causes of success and failure may be found within the organisation, but they are just as likely to be found in the firm's environment. Let us take a simple example to illustrate that point.

It is widely believed that there is a connection between smoking and certain respiratory illnesses. A tobacco firm may therefore have difficulty in maintaining sales of its product, even though the firm is efficiently run by a caring management. This was very much the problem faced by Imperial Tobacco (now Imperial Foods) in the 1960s. Public and governmental attitudes to smoking hardened. Taxes were increased and advertising restricted. Imperial's answer was to reduce their dependence on this market by diversifying into other products. But history is replete with examples of firms or industries who have failed to note a change in their environment and take corrective action in time. Consider the case of the British textile or the Swiss watch industry.

Figure 4.1 illustrates the point we have made – the firm is working within its environment. To carry on its business the firm needs certain

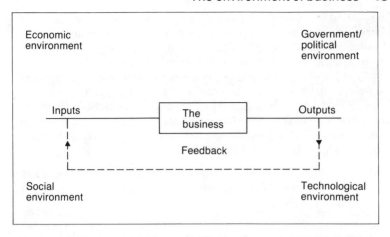

Fig. 4.1   The organisation and its environment

inputs from society. While raw materials, labour, and capital immediately spring to mind, there are many others. Perhaps the organisation needs licences from central or local government to carry on its business, or may be it needs government help to finance exports or limit competition – these are as much inputs into the firm as raw materials and labour. Other environmental inputs may place limitations upon the freedom of the firm. Consider the restraints imposed by law to protect employees and consumers, or market forces which prevent firms charging exorbitant prices for their products.

For the business to be successful it has to transform the inputs received from the environment into an output which is acceptable to that environment. How successful it is in obtaining the necessary demand for its product depends on a large number of factors. The price and quality of its products is of prime importance, especially in a highly competitive market. Consider the case of the British car manufacturers who have been losing their share of the UK market to products from the rest of Europe and Japan. The judgement of many consumers has been that the foreign car is both cheaper and at the same time more luxurious. Changes in taste may also affect the level of demand. Long hair for men has thrown many a barber out of business, but rising demand for desk-top computers has created a growth industry.

The success of the business though, does not only depend upon the goods and services it produces but also upon the way in which they are produced. Throughout the twentieth century there has been a trend requiring business to become more socially responsible than before. This is reflected in the growth of pressure groups and their success on such issues as consumer protection, employee welfare, and the environment. Products of certain companies have been unofficially boycotted because of links with South Africa or Israel, or alternatively because of the low wages paid in some of their factories and plantations in Africa and Asia. We shall return to the problem of social responsibility at a later point in this chapter.

All successful companies are aware of their environment. Figure 4.1 shows the successful business monitoring the feedback that it receives from the environment regarding its product and practices. In practice the environment is always changing, creating opportunities to exploit and threats to be avoided. Businesses are constantly responding to these changes. The response is twofold:

(a) adjusting to the new environment – perhaps by producing a new or improved product, by improved labour practices, or reducing pollution; and

(b) changing the environment in favour of the business – falling sales may be reversed by advertising, trade associations may pressure governments for changes in the law, while large multinational companies may even be able to cover losses on trading by negotiating subsidies (e.g. the Chrysler Corporation and the British Government in 1975).

The environment of business is complex, nor is the environment the same for different firms, yet the variables are the same – economic, governmental, social, and technological. These are discussed in more detail below.

The economic environment

The economic environment can be seen to work at two different levels. First, the state of the economy, the rate of inflation, the level of unemployment, trading arrangements, and economic growth force the Government to act in a particular way. Thus action to reduce the rate of inflation by monetary controls or fiscal policy will often result in a firm's sales being reduced. Conversely, attempts to encourage the growth of exports or reduce the level of unemployment may result in opportunities to increase sales. Economic trends within an economy are studied closely by corporate planners in an attempt to predict the direction and level of economic activity, together with the Government's response.

At a more immediate level managers are concerned with costs and inputs, and the degree of competition within the industry. The major inputs for most organisations are raw materials, labour, and capital. Over each of these, two questions have to be answered – where do we get the input from, and how much will it cost? The fact that we are able to obtain raw materials easily now and for a reasonable price does not necessarily mean that this will always be the case. Many firms have bought up their suppliers of raw materials in order to ensure continuity of supply (e.g. Ready-Mix Concrete took over Hallham River Limited, a company owning sand and gravel quarries). Similarly, changes in relative wages paid in different industries or new technology may mean labour skills are not available or become more costly. The attitudes of workers and the actions of trade unions must be taken into account when considering changes in organisation or production processes.

The degree of competition in an industry will also have important implications for the organisation. Markets in Western economies vary from highly competitive through to pure monopoly. In highly competitive markets producers have little control over price and output, and are therefore very concerned with product design, price, quality, and after-sales service. Concern over declining sales may force firms to integrate forwards and take over outlets for their products (e.g. Singer Sewing Machines, Leyland Paints, Ready-Mix Concrete).

Many more markets though are oligopolistic: that is, controlled by a few firms. Here private agreements on price and output (although illegal in many countries) are often made with competition being reduced to claims on quality, after-sales service, and social responsibility. Pure monopoly, that is, a single supplier of a product or service from whom we have to buy, may arise through the development and patenting of a product or process (e.g. Xerox Copiers) or through nationalisation. Traditionally, such sellers are motivated by self-interest and maximisation of profits, though in practice the watchful eye of the Government prevents too obvious abuse of a monopoly position.

The political environment

Attitudes of the Government have a direct impact on the environment of business. In Britain the attitudes towards business have ranged from distrust and antipathy to enthusiastic support. Potential governments' attitudes can be gleaned from the political parties' manifestos – their blueprints for action if elected.

The twentieth century has seen increased involvement by the Government in the affairs of business. The legal framework within which businesses operate has become increasingly complex. The Government has acted to regulate economic organisation by licensing business activity, nationalisation, monopoly and merger legislation, and company law. Both the consumer and the employee are better protected than ever before.

Yet activities of the Government seek not only to constrain business but also to provide it with opportunities. The Government seeks to promote research and development through the British Technology Group, and the Science Research Council, the use of robotics through direct government grants, the growth and efficiency of small business through subsidised consultancy and the Small Firms Service, a separate division at the Department of Industry. There are many other examples covering the protection of home industry, the encouragement of trade, the finance of industry, and the provision of college-based courses providing skilled personnel for industry and commerce.

The social environment

The attitudes of society provide a framework within which an organisation operates. These attitudes can be reflected in law – perhaps relating to the freedom of the individual, competition, or the protection of the consumer. They are equally likely to be found in the unenacted customs of society – the value that is placed upon education, the role of women in society (or the workforce), even our attitudes to work, leisure, and the environment. These attitudes are not constant, they vary over time. Indeed all the attitudes mentioned above (embodied in law and custom) have undergone recent change.

Attitudes also affect the internal workings of the organisation. The Japanese believe that the firm offers the worker a job for life. This results in the Japanese worker having a more positive attitude towards his employer, who in turn involves him in the policy and decision-making more frequently than in other countries. Relationships in France tend to be more formal than in the United States, which again is reflected in the rather more formal structure of French organisations.

The technological environment

The past century has seen a rapid growth in the use of technology. The application of scientific principles to industrial problems has resulted in a dramatic increase in the goods and services available for ordinary people. If we consider people's way of life fifty years ago with that now, we cannot fail to be impressed by the changes brought about by technological progress.

Technological progress has provided opportunities for firms to provide not only new products but market existing products at markedly reduced prices. Improvements in transport and communication have allowed the growth of larger firms – multinational companies – and encouraged the growth of international trade.

But the speed of technological progress is so great that it is seen not only as providing opportunities to firms and benefits to society but also as a threat. New developments can threaten established industries, for example digital watches caused major unemployment in the traditional Swiss watch industry. New technology exists which could destroy three-quarters of the jobs in the mining industry and not even white-collar workers are immune, the use of computers in business threatening to replace many a middle-managerial job.

Social responsibility

An organisation is not only affected by its environment, it in turn can affect that environment. By advertising it may change people's demand for goods and services, perhaps it may pollute the atmosphere or river, or by bribery secure some advantages it would not otherwise receive. It is the ability of the organisation to alter its environment which has caused increasing concern. If this power is not effectively controlled the unscrupulous firm can appropriate an unfair share of social benefits. Thus large firms may be under little competitive pressure, leaving them free to negotiate beneficial terms with both customers and suppliers. Moreover, its decisions may have an important impact upon the local community and may even determine central government allocation of resources.

Increasingly, therefore, business has been required to become more socially responsible to the community which has allowed it to engage in business activity. A socially responsible business organisation is one which has an awareness of the 'social' problems which arise out of its relationships with customers, employees, suppliers, the Government, and the community, and is willing to commit resources to solve some of these problems.

Yet even when a business accepts social responsibility as one of its objectives it may still be criticised. Consider a chemical company, a major employer in an area of high unemployment. The company discharges effluent into the river which kills all living organisms in and around the river. It has received an order from a statutory authority requiring it to stop this pollution. The cost of treating the effluent would raise the firm's costs so much as to make it uncompetitive. The firm has a choice, close down with all the consequences for the local community, or negotiate agreement to continue polluting the river. In which course of action is it being socially responsible?

The point which is being made is that there is no acceptable definition of what constitutes socially responsible action. Social responsibility varies according to your attitudes. However, a majority of people would accept the following as being areas of concern for the socially responsible firm:

1. Employee relations

(a) The education and training of staff.

(b) The working environment.

(c) Job satisfaction.

(d) Attitudes to disadvantaged groups.

2. Consumer protection

(a) Product safety.

(b) Misleading advertising.

(c) Complaints from consumers.

3. The environment

(a) Pollution.

(b) Noise.

(c) Restoration of land to natural uses.

4. Financial honesty and openness

(a) Bribery and corruption.

(b) Company control and ownership.

(c) Executive pay and compensation.

(d) Contributions to political parties.

Most organisations accept that they owe a responsibility to society, but in many cases this has not been translated into action as fully as we would like. There is, after all, a basic conflict between social responsibility and profitability. Money invested in social responsibility comes out of the company's profits, and if the shareholders do not receive what they believe to be a fair return on their investment they are unlikely to contribute to the future capital requirements of the company. Moreover, while managers as individuals may believe in social responsibility, as managers of the business they are evaluated strictly upon economic performance. The rewards go to the managers who keep costs down most successfully – and that includes the cost of social responsibility. The conclusion must be that social responsibility cannot be left to the whims of individual firms and managers but must be enforced by legislation. The growth of consumer and employee protection legislation is part of this process.

Examination questions

1. What do you understand by the term 'economic environment'. Why is it so important in the operation of business? *(PSC Dec. 1980)*

2. Selecting an organisation of your choice, describe the environment within which it works.

3. Explain how the environment can provide opportunities for, and threats to, an organisation.

4. It is said that businesses must act responsibly in their dealings with the community. Using examples explain what you understand by this statement.

The economic environment

Part II

Economic growth

Chapter 5

The measurement of economic activity

Economic activity is the process by which scarce resources are changed into the goods and services demanded by that country's population. Generally speaking, the more resources there are for this transformation process and the more effectively they are used the larger is that country's national income.

Official estimates of national income for the UK are compiled and published annually by the Central Statistical Office and appear under the title of *National Income and Expenditure.*

The national income for the UK is calculated in three different ways. First, it can be calculated by summing up all the incomes earned by different people in the UK. Secondly, by calculating the output of each industry, and lastly by looking at how we spend the money which we have earned.

The output measure

For each product or service which is produced within the country we calculate the total output, the average price per unit of output, and the total market value. Thus, a purely hypothetical section of the calculation of Gross Domestic Product (output) (GDP(O)) would appear as shown in Table 5.1.

Table 5.1   Calculation of national income by the output measure

Product/Service	Ave. price per unit/ output	Units/ output (m.)	Total market value (£m.)
Cars	£7,000	1	7,000
Eggs	60p (doz)	300	240

When calculating GDP(O) – which is defined as the value of all the goods and services produced in a country during a given period of time – it is important to ensure that only final output is included. Final output is those goods and services which are sold to an end user and do not become part of any other product. Goods which are incorporated into other products are classed as intermediate goods. The inclusion of such goods in the calculation of Gross Domestic Product Output (GDP(O)) would lead to an inflated figure. This can be seen from the example in Table 5.2. The final value of the bread produced is the figure that should be included in the calculation of GDP. To include the value of transactions at previous stages in the production process would be to double and treble count costs that are already included in the £1,000 final figure for bread produced.

Table 5.2   Stages in the production of bread

	£
Company 1 supplies wheat to farm	100
Company 2 (farm) sells wheat crop	300
Company 3 (mill) sells flour	600
Company 4 (bakery) sells bread	1,000

The method by which the final figure of £1,000 is included in the calculation of GDP(O) is to consider the value added by each firm or industry in the production process. Value added is the difference between the value of the firm's output and the cost of its inputs. From the example above we can calculate value added as shown in Table 5.3.

Table 5.3   Calculation of value added

	Value of output (a)	Value of inputs (b)	Added value (a) – (b)
Company 1	100	—	100
Company 2	300	100	200
Company 3	600	300	300
Company 4	1,000	600	400
		Total added value	1,000

In Table 5.4 we can see the contribution certain industries made to GDP, the calculation being made as explained above.

Both the output and expenditure approaches to the calculation of GDP are based on the prices charged to the consumer. These prices often contain a tax element altering their true value. Gross Domestic Product at market prices (MP) may therefore either over- or underestimate the true value of output or expenditure. A more correct

Table 5.4   National income (1980) – the output approach

	£ bn
Agriculture, forestry, and fishing	4.3
Petroleum and natural gas	7.6
Other mining and quarrying	3.2
Manufacturing	48.0
Construction	13.0
Gas, electricity, and water	5.8
Transport	10.1
Communications	5.3
Distributive trades	19.3
Insurance, banking, finance, and business services	18.3
Ownership of dwellings	12.0
Professional and scientific services	25.6
Miscellaneous services	18.7
Public administration and defence	14.0
Total	205.2
Adjustment for financial services	9.7
Residual error	2.0
Gross Domestic Product at factor cost	193.5
Net property income from abroad	–0.04
Gross National Product at factor cost	193.5
Less capital consumption	–27.0
National income	166.4

figure can be arrived at by deducting from GDP (MP) the net value of expenditure taxes (expenditure taxes minus subsidies). The resulting figure is termed GDP at factor cost.

Not all goods and services which are produced within an economy are produced with resources owned by that country. For example, many American firms have subsidiaries in the UK and Western Europe. Historically, the UK has invested heavily overseas and now receives income from these investments in the form of rent, profits, and interest.

To take account of this fact an adjustment is made to the previous calculation of GDP by deducting all payments made to overseas countries resulting from their investments here, and adding to it payments made to the UK arising from our investments overseas.

Gross National Product as this figure is called, is the value of all final goods and services produced as a result of resources owned by that country wherever they are at work. For the UK this adjustment to GDP is positive, with GNP being larger than GDP. This reflects the investments made by the UK overseas in previous years. For many countries though, especially among the developing nations, the adjustment results in a national product smaller than the domestic product.

Approximately 80 per cent of the GNP of the UK is used for consumption. The remainder we term investment. Investment is required in order to maintain and enhance the flow of goods and services in the economy in future years. It is required to replace the existing stock of capital equipment which has been depreciated in value by use over the past period. Approximately 10 per cent of GNP, or nearly half of total investment, is used to replace the capital stock used up. The figure which is left after allowing for depreciation of capital stock (i.e. 90 per cent of GNP) is referred to as Net National Product.

Net National Product (NNP) is, technically, the goods and services available in any year to satisfy consumption without sacrificing future for present consumption. Yet many countries seek to invest more than this minimum amount in capital stock because they wish to improve on their present standard of living. This requires extra investment in new techniques and processes. The extra investment required is termed Net Capital Formation (NCF).

Figure 5.1 shows the relationship (for the UK) between GDP and GNP, and how depreciation and NCF reduce the goods and services available for consumption.

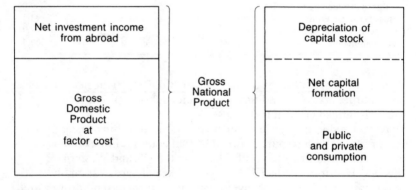

Fig. 5.1   Relationship between GDP and GNP in the UK

The expenditure measure

Gross Domestic Product can also be calculated by looking at the expenditure of the people and organisations within the economy (see Table 5.5). As before we must take care not to double-count. The purchases we wish to include are for final consumption or capital investment. Consumers' expenditure is by far the most important component of GDP (expenditure) (E), amounting to 47.8 per cent of total final expenditure. General government consumption is 17.1 per cent and covers expenditure by both central and local government.

Investment can take a number of forms. First, the investment may be in fixed assets (e.g. buildings or plant machinery) by either the public or the private sector. In 1980 the private sector investment was 9.8 per cent of total final expenditure, while that of the public sector

Table 5.5   National income (1980) – the expenditure approach

	£ bn
Consumers' expenditure	135.4
General government final consumption	48.3
Gross fixed investment	40.1
Value of physical increase in stocks	−3.6
Exports of goods and services	63.2
Total final expenditure at market prices	283.4
Imports of goods and services	−57.8
Gross Domestic Product at market prices	225.6
Taxes on expenditure	−37.3
Subsidies	5.2
Net property income from abroad	−0.04
Capital consumption	−27.0
General government final consumption	48.3
Gross fixed investment	40.1
Value of physical increase in stocks	−3.6
Exports of goods and services	63.2
Imports of goods and services	−57.8
Gross Domestic Product at market prices	225.6
Taxes on expenditure	−37.3
Subsidies	5.2
Gross Domestic Product at factor cost	*193.5*
Net property income from abroad	−0.04
Gross Domestic Product at factor cost	*193.5*
Capital consumption	−27.0
National income	*166.4*

was 4.3 per cent. Investment may, however, take the form of stock-building. Goods that are not sold become part of that firm's investment in stock. Changes in the level of stocks held by firms may result in either positive or negative stock-building. In 1980 stock-building was −1.3 per cent, representing a reduction in the level of stock held by industry and commerce.

The items mentioned so far, when added together, form Total Domestic Expenditure (TDE). They represent the final purchases of UK nationals as consumers and investors. Total final expenditure (TFE) is arrived at by adding to TDE the spending of overseas consumers on British goods (exports). Exports accounted for 22.3 per cent of TFE in 1980. When imports of goods and services are deducted from TFE the resulting figure is GDP(E).

Adjustments to GDP(E) at market prices are made for net expenditure taxes, net property income from abroad and capital consumption, as shown under the output measure to arrive at a figure for national income.

The income measure

When goods and services are produced, the people who help create those products or services are rewarded for their effort. Such payments are known as factor incomes because they are paid to the factors of production – land, labour, capital. The aggregate of such income is called Total Domestic Income (TDI) and is made up of incomes from employment and self-employment and the trading profits of companies and state enterprises, together with income from rent. Of these, income from employment is by far the most important, accounting for approximately 68 per cent of TDI. (See Table 5.6).

Not all incomes are included. State benefits paid out of National Insurance contributions and taxation are excluded. They have not been generated by employment, but are a compulsory transfer from the person earning that income to the person receiving it. To include the transfer payment as income of the person who originally gave value for it and also the state beneficiary would be double-counting.

Table 5.6   National income (1980) – the income approach

	£ bn
Income from employment	137.1
Income from self-employment	18.4
Gross trading profits of companies	24.9
Gross trading surplus of public corporations	6.0
Gross trading surplus of general government enterprises	0.2
Rent	13.2
Imputed charge for consumption of non-trading capital	2.1
Total domestic income	202.0
Stock appreciation	–6.5
Residual error	–2.1
Gross Domestic Product at factor cost	193.5
Net property income from abroad	–0.04
Gross National Product at factor cost	193.5
Capital consumption	–27.0
National income	166.4

An adjustment is also made to TDI to allow for the efforts of inflation on stocks. The process of rising prices increases the book value of stocks even though there has been no physical increase in the stocks held by companies. When the stock is sold the inflated price is reflected in the companies' profits. To be consistent with other measures we must discount the companies' profits by the amount stock has appreciated. This is termed 'stock appreciation' in the calculation of GDP (income) (I) and will be positive as long as prices are rising (which will of course result in a negative adjustment being made to GDP(I).

To GDP(I) at factor cost are made the adjustment for net property income from abroad and capital consumption, as discussed previously.

The use of national income statistics

The annual Blue Book, *national income and expenditure*, appears some nine months after the end of the year to which it relates. It is an important source of information which can be used for many purposes.

The Government, in its attempts to control the economy, will use the accounts to determine how the economy has performed over the previous periods, and whether government objectives (inflation, growth, unemployment, international trade) have been achieved. A trend established over a number of years may be revealed by the Blue Book, and the Government may adjust its policies to meet these changed conditions. Firms in the private sector will similarly benefit from the use of national income statistics.

If, for example, the Blue Book revealed a change in pattern of consumer spending this would have implications for both business and the Government. Some possible implications are as follows:

- Taxation – effect on VAT – Customs and Excise – corporation tax.
- Impact upon unemployment – regional problem.
- Health and welfare – employee and consumer.
- Effect on imports of raw materials or finished goods.
- Increased need for education and training.
- Private and public investment decisions.
- Protection of home industry.
    Listed below are some of the tables contained in the Blue Book; their relevance to the Government and business does not need explanation. Similar information is published in many other countries.
- Analysis of income (sources).
- Analysis of expenditure.
- GDP by industry – subsidies to industry, investment by industry, profitability of industry, employment by industry.
- Public corporations – profitability, employment, investment.
- Central government – current and capital expenditure, sources of income.
- Local government – cost of services provided, capital expenditure, sources of revenue.
- International trade – imports and exports.

At this point it must be made clear that it would be wrong to claim that past trends are a perfect indicator of what is going to happen in the future. They are not, but the information provided in the Blue Book is a sound base upon which to base government policy decisions for the future. Neither must it be thought that the Blue Book is the only source of information available to the Government – it is one of many, but its comprehensive coverage of all aspects of the economy should indicate its importance.

The need for care in using national income statistics

1. Increases in national income from year to year reflect not only the growth in output but also the process of rising prices. Consider the following situation:

Country X	Year 1	Year 2
National income	100	108
Retail Price Index	100	105

The growth of national income in money terms is 8 per cent. However, as inflation during the same period has increased by 5 per cent the real growth in income or output is 3 per cent.

Thus, if we wish to compare national income over a period of time (and perhaps establish a growth rate) we need to find how prices have moved in the same period and use this to discount money national income. Table 5.7 shows just how important is the distinction between real and money national income. Measured in money terms the UK national income grew by 136 per cent between 1975 and 1981. In real terms (constant prices) though, the increase was a mere 6 per cent with national income actually declining between 1979 and 1981.

Table 5.7 United Kingdom GNP at market prices

	Money national income (£m)	% Increase on 1975	Real national income (£m)	% Increase on 1975
1975	105,533	100	105,533	100
1976	125,911	119.3	109,662	103.9
1977	143,893	136.3	110,020	104.3
1978	165,990	157.3	114,423	108.4
1979	194,260	184.1	116,451	110.3
1980	225,839	214.0	113,502	107.6
1981	249,402	236.3	111,955	106.1

2. Two countries may have very similar national incomes and yet their populations enjoy considerably different standards of living. This can occur for the following reasons:

(a) The national income statistics do not show the effect of better-quality goods, improved conditions of work, or a shorter working week, yet all these contribute to a higher standard of living.

(b) Where the size of the population is different we can say that normally the economy with the higher population will have the lower standard of living. This point is easily understood if we express national income as a figure per head of population. See the following example.

Both country A and country B have a national income of
£1,200 m. The population in country A is 20 million and in country
B 50 million.

		National income per head (£)
Country A	$\dfrac{1,200}{20}$	600
Country B	$\dfrac{1,200}{50}$	240

(c) Not all of the national output is available for consumption. Some
is required for the replacement of existing capital stock and some
for new investment projects. There is no requirement that
countries should invest the same amount of their national output,
and in practice it is very unlikely to happen.

---

*The standard of living of a country depends primarily on the goods and
services consumed in that country. As the national income measures the
amount of goods and services produced it is a relatively good indicator of
the standard of living. National income per head of population is often
used to illustrate living standards.*

*But the standard of living is more than a reflection of material
possessions; there are other intangible factors which contribute greatly to
the quality of life we enjoy. Consider the hours men worked a century
ago, compared with today. The pleasure derived from greater leisure
contributes as much to our standard of living as does that obtained from a
new watch or radio. Other items which are excluded from the calculation
of national income yet which contribute to our standard of living would
include beneficial working conditions, the beauty of the environment,
liberty, and cultural heritage.*

(d) The distribution of wealth in an economy is an important factor in
determining the standard of living. The calculation 'per capita
income' assumes an equal distribution of wealth, yet there are
countries where wealth and riches are concentrated in the hands of
a few, leaving the majority with an extremely low standard of
living.

(e) The national income may be underestimated because not all transactions undertaken within an economy are recorded. This is a particular problem for developing countries because a substantial number of transactions will be on a barter basis.

Economic growth

Is economic growth desirable? Certainly governments believe so, as would many ordinary people. The major argument in favour of pursuing a policy of growth is that if it is successful living standards rise. As we can see from Table 5.8, a sustained annual increase in national income of 3 per cent will result in living standards doubling in less than thirty years.

Table 5.8   Effect of varying growth rates – percentage of growth p.a.

| Year | % Rate of growth p.a. | | | |
	1%	3%	5%	7%
0	100	100	100	100
10	110	134	163	197
30	135	243	432	761
50	164	438	1,147	2,946

But often more important than how one country does over a period of time is how it compares against its neighbours (see Table 5.9). A consistently higher rate of growth by one country can lead to a very dramatic difference in national income within a short period of time.

Table 5.9   Comparative growth rates – percentage change p.a. in GDP

	1975	1976	1977	1978	1979	1980
United States	-1.0	5.6	5.1	4.4	3.2	0.2
Japan	1.4	6.5	5.4	5.9	5.6	4.2
W. Germany	-1.8	5.2	3.0	3.3	4.5	1.8
Switzerland	-7.3	-1.4	2.4	0.3	2.2	4.1
Australia	2.4	3.6	0.9	1.7	3.0	1.7
Brazil	5.7	9.0	4.7	6.0	6.4	7.8
United Kingdom	-0.8	4.2	1.0	3.6	0.8	-1.6

Source: OECD

Governments, perhaps naïvely, believe that higher growth rates will impress other countries and persuade them to adopt a similar political/economic system. Certain is the fact that higher growth rates allow a country to strengthen its military capability and defence systems, eases the burden of investment for the future, and enables redistribution of income to proceed without anyone experiencing an absolute cut in their standard of living.

Yet there is a cost to economic growth. Growth requires an investment in education, health, and technology. This investment can only be achieved by consuming fewer goods and services today, a reduction in everyone's standard of living. Moreover, this denial of consumption, if it is to make any significant impact on future standards of living, must be continued for many years. Many countries, though, have followed this path – the Chinese under Mao Tse-tung, Stalin's Russia, and Hitler's Germany all adopted five-year plans which moved resources from production of consumption goods to capital investment goods. Today most developing countries have such plans.

There may also be certain social and environmental costs resulting from economic growth which are not adequately reflected in estimates of national income. A rapid rate of growth requires adjustment in terms of technology and human skills. The change to more sophisticated techniques of production leaves obsolete machinery in its wake, means that less jobs are around for unskilled workers, and that even highly trained workers may find their skills redundant. The costs of this increasing degree of structural unemployment may be difficult to quantify, but they are real and include a higher incidence of mental and physical illness, family problems, and crime.

E. G. Mishan (*The Cost of Economic Growth*) also points to increased pollution, traffic congestion, the erosion of the countryside, and rapid depletion of raw materials as problems arising from fast growth rates.

Factors leading to growth

For most people the case for economic growth is compelling, associated as it is with increased consumption of goods and services and increased leisure. Governments have, therefore, sought to pursue those policies which would encourage growth, yet major disagreement exists over exactly what causes economic growth, and as many as twenty-three potential sources of growth have been identified. In the following sections we will look at a few of the major factors which are thought to lead to growth.

Capital accumulation

For many years economists have noted a correlation between those countries with high growth rates and high investment/GDP ratio. For example, since the Second World War, Japan has had exceptionally high growth rates – often in excess of 10 per cent. At the same time observers have noted that Japan has been investing 28 per cent of her national income in renewing and expanding her capital stock. In the

UK the corresponding ratio has been 14 per cent (likewise with many of her European counterparts), and the growth rate has averaged a disappointing 2 per cent.

Yet for many economies the sacrifice needed to raise the investment/GDP ratio even to that of the UK would be too much. In a subsistence economy consumption is already low and a transfer of resources from consumption to investment will cause extreme hardship, if not death from starvation. In such circumstances it is not surprising that some commentators believe that the gap between rich and poor countries is growing.

Human capital

Neither capital accumulation nor technical change is worth while unless there is the necessary manpower to work it. Economic growth depends upon having a pool of skilled labour available. To talk of human capital may seem odd, but all societies invest money in their workforce. The investment made would be in general education (the majority of workers are, after all, required to be both literate and numerate), the more specific skills required by industry (e.g. craftsmen, technicians, and managers), and health programmes.

Moreover the investment has increased hand-in-hand with the greater complexity and sophistication of industry. Consider the technology used today with that of a century ago and the wide range of skills and specialisms now required. Activity rates for young males in Britain are lower now than they have ever been – reflecting the need to stay on at school, or technical college, longer or enter higher education so as to obtain those qualifications required by industry.

The level of investment in education and skills training also depends upon the speed of industrial change. The greater the speed of change the greater the level of structural unemployment which occurs. Workers with unusable skills need to be invested with new skills to become valuable members of the workforce once more.

Technological change

The progress of technological change involves: (a) taking an idea – a pure scientific advance – and (b) identifying and developing its commercial applications to the point where (c) a new product or process is brought to the market.

Invention and innovation provides sources of new growth which prevent economic stagnation within a society, and the ability of an economy to absorb these changes quickly may be a major factor in determining a country's rate of growth. Where the process of technological advance is slow the major problems would seem to be in identifying the commercial applications arising from the scientific discovery and in overcoming opposition to change, from both management and union.

Technological transfer

It is not necessary for a country to invent a process or product to benefit from its development. If another country exploits that invention more quickly than the one where the discovery was made the second country will reap most of the benefits. One cause of high economic growth in Japan has been its ability to borrow and exploit Western technology for commercial purposes more quickly than we ourselves could.

Governments can also encourage the process of growth by providing sufficiently high incentives for business to 'write-off' existing machinery and invest in and expand new capital equipment. Although there are difficulties in calculating accurately the rate of technological change, the measure used most widely is labour productivity. Productivity itself is a measure of the quantity of output – goods or services, which can be obtained for a given input – land, labour, capital, or entrepreneurship. In practice, because of the problems of measuring the inputs of capital or raw materials it is the ratio of output to labour which is most often quoted. In official publications you will find two important definitions of labour productivity.

1. *Output per head* – the volume of output produced on average by each person employed.
2. *Output per man-hour* – the volume of output produced by each person employed in each hour.

The trend of labour productivity in terms of output per employee has shown major variations between OECD countries over recent years (1971–79). By far the most outstanding performance has been that of Japan whose productivity has increased by 54 per cent. The UK's European competitors have averaged 34 per cent while the USA and the UK languished behind with 25 and 16 per cent respectively.

In the UK's case the problem of low productivity arises because of ineffective utilisation of new plant and equipment. Commentators have also pointed to labour and material shortages, inadequate machine maintenance, quality faults, and overmanning.

Demand
The level of demand for goods and services plays an important part in determining the businessman's outlook for the future. A high and stable level of demand encourages the businessman to believe that he is able to sell all he can produce. Accordingly he will expand production and investment in plant and machinery. Moreover, an expansionist economy encourages the businessman to search for better and more efficient methods of production, resulting in greater labour

productivity. High levels of demand serve to perpetuate economic growth in that the increased investments lead to more employment possibilities and further increases in the general level of demand.

Examination questions

1. What do you understand by the term 'national income'? Selecting a method of your choice, show how it is calculated.

2. Why is it important to measure a country's economic activity?

3. By what methods is it possible to measure a nation's income?

4. Using either the output or expenditure method explain how the national income is calculated. In your answer you should ensure you distinguish between the following terms:

GDP	GNP
GDP (factor cost)	GDP (market price)
GNP	NNP
Money GNP	Real GNP

5. What are the major factors affecting a country's growth rate?

6. Why do some countries grow much faster than others?

7. What difficulties are there in comparing national income?
    (a) in different countries;
    (b) over a period of time.

8. Why do countries seek economic growth? What are the costs of economic growth?

9. What factors determine the incomes of nations and individuals? *(PSC Dec. 1977)*

10. Why is the economic growth important? How may it be encouraged?
    (PSC Dec. 1980)

11. Explain the terms 'cost' and 'standard of living'. What forces can raise the cost of living *or* the standard of living?

Inflation

Chapter 6

Inflation is a rise in the general level of prices. Try to think of any goods or services which you regularly buy which cost less now than they did say three or four years ago. The answer is that there are very few – the prices of most things we buy have risen. Inflation results in a fall in the value of money, or its purchasing power – we could also say that the cost of living has increased.

But while the process of inflation implies that items which cost £10 now will sooner or later cost £11 or £12, we must distinguish between the movement in the price of an individual product and the general price level. The price of an individual product is determined by its costs of production, and what consumers are willing to pay for it. This may move independently of prices generally. For example the prices of home computers are actually falling at the moment while the overall price level is rising. Equally a sudden increase in demand or shortage in the supply of a product may produce a price rise for that product which is in excess of price increases generally.

The reduction in the value of money is not a twentieth-century phenomenon. Throughout history there has been a tendency for prices to rise. It is estimated for example that prices in England doubled during the eighteenth and nineteenth centuries. Where, as in England during the period 1700–1900, inflation was persistent but gradual it is defined as 'mild' or 'creeping' inflation.

The constant worry of governments is that mild or creeping inflation will get out of hand and accelerate to alarming levels. Several countries in Europe experienced this problem (it is called hyperinflation) after the First World War. Hyperinflation exists when public confidence in money drops to such an extent that people are no longer willing to save or hold money. When inflation reaches these levels it is uncontrollable. People expect prices to rise – indeed rise rapidly. In their anxiety to avoid holding notes and coins they actually fuel the inflationary process by bidding up the paper price of any tangible commodity with real value. The normal solution is to abandon the existing unit of currency and create another.

During 1923 the value of money in Germany declined so rapidly (at one stage prices were rising at 5 per cent *per hour*) that at one stage workers were paid twice a day, and used to spend their morning's wages at lunch-time rather than accept the fall in the value of their money which would have occurred by tea-time! Eventually people refused to accept notes and coins in payment of debts. Barter became the order of the day, and other commodities such as cigarettes took over the role of money. In 1918 1 mark was worth about 1p, by 1923 1p would buy 200m. marks!

More recently Argentina, Brazil, Chile, and Israel have also experienced sufficiently high levels of inflation to be termed hyperinflation.

Throughout the twentieth century the UK has experienced a fall in the value of money. While in comparison with the levels of inflation we have just discussed the annual increases in this country have been modest, prices have been rising more rapidly than at any other time during our history. In particular in the last decade 1973–83 we have seen the highest rates of inflation ever recorded in this country (see Fig. 6.1) with annual price rises peaking in 1975 at 24.2 per cent. Over the decade as a whole the annual rate of increase has averaged 13 per cent, or put another way there has been a threefold increase in prices. Since 1980 the inflation rate has fallen markedly and at present is running at approximately 5–6 per cent per annum.

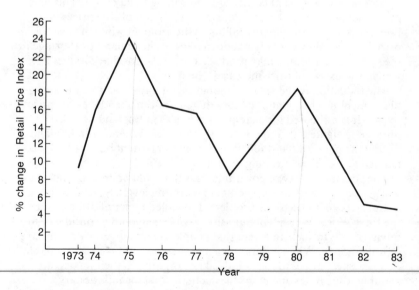

Fig. 6.1   United Kingdom inflation record, 1973–83

The effects of inflation

1. Mild inflation encourages businessmen to maintain and expand production. Rising prices are associated with a high and buoyant level of demand, often termed 'boom conditions'. Unemployment may be reduced as businesses expand production and the rate of economic growth increased as firms invest for the future.

2. Business profits benefit from mild inflation. Buoyant trading conditions result in a high level of demand for most products, while the process of rising prices tends to result in profit margins being larger than anticipated. The rise in profits is normally greater than the increase in the cost of living, and efficient producers make large profits. Share prices also reflect the increase in the level of profits. During the upswing of the business or stop–go cycle, share prices rise as investors first anticipate and then receive enlarged dividends.

High levels of inflation though, are counter-productive. Business confidence in the future is undermined. Businessmen anticipate government action to reduce inflation, including a cut-back in state spending, and are less willing to invest. Moreover, while business profits in monetary terms may be at an all-time high, in real terms they may be extremely low.

3. For the majority of employees a period of mild inflation is a period of prosperity. Unemployment is low and economic growth provides the worker with a rising standard of living. Not all workers benefit equally though. Those with industrial muscle will secure themselves wages and salary increases far in excess of rises in the cost of living. Employers are willing to grant these increases in the belief that they will be able to pass most of them on to the consumer in the form of higher prices. Those whose bargaining position is not so strong, or who do not care to use their power, will find the increases they obtain considerably less. The growth of unionism among office and other professional workers is, in part, an attempt by these groups to prevent further erosion of wage differentials between themselves and industrial workers.

The power of inflation
If we assume an annual inflation rate of 5 per cent the textbook which costs £10 today will cost:

> *£12.75 in 5 years' time*
> *£16.30 in 10 years' time*
> *£34.00 in 25 years' time*
> *£115.00 in 50 years' time*

---

4. It is those people living upon fixed incomes – incomes which do not rise as the cost of living increases, who are hit hardest by inflation. The major group involved are pensioners. The UK inflation of the 1970s which reduced purchasing power to one-third of what it was at the beginning of the period has prompted many unions to negotiate agreements linking pensions to increases in the Retail Price Index (RPI).

5. In a period of inflation the real value of any sum borrowed declines. The man who borrowed £6,000 in 1970 to purchase a house found the real value of the £6,000 he had to repay in 1980 had dropped to a mere £2,000. Conversely, in 1980 the lender would have had to receive not £6,000 but £18,000 to make up for the loss of purchasing power since 1970. We can say, as a general rule, that in inflationary times borrowers gain and lenders lose. Not surprisingly, inflation may discourage saving and encourages people to spend their money now in an attempt to obtain full value from it.

In the long run rates of interest may be forced up in order to attract savings. When inflation in the UK was at its highest in the 1970s the UK Government was paying in excess of 15 per cent p.a. to attract long-term funds – and yet the investor, with inflation running at more than 15 per cent was still not receiving a real return on his loan. But should the inflation rate and interest rates fall the Government may very well find itself committed to paying unnecessarily high interest payments. (It was for precisely these reasons that in March 1981 the UK Government started issuing index-linked 'gilts'.) Interest and redemption values are linked to inflation – as measured by the RPI. There are now (January 1984) nine issues of index-linked gilts accounting for approximately 6 per cent of all gilts issued.

6. As the largest borrower in the country the Government benefits greatly from inflation. Over a period of time the real burden of the National Debt is reduced substantially by inflation. The Government also benefits through increased tax revenue. Wage increases result in poorer sections of society who were previously exempt from tax being dragged into the tax net (even though in real terms they may be no better off than before). For the same reason higher wage-earners find themselves paying more tax.

7. Inflation may also adversely affect a country's trading relations with the rest of the world. Where a country experiences inflation at a rate greater than that of its trading partners it will find that:

(a) its exports decline as they become uncompetitive when compared with the overseas-produced product;

(b) its imports increase as nationals find that foreign goods are relatively cheaper; and

(c) overseas investors remove capital from that country in the expectation of a fall in its exchange rate.

Apart from Spain and Italy the UK rate of inflation has of recent years been consistently higher than that of its major trading partners and other Organisation for Economic Co-operation and Development (OECD) countries, with results the same as those described above.

Calculating changes in the value of money

There are many groups who are interested in this information. They include:

(a) employees and trade unions who claim increased wages because of a rise in the cost of living;

(b) employers, who wish to limit employee wage claims to the cost of living increase;

(c) public sector pensioners whose pension increases are based upon the rate of inflation;

(d) companies who wish to see whether the growth of profits has kept pace with inflation;

(e) the Government, who is concerned with the impact of inflation upon international trade, the balance of payments, savings, investment, and wage increases.

Changes in the value of money are reflected in the prices of goods and services we see around us every day. The RPI (this is also referred to as the 'cost of living' index) is the most commonly used measure of these changes. The index is calculated as follows:

(a) By selecting a base year on which to make price comparisons. The RPI in the base year is given the value of 100.

(b) Approximately 600 goods and services are selected. These represent a typical family's monthly pattern of expenditure. Each item in the index is given a weighting which reflects its importance in the average household budget.

(c) The list of goods is priced at monthly intervals – approximately 130,000 observations (i.e. prices) for the 600 goods and services are collected each month by the Department of Employment.

(d) The percentage change in price for each item (since the base date) is then calculated. This, when multiplied by its weighting, provides the figure which is included (along with the calculations made for all other goods and services) in the RPI.

Let us take a simple example and assume that the average family spends its money on just three items – food, shelter, and clothing which have doubled, trebled, and quadrupled respectively in price over the previous period. Let us further assume that food accounts for 50 per cent of the family budget, shelter 30 per cent and clothing 20 per cent. To obtain the new average price level we multiply each price index by its weighting.

	Weight	New Price index (last year = 100)	
Food	0.5 (50%)	200	100
Shelter	0.3 (30%)	300	90
Clothing	0.2 (20%)	400	80
	Average price level	270	

The average price level has risen by 170 per cent in the past period. The rise is smaller than that for two of the items in the index – shelter and clothing – because the item with the largest weighting – food – has only increased by a modest amount compared with the other two.

There are obvious drawbacks in the calculation of the RPI. First, the choice of goods and their weighting is related to what the average family buys. People who do not fall into this group, and there are many of them, must realise that the RPI is only a general indication of how their cost of living has risen. In practice there are many poor families who find particular price increases very much more significant than the average price level.

Secondly, our tastes and therefore expenditure, change over time (see Fig. 6.2). For example, as a country's standard of living rises its inhabitants will spend less on food and more on clothing, shelter, transport, and leisure. In the UK the CSO changes the weightings on the cost of living index annually after undertaking a family expenditure survey. Over a long period of time the RPI has very little significance because the goods purchased and their weightings will be fundamentally different.

Thirdly, the RPI takes no account of variations in price or quality. There may be significant regional variations in prices with many remote districts paying considerably more for all kinds of goods and services. Improvements in quality may also account, at least partially, for an increase in the price of a product. Cars today, although higher in price than a few years ago, are considerably more fuel efficient, go longer between routine services, and are generally more reliable.

Lastly, the present UK Government has argued that the RPI is not a fair indicator of changes in the cost of living because it does not take into account the impact of direct taxes upon consumer purchasing power. When in 1979 the UK Government cut direct taxes but increased indirect taxes, from 8 or 12½ per cent to 15 per cent, the

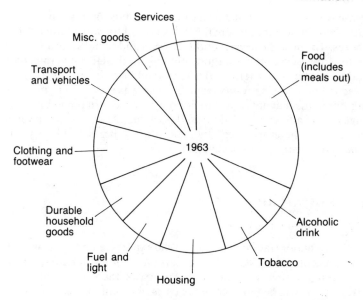

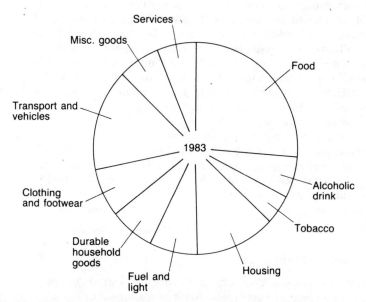

Fig. 6.2 The weighting of main categories of expenditure in the RPI, 1963–83. (*Source:* Adapted from *Economic Progress Report,* Nov. 1983)

immediate effect was to raise the cost of living by $3\frac{1}{2}$ percentage points. Yet had the RPI been adjusted for the reduction in direct taxes the increase would have been reduced to $1\frac{1}{2}$ percentage points. This is obviously of importance where the index is used for wage-bargaining purposes. To show the impact of direct taxes and social security benefits (for which a similar argument applied) the UK Government introduced a new index termed the Taxes and Price Index (TPI). This showed the increase in pre-tax income which was necessary to maintain living standards, having regard to not only increases in prices but changes in tax allowances and rates. It is calculated for various levels of income and therefore gives a more accurate indication of how your *personal* circumstances have changed.

Causes of inflation

Cost push – imported inflation

The UK is a major trading nation. In 1980 exports and imports were 33 and 30 per cent respectively of GDP. It is impossible, therefore, for the UK to avoid the effects of rising prices overseas. Increases in the prices of UK imports will be reflected in the costs of production of British industry and eventually (unless the industry absorbs the increased costs through improvements in efficiency) prices in the shops.

Most of the major changes in the RPI this century have been associated with changes in import prices. In 1920/21 import prices nearly halved and retail prices fell by over a quarter. Increases in import prices during the Second World War and the Korean War caused sharp increases in the UK cost of living. Similarly, it was the spectacular increase in oil prices together with the increased cost of raw materials and food in 1973/74 which was largely responsible for the high inflation rates of the 1970s.

But changes in import prices occur not only because of the actions of overseas producers. Changes may also be brought about by fluctuations in exchange rates. Thus a country which experiences balance of payments difficulties may seek to remedy the situation by devaluing the domestic currency against other currencies. The effect is to make that country's exports cheaper, but also – and in this context more importantly – to raise import prices.

Cost push – wage inflation

Many economies see excessive wage demands by strong unions as a major contributor to many inflationary situations. The argument is that powerful trade unions are able to obtain large increases for their members through the threat, or use, of industrial action. Firms, too, it is argued, have been culpable in granting these increases in the belief that they could be passed on to the consumer.

Unfortunately the higher the cost of living which is the result of granting these wage claims then forms the basis of further wage claims by the unions. In this way inflation is self-perpetuating. An increase in wages causes an increase in prices, causes an increase in wages, and so on. This is commonly referred to as the wage–price spiral.

The increase in wage costs would not be so worrying if there was a corresponding increase in productivity. An increase in wages would not then necessarily result in an increase in prices. Unfortunately, wage increases have seldom been accompanied by agreements designed to raise productivity. And even when productivity deals were negotiated the effect could be inflationary where other groups sought and obtained similar wage increases without improvements in productivity.

Demand pull

Demand pull or excess demand inflation occurs where at a given price level buyers are keen to purchase more than the amount being produced. It is normally associated with a near full-employment situation where the industry finds it difficult to expand production. It is then that the excess demand is absorbed by an increase in the price of goods generally (inflation).

Where there is full employment excess demand may also occur in the labour market. Firms find it difficult to fill current vacancies, and offer wages that are higher than those currently being paid. In this way employees are persuaded to switch employers. The only alternative open to the employer is to use less efficient labour. In either event prices are likely to be increased to cover the increased costs.

Demand-pull inflation can also arise below levels of full employment when it is often termed 'bottleneck inflation'. Inflation is caused by shortages of key workers or materials preventing production of the finished article. For example, since the Second World War a lack of investment in the training of skilled workers by business generally, and the erosion of wage differentials between skilled and unskilled workers (combined with an unwillingness on the part of young men to serve long apprenticeships) has resulted in shortages of skilled employees, especially in the engineering industry. As before, firms are likely to offer more money to obtain the resources they need.

Equally, in wartime as resources are absorbed into the war effort and production of consumption goods declines there is a tendency for prices to rise. It is likely that the Government in such a situation will introduce rationing and maximum prices to control the inflationary pressures. Unfortunately, once the controls are lifted wartime savings compete for the consumer goods available causing prices to rise.

Government induced

Government action may cause or fuel inflation in several ways. A switch from direct to indirect taxation will cause the RPI to rise. Even if increases in taxation do not affect the RPI the effect may be inflationary should employees attempt to offset the reduction in their standard of living by higher wage claims. Equally, the above-average rises in nationalised industry prices, council house rents, and local authority rates of recent years are a result of changes in government policy designed to curb public sector borrowing.

But by far the most telling attack on government policies has come from a group of economists labelled the 'monetarists' who believe the prime cause of inflation is increases in the supply of money. The basis of their argument rests upon the work of an economist, Irving Fisher, who propounded the equation $MV = PT$ otherwise called the quantity theory of money. Briefly M (the quantity of money) when multiplied by V (the velocity or speed at which it changes hands) is equal to P (the general level of prices) $\times T$ (the number of transactions or output). Monetarists argue that V is relatively constant and that therefore increases in the supply of money will result in either an increase in T (output) or at full employment by rising prices (P).

Monetarists believe that Government attempts to maintain full employment through budget deficits have over-stimulated the economy by ignoring the deficit's expansionary effect on money supply (commonly defined as notes and coins together with bank deposits).

A budgetary deficit can be financed in a number of ways. Long-term government stock may be sold to members of the public – a method which merely transfers money from the public to the State and does not involve an increase in money supply. It is all too easy, however, for the Government to avoid this increase in indebtedness by creating new money – that is, printing more pound notes or dollar bills. This was the start of the German hyperinflation of 1923/24. Closer to home, the UK Government expanded notes and coins in circulation with the general public threefold during the 1970s.

An even greater impact on money supply arises when the Government sells Treasury bills to finance the deficit. In the hands of the banking system Treasury bills are almost the same as cash and may be used to increase lending. For each £1 of Treasury bills held the banks can lend up to £7 to the public. Monetarists have amassed a large amount of statistical evidence to prove the link between money supply and inflation. If we accept their argument that the increase in money supply takes approximately two years to work through the system before appearing as higher prices, there does appear to be a remarkable correlation between the two for the UK between 1970 and 1980 (see Fig. 6.3).

Stagflation

In a study of the UK economy between 1862 and 1958, Professor A. W. Phillips found there was a close correlation between the rate of change in

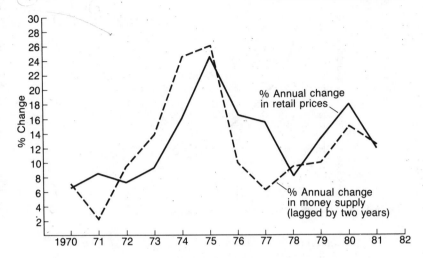

Fig. 6.3 Comparison of annual changes in retail prices and money supply (lagged by two years)

wages and prices and unemployment (see Fig. 6.4). The ability of labour to increase wages depended upon the level of unemployment. When unemployment was high labour bargaining power was reduced, and so were increases in wages. Indeed, at times during the period wages were stable or actually fell. But as unemployment fell annual increases in wages rose. In short, the rate of increase in wages was inversely related to unemployment. Put another way, there was a trade-off between inflation and unemployment. When inflation was low unemployment was high and vice versa. Phillip's work suggested that an unemployment level of between 5 and 6 per cent could be sufficient to guarantee stable prices.

From around 1970 though, the relationship between inflation and unemployment has broken down. Many Western economies have experienced far greater annual increases in wages and prices for a given level of unemployment than previously. For this new experience the term 'stagflation' has been coined by putting together STAGnation and inFLATION.

Diagrammatically we can say that the Phillips curve has shifted bodily to the right. While the reasons for the shift are not completely understood the following possibilities have been suggested:

1. By reason of age and skills large numbers of the unemployed may be unemployable. The problems of full employment therefore become apparent at higher levels of unemployment.

2. Trade unions have discovered that their bargaining power is not so greatly affected by high levels of unemployment as was once thought.

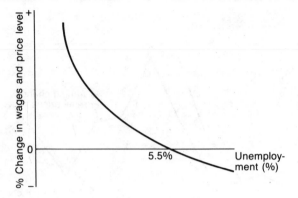

Fig. 6.4 The Phillips curve

3. *Higher unemployment pay and social security benefits cushion the worker from the effects of unemployment.*

4. *Workers are now taking into account the movement of prices when negotiating wage rises.*

The control of inflation

Government action which is designed to reduce the speed at which prices are rising is termed 'deflation'. Deflationary action may take one of three forms, fiscal policy, monetary policy, or direct controls such as a prices and incomes policy. Commonly, the policies are used in conjunction with one another in what has become known as a 'package deal'. The aim of the package deal was to affect, through a whole series of measures, all parts of the economy simultaneously, and to convince businessmen, financiers, investors, foreign governments, and other international institutions of the Government's determination to reduce the inflation rate.

Fiscal and monetary policy both act to reduce purchasing power within the economy. Fiscal policy will act upon the level of aggregate demand through the Government's revenue-raising and expenditure plans. Should the Government wish to siphon off excess purchasing power it will plan for a budget surplus – that is, raising more revenue than it will spend during that year. To do this the Chancellor of the Exchequer may decide that he will reduce government spending but maintain taxation at its current level. But a substantial proportion of government expenditure is planned several years in advance and in consequence is difficult to reduce. It is therefore more likely that the

Government will hold its expenditure at present levels (or merely make modest reductions) and increase taxation instead.

Monetary policy aims to curb inflation in two ways. First by announcing monetary targets in advance it acts upon people's expectations regarding future levels of inflation. Should the public expect inflation to fall trade unions may moderate wage claims yet still preserve their members' living standards. Similarly, firms need not increase prices by as much to achieve a predetermined level of profitability. Secondly, by controlling its own borrowing requirement, and the activities of the banking system the Government can achieve a reduction in money-supply growth, reducing demand for both goods and labour.

Governments have been reluctant to use monetary and fiscal policy to reduce inflation. To have the economy working at below full capacity is a waste of valuable resources. Deflation also damages business confidence, retards economic growth, and implies a rejection of the commitment to full employment.

Direct controls on prices, or incomes, and at times both, have been the most common alternative. The controls which may be statutory or voluntary seek to restrain price or wage rises, thus breaking the wage – price spiral and moderating the rate of inflation. The British experience of such policies does not hold out much hope for their success. For virtually all of the period 1960–80 some form of control on prices or incomes was in operation. While the policies achieved some short-term success, in the longer term they failed to prevent the UK from having a higher rate of inflation than her major trading partners.

To be successful the policy had to be accepted by both employers and unions. Yet employers disliked having their pricing policy determined by the Government while unions were reluctant to surrender their right to free collective bargaining. Acceptance was often grudging and once the period of restraint was over both parties took steps to make up lost ground. Lastly, policies were seen to be inequitable. Those who had obtained a large pay increase just before the introduction of wage restraint gained against all other groups of workers. Moreover, pay policies often hit workers in the public sector harder than those in private industry – the Government wishing to lead by example.

Examination questions

1. What do you understand by the term cost of living? How is it measured? What forces can raise the cost of living?

2. Outline the extent of inflation in your own country and the measures being taken to control it. *(PSC 1980)*

3. What is the problem of inflation? *(PSC 1977)*

4. Why do a majority of governments wish to control inflation? What measures may be used to control it? *(PSC 1978)*

5. Examine the effects of inflation upon:
   (a) an individual;
   (b) a manufacturing firm;
   (c) the economy.

6. What is meant by inflation? How will inflation affect:
   (a) a young married secretary;
   (b) an investor;
   (c) the sterling exchange rate.

7. Examine the effect upon the business community of:
   (a) deflation;
   (b) devaluation.

8. What are the reasons for the continuous rise in prices experienced by most countries?

9. In discussing rising prices the following terms may be used: cost-push inflation; demand-pull inflation; 'stagflation'; hyperinflation; deflation. Clearly and concisely explain what is meant by each term.

The problem of unemployment

Chapter 7

Full employment

In 1944 the British wartime coalition government issued a White Paper entitled *Employment Policy* This committed all post-war governments to the maintenance of a high and stable level of employment. Full employment was defined as a situation where 97 per cent of those available for work were, in fact, employed.

For nearly thirty years after the Second World War British Governments' attempts to achieve full employment were extremely successful. The mass unemployments of the 1930s (when unemployment in the UK reached a peak of 22 per cent in 1932) seemed to be a thing of the past. Jobs were plentiful, workers could pick and choose between them. In many areas there were more jobs than workers available to fill them. It was not until the end of the 1960s that unemployment as a percentage of the working population rose above 2 per cent, nor was it until 1975 that unemployment topped 1 million workers or 4 per cent.

Indeed, it could be said that post-war government policies were too successful. The use of fiscal policy to iron out the periodic variations in the demand for goods and services often created a situation of over-full employment. This caused several problems. Inflationary trends were exacerbated by workers using their enhanced bargaining power to push for higher wages. Businessmen were willing to grant these claims in the knowledge that at least part of the extra cost could be passed on to the consumer in the form of higher prices.

Shortages of labour also had their impact on the balance of payments. First, the high prices of UK goods reduced their competitiveness in the international market. All too often the imported product was cheaper than the home-produced equivalent. Secondly, shortages of labour prevented UK industry from producing the quantity of goods required by the home market – the deficit again being made good by imports.

Economic growth too was hampered by the emphasis on full employment. First the stop–go policy associated with the maintenance of full employment reduced entreprenurial confidence and therefore the willingness to invest. Secondly, in so far as wages rose faster than prices the profit margins of businesses were squeezed, reducing the money available to invest in new improved machinery or new expanding industries.

Since 1975 unemployment has risen dramatically (see Fig. 7.1). Today unemployment in the UK has reached approximately 3 million, nearly 13.0 per cent of the working population. In part this increase in unemployment is attributable to the problems discussed above. However, the position has been exacerbated by the Government's monetary and fiscal policies – high interest rates and curbed public

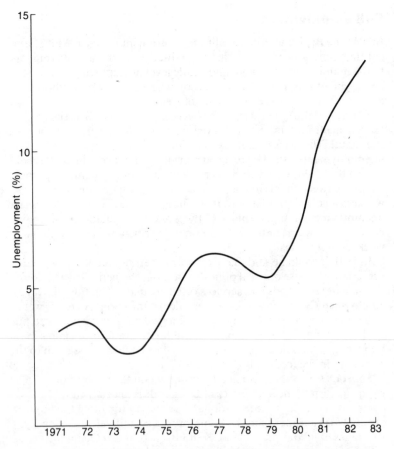

Fig. 7.1 Unemployment in the UK since 1971 (annual averages). (*Sources: Annual Abstract of Statistics 1983; Employment Gazette,* Oct. 1983)

spending, and also the world recession with its reduction in the demand for goods and service generally.

Employment in the UK

The collection of information on the British labour market is the responsibility of the Department of Employment. Such information will be used in both manpower and economic planning. Thus information on vacancies available, and industries which are expanding employment will have implications for the courses run in government skill centres and further and higher education. Equally, unemployment statistics may be used to make a case for giving help to a particular region or group of employees.

Table 7.1   Analysis of UK working population

	'000
Employees in employment	20,644
Self-employed	2,118
Unemployed	2,984
HM Forces	322
Working population	26,068

Source: Employment Gazette, October 1983.

The working population of the UK is approximately 26 million or slightly under half the total population. Two groups – the young and the old form the bulk of those not included in the working population. However, it is not too true to say that the working population comprises of all men between the ages of 16 and 65, and women 16–60. Approximately 7,500,000 in these groups will not be available for work. Two examples will illustrate why. Many young people remain at school or college after the age of 16, while many married women retire (at least temporarily) from the workforce in order to have a family.

The proportion of people who are active out of the total population of each group, classified by age and sex, is shown in Fig. 7.2. Two trends stand out. First that male activity rates have declined in all age-groups. This is not surprising. The demand for a more highly skilled workforce has persuaded many young men (and also young women) to remain in full-time education and study for higher qualifications. Older men retire earlier, primarily because of improved pensions schemes.

Secondly, female activity rates have expanded strongly between 1961 and 1981. In 1961 women formed 32 per cent of the working

	Female				Male		
	1961	1971	1981		1961	1971	1981
15–19	71.1	55.9	64.2		74.9	70.9	70.9
20–24	61.8	60.1	68.9		91.9	89.9	88.9
25–44	40.3	50.6	61.4		98.5	97.9	97.0
45–59 (woman) 45–64 (men)	41.4	57.4	63.6		96.8	94.5	88.4
60–65 +	10.0	12.4	6.5		25.0	19.4	8.0

Fig. 7.2 A comparison of male and female activity rates over two decades. (*Source: Social Trends*, 1983)

population, but by 1981 had increased their share to about 40 per cent. Married women of all ages figure particularly strongly in this trend, increasing their overall activity rates from 29.7 per cent in 1961 to 48.8 per cent in 1981. Several reasons are advanced for this. Women have more control over their lives now due to contraception. The advent of the smaller family has given the married woman more spare time. Spare time has also been increased by the large number of household labour-saving gadgets available. But this can only be a partial answer as we have also seen a growth in the activity rates for women with young children – the presumption must be that social attitudes have moved in favour of the working wife and mother. Additionally, as we shall shortly see, the changes in the structure of business have also been conducive to greater participation in working life by women.

Let us now turn to look at where these people are employed. Economic development is characterised by changes in the structure of industry, and therefore changes in employment opportunities too. Figure 7.3 shows the changes which occurred in the UK between 1901 and 1983. First we note the demise of employment in the primary sector, largely due to the decline in agriculture. Today agriculture, employs only 1.7 per cent of the working population, in 1901 it was over 10 per cent. Secondly, we can see a small but significant decrease in the secondary sector, and lastly a large increase in tertiary employment. The experience of the UK is not unique. Similar changes have been well documented in other industrialised countries.

The reasons for the decline of the UK manufacturing base and the transfer of employment to the service sector are complex. However, one major factor would be the increasing use of automated equipment, allowing manufacturers to increase output and at the same time reduce employment. Equally important has been the growth of manufacturing capacity in developing countries and the consequent increase in competition – especially in traditional industries such as textiles, shipbuilding, and iron and steel.

As regards the growing importance of the tertiary sector we may

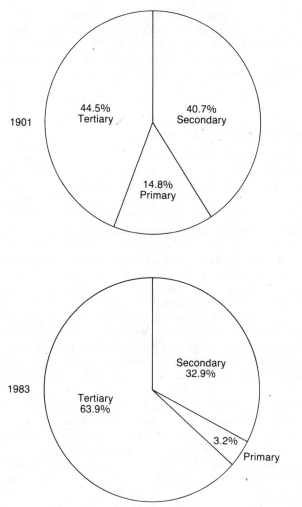

Fig. 7.3 Percentage of total labour force employed by sector – 1901 and 1983

point to the fact that until recently there were fewer opportunities for technical innovation – this sector was labour intensive and productivity was low. But perhaps the most important reason for tertiary sector growth has been the expansion of employment in the public sector, employing 23 per cent of the working population in 1961, but 31 per cent in 1981. By far the greatest part of the increase is attributable to the expansion of education and the National Health Service each of whom doubled their employees during this period.

The expansion of the tertiary sector has had important implications for the employment of women. Women are twice as likely to be employed in the service as in the manufacturing sector. More importantly the education and health services have traditionally recruited a high proportion of women. In 1981 approximately 60 per cent of all employees in central and local government were women, one-fifth of whom were working part-time.

Measuring unemployment

Since October 1982 unemployment in the UK has been measured by calculating the number of people who claim benefit as a result of unemployment. Two classifications are produced monthly. Unemployment is first analysed on a *regional* basis – that is, the region in which the unemployed person claims benefit. Secondly, the *industrial* classification indicates the industry in which the unemployed person last worked. A further classification, *occupational*, showing the occupations the unemployed wish to enter, is published quarterly, while unemployment classified by *age* is issued twice a year.

Two major groups are not included in the unemployment statistics. First there are those who although actively seeking work – full or part-time – are for some reason unable to claim benefits. The 1971 Census of Production estimated that nearly a quarter of a million women (the majority married and supported by their husbands) were searching for work but were not included in the unemployment statistics. Secondly, school-leavers – young people seeking their first job – are also excluded.

There are, however, other factors which serve artificially to inflate the statistics. For example the figures include those who are fraudently unemployed – that is, claiming benefit but at the same time having some form of undeclared employment. Moreover, there are also those who are unsuited or unwilling to work (though there is little evidence to show that this group is as large as some people would have us believe).

The Department of Employment makes adjustment to the crude figures collected monthly to allow for seasonal factors. For example, in the summer months unemployment will fall with the expansion of tourism and building work. Yet this apparent fall may in fact mask a rising trend in unemployment. Unemployment figures are therefore adjusted to eliminate seasonal variations and reveal the real trend.

The Department of Employment Job Centres and Employment Offices also maintain a register of vacancies based upon information supplied to them by local employers. Each month the *Employment Gazette* publishes statistics on unfilled vacancies, classifying the information by industry and region. An occupational analysis is also published quarterly. The published statistics are, however, not a complete record of all unfilled vacancies in the country – employers do not always recruit through the Employment Offices. They may prefer to use press advertisements or private employment agencies instead.

But taken together the monthly statistics on unemployment and vacancies are a reasonable barometer of the state of the labour market. As business activity falls, for example, we would expect to see a rise in the level of unemployment and a fall in the vacancies notified to Employment Offices. Equally, when the level of economic activity rises the opposite occurs.

By measuring vacancies as a proportion of unemployment, vacancies/unemployment, it is possible to obtain a good indication of the extent of the unemployment problem. Where the result is a figure close to 1.0 unemployment is not so worrying for there are nearly as many vacancies as there are unemployed. As the figure declines though, our concern grows because the supply of labour outstrips the demand. The great advantage of this technique is that it may be used to measure the state of the labour market not only for the whole country but also for a region, industry, or occupation.

Unemployment and its remedies

There are several categories of unemployment. It is important to distinguish between them as they have different causes and therefore require different treatment.

Transitional unemployment

There will always be some people changing their jobs. Some will have been made redundant by their employers. Other people will leave one job, subsequently searching for and finding another one. These workers 'between' jobs may form a substantial proportion of the unemployed workforce in prosperous times and provide a pool of labour from which vacancies are filled. Indeed, it is very necessary for this pool of labour to exist so that industry can adapt to changed circumstances – for example increases in product demand, or labour to work 'new technology'.

This category will also include a number of people, who although classified as unemployed are not really seeking work and those who, through mental or physical disability, are unfitted for work.

Government help to the transitionally unemployed has taken two forms:

1. *Financial aid* – so that the unemployed person is not forced to accept the first job that comes his way, but may find a position which best fits his skills and aspirations.

2. *Search aid* – information on current vacancies and an employment placement service speeds the process by which the unemployed person finds a job.

Seasonal unemployment

Seasonal unemployment arises when the demand for labour varies throughout the year. For example, employment in the building, tourism, and agricultural industries may increase dramatically during the summer months.

The degree of unemployment in these industries can be lessened by having a small core of workers who are willing to work long hours in the peak season and accept short-time working at other times of the year. This core workforce may also be supplemented in busy times by casual workers. Thus students often find holiday jobs in hotels or on farms picking fruit. Such intermittent work may also suit other people who are unable to take up permanent employment. Attempts to reduce unemployment in seasonal trades often concentrate on developing the market for goods and services concerned – tourists may be persuaded to take holidays out of season through low prices, or perhaps advertising may persuade people to buy turkeys at times other than Christmas! Alternatively, it may be possible to combine two seasonal trades whose peak periods do not coincide.

Structural unemployment

As with transitional unemployment (sometimes termed frictional unemployment) structural unemployment is caused by changes in the structure of industries. But whereas frictional unemployment is a situation in which the displaced workers will be absorbed into new jobs within a short time, structural unemployment may very well give rise to high levels of long-term unemployment.

A decline in demand has affected many of the industries on which Britain's prosperity was built. Thus the export of Lancashire's textile products were decimated by the growth of the cotton industry in the Far East. The increasing use of oil as a form of power has thrown many Welsh and Scottish miners out of work. Where the change is slow, labour can adjust to the changed circumstance satisfactorily. The workers who retire from the industry concerned are not replaced, those who are unfortunate enough to lose their jobs will find employment in new expanding industries. However, it is where the change is rapid that we have true structural unemployment. New expanding industries are unable to absorb all those made redundant. Moreover, the jobs which are available may demand skills of a very different nature to those of the unemployed worker.

Structural unemployment is often extremely localised. Where an industry is heavily concentrated in an area any downturn in the demand for its products is likely to have a dramatic affect on unemployment. Thus by 1934 the decline in the prosperity of the British coal-mining, shipbuilding, and cotton industries had resulted in unemployment of over 35 per cent in parts of Wales and 30 per cent in parts of northern England and Scotland (when the national average was 16½ per cent). These exceptionally high unemployment rates reflect not only the collapse of work in the industry concerned, but also where these workers spent their wages. Employment in shops, clubs, transport – in virtually every walk of life – was affected as the reduction in purchasing power was felt in these regions.

This unemployment imbalance is still with us today. Regions such as Scotland, Wales, Northern Ireland, and northern England still suffer higher levels of unemployment than the rest of the country (see Table 7.2). Nor is the problem unique to the UK. Italy, Sweden, the USA, and indeed most other industrialised countries have a similar problem.

Table 7.2   Comparative rates of unemployment in different regions of the UK

	1978 (%)	1983 (Sept) (%)
South-East	3.9	9.6
East Anglia	4.8	10.4
South-West	6.2	11.2
West Midlands	5.3	16.0
East Midlands	4.7	11.9
Yorkshire and Humberside	5.7	14.5
North-West	6.9	16.2
Northern	8.6	18.0
Wales	7.7	16.5
Scotland	7.7	15.2
Northern Ireland	11.0	22.2

Source: Employment Gazette, October 1983.

In the UK government policies to alleviate the problem of regional unemployment have existed since the 1930s. These policy measures have centred on either 'taking work to the workers' or alternatively 'taking workers to the work'. This latter policy of persuading workers to move to those areas where jobs were available was never particularly successful, because of the strength of family and social ties. Moreover, because such a policy results in the under-utilisation of social capital (schools, hospitals, roads, etc.) in the donor region and the over-utilisation of the same resources in the host region it has, of recent years, fallen into disrepute.

Present government attempts to aid the unemployed to search for work in another region are twofold. Under the Job Search and Employment Transfer Scheme financial help is given towards visiting new areas to look or work, attending interviews, and moving home to a new area. Secondly, a national mobility scheme has been introduced to ease the movement of public sector housing tenants.

The policy of 'taking work to the worker' presently rests upon the concept of an 'assisted area' – that is, an area of high unemployment where the Government aids industry. At present there are three categories of assisted area – special development, development, and intermediate areas – covering approximately 25 per cent of the working population (see Table 7.3). Various financial incentives are given by the Government to encourage industrial investment (and therefore employment) in these areas. For example, manufacturing firms receive a grant towards the cost of new fixed assets of 22 per cent in special development areas and 15 per cent in development areas. Selected financial assistance is also available where a project undertaken will create employment, safeguard employment, or is 'in the national interest'. Firms in the special development and development areas may also be given preference when tendering for public sector work.

Table 7.3   Assisted areas, 1984

| Northern Ireland |
| North and West Scotland |
| North-West England |
| Humberside and West Yorkshire (parts) |
| North Wales |
| South Wales |
| South-West England |

Until 1982 a further negative control also existed. Industries wishing to expand outside the assisted areas were required to apply to the Government for an Industrial Development Certificate prior to seeking local planning permission. It was generally recognised that certificates were more easy to obtain in the assisted rather than other areas. The hope was that potential developments which were refused a certificate in a prosperous region would then take place in the assisted area.

It is difficult to quantify the affect of regional policy. In two decades over £20 b. has been spent on regional aid, but the poor North, rich South problem with the widely disparate levels of employment continue to exist (if we were to bisect the UK by a line drawn from Bristol to Humberside, the working population would be roughly halved and the unemployment rate in the southern sectors and northern sectors would be approximately 11 and 17 per cent respectively).

Much of the industry which went to the regions was capital intensive, creating only a handful of jobs for skilled personnel while being extremely expensive in terms of grants and other aid.

Additionally, much of the employment created was for female labour. The overall effect was to leave, virtually untouched, a hard core of unskilled male labour. Moreover, much of this industry has proved to be highly marginal in the present recession as parent companies cut back on output. Since 1978 factories in these regions have closed at an alarming rate.

Cyclical unemployment

This type of unemployment arises because of variations in the general level of economic activity – the booms and slumps that are often termed the trade or business cycle. The UK has experienced these fluctuations since the Industrial Revolution. The complete cycle may vary in length between four and eight years. A decline in the general level of economic activity – when all businesses suffered a reduction in the demand for their goods and services – was the main cause of the mass unemployment during the 'Great Depression' of the 1930s. It is also a major factor in our present recession.

It is not only the UK that experiences the trade cycle. All industrialised and developing economies are similarly affected. Indeed, as economies have become more and more linked with one another the trade cycle has taken on an international character. Even in the nineteenth century fluctuations in economic activity among the major trading nations (USA, UK, France, West Germany) followed each other closely. The effects of an increase or decrease in the level of economic activity in one country are quickly transmitted to others.

The impact of a recession, for example, in the USA will rapidly be felt by all countries with whom she trades. Imports of raw materials and finished goods into the USA will be reduced, forcing the exporting nation to cut back on production and therefore employment. Similarly the expansion of economic activity in one country may through its increased demand for imports lead to the expansion of output and employment in other countries.

Since the 1930s the severity of the trade cycle has been mitigated by government action on the lines advocated by Lord Keynes. Briefly (this is discussed in more detail in Ch. 9 p. 119), Keynes believed that a government should regulate its spending so as to make up any deficiency in the level of aggregate or total demand needed to maintain full employment. Therefore, during a recession, the Government should expand its spending and conversely during a boom period reduce its spending.

But the traditional remedy is not available to the present UK Government. The Public Sector Borrowing Requirement (PSBR) and public spending are being restricted in order to control inflation. There are also serious doubts as to whether reflationary action by just one government would be successful in raising employment in that country, rather than being dissipated among many others. For these reasons the major thrust of the Government's attack on unemployment has been through a series of special employment measures which in 1982/83 cost nearly £1,600m. These measures are designed to:

(a) create jobs especially for young people and the long-term unemployed;

(b) subsidise the cost of employing a young worker thereby increasing his attractiveness to an employer;

(c) provide all unemployed 16-year-olds with a programme of education, training, and work experience;

(d) reduce the working population by encouraging early retirement;

(e) reduce unemployment by means of work-sharing.

Technological unemployment

This is a special case of frictional unemployment. Economic growth and a rise in the standard of living are often based upon the introduction of new and improved methods of production. But all too often technological advance is a cause of unemployment – the worker's skills being rendered obsolete by the new technology. So, during the Industrial Revolution the process of mechanisation destroyed many skilled jobs, replacing them with a demand for unskilled labour to operate the machines.

This process continues today, though it is argued that the nature of technological advance has changed. Previously the displaced worker was able to find another job, even though it may not have suited his skills and may have resulted in a drop in wages. Today the introduction of microelectronic circuitry has resulted in many operations becoming highly automated. Many unskilled jobs are lost in the process of automation. A handful of skilled operatives can now control the production process which previously employed scores of semi-skilled or unskilled workers. As the process of computerisation and automation continues it will become increasingly difficult for the unskilled workers to find employment. Technological change will leave in its wake a force of unskilled workers who face the grim prospect of long-term unemployment.

Nor is it just the unskilled who are vulnerable. Automatic cash machines will reduce the demand for bank tellers, while in the office the photocopier and the word processor have already eliminated much of the necessity for routine typing. Moreover, the same machine which is used for word-processing may be used to maintain the book keeping records, to send and receive electronic mail, or telex messages. In the not too distant future it is anticipated that voice typewriters capable of turning dictation directly into a page of finished text will be operating in many offices.

Many people have voiced concern about the impact of microelectronics on unemployment. Yet the overall effect is uncertain. As we have already seen many jobs will be lost, but others may be created. In particular the reduction in cost of many goods through using the 'new technology' will increase demand for those goods (and therefore the employment of the people who make them). Extra jobs will be created in the electronics industry to satisfy demand for microelectronic technology. We will see the development of many new products incorporating microelectronic technology. Lastly, increasing wealth and leisure time will enhance demand for many services in the tertiary sector – an area which is labour intensive.

The pessimists who foresee a net job loss arising on the introduction of microelectronic technology may be correct in their prognosis, but the impact of a failure to implement it would be even worse – for it is certain that our competitors will adopt the new technology. A delay or refusal on our part to implement microelectronic technology will mean that British goods rapidly become uncompetitive in world markets, with dire consequences for employment and our standard of living.

Examination questions

1. What do you understand by full employment? Can it be achieved?

2. Many countries have regions in which unemployment is significantly higher than the national average. How has this come about, and what can we do to remedy the situation?

3. How is the level of unemployment measured? How accurate is the measure?

4. While all forms of unemployment cause concern, some give rise to greater concern than others. Discuss.

5. Outline the nature and extent of unemployment within your own country. What steps should be taken to reduce unemployment?

International trade

Chapter 8

The importance of trade

The principle of specialisation plays an important role both within an economy and internationally. Within an economy we find it more efficient if people specialise and gain expertise in a particular trade or profession. Firms, too, find it profitable to produce only a limited number of products, while even regions may become famous for certain products or services.

The principle of regional specialisation is easily extended to specialisation between countries. International trade then, exists to iron out the deficiencies and surpluses of goods between countries.

A certain amount of trade takes place because of the uneven distribution of raw materials throughout the world. Australia is well endowed with mineral deposits, the UK has North Sea oil, while South Africa has gold.

Variations in climate may also result in trade. It is impossible for the UK to grow those products needing a subtropical climate such as tea or coffee. Equally it is impossible for subtropical countries to grow those crops needing a temperate climate.

Yet the greater part of trade takes place for neither of these reasons. Countries find that they are more efficient at producing some goods than others. This efficiency is reflected in their costs of production and the final prices charged. It is logical for countries to concentrate on making the goods at which they are most efficient, exporting the surplus and using the foreign currency earned to purchase those goods which other countries can produce more cheaply.

Taking the simplified example of two countries producing two products, the theory of comparative advantage shows the benefits of specialisation clearly. Using the same resources, Canada and the UK can produce either of the following:

	Country	
	Canada (units)	UK (units)
Agricultural products	6	4
Machinery	4	8

Now the UK and Canada need both agricultural products and machinery. Without specialisation and presuming both devote half their resources to each product we reach the following situation:

	Canada	UK	Total production
Agricultural products	3	2	5
Machinery	2	4	6

Let us now assume that trade takes place and each country specialises on that product in which they are most efficient and have a comparative advantage. Canada will specialise in the production of agricultural products because she can make six units of agricultural products and Britain only four units. Conversely, the UK, using the same amount of resources, can produce eight units of machinery whereas Canada produces four units. The UK will therefore concentrate on the production of machinery. The effect, as shown below, is that world production of both goods has been increased by specialisation:

	Canada	UK	Total production
Agricultural products	6	—	6
Machinery	—	8	8

Now Canada needs machinery and previously it cost her three units of agricultural products to produce two units of machinery. As long as trade results in her obtaining more than two units of machinery for her three units of agricultural product she has benefited from specialisation and international trade.

The UK has concentrated on the production of machinery because she can produce two units of machinery for each unit of agricultural product, and as long as she obtains more than one unit of agricultural product for two units of machinery she also will have benefited.

If we assume a trading ratio of one unit of agricultural product to one unit of machinery, then both countries are satisfied, and the final position may be something like this:

	Canada	UK	Total production
Agricultural products	3 (6–3)	3	6
Machinery	3	5 (8–3)	8

Even where one country has an absolute advantage – that is, better at producing both goods, trade will still be beneficial, as long as there are differences in the relative efficiencies of production. The more efficient country will produce that product at which it is most efficient, leaving the other to produce the good in which it has the least disadvantage.

Even in the unlikely event of two countries having the same cost structure, trade may still be advantageous if specialisation leads to economies of scale and falling prices.

Free trade therefore, is encouraged because it increases real output throughout the world. It provides consumers with a wider choice of goods and a higher standard of living, while the worker has greater employment possibilities. Trade also speeds the introduction of new and advanced technology with its potential for even greater efficiency.

Restrictions on trade

Although we have seen a liberalisation of trade in the years since the Second World War all countries still restrict trade in some way. Traditionally, tariffs and quotas have been the most important means of controlling imports. A tariff is a tax imposed on imports. It may be levied on an *ad valorem* basis – that is, a percentage of the value of the import, or alternatively on a specific basis as an amount per unit – £1 per bottle of wine. The tariff has the advantage of producing revenue for the Government though this is not normally the main reason for imposing it.

A quota is a quantitative restriction on imports. The restriction may be in terms of units to be imported (e.g. 10,000 cars only) or the value of imports (only £20 m. worth of textiles).

More recently, concern has been growing at the increasing number of non-tariff or administrative barriers on trade. It is impossible to catalogue a complete list, but amongst the major restrictions are:

(a) establishment of norms and standards different to those used elsewhere;

(b) discrimination in public sector purchasing;

(c) bonds to be deposited with the government of the importing company to cover claims against those goods;

(d) retesting of products in the importing country;

(e)   tax discrimination in favour of local manufacturer;

(f)   slow customs clearance procedures;

(g)   publicity campaigns, e.g. buy British, or in some cases buy British last!

Reasons for limiting trade

1. Countries may argue that it is necessary to protect home industry because it is newly established. Young industry may very well need protection initially. Neither labour skills nor production systems are fully developed and their costs of production are therefore higher than older-established industries in other countries. Yet the danger of protecting these 'infant' industries is that they come to rely on the high tariff barrier and never become fully efficient (and paradoxically until they compete internationally in a larger market they will never obtain those economies of scale necessary to become more efficient).

2. A country, for strategic reasons, may decide to ensure the continuity of supplies for certain products. Thus steel is necessary to the production of so many items that even if other countries (e.g. West Germany) have a comparative advantage we should not allow free trade to put our own steel industry out of business. We are willing to accept and even encourage high-cost domestic production.

3. Surplus goods produced in one country are sometimes dumped in another country. By dumping we are referring to the practice of selling goods in a foreign market at a price less than that which is charged in the home market. The aim of dumping is to protect the price of the product in the home market by restricting the amount available there. The danger for the receipient is that the home-based industry may be forced out of business (with a consequent loss of jobs) and that the country is then reliant on imports whatever the price charged.

4. Unfair competition also arises from the subsidising of an exports industry by a government. Thus Eastern European countries, anxious for foreign exchange to buy Western technology, often subsidise and sell goods at less than their true cost. Once again the importing country obtains an immediate benefit in the form of cheaper goods, but this may be outweighed by the monopoly position established by the exporter in the longer term.

5. In times of economic depression, when unemployment is high and demand for goods and services is low, governments often impose restrictions on trade. The argument is that by restricting imports we are providing jobs for workers in our domestic industry. This tactic may succeed if we can persuade our competitors not to take retaliatory measures. In the more likely event of our competitors taking similar measures against us the demand for our goods and services is once more reduced and unemployment rises. Thus during the Great

Depression 'beggar-my-neighbour' policies reduced international trade by 67 per cent between January 1929 and June 1933.

6. Where a country experiences an adverse balance of payments, restrictions on imports may provide temporary relief. The imposition of a tariff on imported goods will reduce demand for imports while at the same time increasing the demand for home-produced substitutes. As before we have to persuade our trading partners that such measures are both necessary and short term if we wish to avoid those retaliatory measures.

General Agreement on Tariffs and Trade

The General Agreement on Tariffs and Trade (GATT) is a multilateral treaty which is recognised by ninety countries accounting for more than 80 per cent of world trade. The basic aim of GATT is to encourage free trade and thereby higher economic growth and rising standards of living. Countries who recognise the treaty accept that:

1. Members should not discriminate against trade with another.

2. Where protection of home industry is necessary it should be by tariff alone, thereby exposing the true extent of the protection.

3. Where changes in the structure of tariffs are contemplated, trading partners should be consulted.

4. Discussions should take place at regular intervals with a view to further liberalisation of trade.

5. Developing countries are not expected fully to reciprocate the reduction in trade values by developed countries but, as their economies grow stronger they should participate more fully in the GATT framework of rights and obligations.

Members of GATT realise that the process of trade liberalisation is a long-term objective and that customs unions or free-trade areas are a means to this end. Numerous free-trade areas and customs unions have been created since 1948, mainly among the members of GATT, e.g. the EEC (Common Market), the Caribbean Economic Community (Caricom), the Association of South East Asian Nations (ASEAN).

The European Economic Community

The EEC is a customs union, that is, it has abolished internal customs duties to create a single market for all those countries who are members. Countries outside the customs union are met by a common external tariff whichever member country they are exporting to. The major distinction between a customs union and a free-trade area is the existence of the common external tariff. Thus the European Free Trade Association (EFTA), of which the UK was once a member, although it has abolished tariffs between members allows its members to decide upon their own level of tariffs for imports from outside the association. By this means the UK was able, while a member of EFTA to continue its system of Commonwealth preferences.

Britain joined the EEC in 1973 after two earlier unsuccessful attempts in 1963 and 1976. Attitudes to joining the Common Market have always been divided. Proponents of the Common Market pointed to the advantages of a bigger market – economies of scale and specialisation, the fact that competition was greater would encourage the introduction of new technology, and there would be more possibility of joint products such as Concorde or the European Air Bus. There were also political advantages. The UK's role as an independent world power was coming to an end – joining the Common Market might bring about a resurgence of the UK's political influence, and even if not there were political advantages in belonging to an economic grouping which was as powerful as the superpowers. Yet again there was the hope that economic agreement between the members could reduce political differences and make the likelihood of war a thing of the past.

Many remained unconvinced. On the political front they pointed to the loss of sovereignty and talked of laws made in Brussels being forced upon us. They also doubted whether British industry could stand the higher degree of competition, or if economies of scale were to be gained. But by far the greatest criticism was kept for the common external tariff (which would keep cheap imports of foodstuffs from the Commonwealth out) and the Common Agricultural Policy (subsidising inefficient foreign farmers).

A decade later the controversy still exists. The Labour Party is convinced that the decision to join the Common Market was a mistake and is committed to withdrawal from membership. Others are less sure that the losses outweigh the benefits and believe that a Britain outside the Common Market would be far poorer than by remaining a member.

The major reason for entering in 1973 was the projected benefits to trade and industry. These have not manifested themselves, though it is fair to add that the raising of oil prices and later the world recession may have had much to do with this.

British trade with the Common Market has increased. Moreover, the gap between visible imports and exports has been reduced. Thus while some sectors have suffered from entry it seems that much of British industry has held its own or even benefited from the increased competition. However, there are two points of obvious concern. The UK expected to gain considerably from free trade in services yet there has been little move towards liberalisation of restrictions here.

Additionally the recession has caused members of the Common Market to maintain existing barriers rather than reduce them and also create other non-tariff barriers to trade.

In the decade before joining the EEC, the UK's growth rate was persistently lower than that of the Common Market members (approximately 65 per cent of EEC members). Since joining the Common Market the UK's rate of growth (along with all other members) has declined. However, the rate of decline has not been as marked as would have been expected if the UK had not joined the Common Market. Between 1973 and 1981 our rate of growth was 71 per cent of that of EEC members, while prior to the recession, between 1973 and 1979, our growth rate was actually 84 per cent of EEC members. Thus the claim that higher European growth rates would enable the UK to grow more quickly may have been borne out.

A major problem from the UK's point of view stems from the EEC budget and the Common Agricultural Policy. British complaints centre on the fact that despite being the third poorest country in the EEC it contributes over 20 per cent of the total budget in levies on agricultural products from outside the Community, duties on other goods and partial transfer of VAT revenues. If moneys paid reflected our GNP then our payments should fall (in 1980) from £2,075 m. to £1,621 m. – a reduction of £454 m. But quite apart from what was considered to be an overpayment to the budget, the UK received very little benefit from that budget. In 1980 75 per cent of the budget was spent on the Common Agricultural Policy. The British farming sector was both small and efficient and could never expect to benefit in the same way as France and Italy. It is true the UK received more than a quarter of the Social and Regional Development Funds, but as these account for little more than 7½ per cent of the total budget the overall effect was small.

In consequence, during 1980, the UK contributed £2,075 m. to the Community budget, but received only £866 m. back in grants and subsidies. It is not surprising that in 1979 both governments – Labour and Conservative – objected to the size of the budget deficit, and that since 1979 we have negotiated budget funds. Thus in 1982 a refund of £650 m. was granted making Britain's net contribution to Community funds £147 m.

Politically the effects of joining the EEC are just as confused. The movement to political unity has been slower than anticipated due to the cumulative effects of the oil crisis and the recession. However, concern has been expressed over:

1. The inadequate scrutiny by the British Parliament of an increasing amount of EEC legislation.

2. The inability of the UK to take unilateral action (monetary or fiscal) to deal with its industrial or regional problems.

The balance of payments

The balance of payments is a summary of the transactions which take place between one country and the rest of the world. It records not only the trading transactions discussed previously in this chapter but other commercial and financial transactions entered into by its people, business, and government. Normally the accounts cover a year, but statistics relating to visible and invisible trade are often issued more frequently. Table 8.1 shows the balance of payments for the UK in 1981. These are discussed in more detail below.

Table 8.1   United Kingdom balance of payments, 1981

	£m.	£m.
Visible trade		
Exports	51,100	
Imports	48,087	
Visible balance (balance of trade)		+ 3,013
Invisible trade		
Shipping and civil aviation	339	
Travel and tourism	(286)*	
Financial and other services	4,697	
Interest, profit and dividends	1,004	
Transfers	(1,956)*	
Government expenditure	(775)*	
Invisible balance		+3,023
Current balance		+6,036
Investment and other capital flows		−7,209
Balancing item		+328
Balance for official financing		−845
Allocation of special drawing rights		+158
Official financing		+687

*Brackets denote net deficit

Visible trade

The balance of visible trade (issued in the UK as the monthly trade figures) indicate the value of visible or tangible exports and imports. Traditionally the UK used to run a deficit on the balance of visible trade, imports of raw materials and foodstuffs being greater than manufactured goods exported. However, the following changes have been noted over the last decade.

1. Manufacturing exports (as a percentage of total exports) have declined from 84 to 72 per cent, while manufacturing imports have

increased (again as a percentage of total imports) from 53 to 64 per cent. This reflects not only the increased specialisation arising through international trade, but also a lack of price competitiveness on the part of British industry.

2. The UK is now self-sufficient in oil. Petroleum exports account for some 13 per cent of all exports. The impact of oil revenue on the balance of payments has obviously been significant. From 1800 to 1979 the United Kingdom only managed to obtain a surplus on the balance of visible trade in seven years. Yet since 1980 oil revenue has been sufficient to turn this deficit into a surplus.

3. Since joining the EEC the UK's trading links have moved in favour of its Common Market partners. Exports to the Common Market have risen from 30 to 45 per cent of total exports, while imports have risen from 28 to 44 per cent. This shift has been at the expense of all other countries except for members of the Organisation of Petroleum Exporting Countries (OPEC).

Invisible trade

Traditionally, Britain has always had a surplus on invisible trade and the deficit on visible trade was always made good by our trade in these invisible items. These are items involving services – the sale of space on ships and aircraft, the movement of passengers for business or pleasure, the repayment of profits, interest, and dividends. We will look at these in more detail below, but first a word of warning – the figures shown in the balance of payments are net items and conceal very large flows of money in both directions (see Fig. 8.1).

1. Tourism. A surplus between 1968 and 1980 reflected the UK marketing herself as a holiday centre. Changes in the exchange rate may affect the size of the surplus – thus in 1977 the devaluation of the pound inhibited British holiday-makers from travelling abroad yet made the UK an extremely attractive place for overseas visitors. A record net £1.26 b. was earned in that year. Conversely, a deficit in 1981 of £286 m. was caused by the high value of sterling against other major currencies.

2. Financial services. Banks, in providing general banking facilities to overseas customers, information on world markets, as well as providing finance for foreign trade, earn valuable currency each year. The insurance industry also earns substantial amounts of foreign currency by accepting risks overseas. The amounts included under this heading are not the only contribution made by banks and insurance companies to visible earnings. Other contributions are included under item (4) below.

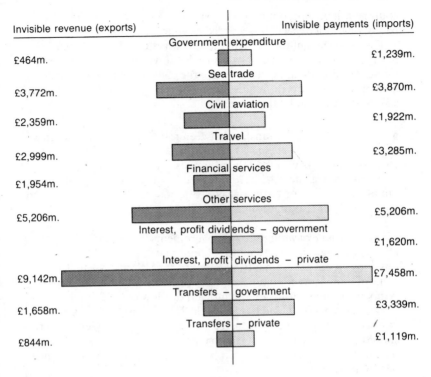

Fig. 8.1 United Kingdom invisible trade, 1981

3. Other services. Items which are not easily classified elsewhere are included here. These include the overseas earnings of:

(a) Civil engineers and construction firms grossing over £800 m. in 1979;

(b) consultancy firms – architecture, advertising agencies, management consultants, accountants and lawyers;

(c) the entertainment industry – films and television programmes produced in this country and sold abroad earn valuable currency, similarly royalties on records. Remember the Beatles? They were awarded the OBE for 'services to export'!;

(d) education of overseas students in the UK.

4. Interest, profit, and dividends. In past years UK companies have invested heavily abroad. Similarly, overseas companies have found it profitable to invest in the UK – perhaps to overcome the EEC tariff barrier – or because of involvement in North Sea oil production. In the year in which the investment occurs the capital amount of the recipient country will benefit, but in future years the repatriation of interest, profit, or dividends will be recorded as an invisible import.

The Government too has lent money (invested) abroad, often to newly developing countries. At times the Government also borrows money from abroad, especially when the country has experienced balance of payments difficulties. Repayments of interest on these loans will be included under this heading.

5. Transfers. Private transfers between residents and non-residents may occur for many reasons. For example, immigrant workers may wish to send money back to their families in another country. Government transfers arise from retired Civil Servants living abroad, but also, more importantly, our contributions to the EEC budget and aid to newly developing countries.

6. Government expenditure. All governments incur expenditure abroad through the maintenance of diplomatic links and trade missions. Some governments, like that of the UK, also spend large sums of money maintaining a military presence abroad. The British Army in Germany leads to a significant outflow of funds each year – over £600 m. in 1979, and has led to the UK Government negotiating various offset agreements with West Germany (e.g. the German Army should buy British tanks). It is also true to say that the UK's balance of payments has benefited considerably from the presence of US armed personnel in Britain.

The capital account

Together, visible and invisible transactions comprise the current balance and are an indication of how well the country is trading. Figure 8.2 shows how the UK current balance has moved in the last decade. The capital account, as its name implies, shows movement of capital between international centres for investment purposes. Thus when British firms, such as Dunlop or Lonhro, decide to extend their operations in Malaysia or Africa, the investment results in a capital outflow being recorded in the UK's balance of payments, but a capital inflow in the accounts of the recipient country. Equally the UK's capital account is the beneficiary when North Americans decide to invest in this country. Traditionally, though, the UK has been a net investor overseas.

Not all investment in an overseas country by firms, or governments for that matter, are for the purposes of producing goods or services there. Both businesses and governments have temporary surpluses of cash and it is logical to invest this surplus until such time as other investment opportunities can be found. The UK has long been the centre for such investments. For example, large sums of money can be

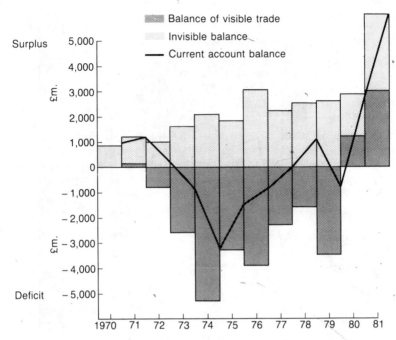

Fig. 8.2 United Kingdom balance of payments current account, 1970–81

lent for as little as a day on the London Money Market and yet earn interest. Normally such investments benefit the UK, but a lack of confidence in the sterling exchange rate, or the ability of the Government to control inflation may cause a sudden and massive withdrawal of this money from the UK. Later in this chapter we will see that this action exacerbates any exchange rate problem.

It is extremely unlikely that the current and capital account of any country's balance of payments will offset each other exactly, and therefore a country will either have a surplus or a deficit on its balance of payments (see Fig. 8.3). A balance of payments surplus arises when we have spent less abroad than we have earned abroad. In 1981 though, the UK ran a deficit on her balance of payments, a favourable current balance being offset by our investing so heavily abroad. Such deficits and surpluses are settled by currency flows between countries. Thus in 1981 the UK paid off her international indebtedness by running down her reserves of gold and foreign currencies to the extent of £687 m. and borrowing from the International Monetary Fund (IMF) of £158 m.

In practice the currency flows recorded by the Government rarely agree with the deficit recorded on the current and capital accounts. This arises because it is difficult to record all international transactions

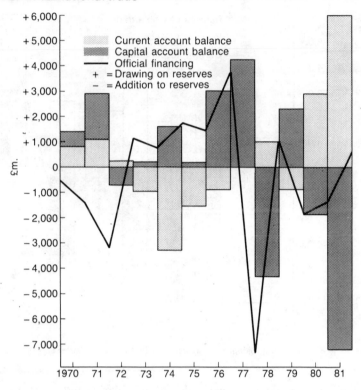

Fig. 8.3 United Kingdom balance of payments, 1970–81

and, moreover, payment may be made at a different time to that of exports or imports. The difference between these two figures is termed the 'balancing item' and is inserted in the balance of payments so that, as its name implies, the accounts balance.

No particular concern is shown when a country experiences the occasional deficit on its balance of payments. After all every country cannot be in surplus at the same time. However, where the deficit is large or persists for a number of years the country concerned is expected to remedy the situation.

In the short term a deficit will be financed by running down reserves of gold and foreign currencies or perhaps by borrowing from abroad. But persistent deficits will soon exhaust these resources and the authorities will have to consider measures to halt the net outflow of funds from the country. These will include trading restrictions, deflation, and even possibly devaluation.

We have already considered tariffs, quotas, and other restrictions which have from time to time been placed upon international trade and noted that the most likely consequences are retaliatory measures from those countries which are affected. Governments may also try to make it more difficult for capital to leave the country. At the time of writing, France has placed restrictions on the amount of currency French tourists can take out of the country and also on investment and other capital flows. As an alternative to restricting imports and other currency outflows, governments have also tried to make their exports more attractive by means of subsidies, or credit facilities.

'Deflation' is the term given to the combination of monetary and fiscal measures which are designed to reduce the level of demand within the economy. By reducing the demand for all goods and services it is hoped that imports of raw materials and finished goods will decline. Monetary measures normally taken will include the restriction of bank and hire-purchase credit, the control of government borrowing, and the raising of interest rates. Higher taxes and lower government spending are examples of fiscal measures. While deflation may secure a reduction in the payments deficit the price paid internally is low economic growth, lower investment, and higher unemployment – results which can be highly embarrassing to a government.

The final alternative open to the Government is that of altering its exchange rate – devaluing the value of the domestic currency against other currencies so that, for example, the pound does not buy as much abroad. Britain, for example, devalued in 1967, reducing the sterling – dollar exchange rate from £1=$2.80 to £1=$2.40. The effect of this, as with any devaluation, was to make:

(a) imports more expensive;

(b) exports cheaper;

The aim of devaluation is thus clear. If exports are cheaper we will sell more, earning greater revenue than before, and with imports being dearer, we are likely to find them less attractive and spend less on them. This will reduce, if not eradicate, the balance of payments deficit.

But a policy of devaluation is not always successful. Exports are cheaper, but to earn more revenue we have to sell far more than previously (readers who have studied economics will realise we are talking about the elasticity of demand for the country's exports). The sterling devaluation of 14 per cent in 1967 effectively meant that we had to sell over 14 per cent more exports to earn the same amount of revenue.

Equally, although imports are more expensive, if the goods purchased abroad are 'essentials', e.g. foodstuffs or raw materials, we are likely to find ourselves buying a similar amount as before from abroad, but this time at a higher price!

Finally, devaluation may also cause inflation. First, because higher import prices for raw materials, foodstuffs, or finished goods will normally be reflected in a higher RPI. Secondly, if demand for exports increases strongly and cannot be met by exporters, prices of these goods are likely to rise.

The International Monetary Fund

This was set up in 1945, its aims were to:

(a) bring stability to international exchange rates; and

(b) help those countries undergoing balance of payment problems.

A subsidiary aim was to encourage the growth of world trade. However, since the movement away from fixed to floating exchange rates the IMF has concentrated on aiding those countries with balance of payments problems.

Members of the IMF are required to contribute a quota of their gold and foreign currency to the fund. This is based upon their volume of trade. In return they receive special drawing rights which may be used by that country to pay off international indebtedness.

Members may also borrow up to 200 per cent of their quota from the fund when they experience balance of payments problems. Loans from the IMF are often accompanied by 'strings' or 'conditions'. For example in 1976 the IMF required the British Government to reduce both the money supply and its own expenditure.

The World Bank

The International Bank for Reconstruction and Development, is also known as the World Bank. Its function was initially to finance post-war reconstruction, but it is now concerned with encouraging international investment in developing countries.

To finance this investment the bank borrows money (quotas) from its members (who must be members of the IMF), and also by issuing its own bonds on the international money market. Interest is charged on the loans to developing countries and the Government is required to guarantee the loans.

The bank also encourages private investment, and may enter into partnership with private investors to complete a project. Since its creation the bank has lent many millions of dollars, the majority being to newly developing countries.

Through a subsidiary, the International Development Association, loans are sometimes made to developing countries on advantageous terms – low rates of interest, and lengthy repayment periods.

Stand-by loans may also be granted by the IMF where it believes there is no real balance of payments problem, and that pressure on the currency is caused by speculation. Often the mere fact that the loan has been granted is sufficient to regenerate confidence in the currency.

Exchange rates

International trade is complicated by the fact that each country has its own currency and exporters wish to be paid in that currency. For international trade to be possible then, it is necessary to determine an exchange rate for these currencies. Buyers and sellers of currencies transmit their orders to dealers who, in marrying the two together, create a market in foreign exchange.

Exchange rates determined on the foreign exchange market reflect the supply and demand for currencies. When we import goods or buy services from abroad we offer sterling on the foreign exchange market so as to obtain the local currency required by the exporter. Conversely, when we export goods we will offer the foreign currency received to the foreign exchange market and demand our own currency. In Fig. 8.4 we can see the effect of trade movements upon our rate of exchange.

Should our imports be greater than our exports the supply of sterling will reduce the price of sterling against the dollar. It is the movements of the exchange rate which equate the supply and demand for currencies.

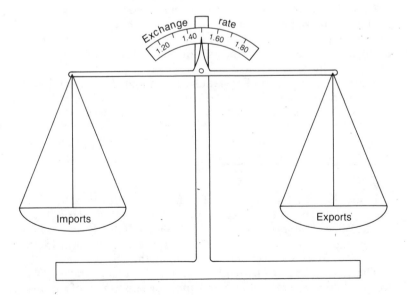

Fig. 8.4   The impact of imports and exports on the exchange rate

Until 1973, most countries adopted a system of <u>fixed exchange rates</u>. Under this system governments stipulated the rates at which they would exchange currencies. For example, the rate between the dollar and the pound was set at £1=$2.40. The rate was, however, allowed to fluctuate within narrow bands. But should there be pressure on the sterling exchange rate to move outside the limits determined by the Government, it would step in to buy or sell sterling as the situation demanded (see Fig. 8.5).

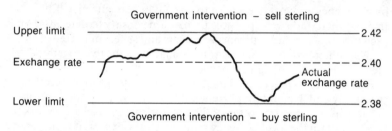

Fig. 8.5 Stabilisation of exchange rates through government intervention

Until 1973 countries adopted fixed exchange rates because they believed that flexible exchange rates might result in such violent fluctuations as to deter trade. Moreover, the market could be destabilised even further by speculation against the currency. But the major advantage of flexible exchange rates was that a country had greater freedom in determining its monetary and fiscal policy. With flexible exchange rates gradual depreciation of the currency took the place of import, investment, and exchange controls, deflation and devaluation. Balance of payments problems were countered by movements in exchange rates.

Since 1973 the great trading nations have adopted a form of flexible exchange rates. Yet exchange rates have not been left completely to the mercy of the market forces but rather have been 'managed' by central banks. While central banks would not normally interfere with an exchange rate, if there were unusual circumstances (e.g. speculation against a currency or a sudden imbalance in trading) they were prepared to intervene and defend what they perceived as the correct rate.

In the UK great attention is paid to the sterling/dollar exchange rate. The inference is that a change in this rate will have a large impact on the value of our exports and imports. Yet, in fact only one-quarter of our trade is affected by changes in this exchange rate – over 75 per cent of our trade is with countries other than the USA.

The Bank of England therefore issues an 'effective' or trade-weighted exchange rate index based upon the importance of various currencies to British trade. This more accurately reflects the impact on the economy of changes in the exchange rate. The movement of both the sterling/dollar and the sterling effective exchange rate is shown in Fig. 8.6.

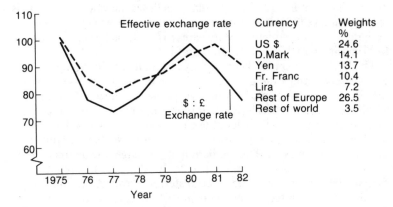

Fig. 8.6 Dollar sterling exchange rate and its comparison with sterling effective exchange rate. June 1975 = 100. (*Source: National Income and Expenditure 1983*)

Exchange rate movements

What causes fluctuations in a country's exchange rates? For example why has the sterling/dollar exchange rate dropped from £1=$4 to £1=$1.30 since 1947. Moreover, why does the same exchange rate – oscillate, sometimes quite dramatically over even a short-period of time? The answer is complex; however, the following factors are important.

1. Inflation. If the rate of inflation is relatively high in Britain compared with other countries the likely result is a depreciation in the value of sterling against other currencies. Inflation has two effects: it makes our exports less attractive as the same goods can be purchased elsewhere more cheaply; imports, because they are lower in price, become more attractive than the home-produced product. Consider the effect in terms of Fig. 8.4: imports are greater than exports, and therefore the supply of sterling on the foreign exchange market is greater than the demand. Currency dealers to equate supply and demand for sterling will reduce its value in terms of other currencies. The balance of payments and exchange rate problems experienced by the UK since 1945 have been caused to a considerable extent by it's higher-than-average inflation rate.

2. Speculation against a currency. A speculator is a person who (in this context) buys or sells currencies in the hope of making a profit by predicting their future prices. Thus if a speculator believes sterling is going to depreciate against the dollar he will convert his sterling holdings into dollars. Later, if he is right, he will be able to repurchase sterling at a lower 'price'. For example let us assume an initial exchange rate of £1=$2. Our speculator believes the value of sterling is too high and sells £300 sterling receiving in exchange $600. If the exchange rate subsequently depreciates to £1=$1.50 he can now buy £400 sterling with his dollars, £100 profit!

The UK's problem has been slightly different. Traditionally, overseas companies and governments have invested surplus funds in the UK. However, should they believe, perhaps quite wrongly, that a sterling devaluation was likely their immediate reaction is to move their funds elsewhere. Consider the effect on the foreign exchange market. Suddenly a vast quantity of sterling is presented for conversion into foreign currencies. The prediction of exchange rate depreciation is self-fulfilling. The actions of the speculators alone cause foreign exchange dealers to mark the value of sterling down. A recent example occurred in the United States where in 1979 speculation against the dollar in favour of gold pushed the price of gold up fourfold to $800 an ounce.

3. Interest rates. Pressure on a currency, for example sterling, which has been caused by a deficit on the balance of payments can be countered by the raising of interest rates. If overseas investors are thereby encouraged to invest more of their funds in the UK the short-term pressure on sterling is reduced. In the longer term, however, the benefits are more doubtful. Should the UK at some stage in the future wish to reduce interest rates or other countries raise their rates, these funds are likely to be transferred from the UK to other more profitable centres. The UK as an international financial centre is particularly vulnerable to such transfers of funds, and the consequent fluctuations in exchange rates.

The pressure of exchange rates mentioned above may be exacerbated if the variations in international interest rates are great. In April 1983 interest rates varied from 5 per cent in West Germany, 10 per cent in the UK to 16 per cent in Italy. Speculators may very well find it profitable to borrow money in West Germany or the UK, exchange it for lira, and lend the money in Italy!

Terms of trade

The relationship between the prices of imports and exports is known as the 'terms of trade'. If export prices increase faster than import prices the terms of trade are said to have moved in our favour because we can now purchase the same amount of imports for less exports.
Conversely, where import prices rise faster than export prices the terms

of trade have moved against – we have to sell more abroad to finance the same volume of imports.

The method of calculating the terms of trade is:

$$\frac{\text{Index of export prices}}{\text{Index of import prices}} \times 100$$

The difficulty in calculating the terms of trade is that the commodities bought and sold all have different measurements (e.g. kilograms, metres, barrels). An index of export or import prices is therefore calculated by weighting the different category of goods according to their importance in trade. In the first or base year the index is valued at 100. If in future years export prices increase relative to import prices then the index value increases (and we can say the terms of trade have moved in our favour), but if the price of imports rise relative to those of export, then the index value falls.

The major reasons for changes in the terms of trade are:

1. Changes in the production cost of goods entering international trade.

2. Changes in exchange rates between countries (devaluation worsens the terms of trade).

3. Action by a cartel or monopolist to increase the price of their product.

Most countries experience changes in their terms of trade. The UK, for example between 1952 and 1972, experienced favourable changes in the terms of trade with export prices of her finished goods rising more rapidly than import prices of foodstuffs and raw materials. However, 1973/4 saw a fivefold increase in oil prices and the doubling of other important basic materials – the effect was a reduction in our terms of trade from 101.3 in 1972 (1970 = 100) to 75.1 in 1974. Since that time there has been a modest improvement in the UK's terms of trade, but the index is still substantially below that achieved in 1972.

Examination questions

1. What is the value of international trade to a country as a whole and its individual inhabitants? *(PSC 1979)*

2. Why is there a need for countries to engage in foreign trade? What factors prevent the operation of a completely free trade system. *(PSC 1977)*

3. Has the UK benefited from membership of the EEC?

4. Imports of cars into the UK have increased significantly in recent years. Why should this be so? How can it be reversed? *(PSC 1976)*

5. Consider the impact of North Sea oil on the UK economy and the balance of payments.

6. Select one country and describe the benefits and problems that have resulted from its joining a 'trading bloc'.

7. What is the relationship between a country's international trade and its balance of payments. How do trading blocs aid international trade?

8. Distinguish between the various components of your country's balance of payments. Explain why it always balances.

9. Why is the Government concerned with the balance of payments of its country? What can it do to improve it?   *(PSC 1980)*

10. Assuming your country has an adverse balance of payments on current account, what measures could you take to correct this?

11. The following terms are often used when discussing international trade. Explain the difference in meaning between each pair.

Visible trade	Invisible trade
Fixed exchange rate	Floating exchange rate
Tariff	Quota
Customs union	Free-trade area

Public finance

Chapter 9

In a mixed economy the State, although acknowledging the central role of private enterprise in the provision of goods and services does, in some cases, see fit to intervene. Thus the State:

(a) supplements the market by providing certain services which private enterprise would not supply, e.g. defence, police, prisons, space, and nuclear programmes;

(b) restricts the market by providing services which can and are provided by private enterprise elsewhere, e.g. roads, medicine, education;

(c) distorts the market by transferring money between individuals and companies, e.g. grants to unemployed, pensioners, company investment allowances;

(d) subsidises the market by providing goods and services at less than their full cost, e.g. losses of nationalised industries, or payment to private firms in financial difficulties;

(e) uses public revenue and expenditure as a means of controlling the level of economic activity within the economy (this is discussed in detail under the heading 'The budget', below, p. 132).

It is not difficult to see that the State plays an extremely important role in our lives (you might consider your actions on an average day, and how you note state intervention). In this chapter we are interested in how the State raises its income, including the role of the budget and how it spends this revenue.

Government revenue

By far the greatest part of government revenue is raised through taxation. A small sum is obtained from trading activities and past investments but this is virtually eclipsed by the amounts raised from taxes on income, capital, and expenditure (see Fig. 1).

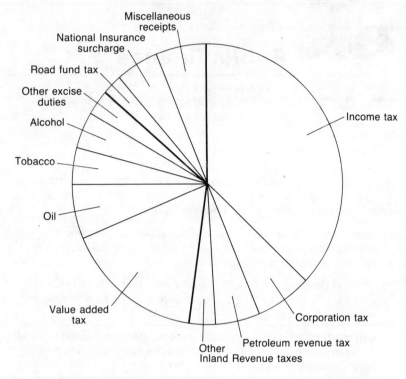

Fig. 9.1 Sources of government revenue

Taxes on income

Income tax
As the name implies, this is levied on a person's income. Not all the person's income is liable to tax – a number of allowances are given for wives, dependants, mortgages, pensions, and life assurance. Personal allowances are also given. The aim of the allowances is to raise the threshold for tax above the amount earned or received by the poorer elements of society. Those members of society who earn more than the 'average' income will pay tax at a higher rate than the basic 30 per cent. In this sense income tax is said to be progressive in that it bears more heavily on those who can afford to pay a greater amount. The budget of 1984 established the following allowances and tax thresholds;

Single person's allowance of	£2,005
Married man's allowance of	£3,155

Income tax at 30% for the first £15,400 of taxable income

40%	from	£15,401 to £18,200
45%	from	£18,201 to £23,100
50%	from	£23,101 to £30,600
55%	from	£30,601 to £38,100
60%	over	£38,100

Normally, allowances against income are changed each year by the Chancellor of the Exchequer in the budget to keep abreast of inflation. Since 1977 a system of automatic indexation has been used to maintain the value of allowances, though this was not implemented in March 1982.

Fiscal drag

A government does not need to raise taxes to increase tax revenue, this happens automatically thanks to inflation. Each year millions of people receive wage increases to cover the increase in the cost of living. Thus poor people who were previously exempt from paying tax now find themselves dragged into the tax net, while higher wage-earners find themselves paying more tax. This happens even though these people may not, in real terms, be better off than before.

Companies are also affected. Corporation tax is levied on money rather than real profits. So if a company buys machinery worth £100 it is allowed to set off £100 as an expense against profits. Yet five years later when the machinery has to be replaced the company has to pay perhaps £250. Because the tax system ignores the effects of inflation the company pays tax on money which is needed to replace fixed and working capital.

In Britain taxes on personal incomes are deducted by means of the PAYE (pay as you earn) system. Employers pay wages and salaries net of tax (and National Insurance contributions) to the employee, remitting the balance to the Government.

Corporation tax

This is levied on a company's profits. However, taxable profit is reduced by a system of allowances for investment in plant and machinery, stock appreciation, and various other expenses. The rate of tax is normally 52 per cent, but smaller firms may benefit from a 40 per cent reduced rate of tax. However, allowances mean that the average firm pays only 16 per cent of its profits in corporation tax. The system of corporation tax is designed to encourage investment and expansion of production. Allowances are granted against the purchase of plant and machinery and these may be claimed fully in the year in which the expenditure is incurred. Thus a firm which retains and reinvests its profits will have a lower tax liability than one which distributes its profits.

Reinvestment of profits is also encouraged by treating distributed profits – that is, dividends to shareholders – as being liable for income tax. Those investors paying tax at higher rates may actually seek out companies reinvesting the majority of their profits. Reinvestment and expansion of business activities, if successful, is likely to lead to an increase in the company's share price, and the capital gain made on the sale of the shares will be taxed at a lower rate than their marginal rate of income tax.

Petroleum revenue taxes

These are levied under the Oil Taxation Act 1975 and are charged on the profits arising from winning the right to drill oilfields in the UK and the North Sea. The rate of tax is 70 per cent and is designed to ensure that the benefits of North Sea oil production accrue to the UK economy.

Taxes on capital

Capital gains taxes

These are levied where the owner of assets sells those assets at a price higher than he paid for them. The rate of tax is 30 per cent, but relief is given by (a) exempting certain assets altogether, e.g. your house and car, and (b) allowing exemption from the tax where total net gains do not exceed £5,000 in any year. This tax, introduced in 1962, was designed to catch the large numbers of people who had 'got rich quick' by speculating in land and shares.

Capital transfer tax

This applies where the owner of assets transfers those assets to some other person during his lifetime or on his death. Lifetime transfers are exempt if under £2,000 annually. Transfers on death are exempt if under £50,000. The rate of tax charged on the balance varies. First, lifetime transfers are taxed at lower rates than transfers on death. Secondly, the rates applied to both types of transfers are progressive – the bigger the transfer the bigger the slice the Inland Revenue takes.

Taxes on expenditure

Value added tax

As its name implies, this is a tax on the value added at each stage of the production process. Consider the following example where we assume the rate of value added tax (VAT) is 10 per cent – in practice it is 15 per cent.

A farmer purchases wheat from a grain merchant costing £550. The grain actually costs £500, but there is the tax of 10 per cent which the grain merchant is responsible for collecting from the purchaser and paying to the Customs and Excise. Now the farmer sows the grain and eventually harvests wheat worth £1550. The value added by the farmer is therefore £1,000 (£1,550 –£550, the cost of his seed) and he will pay tax on this of 10 per cent, that is, £100. Thus the bakery which purchases the wheat will pay £1,650 in total. When the bakery has processed the wheat and produced the bread it is worth £2,400. The value added by the baker is £750; he will pay tax on this of £75, and consumers pay the full price of £2,475. The example is summarised below:

	Value added (£)	Tax at 10% (£)	Total (£)
Grain merchant	500	50	550
Farmer	1,000	100	1,100
Bakery	750	75	825
	2,250	225	2,475

In the UK the effect of VAT is limited in a number of ways. First, certain basic products and services are zero rated. Examples include food, fuel, buildings, and public transport. Where goods are zero rated the vendor does not have to charge VAT on his sales and may also claim a refund of the tax paid by his suppliers and included in the price charged to him. Another group of goods are tax exempted, which means that the vendor does not have to charge VAT on his sales but is not allowed to claim a refund of taxes paid at previous stages of 'the production' process. Exemption applies to land, rents, insurance, finance, education, and health services.

Excise duties
These are taxes placed upon goods for revenue-earning purposes and are levied in addition to VAT. As the Government is committed to spending very large sums of money each year it has to be sure that the revenue it plans to raise from taxes on goods does in fact materialise. The Chancellor of the Exchequer does not wish to tax goods only to find that the higher price leads to a significant reduction in the quantity demanded and therefore tax revenue being less than anticipated. In consequence the Government looks for goods which we will buy in roughly the same quantity even though the price has risen. Food, clothing, and shelter are obvious examples, yet as taxes on these goods will bear most harshly on the poor the Government seeks instead to tax goods which are by convention, rather than nature, necessities. Experience has shown that even though high taxes are placed upon oil,

tobacco, alcohol, and cars, people continue to buy these items in large quantities. Figure 9.2 shows the proportion of tax in the final price of selected goods sold in the UK during 1981.

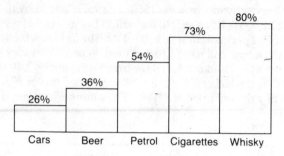

Fig. 9.2 Tax paid as a percentage of retail price, 1981

Protective duties
These are levied on commercial and agricultural products entering the Common Market through the UK. Duties raised by way of the common external tariff are remitted to Brussels and become part of the Community's income.

The principles of taxation

While no tax system is liked, most of us accept that taxes have to be levied and our consideration therefore turns to ensuring that the tax system is just. In practice that is no easy matter as it involves moral, political, and economic judgements, but its importance is indicated by the fact that the UK lost her American colonies through the imposition of unjust taxes!

Adam Smith argued that there were four basic principles which a government should work to: economy, equality, certainty, and convenience.

1. Economy. Taxes should be collected as efficiently as possible; moreover, we should avoid situations where the tax raised is less than the cost of its collection. In the UK the collection of direct taxes is particularly efficient, costing the State just over 1p for each pound collected.

2. Equality. This can be interpreted in different ways. Obviously, two single secretaries each earning £5,000 should pay the same amount of tax. The tax system should have no favourites! Smith went further though. He suggested that taxes should be proportional to income, and that we should all pay, say, 15 per cent of our income, whatever its level in tax. A more modern argument is that the burden of tax should be similar. The rich man, because of his larger income can afford to pay more than the poor man. The system of income tax with its progressively higher rates is an example of the latter point.

3. Certainty. Each taxpayer should know what taxes he is liable for, the amount he has to pay, and when it is to be paid. Unfortunately, a degree of uncertainty often exists with people not understanding how a complicated system of allowances and deductions applies to them.

4. Convenience. A tax is said to be convenient if its collection causes the taxpayer no problem. While the timing of tax payments will never be wholly convenient, measures can be taken to minimise the inconvenience. Thus the PAYE system deducts tax from wages and salaries before payment is made to the recipient. Compare with that local government rates which many people still pay as a lump sum in April of each year.

To these four well-established principles of taxation others have been added:

5. Economists suggest that flexibility or the power to vary taxes at short notice is necessary in order to control the level of economic activity within the economy. So, for example, at the present time the Chancellor has the power to 'regulate' or change the VAT rate by 10 per cent in either direction (i.e. VAT may vary between 13.5 and 16.5 per cent).

6. Taxes should not act as a disincentive to effort. While people expect to pay taxes it has been suggested there is a limit to what they are willing to pay; this is sometimes referred to as 'taxable capacity'. Should taxes extend beyond this limit we find workers are not willing to accept overtime, managers do not find it worth while to move to new jobs, and many will try to evade paying the tax due.

Attempts to prove that high tax rates discourage people from working harder have not been particularly successful. Money is only one of a number of motivators. Power and prestige are two others which are considered to be important. However, it is only fair to say that until 1979, when the highest band of income tax was reduced to 60 per cent, some people in the UK faced a uniquely high marginal tax rate of 80 per cent.

It is at the other end of the income scale that attempts to prove the disincentive effect have been more successful. In the UK we have a system of benefits which are available to people on low incomes. These benefits are withdrawn as income rises. It has been shown that a person on a low income, who takes on extra work or overtime may find that the means-tested benefits withdrawn and tax deducted are together greater than the income received – a marginal tax rate of over 100 per cent.

Direct and indirect taxation

A direct tax is one where the taxpayer makes payment directly to the tax authorities. Taxes on income and capital are examples of direct taxes. An expenditure tax is cited as an indirect tax because the tax is paid by the bearer of the tax through someone else. As we have already seen, VAT is remitted to the Customs and Excise by each firm in the productive process.

Economists and politicians are divided over whether it is better to use direct or indirect taxes. Readers are advised to consider the points made below and make their own assessment.

Advantages of direct taxes
1. Direct taxation is certain in its impact. Income tax or capital transfer tax is levied on the individual, who is unable to pass this liability on to someone else.

2. Because such taxes are normally progressive and take account of individual commitments they are deemed to be equitable. Moreover, the tax system can be arranged so as to relieve low earners of any liability.

3. It is easier to estimate the yield from direct taxes because people cannot avoid paying the tax.

4. Direct taxes are easy and cheap to collect.

5. Direct taxes do not affect the cost of living index and will, therefore, not lead to inflationary wage claims. Over a number of years direct taxes may even be deflationary if the Government does not adjust allowances to keep pace with inflation.

Disadvantages of direct taxes
1. Direct taxation may be a disincentive to effort and saving.

2. Direct taxes do not have the flexibility of indirect taxes – consider the problems the Inland Revenue have faced changing house purchasers' assessments when the mortgage interest rate has changed. As a result of this inflexibility direct taxes cannot easily be used to reflate or deflate the economy.

3. The system of allowances creates difficulties of assessment. Professional advice is often required, especially by businesses to ensure that their tax liability is minimised. A less complicated system would release these 'tax experts' for other work.

Advantages of indirect taxes
1. An individual can avoid paying the tax by not purchasing the goods on which the tax is levied.

2. Expenditure taxes do not have a disincentive affect on work and enterprise. The workers or entrepreneurs do not see the fruits of their labour taxed away.

3. These taxes are concealed in the price charged and the consumer often does not realise that he is paying them. Thus the Government can raise its revenue and yet avoid the criticism that it is taxing people heavily – though in fact it may be.

4. Indirect taxes may be used for social purposes. Taxes on tobacco and alcohol not only raise revenue but discourage increased consumption of these items.

5. They can be used as an economic regulator by the Government quickly to increase or reduce the spending power of the consumer. Alternatively, import duties may be used to regulate trade in specific products or with certain countries.

Disadvantages of indirect taxes
1. They are said to be regressive because they do not reflect a person's ability to pay tax. Each of us, whether rich or poor, will be paying the same amount of tax on items purchased.

2. It is an inflationary tax. An increase in the tax is likely to affect the final price of the product and therefore the RPI. This has adverse implications for the balance of payments, and those groups with little bargaining power.

3. The tax yield is uncertain. No one knows for sure what effect the tax will have on sales of the product. If many people are deterred from buying because of the increase in price the anticipated revenue will not be forthcoming. Even with goods which are conventional necessities the tax revenue is by no means certain. Thus, increases in taxes on cigarettes have led to reductions in tax revenue.

Public expenditure

Public expenditure is defined as all expenditure which has to be financed from taxation, National Insurance contributions, and government borrowing. In practice there are three components:

1. Current expenditure of central and local government.

2. Capital expenditure of central and local government.

3.   Grants and loans to the nationalised industries.

The control of public expenditure

The twentieth century has seen an explosive growth in the public sector and its spending, public expenditure in 1980/81 accounting for 56 per cent of national income. Not surprisingly therefore, interest has been growing in the possibility of controlling public expenditure. This interest has settled on four issues, namely to ensure:

1.   The right balance between public and private expenditure.

2.   The best allocation of resources between alternatives.

3.   That money is spent in the way Parliament intended.

4.   That money is spent efficiently without waste.

Both issues (1) and (2) are essentially political. Issue (1) revolves around the position of the State in the economy. Some Socialists would argue that the level of state intervention has to be high to remedy the deficiencies of the private sector. Yet Conservatives believe the existence of a large public sector inhibits the growth of private enterprise.

Readers should also be aware that the various political parties would use the resources at their disposal in different ways – what is the best allocation is very much a political question. Figure 9.3 shows how the UK Government utilised its income during 1983–84. However, the Government does undertake a number of policy reviews, the aim being to question the relevance of policies adopted in the past, and often the opinions of the various interest/pressure groups are sought.

On the more technical questions of whether money allocated by Parliament has been spent correctly and efficiently, a number of checks exist. Initially the prime responsibility for ensuring public moneys are spent properly rests with the department concerned. To aid the departments 'expenditure profiles' or budgets are prepared, and deviations from the planned profile have to be explained to the minister in charge. Similar statements are also used in local government and nationalised industries.

With high levels of inflation causing considerable overruns on government expenditure, especially capital programmes, systems of cash limits, that is, ceilings on expenditure, have been introduced. The Government will review these limits only if inflation is substantially different to that on which the limits were based. Local authority expenditure is also subject to a cash limit while nationalised industries' borrowing requirements have been subjected to a similar ceiling.

Lastly an audit of central government expenditure is carried out for the Crown by the Comptroller and Auditor General and his staff in the

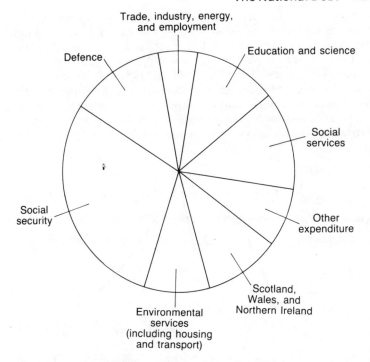

Fig. 9.3 Public expenditure

Exchequer and Audit Department. The role of the Exchequer and Audit is not only to verify the accuracy of the records kept by each department by checking a sample of transactions but also that the money has been spent as Parliament intended. Audit reports are presented to the Public Accounts Committee of the House of Commons. Chaired by a senior member of the Opposition the committee vets the reports presented to it and summarises the findings for debate in Parliament.

Similar audit procedures are carried out in local government, where district auditors employed by, but independent of, the Department of the Environment confirm the accuracy of the records. The ensuing report is made to the local authority concerned, but is also available to the public. The accounts of nationalised industries are audited in the same manner as public limited companies, the audit being presented to Parliament along with the annual report and accounts.

The National Debt

In March 1980 the UK National Debt amounted to £96 bn. or £17.2 m. for each inhabitant of the UK. The debt arises because, at certain times, the Government, local authorities, and nationalised industries have been unable or unwilling to cover all their expenditure from current revenue. Figure 9.4 shows the history of the debt in the last 125 years. The impact of the two world wars on the debt is dramatically illustrated. Between 1945 and 1951 the National Debt also rose because of government stocks issued to shareholders of firms and utilities nationalised during this period. The decline since 1955 has occurred because the National Debt (i.e. government-sector borrowing) rose less quickly than money GDP – the effect of inflation.

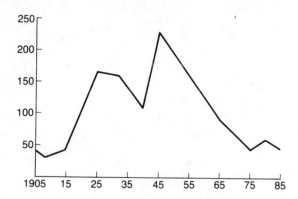

Fig. 9.4   Ratio of National Debt to GDP 1905–85 (estimated) (*Source: Economic Progress Report*, July 1982, adjusted)

In Victorian times, the National Debt though small, compared with that of the twentieth century caused considerable worry to Parliament and great efforts were made to reduce its size. In fact they were successful for by 1914 the debt had been reduced from a peak of £840 m. to £650 m. More recently though, people have questioned whether the National Debt is really a burden.

Of the total National Debt of £96 bn., £85.9 bn., is owned by British organisations and individuals. In so far as payments of interest and repayments of capital are from one resident to another there is no burden on society as a whole. The necessary interest payments which amounted to 11.2 per cent of total government expenditure (source: CSO, *Economic Trends,* March 1983) are merely transfers, redistributing income from one resident to another. However, a burden may be said to exist within society in that those who make the capital and interest repayments may be a substantially different group to those who receive the payments. Yet another argument which has been put forward is that excessive government borrowing dries up finance (which is badly needed by private enterprise), or at least increases the cost of borrowing. Thus the National Debt may both inhibit growth and increase inflation.

Having regard to the external debt though, payments of interest and capital do represent a real burden to the community. Both the interest and the eventual capital repayment must be met from surpluses in the balance of payments.

National Debt and the developing countries

Under the influence of Keynesian economics most countries have from time to time run budget deficits and financed these by borrowing – and, more importantly, often from abroad. Developing countries trying to raise the rate of economic growth have again borrowed heavily from abroad. Figure 9.5 shows the almost impossible difficulties of three developing countries. In each case interest and capital repayments due to overseas financiers annually are greater than that country's annual export earnings. This is caused by:

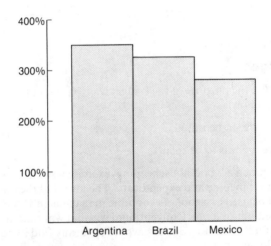

Fig. 9.5 International debt as a percentage of export revenue. In all three cases annual interest and capital repayments are greater than export revenue

1. *Borrowing at low rates of interest and being caught out by rising rates.*

2. *Banks lending without really considering the ability of the borrower to repay.*

3. *The recession, leading to a decline in the demand of the developed countries for the developing country's commodity and raw material exports.*

4. *Investment in non-revenue-earning sectors, e.g. hospitals, houses, roads.*

In financial circles Mexico, Brazil, and Argentina are collectively referred to as the 'MBA problem', but their difficulties are by no means unique; many developing countries are quietly negotiating the rescheduling of interest and capital repayments.

Finally, whatever burden exists is reduced to the extent that government borrowing is backed by revenue-earning assets, for example gas, steel, rail, etc. Not all UK nationalised industries are profitable, yet many do make a contribution to government revenue. Moreover, it is always open for the Government to resell these assets and reduce the overall level of government borrowing.

The budget

Traditionally, the purpose of the budget was to present to Parliament proposals on how:

(a) revenue was to be raised;

(b) the revenue was to be spent.

It was very much a 'good housekeeping' exercise in which the objective was to balance income and expenditure. The idea that the budget could and should be used as a tool of economic management would have been rejected out of hand. Conventional wisdom was that the economy, if left to its own devices, would naturally find its equilibrium at full employment.

It was not until after the Great Depression of the 1930s that people came to realise through the writing of Keynes, that conventional wisdom was wrong, and by 'unbalancing' the budget and running a deficit or surplus the level of economic activity could be regulated.

Briefly Keynes's idea was that the Government should, in a recession, expand its own spending to counter the reduction in spending by business and consumers. By extra spending on special projects, or even by giving more money to the unemployed, the Government was going to increase the demand for goods and services, and therefore output and employment.

Keynes's idea is illustrated diagrammatically below. The level of spending needed to ensure full employment is shown by boxes A and B

| Planned increase in government spending | B | Deflationary gap |
| Level of demand for goods and services to guarantee full employment | A | Current level of demand for goods and services |

together, yet the current level of demand (box A) is insufficient to ensure full employement of labour. The difference between the current level of demand and that needed for full employment (box B) is termed the 'deflationary gap'. This is the amount of extra spending required from the Government. Now assuming that previously the Government had balanced its budget (i.e. revenue = expenditure) it now needs to budget for a deficit (i.e. expenditure greater than revenue). The budget deficit is financed by government borrowing.

A budget surplus arises when the Government raises more in revenue that it spends. A budget surplus is deflationary and is used when the Government wishes to reduce the level of economic activity. Let us consider the diagram below. Box X represents the level of demand necessary for full employment.

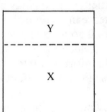

| Excess demand | Y | Planned reduction in Government spending |
| Level of demand for goods and services to guarantee full employment | X | Total or aggregate demand |

But total demand (boxes X and Y) is in excess of this. Box Y is termed 'excess demand' because there is no labour available to provide the extra goods and services demanded. The likely outcome is that either the excess demand will be mopped up by rising prices, or will be satisfied by imported goods. As neither of these results is particularly appealing to the Government it may decide to reduce its own spending sufficiently to offset the excess demand.

It should be obvious by now that the budget is far more than a statement to Parliament on sources of tax revenue and expenditure. The Chancellor in his budget speech analyses the economy's progress during the past year and its prospects for the future. The measures then announced by the Chancellor on revenue and expenditure are designed to ensure that the prospects for the future accord with the Government's macro-economic objectives. These attempts to control the economy through taxation and expenditure are termed 'budgetary' or 'fiscal' policy.

How fiscal policy may be used

1. Full employment. To stimulate a greater demand for goods and services the Chancellor can reduce taxes on income or goods and services. Alternatively, government expenditure may be increased. Measures may be designed to aid recovery in areas of high unemployment. Special allowances may be given to firms operating in such areas – employment subsidies or perhaps higher investment allowances. Government expenditure may also be concentrated on projects in these depressed areas. Alternatively, measures introduced can be designed to help specific industries, for example a reduction in car tax or duties on petrol.

2. Stable prices. Should aggregate demand be so high as to cause inflation the Government may reduce the level of demand by increasing taxes – income, capital, or expenditure. Excess demand may also be creamed off by the Government reducing its own expenditure on goods, services, or capital projects.

3. Satisfactory balance of payments. Where a country is suffering a balance of payments deficit, imports may be discouraged by raising customs duties. An increase in income and expenditure taxes generally may reduce demand for all goods and release production for export. Export industries can be helped by larger investment allowances, subsidies, and increasing information to exporters. Government expenditure on overseas aid and representation may be reduced.

4. Economic growth. By maintaining a high and stable level of demand, businesses are encouraged to expand production and also invest in new plant and machinery. Yet again, new investment may be made more attractive by raising investment allowances. Additional expenditure on education and training will provide the extra skills needed by industry.

5. Equality. Fiscal policy is the major means by which inequality of income can be reduced. Income tax can be graduated so that high-income earners pay most tax. Necessities, such as food and clothing, may be zero rated or exempted from VAT while luxury goods may be taxed more heavily than other goods.

It may have occurred to readers by now that the application of fiscal policy to a particular macro-economic objective has important implications for other policy goals. Two examples will illustrate this point. Since 1944 all UK governments have been committed to maintaining full employment. Often this has meant the Government expanding its own spending to fill the deflationary gap. Yet for a majority of the period since the Second World War the UK balance of payments has been in deficit, and the Government to counter this problem has needed to reduce the level of demand by raising taxes and cutting expenditure.

Here then, lies the heart of the problem. Two policy goals may conflict and the Government has the unenviable task of choosing which to implement. In the above situation, governments have chosen to remedy the balance of payments deficit rather than promote full employment. A similar conflict exists between inflation and employment as policy goals. To cut the rate of inflation we reduce the level of demand, but in doing so it is almost inevitable that we increase unemployment.

The conflict in policy objectives has been characterised by the 'stop – go' cycle (See Fig. 9.6). During a period of rising demand, imports would flood into the UK and prices would rise (making exports less attractive). The ensuing balance of payments difficulties then caused the Government to reduce the level of demand by tax increases and expenditure cuts leading to a sharp increase in unemployment. The commitment to full employment eventually leads to a reversal of the policy measures and once more a period of rising demand.

Clearly, fiscal policy has not been as successful as we would like. In part the answer lies in predicting the future course of the economy. Our

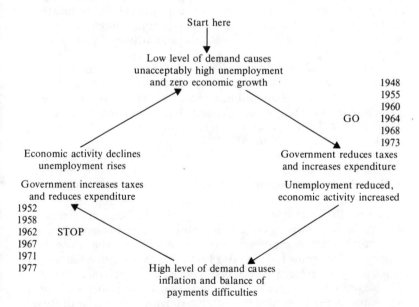

Fig. 9.6 The 'stop–go' cycle

understanding of the workings of the economy and our forecasting techniques were such that the information provided for the Government to act upon was generally too little and too late. Thus measures to correct a slump in economic activity were taken when the economy had already turned the corner. Consequently, government action to mitigate fluctuations in economic activity may, in fact, have aggravated it. Moreover, as a consequence of the inability of the Government to control the economic environment, businesses were unable to plan and invest for the future with any degree of confidence.

The making of a budget

Each year the Chancellor has to make decisions on revenue, taxation, and any borrowing for the forthcoming year. These decisions which are announced in the budget are the end of a planning cycle which is, in fact, continuous.

Since 1980 the starting-point for any UK budget has been the Medium Term Financial Strategy (MTFS). The MTFS outlines in broad terms the Government's macro-economic objectives – the position it would like the economy to be in, say, four years from now. It then states again in broad terms the fiscal and monetary policy necessary to achieve that objective. The MTFS therefore provides the underlying theme to budgets for a number of years. For example the Thatcher Government's economic strategy has been to reduce inflation (as a prerequisite to sustainable economic growth) by controlling the money supply. The fiscal policy identified as being consistent with this strategy was reducing the PSBR – in practice partly by the cutting of government expenditure.

It must be apparent that as each individual budget has to be consistent with MTFS the range of options open to the Chancellor are more limited than is often assumed. Measures taken in the budget will, first and foremost, be designed to check deviations from the MTFS. The budget will also deal with other issues in so far as measures needed are not inconsistent with the MTFS.

Let us now look at how the decisions taken in the annual budget are arrived at. The decision making process is illustrated diagramatically in Fig. 9.7. The information upon which decisions are taken is derived from a series of forecasts produced by the Treasury computer. Treasury officials feed into the computer information on the British and world economies together with specified policy measures. The predictions are then appraised for their compatibility with government objectives. Under the Industry Act 1975 the Government is required to make public two forecasts. The first is issued as a supplement to the Chancellor's budget speech, while the second in November/December accompanies the Government's autumn statement. The issue of these forecasts is intended to increase public understanding of government

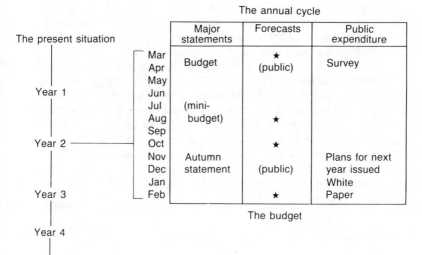

The annual cycle

The present situation		Major statements	Forecasts	Public expenditure
	Mar	Budget	★ (public)	Survey
	Apr			
	May			
Year 1	Jun			
	Jul	(mini-		
	Aug	budget)	★	
	Sep			
Year 2	Oct		★	
	Nov	Autumn		Plans for next
	Dec	statement	(public)	year issued
	Jan			White
Year 3	Feb		★	Paper

The budget

Year 4

Where we want to be, e.g. reduction in inflation increase in employment, satisfactory balance of payments, sustainable economic growth

Fiscal and monetary policy consistent with macro-economic objectives – the Medium Term Financial Strategy

★ = Treasury forecast not available to general public

Fig. 9.7 The British economy

policy and provide a more informed basis for parliamentary and public debate.

At the same time as forecasts are being made monitoring the economy's progress the Treasury is also involved in the process of determining public expenditure for the next financial year. Plans for public expenditure are discussed with the various departments against the background of economic forecasts and in total for compatibility with the MTFS. Final decisions on next year's public expenditure are taken by the Cabinet during the autumn and are announced as part of the Autumn Statement. By now the Chancellor has a fairly clear picture of the shape of the next budget. Forecasts have indicated the measures he needs to take to maintain the MTFS – the raising or lowering of aggregate demand, and the level of public spending has been decided. It remains to be decided how the revenue is to be raised – how much borrowing, what taxes?

Changes in most taxes are considered in the following months, but many are quickly rejected on the grounds of cost or administrative difficulties. The Chancellor's final decisions are based upon the computer forecasts of how the economy will react to different policy measures, together with the representations made by companies, trade associations, the CBI, and the Trades Union Congress (TUC). During this period the computer forecasts are being continuously updated. The final choices are delayed as long as possible, but eventually a few days before the budget the decisions are made.

Interest tends to centre on the budget speech itself, but the Chancellor still has to guide the budget proposals through four days of detailed scrutiny by Parliament. Indeed, there have been occasions when it has become clear during the debate that the Chancellor could not rely on a majority of MPs to support specific measures and has amended his proposals accordingly (for example in 1981, the Chancellor halved to 10p his original proposal to increase the duty on diesel oils). The budget resolutions passed by the House of Commons at the end of the debate form the basis of the Finance Bill which normally becomes law in July.

The finance of local government

Many of the public services which we take for granted within the UK are provided by the local authorities. A description of these services is part of Chapter 15. Our interest here lies in the financing of these services. Figure 9.8 shows how the money was raised in 1980.

Planned expenditure by local authorities in 1983/84 amounted to £31,213 m. This current expenditure, which accounts for three-quarters of total spending is dominated by education (approximately two-thirds of current expenditure). This is followed by expenditure on police, social services, roads, and public health. The major item of capital expenditure is housing.

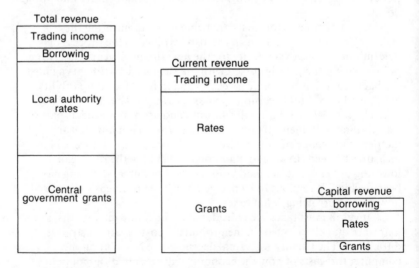

Fig. 9.8 Sources of local government revenue

Central government grants

Local authority expenditure increased dramatically during the 1970s, reflecting, it is thought, not only improvements in the services offered, but also a decline in the efficiency of the sector as a whole. The bulk of this increased expenditure was financed by central government through the rate-support grants. Since that time reliance on central funds has been reduced to approximately 50 per cent by the introduction of a system of cash limits on the level of government help for local authorities. The burden of increased local authority spending has, therefore, fallen more heavily on the local ratepayer with rates rising by 110 per cent between 1978 and 1982.

Rates

Owners and occupiers of land and property pay rates, a local tax, to meet the cost of local services. All property in the locality is inspected by the Inland Revenue who place a value upon it (based upon the property's annual rental value). The local authority uses this as the basis for determining each ratepayer's liability by declaring the amount of tax which has to be paid on each £1 of rateable value. Householders are charged a lower rate than owners of commercial or industrial property. The extent to which local authorities rely on rates as a source of revenue varies between areas. Local authorities with large towns or cities within their area find rates an important source. Rates in the City of London are sufficient to cover expenditure several times over. Conversely, agricultural areas where the total of rateable values are low tend to rely more heavily on central government funds (rates in Powys yield less than 20 per cent of all revenues). As a form of taxation, rates have the advantage of providing local authorities with a predictable amount of revenue which is easy to collect. However, rates may be regressive in that there is no necessary correlation between rateable value and ability to pay. A government report, *The Impact of Rates on Households,* as long ago as 1965 argued that rates were unfair upon houses occupied by pensioners, or where there was only one income coming in. As a separate point the wide disparity in rates paid by the householder in different localities also causes a high degree of resentment. The present Conservative Government was committed to abolishing the 'rates system', but has been unable to find any viable alternative. In other countries finance for local services is often raised by means of a local sales or income tax.

Trading income

Most local authorities obtain income from services they provide. One important source is council housing. Charges are also made for entrance to sports centres, museums, car parks, and evening classes.

Examination questions

1. In what ways, and for what reasons does the Government intervene within the economy?

2. What is the budget, and what is its relationship to the smooth running of the economy? *(PSC Dec. 1978)*

3. How can the budget be used to influence economic activity? *(PSC June 1975)*

4. What is the purpose of the budget? *(PSC Dec. 1980)*

5. Outline some of the major considerations influencing a government in the formation of a budgetary policy. *(PSC June 1977)*

6. Explain the following types of taxation, giving example:

   (a) taxes on income;

   (b) taxes on capital;

   (c) taxes on expenditure. *(PSC Dec. 1978)*

7. Selecting a firm of your choice, show how the ways the Government raises and spends money affect that firm.

8. What are the objectives of central government in managing the economy? Do they conflict? *(PSC June 1979)*

9. How may a central government move an economy towards full employment? What are the advantages to be gained from full employment? *(PSC June 1979)*

10. What is meant by:

    (a) Monetary policy?

    (b) Fiscal policy?

   In what circumstances is the Government likely to adopt a deflationary economic strategy?

11. What is a country's National Debt? Should we attempt to reduce its size?

The organisation of business activity

Part III

The organisation
Chapter 10

There are two ways in which we use the word 'organisation'. The first implies a functional group, that is, a group created for a purpose. Businesses, whether they be sole traders, partnerships, or limited companies, are prime examples of organisations. Equally the clubs, societies, and charities we belong to in our private lives and the central or local government departments we may deal with from time to time are also organisations. The importance of business and governmental organisations is discussed elsewhere in this book. But the term 'organisation' may also refer to the process by which men, materials, machines, and management are brought together and co-ordinated so as to achieve efficient production of goods and services. It is this aspect which we wish to consider in this book.

Approaches to organisation design

Prior to the Industrial Revolution little thought had gone into organisation design. That was because apart from the Church most organisations were small scale. However, with the growth of large-scale industry problems of co-ordination and control increased and the need for research into organisation design became obvious.

The classical approach

Classical writers were convinced that there was one best way to structure an organisation and sought to find a set of principles which if implemented would guarantee an efficient organisation.

F. W. Taylor (1856–1915) is often said to be the father of the classical school. He was a production engineer who spent his working life in the American steel industry. His interest was in work and productivity which he believed could be raised significantly by what is now known as method study and work measurement. As a result of his studies he published a number of books and propounded the four following principles for job design:

1. Job design should be undertaken scientifically (see Ch. 12, p. 209 for a detailed description of method study and work measurement).

2. Workers have different attributes and abilities – select the proper employee for the job, and ensure he is trained properly in the correct method.

3. Workers are motivated primarily by money. The introduction of incentives can increase productivity.

4. Each task has both a 'planning' and a 'doing' element. It is the function of the manager to plan, thus allowing the employee to concentrate on doing the job.

These principles may not seem particularly significant to us today, but at the turn of the century they were thought revolutionary. They rapidly became standard practice.

While Taylor focused his attention at the base of the organisational pyramid, Henri Fayol (1841–1925) a French mining engineer sought to establish principles which could be applied throughout the organisation. They were:

1. The principle of the objective – all parts of the organisation must contribute to its objectives otherwise they are redundant.

2. The principle of specialisation – each member of the organisation should be allocated a single role which is well defined in terms of authority, responsibility, and relationships.

3. The principle of co-ordination – the structure established should ensure united efforts towards the goals of the organisation.

4. The principle of authority – a clear chain of command should exist from the most senior executive to all employees in the organisation.

5. The principle of responsibility – a superior cannot avoid responsibility for the acts of his subordinates.

6. The principle of correspondence – the authority given should always be sufficient to discharge the responsibilities undertaken.

7. The span of control – there is a limit to the number of people whose work a manager can supervise. A manager's subordinates should be limited to a maximum of six where their work interlocks.

The acceptance of these principles brought a growing realisation that managerial skills could be learnt, and the subsequent development of management courses in colleges and universities.

Max Weber (1864–1920) provided the third pillar in the development of classical organisation theory. Like Taylor and Fayol, Weber believed that there was a logical framework for organisations which could be used to improve efficiency. He believed such an organisation had the following characteristics:

1. Official duties – each employee would be allocated very specialised tasks leading to greater expertise among staff.

2. Hierarchy of authority – there are clear levels of authority with the higher positions controlling and supervising those below them. This enables activities to be co-ordinated.

3. A system of rules and regulations – all decisions will be based upon the rules which have been established. This ensures uniformity of decision-making.

4. Impersonal attitude – rational decision-making is promoted by disregarding all personal or emotional considerations.

5. Technical qualifications – employment is based on qualifications and experience (merit). It is expected that the organisation will employ the worker throughout his working life. Greater expertise is thus developed and the employee is more able to resist external pressures.

Such an organisation Weber termed a 'bureaucracy'. The term, to him, did not have the negative connotations which it has to us today. To Weber it was like a highly efficient modern machine.

Bureaucracies are very much a feature of modern life. Many large organisations and government departments exhibit all the characteristics discussed above. The growth of bureaucracies has arisen because of the following:

1. *As the firm increases in size there is a greater specialisation, and the need for more careful co-ordination of activities.*

2. *The greater complexity of the environment in which the organisation operates, for example the increasing number of ways in which the Government tries to control the activities of business.*

3. *Their system of rules and regulations, levels of authority, job design, is seen to be efficient.*

4. *Claims for equality of treatment result in the establishing of rules to be followed in all cases.*

The classical approach to organisation theory has been criticised for a number of reasons. Firstly, classical organisation theory takes no account of the individual. Taylor, for example, regarded man as an adjunct to the machine who could be manipulated as management wished. Secondly, the classical writers ignored the impact of the environment upon the organisation. Thirdly, the classical organisation principles seem less valid in today's complex and unstable environment. For example, our bureaucracy with its formalised structure and procedures is unable to respond adequately to rapidly changing conditions. Lastly, in large organisations many principles seem too general. Lines of authority often become blurred with employees receiving orders and being responsible to more than one superior.

The human relations and behavioural science approach

This approach to organisation design arose out of what was seen as the major defect of the classical approach – its dehumanising attitude towards workers. Human-relations researchers believe that organisations should have two objectives – firstly business efficiency, but also secondly workers' satisfaction.

The first major contribution was made by Elton Mayo (1880–1949) a Scottish psychologist working in America. Mayo conducted a series of experiments at the Hawthorne Plant of the Western Electric Company between 1927 and 1932. These experiments are generally known as the 'Hawthorne Experiments'.

The initial experiment conducted sought to establish a relationship between output and illumination. Researchers found that as illumination increased output rose, but were dumfounded to see productivity rise still further when illumination was decreased (Fig. 10.1).

Further experiments followed in which researchers varied salaries, rest periods, and working days with an experimental group while maintaining normal established working conditions in a control group.

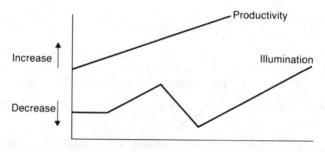

Fig. 10.1 The Hawthorne Experiments — impact of changes in illumination on productivity

The researchers now found that productivity rose in both the experimental and control groups. Mayo believed that something other than working conditions and financial incentives had affected their motivation to work – these he believed to be social and psychological factors. The interest shown in the groups by the researchers, the group cohesiveness, and the mutual co-operation of the researchers and groups being the major motivators.

But group cohesiveness did not always result in workers striving to achieve organisational objectives. In the bank wiring room at Western Electric Mayo found a group of workers who restricted output, ignored financial incentives, had their own code of conduct, and had selected a leader who was different to the official one. Eventually Mayo concluded:

1. Man is motivated by social needs.

2. The division of labour or specialisation had destroyed much of the meaning of work. This now had to be found in social relationships at work.

3. The work group will have more effect on worker behaviour than organisational incentives and controls.

4. Managers and supervisors concerned with the attainment of organisational objectives must also ensure that the workers' social needs are met.

Mayo's contribution to organisation theory cannot be underestimated. As a result of the Hawthorne experiments a new approach to the problem of organisation design and managerial effectiveness grew up. Many organisations modified their structure and work practices in the belief that satisfied workers would be productive workers. Unfortunately the increases in productivity which were expected often failed to materialise and later writers such as McGregor, Argyris, and Maslow pointed out that the link between organisation design, motivation, and productivity was far more complex than previously imagined.

McGregor, for example, believed that much of the formal organisation structure was based on a set of negative assumptions about workers. These assumptions which he referred to as Theory X were:

1. Man dislikes work and will avoid it if he can.

2. Man wishes to avoid responsibility and prefers to be directed.

3. Above all else man demands security.

The role of the manager therefore is to direct and control their work, if necessary threatening them with punishment should they fail to produce sufficient effort.

Diametrically opposed to Theory X is Theory Y which takes a much more positive view of individuals:

1. Man enjoys and finds real satisfaction in work.

2. Man accepts and even seeks responsibility.

3. Man can be committed to and strive for organisational objectives without the threat of punishment.

4. Modern industrial life uses only a small part of the average worker's ability.

The role of the manager under Theory Y is to provide an environment in which employees can best achieve their own goals while striving to attain the organisational objectives. Thus the organisation would be structured to allow employees more independence, greater communication with managers, and more participation in decision-making.

For the many employees, who McGregor believed fitted Theory Y, the near-complete control which managers exercised over their activities resulted at best in apathy, or worse still dissatisfaction and frustration. In these circumstances absenteeism and labour turnover were likely to be high, morale low, and the organisation have difficulty in attaining its objectives.

The human relations and behavioural science approach to organisation design, like that of the classicists, has been criticised for several reasons. Like that of the classicists it suffers from the deficiencies of believing there is one best approach to organisation design and ignoring the impact of the environment. Moreover, in practice it is often extremely difficult to structure an organisation so that all jobs are challenging and rewarding, and yet maintain that high degree of efficiency required in today's harsh economic climate.

Contingency approaches

Later approaches to organisation design emphasise that there is no one best method of structuring an organisation. Instead the approach used will depend upon the particular circumstances in which the organisation finds itself. The approach does not reject the classical and human relations approaches – it will draw upon them as appropriate, but believes that there are other factors which have to be taken into account. These would include:

1. The strengths and weaknesses of the organisation.

2. The objectives of the organisation.

3. The external environment of the organisation.

Establishing the structure

Defining objectives

All organisations have objectives – that is, end results towards which the organisation directs its activities. These may be primary or secondary. A primary objective is a broad statement indicating in very general terms what the owners or managers of an organisation wish to achieve. Thus a non-profit organisation may express this in terms of providing a service – perhaps educating our children, aiding the handicapped, or relieving pain and suffering. A pressure group would express its desire to influence government and public opinion. A business would emphasise survival, profitability, and growth.

But primary objectives tell us little about the way in which the organisation will achieve its aims, and therefore need to be broken down into more specific statements which are capable of being translated into actions by individuals on a daily basis. These specific statements we term secondary objectives. Our non-profit-making school may, say, educate our children by providing classrooms, teachers, books, and syllabuses, while the pressure group will identify the need to raise money, and to place supporters in positions of influence. The business will state its secondary objectives in terms of production, marketing, innovation, and efficiency.

Developing the formal organisation

The formal organisation refers to the structure which is developed to aid the organisation in meeting its objectives. We can see the formal organisation in the way in which the organisation has:

1. Grouped activities into departments such as marketing, production, and finance.

2. Divided work so that employees contribute fully to the work of the organisation.

3. Defined relationships between employees.

4. Established rules and procedures which are to be followed.

5. Determined where decisions are to be made.

6. Created channels of communication for the passing of information.

The informal organisation

While the formal organisation is an attempt on the part of the managers to structure the organisation and establish relationships which will meet organisation objectives effectively, the informal organisation arises out of the activities and interactions of employees. Virtually all organisations have an informal organisation. It is after all a perfectly natural thing for people within the organisation to be drawn together by job, work, seniority, age, interests, and so on. We can see the informal organisation functioning in the group that always sit and have coffee together, the grapevine that passes information around the office, or the group of employees who restrict output whatever incentives are offered by management.

The informal organisation arises because companionship and social relationships are important to the individual. It is a means by which he shares his own experiences and shares in the experiences of others. It gives him a sense of belonging, a group identity – perhaps making an otherwise boring job bearable. An element of security is also provided by the informal organisation. Workers may agree a common response to new requirements of the formal organisation. They can prevent competition among themselves, which could result in the least efficient workers being laid off. Lastly the competence of the new or inexperienced worker may be increased through the help and advice of the informal group members.

To the organisation though, informal groups are a double-edged sword. They may benefit the organisation through the higher morale of its members. Informal arrangements and agreements may also reduce the deficiencies of the formal structure and provide an additional management/employee channel of communication. However, against this must be placed the fact that sometimes informal group objectives run counter to the goals of the organisation. For example, employees may restrict output, or alternatively the ties of the group which bind the members together may limit labour mobility.

Types of organisation

The formal structure of an organisation is the means by which it co-ordinates its activities and thereby attains its objectives. The structure adopted reflects the particular requirements of the individual organisation. It should not surprise the reader, therefore, that there is no one correct way of structuring activities or that organisation structures will alter as objectives change. However, most structures will fall into one of the following three broad classifications: line; line and staff (including functional organisation); matrix.

Line organisation
There are certain activities which are essential if an organisation is going to survive as an efficient unit. These we will term line activities. Other activities carried on within the organisation are designed to improve the efficiency with which line activities are carried out. A line

organisation exists when the formal structure of the organisation consists of departments based upon line activities.

Let us consider an engineering firm. Should this business adopt a line structure, what would it consist of? Put another way, what activities are essential in order to achieve its primary objectives (survival, profitability, growth). Certainly the business needs to be able to raise the finance necessary to start or expand the business. It must be able to manufacture the products it plans to sell. The products must, in fact, be sold, while in the longer term the business should develop new or improved products. All other work carried out by the business merely seeks to improve the efficiency of these activities. Figure 10.2 illustrates a line organisation we have described.

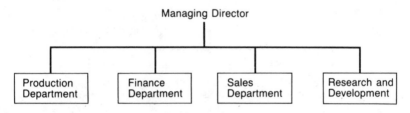

Fig. 10.2 Line organisation in an engineering firm

Other businesses will of course have different line activities and therefore a different line-organisation structure. Thus a retail organisation adopting a line structure will group its activities around purchasing finance and sales, and an insurance company around claims, sales, finance, and underwriting.

The line organisation has a number of advantages:

1. The structure is easy to understand.

2. Responsibilities are well defined.

3. Employees can see the value of their contribution (and other peoples) to the organisation.

4. The simple structure makes for few communication problems.

5. It aids the development of all-round managers rather than specialists.

Line and staff organisation
A line organisation is primarily suited to the small organisation. As an organisation grows the managers of line activities find that more and more of their time is taken up with peripheral activities. Thus the production manager rather than concentrating on the problems of production will be devoting time to industrial relations, quality

control, and the purchasing of raw materials or components. The production manager's attempts to deal with these other problems are a waste of his time and expertise. His efforts may be being duplicated elsewhere in the firm, while more importantly he may not have the expertise to deal with these problems effectively.

Once we have recognised that the appointment of specialist staff and the creation of specialist departments may aid organisational efficiency, a line organisation no longer exists.

A line organisation becomes a line and staff organisation once the structure incorporates (Fig. 10.3):

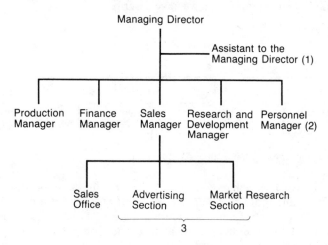

Fig. 10.3 Line and staff organisation in an engineering firm

1. An assistant to a senior executive who does not have line responsibilities – a senior secretary or a personal assistant may adopt this role (these are termed general staff).

2. New departments with specialist responsibilities are created, for example, purchasing, personnel, work study, or computer departments (these are termed specialist staff).

3. Line departments are modified to accommodate specialist activities, for example the production department may include, as a distinct activity, purchasing or quality control while the sales department may create sections dealing with advertising or market research (these are termed specialist staff).

(a) General staff. It is important to distinguish between an assistant to a senior manager, for example assistant to the managing director and an assistant managing director. The latter has line authority given

to him – he will have specific duties allocated to him for which he is responsible and will be able to give orders to subordinates. In the absence of the managing director the assistant managing director will take over his responsibilities. On the other hand the assistant to the managing director has <u>no formal authority</u>, his duties are those allocated to him by his superior from time to time and he is unable to issue orders in his own name. In organisational terms the difference is illustrated in Fig. 10.4.

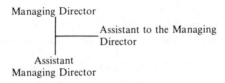

Fig. 10.4 Example of a general staff assistant

The appointment of general staff assistants can be beneficial for a number of reasons. The assistant can relieve the overburdened executive by taking over responsibility for certain parts of his work, or undertaking the detailed work necessary to implement a decision made by a senior executive. The general assistant may also act as a co-ordinator, making arrangements in the superior's name. Alternatively, the role of the general staff assistant may be used to provide a loyal member of staff with employment, rather than making him redundant when organisational change occurs. It may also be used to enable a young executive to learn the job he is expected to take over shortly or to give him support while he is learning the job.

Although we may support the appointment of general staff assistants in principle, careful consideration of all the factors should always be made before making such an appointment. Personal assistants can be something of a status symbol, and the appointment of one to a manager on the same level as you may cause friction if your claims to equal treatment are turned down. The appointment of a personal assistant to a manager may also cause friction within his own department. Subordinates may feel the work allocated to the personal assistant should have devolved to them, or that an extra subordinate position should be created. We may question why the manager is overburdened – perhaps he will not delegate – and point out the danger of the manager developing too close a relationship with his personal assistant to the detriment of his subordinates. For these reasons general staff assistants have always been used sparingly.

(b) Specialist staff. Specialist staff are appointed for their expertise, an expertise which it is believed will enable the line departments to do

their work more efficiently. Their work within the organisation, whatever their expertise, may be classified as advisory, service, or control. In their advisory function the specialist will advise the line manager on some proposed course of action. The maintenance engineer may advise the production manager against purchasing a certain make of machinery because of the difficulty of servicing or of obtaining spare parts. The personnel manager may advise the production manager on aspects of health and safety legislation. Of course the line manager is not compelled to accept this advice – he may already have received conflicting advice to that of the maintenance engineer from the purchasing department, but he will listen carefully and consider all that is said.

Should a staff specialist be convinced that the decision of the line manager is incorrect he may appeal to their superior who then has to mediate between the two. Should the senior manager accept the advice of the staff specialist that advice then takes on the form of a line order from a superior to (in this case) the production manager. Unfortunately, whatever decision the superior reaches the relationship between the two subordinates is impaired.

The specialist's second function is to provide a service from which the line departments may benefit. Thus the personnel manager may provide a recruitment service for the whole organisation, or the maintenance engineer establish a programme of planned maintenance. But it must be remembered that the service function is not an end in itself. It exists to enhance the efficiency of line departments. Indeed for line departments to operate with maximum efficiency, service functions may have to operate below this level. For example, production should not be impeded by maintenance work. It may be necessary to bring in maintenance staff on overtime at night or weekends to avoid interference.

Lastly, staff departments have a control function. In his capacity they will introduce a system for the line manager's use and ensure that the system is used properly throughout the organisation. Thus the personnel manager may establish the procedure to be followed in the disciplining and dismissing of employees so as to avoid unfair dismissal claims. He must ensure that the procedure is in fact understood and followed by all departments.

The major disadvantage of line and staff structure arises from its greater complexity of relationships – a complexity which often causes friction between line and staff personnel. For example:

1. The line manager finds his authority and responsibility curtailed by the appointment of the specialist. He feels his status is threatened.

2. The line manager may feel the specialist is being used by senior staff to monitor his work.

3. Line managers feel that specialists have a narrow outlook and are unable fully to understand the problems of line management.

4. Specialists talk a different language and often use highly sophisticated techniques which are incomprehensible to the layman.

5. Specialists may introduce change to justify their position.

The role of the staff specialist within the line and staff organisation is purely advisory; where, however, he is given authority over others in respect of his specialism he is said to have a functional role. Under this form of organisation an employee may be responsible to more than one superior.

The concept was popularised by F. W. Taylor during the early part of the twentieth century. He believed that the work of foremen in engineering workshops demanded so many different skills that one man could not do the job efficiently. Taylor's solution was to divide the work of the foremen into eight different activities, allocating one function to each foreman. The worker thus became responsible to eight supervisors – each for a different part of his job. Although examples of this structure do exist, functional organisation has never been popular largely due to the potential conflicts the worker could face in being responsible to so many different people.

Matrix organisation

This structure was developed first in the United States in the aerospace industry. It is an attempt to break down the communication and authority/responsibility barriers which exist in a line and staff organisation by integrating personnel into a project team. Today the concept of the matrix organisation is widely used in the construction industry and also in many other situations where a high degree of co-ordination is necessary.

Figure 10.5 illustrates a typical matrix organisation. It is in fact two organisations in one. The departments are a permanent feature of the organisation responsible for their specialism throughout the business. Project teams, however, are created as necessary – that is, when a contract calling for a high degree of co-ordination and multidisciplinary skills is obtained.

The members of the project team are drawn from the various departments and are, for the duration of the project responsible to the team leader. The team members will draw from their parent departments such resources as are necessary for them to carry out their jobs as team members. The project leader is responsible for co-ordinating their efforts and ensuring that the project is completed successfully. Once the project is finished the team members and leader will return to their parent departments until they are assigned to another team.

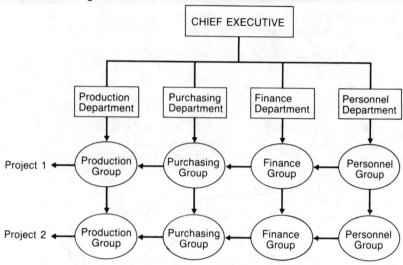

Fig. 10.5 Matrix organisation

The matrix organisation structure has several advantages of which the most important is the efficiency with which the project is carried through. Interdepartmental barriers are broken down by the team approach, team members can devote their skill completely to the project, and are more likely to co-ordinate their activities. The appointment of a team leader has the dual advantage of ensuring tighter control of the project and providing a contact to whom the client can always refer to (thus ensuring a better client/organisation relationship). Lastly, the integrated approach to problem-solving aids manager development, and may reduce barriers between the parent departments.

However, matrix organisations are much more complex than other organisation structures, and often result in a less efficient use of resources in the parent departments. Moreover, the assignment of staff to project teams unless carefully planned may disrupt or even prevent staff management development.

Organisation charts

The most common method of describing an organisation structure is by means of an organisation chart. This pictorial method is used because of the complexity of most structures and the difficulties of describing them verbally. Let us look at an organisation chart for Condor PLC., a typical manufacturing concern (Fig. 10.6) and see what it tells us:

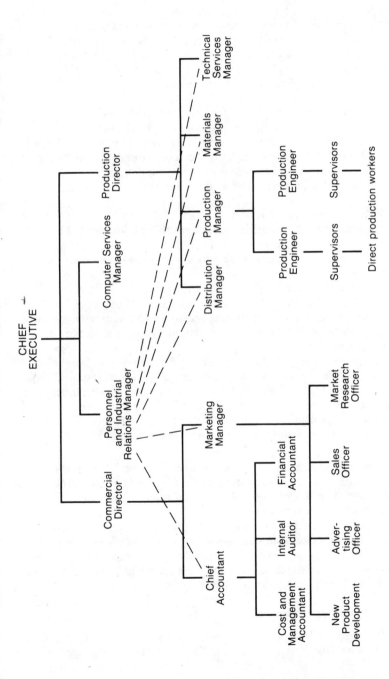

Fig. 10.6 Organisational chart for Condor PLC – a typical manufacturing concern

1. The grouping of activities. The chart shows how Condor's activities have been split up. The individual units or departments are shown by boxes and indicate work on the basis of functions – accountacy, marketing, personnel, production, materials, and so forth. There are, of course, many other bases on which work could be grouped, for example region, market, product, or process.

2. Division of labour. Each title represents an individual who is responsible for a part of the organisation's work. The title indicates in very general terms the area of his responsibilities. It indicates the extent to which specialisation is being used. Thus the work of the marketing department is broken down into four parts – market research, advertising, sales, and new product development.

3. Chain of command. The unbroken line extending from the top to the bottom of the organisation chart shows that all workers are linked to the chief executive by the chain of command. This is the means by which orders are passed and work allocated to each individual employee.

The organisation chart also indicates the superior – subordinate relationships. Thus we can see that the Marketing Manager of Condor PLC receives his orders from and reports to the Commercial Director, while the Personnel and Industrial Relations Manager reports direct to the Chief Executive.

Managers not only have a responsibility for the work within their own department or section, many also have a functional responsibility for their specialism throughout the whole organisation. This functional responsibility is denoted by a broken line. Thus the Personnel Manager's responsibility for 'personnel' throughout Condor PLC is shown by a broken line linking him with all other departments.

4. Communication channels. The unbroken line also indicates the formal channels of communication within Condor PLC and shows how information is processed by the organisations. A modern organisation, however, does not rely solely on vertical lines of communication, to do so would be a waste of time and money. Instead the organisation establishes procedures by which employees can pass information to one another without involving their superiors each time – although at the same time provision is also made to keep superiors informed of any problems or difficulties which may arise.

Advantages of organisation charts

1. It provides information on the formal structure of the organisation in a form that is easily understood by all. It may be displayed on staff notice-boards thus providing a focal point for information on changes in organisation structure or personnel.

2. The preparation of the chart draws attention to organisational defects, for example areas of conflict, areas of duplication, an excessive span of control or an excessively long line of authority.

3. The organisation chart is also the basis from which any proposed changes to the organisation structure are made.

Disadvantages of organisation charts

1. The chart is a picture of the organisation at a certain time and is rapidly outdated by changes in structure or personnel.

2. The designer faces the difficulty of showing the organisation structure in full, in which case the chart is complex and confusing, or simplifying the structure and thereby presenting an inaccurate picture.

3. The organisation chart may cause employee discontent. Employees often believe status within an organisation is implied by their distance from the Chief Executive, or the size of their box!

4. Organisation charts do not reveal the different degrees of responsibility borne by executives.

5. They do not show the unofficial relationships and chains of communication without which the organisation would not function properly.

Types of organisation chart
The traditional method of portraying the structure of an organisation is the vertical organisation chart. Attempts have been made to show the structure in a different way to avoid the emphasis on status or levels of management. Figure 10.7 and Fig. 10.8 depict the upper levels

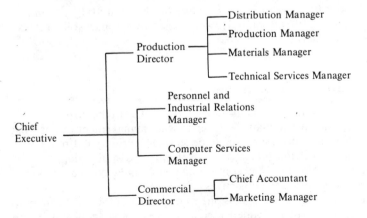

Fig. 10.7 Horizontal organisation chard for Condor PLC

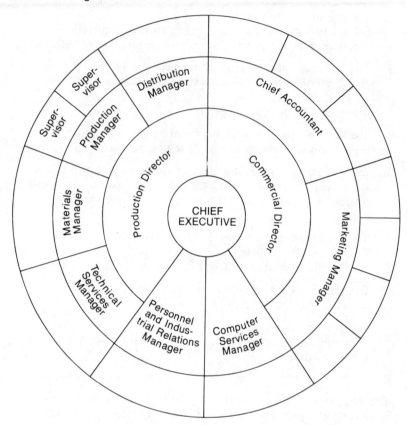

Fig. 10.8 Circular organisation chart for Condor PLC

of Condor PLC organisation structure in a horizontal (Fig. 7) and circular (Fig. 10.8) fashion. However, the vertical chart still remains the most widely used.

The role of the manager

As with the study of organisations, it was not until the turn of the century that any thought was given to what management was or what managers do. The first person to do so was Henri Fayol. From his work we may define management as the process of planning, organising, directing, and controlling people and resources so as to achieve organisational objectives.

It follows that a manager is one who carries out these key functions. The term 'manager' is widely used in business, but of course there are other people as well who carry out managerial activities within the firm and yet have a different job title. Examples could include director, controller, supervisor, or section leader. Moreover, managers, whatever their job title, are not only needed in business but wherever there is organised activity – the Church, armed forces, government departments, or charitable bodies. We will now consider each of the managers key functions.

Planning

Initially, planning is needed to establish the objectives of the organisation. It is also needed to establish the policies, programmes, projects, and procedures by which these objectives will be achieved.

Planning involves four steps:
- Establish objectives.
- Determine how the objectives may be achieved.
- Evaluate the different sources of action.
- Decide upon the course of action and detail plans and procedures to implement it.

Planning is said to be the starting-point of all managerial activity; without it there can be no logical organisation structure, directed activity, or means of control. Planning has become even more important because the increasing size of organisations has created the problem of co-ordinating work effectively. Increased uncertainty in the environment facing organisations has been an additional factor.

Organising

The manager's role in organising is to draw together the resources of the organisation:

- men;
- materials;
- machines;
- money;

in such a manner that the objectives of the organisation can be achieved. We can say that management is the resource which unifies the other four.

Let us take the example of a distribution manager in an engineering firm. Goods for distribution will have to be packed. Schedules will have to be drawn up establishing when the goods will be transported and where they are destined for. Vans and lorries will have to be maintained. Drivers, clerks, typists, and maintenance men all have to be employed and receive instructions as to their duties. In some way the manager has to co-ordinate all these operations.

The results of the manager's efforts may be seen in the ways in which activities are grouped, work divided, and communication channels established – in short the formal organisation structure.

Directing

The work of the manager is sometimes described as 'getting things done through people'. Although this is by no means a complete description of the manager's work it does have the merit of pointing out that all the planning and all the organisation are of no use if the employees do not work in the way required. To obtain co-operation the manager will need to communicate, motivate, lead, and discipline his staff.

Motivation

There are many theories of motivation which attempt to explain a worker's reaction in a particular situation. Some emphasise the importance of the work environment, some the need for work to be interesting and challenging, and some the importance of financial incentives. What is clear is that what may be a motivating influence for one person may have little effect upon another person. The task of the manager must therefore be to know his staff thereby identifying and hopefully providing the motivating influence which they require.

Leadership

It is generally agreed that leaders have an important role in helping organisations achieve their objectives. The function of the leader is twofold. In his task-related function he will (1) co-ordinate the work of others, (2) plan for the future, and (3) solve present problems. In his 'group maintenance' or social function he provides the unifying force that welds the group together and helps it operate smoothly. He may encourage or give support to subordinates; alternatively, he may act as a mediator in disputes.

Communication

The communication process is at the heart of the effective organisation. A large percentage of the time that managers spend in organisations is devoted to the passing of information between people, for example face-to-face discussions, memos, letters, reports, telephone calls. In fact both as individuals and employees we are constantly involved in the receipt, evaluation, and distribution of information.

Yet while all organisations want good or effective communication a 'breakdown in communication' has often been cited as the cause of failure to achieve objectives. For example it is possible for the message to fail to reach its destination. In large organisations it is very easy for the mail to go astray, a phone message to be lost on an untidy desk, or the right person to be away from the office at the important moment. It is also possible that the message is distorted. The communication may be ambiguous. Words have a variety of meanings and may be interpreted in different ways. As information is passed through a number of recipients its meaning and content may change significantly. The probability of distortion will increase where communication is between employees with different specialisms (e.g. accounting and marketing), or where communications are reduced in length. Lastly, people often have preconceived ideas about what is going to be said to them. These expectations can distort the interpretation of the communication.

Discipline
For organisations to function efficiently a large number of people will be required to work in a predictable fashion. Thus employees have set hours for work, they are instructed what work to carry out, and in many cases the procedures by which it is to be undertaken. To ensure that employees conform to these requirements managers have various sanctions at their disposal. Managers, for example, have considerable discretion in the work that they allocate to subordinates – some of the jobs may be interesting some boring. The deviant employee will obviously not receive the 'plum' jobs. There are also formal procedures in most organisations whereby the deviant can be warned regarding his work or attitude, and eventually if necessary dismissed.

Today though the movement is away from discipline imposed from above towards self-discipline. Thus subordinates in conjunction with their superiors will agree targets against which their performance will be measured. In effect the superior says: 'Here is the target which we agreed, how you achieve it is your responsibility, but you will be judged by the results.'

Semi-autonomous work groups are another example of the movement away from imposed discipline. In this situation a work group is made responsible for a particular task, but is left to determine how the task should be undertaken. Discipline is imposed by the group.

Organisational levels

Virtually all organisation structures are shaped like a pyramid (See Fig. 10.9). This reflects the narrowing number of jobs at each level until eventually there is only one at the top – that of the chief executive.

Although all managers perform the same functions – planning, organising, directing, and controlling – the emphasis which is placed on each function will vary according to the manager's level in the organisational hierarchy.

Top management. *Senior management is responsible for long-term planning and policy decisions within the organisation. Planning involves determining the organisation's profit and growth objectives. Organising* *involves deciding upon the basic structure of the organisation – what divisions or departments to create, whether to organise by product or territory. Directing includes providing the motivation for lower-level employees to strive for organisational objectives, while controlling is through measurement of achieved results against objectives.*

Middle management. *Middle managers are required to implement on a day-to-day basis the policies decided by senior management. Planning requires formulation of plans and procedures to ensure that activity is directed towards organisational goals. Organisation requires the delegation of specific activities to subordinates, the co-ordination of their work, and the development of horizontal relationships. Directing involves creating situations where the employee can satisfy personal goals while at the same time meeting organisational goals. Controlling is based upon a comparison of budget results in relation to plans.*

Supervisory management. *Sometimes called first-line management, supervisors or foremen are the managers in daily contact with the workers. Planning by supervisors is limited to developing detailed schedules of work for employees. Organisation requires implementation of these schedules. Directing involves the application of motivation and discipline to overcome employee resistance, the recognition of outstanding work and sometimes acting as friend and counsellor. Control lies in ensuring that work is completed satisfactorily and according to schedule.*

Controlling

Finally the manager needs to ensure that the system he has devised is working successfully. The performance of the organisation,

Fig. 10.9 The shape of a typical organisation structure

department, or section will be measured against objectives which were established in the planning stage. Controls are established in virtually all parts of the organisation. For example:

Marketing sales volume; advertising expenditure; new product development; new outlets or customers.

Production Cost; quantity; quality; waste.

Personnel. Labour turnover; illness and absenteeism; industrial disputes; industrial accidents.

Financial. Profit levels; budgets; cash flow; cost of finance.

Controlling involves not only checking performance against targets but taking whatever corrective action is needed to bring performance back on to line. Alternatively the plan may be revised.

For the sake of simplicity we have considered the function of managers separately and as part of a cycle. Unfortunately, in reality it is not so simple. First, except in a completely new organisation the functions will not necessarily occur in the order illustrated in the cycle. Moreover the manager is involved in many projects all in different stages of completion and will perform all functions on a typical day.

Secondly, in practice it is difficult to distinguish the four functions. Plans are used to control employee activity (organisation and direction), or control activities may lead to the revision of plans. Finally, the manager's ability to plan, organise, direct, and control is often impaired by restrictions on his authority or the use of resources. It would be extremely rare for any manager to have complete freedom of action.

Delegation, decentralisation, and committees

Delegation

It is unlikely that any manager is capable of making all those decisions which are necessary for the smooth running of his part of the organisation. It is therefore essential that the manager assigns some of his duties to subordinates. In doing so he is able to concentrate on those tasks which are most important to the organisation. At the same time the assignment of tasks trains and develops the skills of the next generation of managers, while also acting as a powerful motivating influence.

The act of assigning work to subordinates is termed delegation. Its importance in the modern organisation can be gauged by considering the complexity of the typical organisation chart.

There are three important aspects to delegation – responsibilty, authority, and accountability. First, in accepting the task a subordinate assumes a responsibility – that is, an obligation to ensure that delegated duties are performed satisfactorily. For delegation to be effective, responsibilities should be clearly defined. The sum total of the subordinate's responsibilities can be seen by referring to the job description for the position he holds.

Secondly, for delegation to work the subordinate must have the authority to carry out his duties. This authority could include spending money, using other organisational resources, the hiring and firing of personnel, or the giving of advice in the name of his superior.

Thirdly, the subordinate having been given the responsibility and authority necessary for his duties is accountable to his superior for performing the work agreed and the results achieved. This accountability is most meaningful where standards of performance have been established beforehand. However, there is another side to accountability. Managers are not only accountable for the duties which have been assigned to them, they are also accountable for the actions of their subordinates. In this way the chief executive of a company is ultimately responsible and accountable to the shareholders for all that happens within that organisation and may be required to resign when things go wrong.

Although delegation has important advantages for an organisation, in practice there are limits to the extent that it can be used. It is unlikely that highly specialised or highly confidential work will be delegated to subordinates. Equally the greater the potential cost of a decision to the organisation the greater the likelihood that that decision will be made by senior managers.

We must also consider the ability and the attitude of both superior and subordinate to delegation. A manager may experience difficulty in controlling the activities of more than two or three subordinates. V. A. Graicunas suggested that a superior's span of responsibility could not efficiently extend beyond controlling the work of six subordinates whose work interlocks. But many superiors are also unwilling to delegate arguing that 'it's quicker to do it myself' or 'I've got to make sure it is done properly'. Other managers may not be able to plan sufficiently far ahead to delegate. Finally, feelings of insecurity – the idea that a subordinate who does a good job may become a threat to his own position may prevent a superior delegating.

The ability of the subordinate to carry out the delegated task is also an important consideration, especially as the superior is ultimately responsible for the actions of his subordinates. Yet while this is a legitimate reason in the short term, in the longer term it is no excuse for the manager should be training his subordinates for these responsibilites. It is also possible that the subordinates are unwilling to accept the extra responsibility delegation imposes upon them. The common reasons for this include wanting a quiet life, fear of making a mistake, or insufficient incentive to take on the extra duties.

Decentralisation

While delegation refers to the extent which individual managers assign duties to subordinates, decentralisation refers to the extent to which the organisation as a whole pushes authority and responsibility for decision-making down into its divisions, departments, and sections. In a highly centralised organisation power is concentrated in the upper-management levels of the organisation with key decisions being taken by a few top-level managers. In a decentralised organisation lower levels of management will have responsibility for many important decisions. However, let us be clear that no organisation is completely centralised for no one person could take all decisions necessary to run the organisation. Equally, no organisation is completely decentralised, to be so would imply a total lack of control and co-ordination.

The major benefit arising from decentralisation is the control top management obtain over the activities of the organisation; there is a greater degree of co-ordination, uniformity of action, and security of information. But decentralisation has been forced on many organisations as they have increased in size and complexity. Senior managers have become overburdened and been forced to delegate.

Decentralisation has the advantage of enabling decisions to be taken quickly, and at the position in the organisation where there is most knowledge. It may also have beneficial effects on employee motivation.

The degree of decentralisation present in any organisation structure will be determined by the following factors:

1. *The philosophy of management* – some organisations have a history of centralisation or decentralisation which reflects the philosophy of its chief executive. Thus Henry Ford once boasted that all major decisions in Ford were made by himself.

2. *Method of growth* – firms that have grown through merger tend to adopt a more decentralised structure than those expanding internally.

3. *The costliness of the decision* – the greater the cost involved the greater the degree of centralisation.

4. *The influence of the environment* – where the environment is unstable a higher degree of decentralisation is often chosen so that the organisation may respond more quickly to those changes which it perceives.

5. *Characteristics of the organisation* – the greater the number of products the organisation makes or markets it serves the greater the degree of decentalisation forced upon it.

6. *The ability of subordinates.*

Committees

A committee is a group of people who have been formally appointed to undertake a specific duty. It is a form of delegation, the members having been charged with responsibility for a task, given the necessary authority, and being accountable to those who created the committee.

Although committees have long been the butt of managerial wit – 'a camel is a horse created by a committee' – they are widely used in business today for fact-finding, problem-solving, co-ordination, decision-making, and advisory purposes.

Standing committees have a permanent role within the organisation and will meet weekly or monthly to deal with their routine business, for example forward planning or finance.

Ad hoc committees are set up for a specific purpose, for example company reorganisation. They have no routine work and once their task is accomplished they are disbanded.

Advantages of committees

1. Co-ordination. Large organisations often find that activities are insufficiently integrated through the formal vertical communication channels. The committee allows managers of approximately the same level to come together, exchanging information and systematically co-ordinating their activities.

2. Decision-making. The diversity of expertise a committee can bring to bear on the topic under discussion is far greater than that of the individual executive. It is therefore possible to obtain a more balanced view and avoid biased decisions.

3. Creativity. Working in a group can stimulate creativity. Ideas put forward by one committee member will be developed by another, or generate a different idea in yet another member.

4. Consultation. A committee is an invaluable method of obtaining specialist advice from subordinates. It also provides a channel through which the views of subordinates and other staff on a wider range of issues can be made known.

5. Commitment. Participation in the decision-making process tends to increase an individual's commitment to the decision reached and his desire to implement that decision effectively. Even where the committee member does not agree to the decision taken, he knows his viewpoint has been considered, and also the rationale behind the committee's decision.

Disadvantages of committees

1. Cost.   Committees cost an organisation dear both in time and money. Try calculating the cost of a three-hour meeting for five middle-management executives each earning £15,000 p.a. But conversely, you might also consider how long it would take to pass the same information and reach the same decision without the committee!

2. Quality of decisions.   As most committees wish to accommodate the views of all participants, the decision is often a compromise which satisfies no one.

3. Indecision.   Many managers argue if you want to delay a decision appoint a committee. Difficulties in arranging times suitable for all participants, and conflicting viewpoints both preclude the fast decision the organisation often needs.

4. Accountability.   Decisions taken are often more risky because committee members are able to avoid individual responsibility for the outcome. For the same reason they may not work as hard to correct the decision when wrong.

Much of the criticism of committees is a reflection of the way they work. All too often meetings are ineffective because responsibilities are poorly defined, bad chairmanship, or incorrect size or structure of the committee. Careful attention to these matters will ensure that committees function as an effective and integral part of the organisation structure.

Examination questions

1. Describe the types of organisations known as 'line', 'line and staff', and matrix. In what circumstances would you consider each appropriate?

2. Distinguish between formal and informal organisation. Why is it necessary for managers to understand the informal organisations?

3. Present an organisation chart showing the structure of a medium-sized manufacturing concern, and either:

    (a)   give a short job description of four managers you have mentioned in your organisation chart; or
    (b)   discuss the extent to which organisation charts are useful in portraying a picture of the firm; or
    (c)   explain the likely structure of one department in detail.

4. To what extent do scientific management and human relations theories provide contradictory guidelines for managers.

5. What do you understand by delegation? Explain its benefits and limitations.

PSC 1978

6. In what circumstances do you think it would be worthwhile delegating work to a committee? What disadvantages, if any, are there.

7. Outline functions of committees. Consider their advantages and disadvantages.

8. Explain the functions of specialist staff within an organisation. For what reasons may difficulties arise between line and specialist staff?

9. Outline the role of a manner within a business organisation.

10. What is the delegation? Describe the conditions necessary for its success.

11. How important is it for a manager to be a 'good organiser'?

12. With the aid of an organisation chart explain what comprises the levels of management in a public limited company with which you are familiar. How may a manager's work vary according to his level in the hierarchy.

Marketing
Chapter 11

The Institute of Marketing defines marketing as: 'The management process responsible for identifying, anticipating, and satisfying customer requirements profitably.'

Success in business is by no means guaranteed. Within a short period of time highly respected organisations may suffer a reversal of fortunes resulting in dramatic losses or even bankruptcy. Equally, companies which were unheard of a decade ago are now the market leaders.

One major reason for these organisations' changes in fortune arises because our affluent twentieth-century consumer is presented with many ways in which to spend his money. Improvements in international trade, transportation, and technology have greatly increased the quantity and type of goods available for purchase. For manufacturers this has meant that they can no longer rely upon the general scarcity of goods as providing a market for their product, but rather the goods they make must be tailored to the consumer's requirements.

Yet this was not always the situation. In earlier times goods were always limited in supply, nor was there any choice between similar products. It was a seller's market with businesses realising that customers would buy almost everything which they produced. We could say that business was production orientated. Gradually, though, the situation changed. Mass production dramatically increased the supply of many products while at the same time reducing their price. Improvements in transport and the relaxation of international trade controls resulted in larger markets being created and an increase in the level of competition between firms. Consumers used the wider choice available to them to select goods which matched their own particular requirements. The successful firm became one which set out to discover what the consumer wanted or could be persuaded to buy, who then made that product (or provided that service), and sold it at a profit. Such firms are said to be marketing orientated.

As we can see, marketing strategy is now more important than it was, say, in the nineteenth century. This strategy will comprise of four elements often called the '4 P's', or the 'marketing mix'. They are:

1. *Product.* The organisation has to identify the products which the consumer wants and consider the ways in which its products can be adapted to meet the consumer's needs more successfully. Consideration should also be given to what new products should be developed.

2. *Price.* A balance has to be obtained between the demands of the consumers for 'value for money' and the organisation's requirements of a satisfactory profit. Discounts for bulk and transport charges may also have to be considered.

3. *Promotion.* What methods are used to generate sales of the product? Possibilities include advertising, sales promotion, or personal selling.

4. *Place.* How do we ensure that the product is the right sales place at the right time so as to capture the maximum sales?

The term 'marketing mix' indicates that we can combine these elements in different ways. The aim of the marketing specialist is to combine them in such a way as to optimise sales revenue. However, the strategy or marketing mix adopted is not static but is adjusted to meet the changing circumstances both within the company and the market. For example, where the business experiences increased competition the natural reaction is to place more emphasis on advertising and promotion, or perhaps competitive pricing. Equally the introduction of new products by our competitors will intensify our company's research into new products, or the modification of existing products.

One critical factor affecting the marketing mix is the position of the products within its life cycle. Products are said to have a life cycle consisting of four stages, as illustrated in Fig. 11.1.

1. *Introduction.* The product is brought to the market, sales are low. The emphasis will be placed on a promotion strategy designed to inform the public of the product's availability. As sales are low we can be relatively selective as to the outlets from which the product is sold, yet at the same time strive for maximum exposure at these points of sale. The price may be relatively high at this juncture due to the newness of the product and the lack of competition.

2. *Growth.* A period in which there is extremely rapid growth of sales and the first signs of competition arise. Prices may be lowered to attract a wider market and the numbers of outlets are increased. The search begins for products which will eventually replace this one.

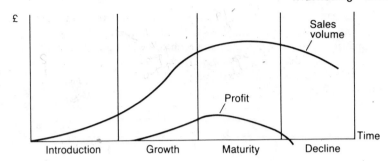

Fig. 11.1 Product life cycle

3. Maturity. Sales and profits reach a peak and eventually decline. The majority of sales are 'replacements' rather than first-time purchases. Prices are reduced further to maintain our share of the market in the face of fierce competition. Advertising seeks to persuade the consumer to buy 'this' rather than the competitor's products. We search for other markets (perhaps abroad) and other uses for this product. The product is examined to see if there are any developments or refinements which can be introduced, giving us a competitive edge and putting off the decline in sales. We introduce those other products which will, in the future, replace this one.

4. Decline. As new products take over the market, sales decline until it is no longer profitable to continue production. Advertising ceases and prices are reduced to the minimum compatible with profitability to stave off the eventual close-down of production.

In Figure 11.2 we see examples of products at different stages in the product life cycle.

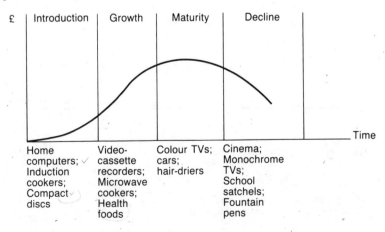

Fig. 11.2 Stages in the product life cycle of selected goods

The organisation of the marketing function will vary from business to business. In large organisations the scale of operations may warrant the creation of several departments each specialising in one aspect of the marketing operation. Each departmental manager would report to a senior manager who may very well be an executive director of the company. (Fig. 11.3).

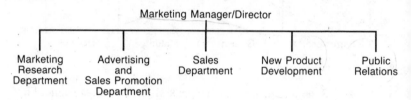

Fig. 11.3 Division of marketing activities in a large organisation

Smaller firms, however, may find it uneconomical to develop a similar range of marketing activities within the organisation. They may, for example, place advertising and other promotional activities or marketing research in the hands of an advertising agency, or a marketing research company. But even where smaller firms carry out similar marketing activities to those undertaken in the larger organisation the structure adopted is likely to differ – normally that of a single department headed by a marketing manager responsible to the marketing or some other executive director (see Fig. 11.4).

Although the organisation of the marketing function will vary considerably between businesses, the responsibilities are broadly similar and include the following:

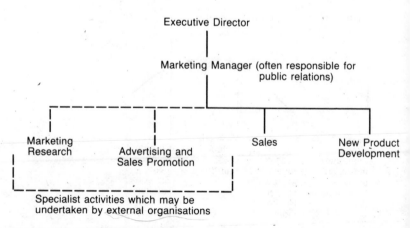

Fig. 11.4 Marketing organisation within the small/medium-sized business

1. To help and advise the board of directors in establishing marketing policy.

2. To provide senior management with marketing information.

3. To predict future demand and prices for products.

4. To research the market for new products.

5. To spearhead the development of new products, or modification of existing products.

6. To co-operate fully with other parts of the organisation so as to ensure co-ordination of effort.

7. To establish and maintain a good image in the eyes of the public.

8. To promote the organisation's products by advertising and other means.

9. To identify and establish the most suitable channels of distribution for the organisation's products.

10. To administer an efficient and cost-effective function.

We will now consider in detail how these responsibilities are discharged by looking at the work of the marketing function under the headings of marketing research, advertising and sales promotion, sales management, new product development, and public relations.

Marketing research

With the growth of large organisations and the introduction of specialist functions the simple relationship which existed between manufacturer and customer has disappeared (see Fig. 11.5(a)). In its place we have the extended chain illustrated in Fig. 11.5(b). The result of this change is that information on markets and products fails to get to those parts of the business which need to act upon it. Marketing research is designed to fill that gap (see Fib. 11.5(c)).

Marketing research aims to provide management with information on which to base its decisions regarding the organisation's future activities. Such information is vital to the success of the organisation, all decisions relating to the marketing mix – products, prices, promotion and distribution – being based upon marketing research. Failure to provide such information leads to an inefficient use of the organisation's scarce resources.

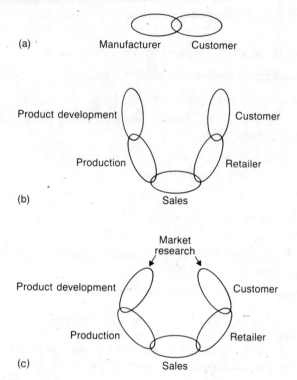

Fig. 11.5 The need for marketing research

Forms of marketing research

Market research

1. Economic, aimed at providing important background information on the country or region under consideration. Examples will include size of population, their income, restrictions on trade, the stability of the government, and business activity. Political and social factors may also be considered.

2. More detailed research on a particular market designed to ascertain what products are being purchased at the moment and the trend in their sales. We are also interested in the degree of competition in the market, the strength of the competitors, their market share as well as the structure of their prices. Should the information obtained so far be encouraging, sales forecasts for specific products may be prepared.

Consumer research

This aims to build up a profile of the person who buys a particular product. We are interested in discovering the critical attitudes and desires which persuade them to purchase that product. It is then possible to design a product which more obviously meets their requirements, or alternatively to create a promotion strategy which is more likely to persuade people to buy that product.

Product research
Product research is concerned to establish the acceptability of new or existing products. It seeks to establish the essential features of the products and the price the consumer is willing to pay for those features. It is then possible to redesign a more competitive product incorporating the essential features, but also reducing costs by eliminating non-essential features or using alternative (cheaper) materials.

Promotional research
This seeks to ensure that money spent promoting goods is used to the best effect. By comparing different forms of promotional activity in terms of cost and sales generated it can identify the most efficient promotional strategy.

Market research techniques

Desk research
This should be undertaken prior to any field investigation. The research team will analyse information obtained from the sources given below.

1. Internal sources. Those which will cover the organisation's records to identify popular and unpopular products, and trends in sales (including seasonal fluctuations). Such information is of limited value; it cannot tell you what the market size is, why our products are not doing well, or the consumer's needs. However, research of this kind does reveal and clarify the nature of the problems faced by the organisation. Other sources or techniques, though, may now be used to discover the causes and remedies for these problems.

2. Published data. Obtained from a variety of sources, it is the basis of most statistics, trade research, and professional associations, and even everyday newspapers can be used to answer questions on:
- market size and trends;
- how our competitors are doing;
- what products are customers buying;
- what are our competitor's costs and prices;
- the effect of advertising; and many others.

Such information should be collected systematically and analysed regularly. It may very well obviate the need for costly field studies.

Field studies
Field studies are used when desk research fails to provide the
information required by the organisation. Three techniques are widely
used.

1. Surveys. A number of carefully selected people, who it is believed
form a cross-section of the market, are questioned. The aim is to
establish from their answers the reactions of consumers generally to
new or modified products. Such surveys may be conducted personally
by telephone or by post.

A personal interview is time consuming and expensive; however, it is
possible to obtain more information by this method – supplementary
questions may be asked while the interview can also enable other
information on the respondent to be obtained merely by observation.

Telephone interviews tend to be shorter and less costly than both
personal and postal surveys. However, telephone costs prevent a
lengthy interview, follow-up questions are restricted, and the call may
be terminated before the end of the interview.

Postal questionnaires are cheap, easy to administer, and speedy.
However, the response rate is normally low, the questions asked have
to be simple, and it is impossible to supplement answers by additional
questions or observation.

2. Observational methods. Data are collected by watching an
individual's reactions in a given situation. The respondent is normally
unaware of the attention being paid to him. By this method consumer
reactions to a certain product or group of products may be tested (this
could of course be followed up by a personal interview) as may his
reactions to certain sales techniques. Alternatively, an interviewer may
pretend to be a customer in order to assess the ability of sales staff or
discover which products they promote.

Observational methods will tell us more accurately than the
respondent himself can, what his actions were at any given moment.
However, it gives us little insight into why he acted in a particular way.
Moreover, as we cannot control the environment within which the
observations are made it is difficult to be sure that the stimuli we are
investigating was, in fact, the cause of the reaction we noted. For this
reason it may be necessary to use experimental records.

3. Experimental methods. The most common application is in test
marketing. Here a control market is established in which a product is
marketed as before. Test markets are then established in which one of
the variables (e.g. price, product, promotional activity, distribution) is
varied. It is then possible by comparing sales in the test and control
markets to see what effect the change in variables has had.

The great advantage of experimental methods is that is the only method of investigation which uses the market situation. Yet the results obtained in the test market are of little value if the test market is unrepresentative of the whole market – herein lies the real problem. Moreover, these tests by their very nature are both lengthy and costly. The tests may also be undermined by the actions of competitors in changing prices or promotional activities in test or control areas!

Conducting a market research investigation

Defining the project
Normally the object of the investigation will be to find the answer to some problem, perhaps why a particular product is not selling well. Alternatively the object may be to discover if there is a problem. For example, how effective is our advertising, or is our product range adequate?

Background research
We have already noted that a large amount of statistical information is available from published sources. Quite apart from the regular study of such information an appraisal of it should be made prior to any field studies. The aim is to become familiar with the literature relating to the research investigation and ensure that the answer to the problem cannot be obtained from these sources. Desk research may also clarify the nature of the problem leading to the formulation of certain hypothesis which can be tested by field studies.

Planning and implementation of field studies
Having identified the group of people who have the information needed, consideration must be given the methods of obtaining this information – personal or telephone interviews, maybe postal questionnaires. Normally the cheapest method commensurate with obtaining the necessary information would be selected; however, speed could also be an important consideration.

Once the methods for gathering information have been decided a questionnaire has to be devised and tested. Testing of the questionnaire is undertaken to reveal such problems as ambiguity, words and phrases which would be unfamiliar to the respondent, impertinent and leading questions. Failure to devote sufficient consideration to testing can invalidate the whole study and even result in future plans being based upon false information.

When the questionnaire has been tested, and if necessary amended, the actual work of collecting the information may begin.

Analysis of results, conclusions and recommendations
Once the data has been collected it has to be collated. Nowadays much of this work would be done by computer, saving time and money. The

results can now be analysed and a report drawn up embodying the findings, conclusions, and recommendations.

The advertising and sales promotion department

The advertising department is responsible for all activities involved in promoting the products or services of an organisation. Thus the department is not only concerned with the production and dissemination of advertisements but also with the design and distribution of brochures and catalogues, special offers (reductions in price of 25 per cent or more, free gifts), sponsorship, special displays, and competitions. There are many ways of promoting sales, but those listed above are those most commonly employed.

It was the rise in large-scale production which prompted business to invest heavily in advertising and other promotional activities. Large-scale production (bringing with it the advent of cheaper products, and the possibility of goods which the average man could never have previously afforded) was dependent upon a large-scale market. Business had to make known to the consumer what was being produced and persuade him to buy. A whole industry, advertising, grew up around the possibilities of increasing demand and even creating demand for goods and services. In short, the advertising industry seeks to change people's attitudes towards a service or product in a way which would be advantageous to the seller.

Today advertising falls into three broad classes – informative advertisements, persuasive advertising and institutional advertising. With each class the general aim is to increase sales, but more specific objectives would arise because of the nature of the product and its position in the product life cycle.

Informative advertisements
Where a new product is brought to the market sales are naturally low at first because few customers know of its existence and perhaps even less its application. Here advertising seeks to inform the public of the product and its uses. Equally, where a product is modified and improved or new uses are found for an existing product, advertising informs the public of these facts.

Other products and services are complex in nature with a large amount of information needing to be digested before purchase is considered. Many industrial products fall into this category, though the purchase of a car or life assurance are also good examples. In these circumstances advertising is designed to highlight the most important or attractive features of the product. Although radio, television, and newspapers are often used for advertising these products, the use of brochures and leaflets is also very common.

Persuasive advertising

This form of advertising will normally be used during the maturity stage of a product's life cycle – a situation where there is normally a high degree of competition with several businesses producing and selling similar products. Experience has shown that the consumers in these situations do not always purchase the same brand of product. Rather they will select the first make of product they see provided the price is right. Persuasive advertising seeks to point the consumer in the direction of a specific product and by that means ensure that sales are maintained at a satisfactory level.

Persuasive advertising is commonly associated with consumer goods. It has been particularly heavily used where the degree of product differentiation is minimal. For example, one make of toothpaste is very like another. Similar comments can be made for soap powders, cans of beans, and many other products which we buy regularly. Persuasive advertising has been criticised for playing too heavily on emotional appeal and exploiting anxieties.

Most advertisements though, are a blend of informative and persuasive communication. Thus an advertisement referring to cut-price petrol (a) informs the market on the details of the offer in such a way that it (b) persuades them this offer is too good to miss.

Institutional advertising

Such advertising is designed to improve the image of the advertiser, rather than to sell a specific product. It is very much a public relations exercise. Many large companies try to show by such advertisements how socially responsible they are – what contribution they have made to society. The aim is to engender a positive attitude to the business in the minds of the shareholders, consumers, and employees as well as the general public.

Ensuring that advertising is effective

A marketing executive is reported to have once commented, 'Half my advertising budget is wasted – but I don't know which half.' No doubt the comments are apocryphal, yet a problem does exist. It is undoubtedly true that not all advertising is successful in generating extra sales, yet it is also true that it is difficult to prove conclusively that a particular advertisement has, or has not, achieved the desired results. The fact that sales rose during an advertising campaign may suggest that advertising has achieved the desired result, but it is not conclusive. Other marketing factors or even external conditions could have affected the outcome.

Although techniques have been devised to measure an advertisement's impact none have the degree of authority we would like. The following points must be considered for advertising to be successful.

1. Business environment. We have already seen that in a recession the level of demand for most goods and services declines. For luxuries though, the drop in demand is much greater and advertising is unlikely to be successful. A similar situation will occur when the Government imposes additional taxes or public attitudes harden against the product advertised.

2. Suitable media. There are many possible media which may be used for advertising, but it is important to select those that are likely to obtain the best results. Thus it is unlikely that an engineering product would be advertised on television. The target audience is more likely to be reached by using specialist magazines.

3. Adequate background preparation. Advertising is most likely to succeed when market research has previously been undertaken to discover the likes and dislikes of the consumer. Consideration must also be given to the style of the advertisement – informative or persuasive – and the method of presentation. Poor presentation may even create resistance to the product advertised.

4. Extent of demand. If there is little demand for a product – perhaps it is in the decline stage of its life cycle and has been superseded by other improved models – advertising is likely to have little effect.

5. Market conditions. Advertising will be the most effective form of promotion when the market is widespread with many customers in different locations.

6. The nature of the product. Where a product is tailor-made to a customer's requirements and has a high unit value or is technical in nature, it is best promoted by personal sales efforts. Conversely, where a product is mass produced (standardised) having a low value and has few or no technical features advertising will be cost effective.

Sales management

The primary function of the sales organisation is to produce that volume of sales which will yield the planned profit. It will also be required to undertake other activities as specified by the marketing manager or the board of directors. These could include sales maximisation of certain product lines, export penetration, or the provision of information for marketing research. Although the organisation structure adopted for sales may vary considerably there are normally three facets to its work, namely selling, distribution, and administration.

1. *Selling* – sometimes referred to as the field sales organisation, selling is concerned with the work of the sales force. This will involve aspects of appointment and training together with motivation and control of sales staff.

2. *Distribution* – potentially there are many ways in which a product or service can be sold to the public. The problem which business faces is to determine which of these channels is most appropriate. The final decision will take into account factors such as:

   (a) the nature of the goods, e.g. weight, size, fragility;

   (b) the nature of the market, e.g. size, distance, competition, profitability.

3. *Administration* – the sales office is responsible for maintaining records and ensuring efficient operation of the administrative system.

Where firms are selling only a small range of products through similar distribution channels a functional structure is often adopted. Figure 11.6(a) shows how specialists responsible to the sales manager are appointed to each of the positions mentioned above. While this structure is popular with small or medium-sized firms, larger firms tend to base their organisation on areas or products.

Area organisations (see Fig. 11.6(b)) are used by many large companies manufacturing relatively few products but which have to be distributed over a wide area. Oil companies, banks, and breweries all

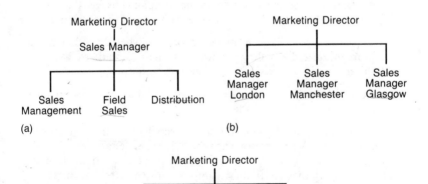

Fig. 11.6 (a) Functional organisation; (b) area organisation; (c) product organisation

adopt this structure, finding it easier to cater for changes in consumer preferences between areas and also to establish and maintain local links.

Industrial companies tend to favour a product-based structure (see Fig. 11.6(c) acknowledging the high degree of differentiation between many of their products and also their technical complexity. The sales organisation will then be responsible for marketing a range of relatively homogeneous products.

Selling

Why do we need sales people? Basically because advertising and other promotional efforts may be unsuccessful in reaching our target group and obtaining a sale. Personal selling, although being far more costly per person reached than advertising, may, because of sales made, be far more cost effective. Personal selling carries with it the opportunity for discussion and clarification on points of misunderstanding, and therefore has far greater persuasive force than other promotional techniques. Moreover, the sales presentation can be tailored to the needs of the individual customer. Yet the employment of the sales force has other benefits for the business too, as enumerated below:

1. It is an invaluable source of marketing research information.

2. Sales staff are able to find new outlets for their company's products, selecting only those which reflect the image the company wants to create.

3. By maintaining a direct link with the customer rather than marketing through a middleman the company ensures that its products are always brought to the attention of the customer.

4. The sales force will promote new products, whereas middlemen are more interested in selling products which are already well known – this after all is the easiest way to earn their money.

5. In establishing a personal relationship with customer repeat sales are more likely to be made.

Supervising the activities of the sales forces is the function of the sales manager. In conjunction with the personnel department the sales manager will be responsible for the appointment and training of new sales staff. Training is particularly important to ensure that the sales representative is well groomed, and has a good understanding of both the products he sells and company's procedures.

The sales manager motivates and controls his staff by means of targets and remuneration. Targets for sales, both monthly and annually, are established. The target should be agreed with the salesman, rather than imposed from above. Skill is needed in setting the target. If it is set too high the salesman quickly loses heart, too low and the company is not using his services efficiently. The target is used as a means of evaluating the salesman's efforts from month to month, but may also be used as a means of generating competition between sales staff (who can exceed their target by the greatest percentage?) and calculating pay bonuses.

The system of remuneration which is operated is normally a basic salary together with incentive/commission payments for achieving high results. The system must be fair and take into account all factors affecting the volume of sales he is likely to achieve. For example, should a salesman in one period be required to spend a large proportion of his time promoting a new or unknown product the value of sales he produces during that period is likely to be far less than normal, and his target should reflect this.

Sales administration
The primary function of the sales office is the maintenance of an adequate set of records, they will include:

1. *Salesmen's records* – showing areas worked in, sales achieved, salary, bonus, and expenses paid.

2. *Customers records* – showing names of contacts within the firm, orders taken in the last few years, discounts given, any special requirements, and credit rating. Records on past and prospective customers will also be kept.

3. *Salesmen's reports* – salesmen spend most of their time away from the office working by themselves. Reports are essential, therefore, to discover how their time has been spent. The report form must be designed so that the maximum information can be obtained in the minimum time, but should indicate the number of calls made, the name of the person met, details of the discussion, orders obtained or the state of negotiations, and any information on competitors.

4. *Statistics* – records on products sold over time and by area should also be maintained.

The sales office will also handle enquiries, orders, and complaints. All must be dealt with speedily. Enquiries and complaints will require individual attention by either the sales manager or the salesman who is normally responsible for maintaining contact with that business (or in whose area the firm is situated). Standard letters for quotations and orders enable information to be supplied promptly – perhaps aided by a word processor, while also facilitating the keeping of records.

Distribution

Traditionally, distribution has been outside the control of the marketing function; however, distribution is an important element in the marketing mix and the marketing department is keenly interested in this area. This paradox may be explained by considering distribution at two different levels.

The marketing department's interest in distribution lies in what channels should be used to obtain an advantage over their competitors, for example whether to sell direct to the consumer or to middlemen. The marketing department has not the same degree of interest in the physical distribution of the goods, for example scheduling and routeing of deliveries, control of stock, and transportation.

Moreover, the blend of skills needed to run such a system efficiently is not normally found within the marketing department. They are more likely to be found within the production department. Again, as distribution follows on naturally from production it is logical to place it within the ambit of the production department.

Channels of distribution

Direct selling.   There are many examples of direct selling to the consumer. Avon and Tupperware are always mentioned, but double glazing and insurance are also examples of selling to the consumer in his or her own home. Another variation is where a producer owns and runs his own retail outlet, such as Singer Sewing Machines or the Burton Group, but the list could also include shoe manufacturers and bakeries. Many industrial products are also sold in this way.

The major benefit arising from direct selling is that by using your own staff and retail outlets you can be sure your product will be properly promoted. Competing products are not at hand to divert the customer's attention and sales staff are fully conversant with the products they are selling. The above points also apply when the place of contact is in the customer's home, with the added advantage that the salesman has a semi-captive audience!

The major disadvantage of direct selling is that selling costs are likely to be high – rent and rates where retail outlets are established, and a higher sales force cost where home canvassing is employed. However, these extra costs are to some extent offset by a higher profit margin.

Producer to retailer.   Very much a compromise between direct selling and selling to middlemen, this method is adopted by large firms selling a number of products to the same kinds of retail outlets. Frozen-food firms and bakeries both have their own distribution network. A large, costly sales force is needed to ensure that orders are obtained from retail outlets; however, this has the advantage that the firm has some control over the way their products are displayed. Indeed some firms will even assist in the presentation of their products within the retailer outlet to ensure that their point of sale display is the equal of, if not

better than, their competitors. One particular problem experienced
both with retail and wholesale distribution is that new products
(because they generate less sales per unit of sale space) are not
promoted sufficiently.

Producer to wholesaler.   This is often chosen by firms who have a
small or incomplete product range and are unable to afford the high
costs associated with an extensive distribution network and large sales
force. The major advantage is avoiding the high selling/distribution
costs associated with the methods described above, though we hasten
to add that some kind of distribution network must be maintained and
some sales staff will be employed. Yet there are major problems
associated with this method of distribution. First, the producer has no
control over the retail outlets – as to how the products are displayed, or
even whether they are stocked at all. Secondly, new products do not
receive the promotion they deserve, and finally the profit margin tends
to be lower than in either of the other two methods of distribution.

Franchising.   A franchise is a concession given by the owner of patents
relating to goods or services to another person allowing him to
produce and sell those products/services. Generally the franchiser –
that is, the person giving the concession – provides a well-known trade
name together with technical and administrative training. The
franchisee – the person to whom the concession is given – undertakes
in return to sell only the franchiser's products and conform to certain
specified standards.

   Franchising is attractive to the franchiser because it offers many of
the advantages of owning your own retail outlets without the capital
cost normally associated with this. To the franchisee it gives the
independence of operating his own business, marketing a successful
product with the aid of the franchiser.

   So far we have concerned ourselves with the marketing of existing
products. Yet our discussion earlier on the product life cycle will have
told us that no business can rely upon existing products to provide an
indefinite future for the firm. For many businesses the search for new
and improved products is a continuous process. Product development
encompasses two ideas: first that an existing product may be modified,
and secondly the development of a new product – let us look at these in
turn.

Product modification

The aim of product modification is to prolong the life of a product by
changes in its quality and features. Consider how motor manufacturers
change specifications and styling at regular intervals after the
introduction of the original model. The effect can be seen by
considering Fig. 11.7.

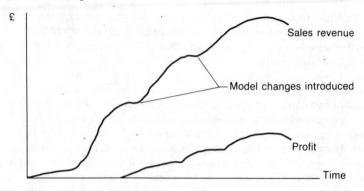

Fig. 11.7 Effect of product modification on sales and profit

Once the original model has been introduced the search begins for modification which would improve the car's standing with consumers. Marketing research is closely involved in this process. Sales of the model are closely monitored and modification will be introduced to coincide with the peaking of demand for the original model. Renewed interest will then cause a further expansion in sales. Production modification may eventually result in the marketing of a model which is totally different to that which was first introduced.

Product development

Product modification does no more than put off the day when a product has to be phased out. Product development is therefore essential to the survival of the business. But although most firms recognise the importance of product development, actually producing a new product which is commercially successful is by no means easy. Even large well-known companies achieve a success rate of less than 50 per cent on the introduction of new products. The following sections outline the procedure which is likely to be adopted for new product development, but must not obscure the fact that most of these products are abandoned even before the launch stage.

Generation of ideas
Ideas for new product development tend to fall into three categories. Products may be entirely new, that is, something for which there is no substitute, for example video-cassette recorders. Other products may replace existing products and yet be significantly different from those earlier products, for example tinned peas replaced dried peas and frozen peas replaced tinned peas. The third category of new product is purely imitative – it apes a product already on the market in the hope of capturing part of that market.

Maintaining the flow of new ideas is both a major problem and a necessity to the business. All departments, but especially marketing and production, have a contribution to make. In some businesses a technique referred to as 'brainstorming' is used. A number of people – preferably from diverse backgrounds but with a general knowledge of the problem – are asked to provide ideas, in this situation for new products. Evaluation of these ideas is suspended, participants are encouraged in a competitive atmosphere to mention all ideas, however wild. It is only after the brainstorming session, and by a different group of people, that these suggestions are evaluated. Many will be rejected immediately, the majority after greater consideration, but perhaps one or two may contain the germ of an idea worthy of development.

Assessment of new product ideas
As development costs escalate sharply once we have passed the assessment stage it is vital that we consider the following:

1. Is there sufficient market demand?

2. Is the product compatible with other products which we produce? In particular do we have the necessary technical expertise, can we use our present sales force and our channels of distribution, and is the product compatible with our business image?

3. Is this product going to be profitable and do we have sufficient finance for its development?

4. Do we have the physical capacity and time to deal with this product?

It is obvious from the questions which have to be answered that new product development draws upon the expertise of the whole firm.

Design and development
By the end of this stage a prototype will have been produced. Technical problems involved in its production will have been identified and ironed out. We are able to cost the finished product more accurately. Yet again we evaluate the product in terms of the criteria established in the assessment paragraph above.

Market and product testing
Now that a prototype has been made we are able to test it. Product tests are designed to ensure that the prototype conforms to certain standards in terms of performance and durability.

Market tests are designed to discover whether the product is acceptable to the consumer. This may involve asking groups of potential consumers to use and evaluate the product. Alternatively, we may market the product in certain areas and conduct tests to discover how closely it conforms to consumer requirements.

As a result of the information obtained here it may be necessary to revert to the design and development stage to change some of the product's technical or style features. But senior management now has as much information on the product as it is ever likely to have and must shortly make the decision whether to market the product commercially.

Market entry

Prior to entry, decisions relating to prices and promotion are made. We have to buy plant and machinery and go into production. The sales force has to be fully conversant with the product. We have to ensure that there are adequate stocks of the product in retail outlets. After the launch the process of evaluation begins again. In what ways can we modify the product so that it more closely meets customer requirements? Is it possible to improve our marketing mix? We will also be considering what other ideas are worthy of our attention. Product development is very much a continuous process.

Studies have revealed there is no one best method for organising product development. Often a separate department is created reporting directly to senior management. The department would be responsible for all aspects of development and would only hand over responsibility for the product to the marketing department after a successful launch.

Alternatively, a committee structure, normally with members from finance, marketing, production, and research may be used. This has the benefit of drawing directly on the expertise held in other departments and involving the whole business in the process of product development.

Public relations

Public relations work is often confused with advertising. This is not surprising as the end result of a public relations exercise may very well be an advertisement extolling the virtues of the organisation. Yet just as advertising is only one form of sales promotion it is also just one facet of public relations.

Public relations can be defined as presenting an acceptable image of the business to members of the public. Through public relations the business seeks to:

1. Persuade customers or 'would-be customers' that it is an organisation with whom they are happy to be associated – thereby indirectly promoting its products.

2. Provide the investing public with information which presents the activities of the business in the best possible light – thereby encouraging investment in the business now through the Stock Exchange, or later when it is necessary to raise capital.

3. Inform employees of the firm's activities, emphasising the contribution of all employees to the success of the business – thereby strengthening employee interest in the business and raising morale.

In a large organisation public relations may form a department in its own right while in smaller organisations either the marketing manager is responsible for maintaining a positive business image, or a public relations officer with a background in journalism may be appointed. The methods used to maintain and develop public relations cover the following range:

1. Press releases and conferences.

2. Participation in exhibitions or trade fairs.

3. The sponsorship of sports and other events.

4. Literature – house magazines, annual reports and accounts, recruitment literature.

5. Information to employees of the firm's activities, emphasising the contribution of all employees to the success of the business – thereby strengthening employee interest in the business and raising morale.

Examination questions

1. For what reason may a business undertake advertising and how may it ensure that its investment is effective?

2. What benefits are obtained by a business from employing a field sales force? With the aid of examples explain how such a force may be organised.

3. Why is a new product development essential for a successful business?

4. To what extent is advertising the key to successful marketing?

5. Explain the role of marketing within a large public limited company.

6. What is function of marketing within a large manufacturing company? Outline the contacts which would take place between the marketing department and other departments.   *(PSC Jan. 1979)*

7. In what ways does an investment in market research and advertising benefit:

    (a) the business making that investment;

    (b) the consumer.

8. What steps may a marketing department take to ensure successful new product development?

9. How would you define marketing? Select and explain some of the major functions of the marketing organisation. *(PSC Jan. 1973)*

10. Explain the phrase 'marketing mix'. With the aid of examples show how the marketing mix may change during the product life cycle.

11. In what ways may marketing research aid the efficiency of a business.

12. What is meant by 'product life cycle'. Illustrate your answer by reference to products and companies.

13. What kinds of questions on products or Services might be answered by the use of marketing research?

14. Briefly describe:

    (a) the means by which marketing research information is obtained; and

    (b) how it is used.

15. What is marketing? How would a manufacturing company *market* a new product? *(PSC Dec. 1980)*

16. How may a large manufacturing company achieve successful marketing. *(PSC Dec. 1981)*

17. Outline the major differences in work carried out between marketing and selling departments within a manufacturing enterprise. *(PSC Dec. 1981)*

18. What do you understand by the term 'marketing mix'?

19. In what ways would you expect the organisation of the marketing mix of a consumer product and an industrial product to differ.

Production

Chapter 12

Production is the process by which we produce a finished product from raw material. The role of the production function is to ensure that this transformation process is carried out efficiently. The decisions which have to be taken are similar whether we consider an organisation employing 50 or 5,000 people. What differs is the number of roles that individuals have to undertake. In a small firm one person may undertake several jobs, whereas the larger firm is able to employ specialists in each of these activities.

In broad terms the activities which have to be undertaken within the production function fall into one of three categories. First, those relating to the manufacturing process itself – decisions concerned with where to produce, what to produce, and the methods and techniques which should be used. Secondly, there are the ancillary or service activities – those which are designed to ensure that the manufacturing process proceeds smoothly without interruption. Finally, we have the control or advisory activities which seek to ensure that the process is carried out as efficiently as possible (see Fig. 12.1).

In the following pages we will use this classification to discuss the workings of the production function in more detail, but first a word of

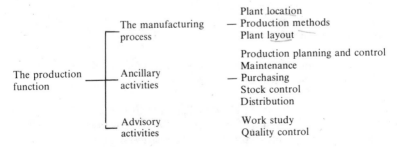

Fig. 12.1 Activities undertaken by a typical production department

warning. The production department does not act in isolation and decisions taken will be based upon information received not only from sources within the function but also other departments in the organisation. Thus decisions regarding what to produce will be taken in conjunction with the marketing department, the personnel department is required to engage employees with the correct skills, while the finance function is required to provide information on costs which may be used for control purposes.

The manufacturing process

Plant location

Decisions relating to the site of a factory are not undertaken every day. Normally such decisions will only have to be taken when an organisation wishes to expand its manufacturing capability and is unable to do so on its present site. However, where such a decision has to be taken the production manager is intimately involved in the discussions which take place.

There are five major factors which affect the choice of site, as listed below.

1. Land Is the land suitable for development?
Is it capable of being developed further in the future?
Does the cost of land and building compare favourably with other sites?
Are there any financial benefits (e.g. government aid) or undue legislative restrictions placed upon development?

2. Labour Is there an adequate supply of labour?
Will the labour require training?
Does the cost of labour compare favourably with other sites?

3. Material Are the materials necessary for manufacture available in this area?
What is the cost of those materials?
If materials are not readily available in the area what is the cost of transportation to the area?

4. Market Is the market for the finished product near?
What is the cost of product transportation to the market?

5. Services Does the area provide adequate water, fuel and power resources, disposal facilities for waste products, transport and communication facilities, educational, recreational, and social facilities?

If any of these services are deficient what is the cost of providing that service?

It is unlikely that any one site will prove advantageous on all points mentioned above, and any selection is therefore bound to be a compromise. Considerable advantages do exist though in siting the business in an area where work of the same kind is already carried out. An adequate supply of labour with the right skills will already exist, as will ancillary services including specialist suppliers and subcontractors to that industry.

However, in most situations the option of relocating the factory is not open to the organisation. The production manager must therefore work to increase efficiency and economy through plant layout and production methods.

Production methods

Job production
This is often a contract for the manufacture of one item to a customer's requirements. Both the shipbuilding and civil engineering industries are examples of this technique. However, the overhaul and repair of a motor car or the servicing of a central heating boiler under contract (which are also examples of this method of production) illustrate its breadth of application and therefore its importance within an advanced economy.

Characteristically, job production requires a large technical sales staff (consider the estimating department in a building or civil engineering firm), a range of general-purpose machines and other equipment, skilled workmen capable of utilising machinery in its many different applications, together with production planning and control systems.

Batch production
Batch production is commonly found in the engineering industry. Many of the components used in motor-car assembly are produced by this method. It is also used for the production of books, clothes, and furniture where small to medium-sized quantities of the product are produced to order or for stock. Many different products will be produced in the factory at the same time.

Batch production, like job production, relies on general-purpose plant and equipment that can be used in a variety of ways. There will be frequent changes in machine set-up as production is switched from one item to another, machines being grouped together according to the processes they fulfil. Demand for each group of machines will vary according to the products being produced as the production process will utilise some but not all of the machinery available. The success of batch production systems is dependent upon highly sophisticated costing, production planning, and production control systems.

Flow production
This occurs where demand for a complex product is sufficiently large to arrange the production process so that all operations involved in product manufacture are carried out continuously. It is possible to arrange production so that it 'flows' along a line through a number of work stations where operations are carried out until it emerges at the other end of the line as a finished product. Flow production occurs in the motor-car assembly industry, papermaking, brewing, and chemical industries. Flow production requires a highly standardised product with few variations from the basic product. The production process is broken down into a large number of very simple operations through which each unit of production passes. Machine utilisation is extremely high and purpose-built machinery is required. A production run of at least a year is required to recover the heavy investment in specialised equipment.

Large-scale production is said to depend on two factors – specialisation and simplification. Let us look at these in turn.

Specialisation, or the division of labour, was first drawn to our attention by Adam Smith an economist who in 1776 published a book titled **An Inquiry into the Nature and Causes of the Wealth of Nations.** *He proceeded to describe the process by which a pin was traditionally made with one worker undertaking all operations. He concluded that by this method it was impossible for that worker to produce more than twenty pins a day. Where, however, making the pins was divided into eighteen different operations and workers specialised in one or two distinct operations output per worker was increased to 4,800 pins per day! That process of specialisation has been taken to its logical conclusion in flow production today where one worker with specialist machinery is responsible for a very small part of the whole production process. The advantage of specialisation is not only the increased output, but also the reduced investment in tools, machines, and materials for each worker. Specialisation, however, requires a stable market and technology, sudden or rapid movements in demand or technology may cause business severe organisational problems and financial loss.*

Product simplification is the process of eliminating marginal lines in the organisation's output. A motor-car manufacturer, for example, may examine sales and find that one particular model is not selling rapidly. The decision to cease manufacture is an example of product simplification. The business will in future concentrate on its most successful product, obtaining longer production runs, reducing its investment in men, materials, and machines, and simplifying

*organisational administration. The consequent savings may be passed on
to the consumer in the form of lower prices. Simplification often brings
the production function into conflict with the marketing group who would
like to see the organisation provide exactly what the customer requires.
This, as previously indicated, is not consistent with flow production or low
prices. Some degree of compromise is often achieved, however, by slight
variations of the basic design.*

*The term 'simplification' is often confused with standardisation. The
confusion arises because the process of simplification is often extended to
the components and materials used in manufacture. The car manufacturer
may simplify stockholding by using the same door handles, plugs,
carburettors, etc. on many of his models. His use of components has been
standardised.*

*However, standardisation is really the process of obtaining agreement
on a standard to be applied to a product and the implementation of that
standard. The standard agreed may relate to performance or method of
manufacture as well as dimensions or composition. Hence, although
standardisation may result in simplification this is not always the case.*

The success of flow production lies in being able to maintain a high
and continuous level of production. Great emphasis is placed on
ensuring that materials and components are always available, plant
maintenance to ensure that breakdowns on the machines on the line
itself are kept to a minimum, and the prevention of labour disputes
through good industrial relations.

Flow production techniques have undoubtedly led to major
improvements in productivity in many industries. However, it has been
suggested that these obvious benefits may be outweighed by the high
labour turnover and absenteeism resulting from breaking down the
manufacturing process into small repetitive tasks. Behavioural
scientists argue that workers seek more than money and security from
their work. They are motivated as much by a sense of achievement – a
difficult job well done – and recognition of their importance to the
organisation. Moreover, the trend of work rationalisation runs counter
to the higher educational levels of today's school-leaver.

Numerous attempts have been made to provide more interesting,
varied and challenging work; for example job enlargement allows
employees to carry out a wider range of activity, so reducing boredom
and perhaps allowing the employee to complete one small part of the
production process. An alternative to loading the employee with more
tasks of the same degree of difficulty is job enrichment. Here the scope
of the job is widened by giving the employee greater responsibility for
decisions relating to his work. Thus he may be responsible for deciding
how to carry out his work, or for ensuring that the quality of his work

is up to standard. Job enrichment unlike job enlargement requires the employee to use skills he has not used before.

There are many recorded instances of jobs being redesigned so that they are enlarged or enriched. Almost without exception they report a reduction in turnover, absenteeism, and other behavioural problems. However, job enlargement and enrichment are not the panacea to all industrial ills. Often the tasks undertaken by workers in the production process are highly specialised and difficult to enlarge or enrich while still maintaining the high level of productivity. Moreover, even where it is possible to maintain high productivity while redesigning jobs difficulties may occur – trade-union opposition to the breaking down of the barriers between skills, or claims by the employees for pay rises to reflect their greater responsibilities!

Plant layout

While the precise nature of the plant layout in an organisation is dependent upon the product being produced and the production capacity required, in general terms it will conform to one of two basic types.

Product layout
This is associated with the production of standardised goods in large quantities. The most obvious example is car production. It is sometimes also referred to as line layout. Its essential feature is that each unit of production will undergo a similar sequence of operations which starts with the drawing of raw material components from stores and ends with the finished product. The success of product layout depends upon maintaining a high output and thus reducing manufacturing costs per unit. Considerable emphasis is placed upon 'line balancing' so that the machines at each stage of operation are just sufficient to deal with the workload. Such balancing prevents bottlenecks occurring at certain stages of production and under-utilisation of machinery at other points.

Considerable use of work study is made to speed up and automate the movement and operation of the production line. This has the advantage of reducing the amount of material in the production process at any one time and the unit labour cost. Product layout also has the advantage of being easier to control than process layout because of simpler routeing of materials and fewer variations of product. Against the undoubted advantages of the product layout must be the the problem of inflexibility. A breakdown in any part of the production line inevitably affects the rest of the line. Line balance will also be affected should the marketing department require changes in product design or specification.

Process layout

Normally associated with firms producing small quantities of product to a customer's order or for stock, for example furniture. Firms will produce a variety of products all requiring slightly different manufacturing operations. Process layout requires machines doing a similar job to be grouped together.

The major advantage ascribed to process layout is its high degree of flexibility. The layout can accommodate the production of several different products at the same time, each following a different production route. Moreover, the disruption caused by a machine breakdown affects only one person and may also be minimised by the holding of buffer stocks.

Service of ancillary functions

Production planning and control

Planning and control lie at the heart of the production process. Because the two activities are so closely related they are normally undertaken by a single section within the production department. The responsibility of this section is to:

1. Bring materials, machines, and labour together in the most efficient way thereby ensuring the elimination of bottlenecks and space capacity.

2. To develop a system of controls for the monitoring of performance.

3. To take whatever corrective action is necessary so that production continues according to plan.

It is difficult to overemphasise the importance of this function to the organisation as a whole. The inability to deliver customer's orders on time resulting from poor production planning and control will quickly rob the firm of its reputation and customer goodwill. Moreover, high production costs arising from frequent production changes, operational delays, and overtime will greatly reduce profitability.

Production planning

Information received from the sales or marketing department on the likely future demand for the organisation's products provides the data from which a production plan is designed. Production planners will not only need information on what to produce but also the quantities required and the date required for completion.

The production plan is drawn up by determining the process which has to be followed in manufacturing the finished article and thereby establishing the workload for each group of machines. Production is then 'routed' so that each product or group of products moves logically from stage to stage through the production process. Production is also 'scheduled' so that sufficient time is allowed to complete each operation before it is required at the next stage, and the final operation is completed before the goods are required by the customer. The production plan is then broken down into very precise instructions to each work process or group of machines explaining what work has to be done, when it has to be done, and which work stations it should be transferred to when finished.

Charts are often an important tool in the planning and control of work. The most widely used is the Gantt chart, an illustration of which is shown in Fig. 12.2. The chart shows a product going through three stages of production planned over a period of ten days. The planned time for each process is indicated by the horizontal broken line against each process. Thus process 2 is planned to take three days and finish on day 6. Once production starts we indicate the present day in the process by a pointer at the top of the chart. The pointer indicates we have just finished day 6 of the production process. Our actual progress is shown by the dark horizontal bar against each process. Figure 12.2 shows that process 1 was completed as planned, but that process 2 which should have finished on day 6 will not be finished to schedule.

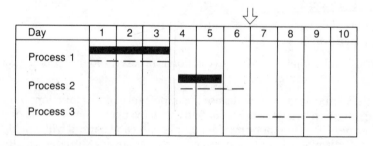

Fig. 12.2 Gantt chart

The advantage of such charts is that they show both the plan and present progress in a form which is easily and quickly understood. Production controllers can rapidly identify these jobs which will require their attention each day.

Production planning requires liaison with many other parts of the organisation. It is necessary to ensure that raw materials will be available when required for use in the production process. The raw material requirements, which are based upon the sales estimates, will be passed to the purchasing/materials management section within the organisation. Production engineers – concerned with the design and operation (rather than the management) of the production system – need to be informed of products to be produced so that the necessary tools and patterns are produced. It may also be necessary to purchase additional plant and equipment for the production process. Yet again we may need to consult with personnel so that the correct mix of labour skills is available, or so that piecework rates (if applicable) where not previously established are calculated and agreed upon by management and unions. Lastly the costing department may be involved in establishing standard costs or prices for any work undertaken.

Considerable skill and compromise is required by production-planners, as it is unlikely that sufficient resources, labour, materials, and machinery will be available to meet all demands made upon them. In these circumstances it may be necessary to agree some form of priority for the work which is to be undertaken.

Production control

Once the production plan has been drawn up it is put into effect by issuing detailed instructions to all those involved in the production process. In flow production industries the instructions might be quite simple as all items of manufacture will go through the same process. However, where job or batch production is undertaken no two orders are the same, and instructions may be exceedingly complex. The action of issuing orders to the production unit is often known as 'dispatching' (not to be confused with despatching which is the physical transfer of goods out of the factory to the next destination). The dispatch clerk not only issues orders to the production process but also ensures that all materials, parts, and tools required for that order are available, and sanctions their requisition from stores.

Once orders have been issued to the production unit the production plan is used as a basis for checking the progress of work through the factory. This work which is often known as 'progressing' is normally undertaken by the dispatch clerks, though some firms may use a separate group of employees known as 'progress chasers'.

Where orders are proceeding according to plan there is little to be done. Unfortunately this state of affairs does not normally exist for very long. Where work does deviate from plan it is the dispatch clerk/progress chaser's job to discover the cause of the problem (e.g. lack of or substandard materials, machine breakdown, labour difficulties) and then:

(a) help in removing the cause of the problem; and

(b) adjust the production so as to bring work back on to schedule, or alternatively revise the production schedule.

In this work the progress chaser is aided considerably by inspection staff concerned with quality control.

Maintenance

Maintenance is defined as work which is undertaken by a person or organisation in order to keep and restore every facility to a reasonable standard. The importance of maintenance to the average organisation lies in the large amount of money it has invested in land, machinery, plant and transport. Without maintenance this investment would rapidly diminish in value. Maintenance of machinery is also required to ensure that breakdowns are kept to a minimum. This is of the highest priority in flow production where the breakdown of one machine can stop the whole manufacturing process, or alternatively in job or batch production where if little spare capacity is available any breakdown will cause an immediate bottleneck.

It must be obvious that in many manufacturing situations it is too costly to wait until a machine breaks down before repairing it, but rather we must plan maintenance to prevent or minimise machine failure. Such a policy is often referred to as 'planned maintenance' or 'preventative maintenance' and a measure of its success is its ability to keep plant running or to repair breakdowns as quickly as possible.

For planned maintenance to be successful an inventory of all plant and equipment must be kept. The inventory should show:

- the type of plant – uses, design, and manufacture;
- its age;
- spares required/carriage/sources;
- likely causes of breakdown;
- a record of past breakdowns;
- the record of planned maintenance.

A schedule of inspection and overhauls (the maintenance plan) will also be drawn up indicating how often a machine has to be inspected and how long can elapse between major overhauls. This information can also be useful in determining the size of the workforce and the skills needed by the maintenance department in order to carry out its work, though some element of overmanning is required because breakdowns will still occur despite all efforts.

Once the maintenance plan has been put into operation it should be revised as experience dictates. Thus it may be possible to extend the intervals between inspection and servicing of certain machines, while others will require more frequent overhaul than originally anticipated.

Planned maintenance has been criticised. Often it involves replacing items which are in perfect working order because statistically it has been calculated that this is the optimum time to replace that item. The alternative is to replace items only when they actually fail with results which we have already noted.

Although by far the most important responsibilities of the maintenance department are to develop and implement a system of planned maintenance there are other important aspects of its work. Many machine breakdowns are caused by the operator using the machine in an improper manner, and in conjunction with training staff the department has a responsibility to instruct operatives in the correct method of use. Similarly the department has a duty to advise the production manager on the replacement of plant and equipment. The advice given will relate to the timing of the replacement purchase and the maintenance cost of different types of machinery.

Where planned maintenance fails to bring a reduction in the number of machine breakdowns two major causes have been identified. First, schedules of inspection and overhaul designed to prevent breakdowns may be defective. Alternatively, the cause of breakdowns may not be covered by planned maintenance, for example metal fatigue in essential parts of a machine.

Purchasing

The role of a purchasing department will vary according to the type of business we consider. In a manufacturing concern over half the total costs may be attributable to raw materials and components. Similarly, in a retailing concern a large proportion of all expenditure will be on goods bought in for resale. Supermarkets and discount stores in particular rely on astute purchasing to provide a reasonable profit margin while retaining their competitive edge. However, a service organisation, for example an estate agent or insurance broker, will not require the sophisticated purchasing function demanded by the manufacturer or retailer.

For many organisations though, the purchasing function may have an appreciable effect on overall profitability. Consider the effect upon the organisation when goods of the wrong type or quality are purchased or where too high a price is paid. Buying too large a quantity leads to an excessive investment in stock and a potential obsolescence problem, while purchasing too little may result in costly production stoppages.

A successful purchasing policy will avoid the problems mentioned above and will take account of factors such as those enumerated below.

1. Estimates of future demand.   The level of stocks held by either a manufacturer or retailer will reflect the marketing department's prediction of future sales. Consider the extra stocks held by retailers during the Christmas period.

2. Price. The aim of the purchasing officer must be to buy as cheaply as possible. Price may, however, have to be sacrificed should any item be needed urgently, though this should only happen on rare occasions. In all circumstances though, care should be taken to ensure that quality is not sacrificed.

3. Quality. Substandard raw materials or components may be purchased cheaply, but in the long run will injure the organisation's reputation with the customer. A system of checks should be instituted to ensure that materials and components ordered are of the quality required and that those received are of the quality ordered. It is equally bad for the organisation to purchase items which are of a higher quality than needed. The organisation will then be paying a higher price than is necessary for quality which is not required.

4. The supplier. The reputation of the supplier in terms of price, quality, service, and reliability should be assessed. Alternative sources of supply should always be identified for all essential raw materials and components.

5. Quantity. The quantity purchased should always be sufficient to meet current demand. Regular purchases of small quantities minimises stockholding costs, but precludes the negotiation of lower prices for buying in bulk.

6. Delivery. All contracts should specify a delivery date, and the importance of adhering to this date should be made clear to the supplier. Lists of alternative suppliers should be maintained in case of non-delivery.

7. The method of purchase. This will not be the same for all items used by the organisation. Where it is necessary to ensure continuity of supply, as in flow production, a contract to purchase an agreed amount over a specified period will be entered into. As part of the agreement it may be stipulated when deliveries are required, thus reducing stockholding costs. Such an agreement may also be used where there is little likelihood of variation in the price of the items ordered over the period of the contract. Apart from ensuring continuity of supply, the organisation is also able to estimate accurately its cost of production for the forthcoming period.

Should market prices of items contracted for fall during that period the organisation will be at a competitive disadvantage compared with other organisations who made 'spot' purchases. Consider the case of the independent oil companies who have been able to purchase surplus oil cheaply on the 'spot' market and pass this saving on to the consumer in the form of lower petrol prices. 'Buying as required' would normally be limited to non-essential items or those for which there is a continuous supply. There is, however, an element of risk as prices may rise as well as fall.

It is also possible to extend the element of speculation by 'purchasing futures'. This is a practice adopted in certain commodity markets, for example copper and cocoa, to purchase a commodity in advance of it being needed or harvested. The belief is that future price rises will result in a saving being made by buying now, or that the commodity can be resold at a profit later. The element of speculation in purchasing futures is great. Extremely large sums of money have been both gained and lost in estimating the future demand and therefore the price of the commodity.

The organisation of the purchasing function varies widely. Where the cost of materials is a high proportion of total cost the purchasing organisation is likely to be complex and its senior executive have similar status to other departmental heads. Alternatively, purchasing may be part of the production department where the purchasing of materials and components for the manufacturing process forms the major part of its work, or the marketing department where, as with the retailer, goods are purchased for resale.

The organisation for puchasing may also be centralised or decentralised, but as a firm grows in size the movement is towards centralisation. The major reason for this is the possibility of bulk buying and obtaining substantial discounts. However, other advantages include:

1. Different departments will often have similar needs, e.g. stationery, furniture.

2. Centralisation establishes a standard procedure for ordering purchases.

3. It is easier to obtain control over the total purchases expenditure of the organisation.

4. Quality is more easily controlled.

5. The needs of one department may be satisfied from a surplus of another department.

6. Specialist buying staff can be utilised.

However, against this must be put:

1. Delays in obtaining purchases and increased paperwork.

2. Specialist requirements of a department are better met by direct negotiation by that department and the supplier.

3. Dealing with local suppliers leads to a stronger relationship and a greater commitment to service on the part of those suppliers.

In practice the answer to the problem of centralisation or decentralisation is normally a compromise. The majority of items are purchased centrally, but each individual unit (whether it be a factory or a department) has the authority to purchase certain items or items to a specified value without the sanction of the purchasing department. Details of such purchases would be transmitted to the purchasing department as a matter of course.

Stock control

This section of the production department is responsible for the control of all purchases made by the organisation from the time of receipt until their issue to the production process or other department. Its work follows logically on from that of the purchasing function, and in some organisations this has led to the creation of a combined department (materials control) embracing both activities. Stock control involves not only controlling and issuing stock but also the inspecting and reordering of stock and checking the accuracy of stock records. We will examine each of these activities in turn.

On receipt of stock items the stores clerk will check what has arrived against the purchase order. This is not a detailed check of individual items but to ensure that the correct number of cases, cartons, etc. have arrived. The materials will then be passed to the appropriate store where after inspection they will be entered on the stores records. The purchasing department will be informed on their arrival. The stores records maintain a running total for each item of stock with 'receipts in' being added to the existing balance and 'issues out' deducted. The information in the stores records is duplicated by the use of 'bin cards' which are found with the storage containers in which the stocks are physically located.

Prior to the goods being placed in their appropriate bins or entered on to the stores records, detailed inspection of the order takes place. It is after all too late to discover that the goods are substandard once they have been issued to production. The nature of the inspection varies according to the item concerned but could include weight, dimensions, colour, hardness, or chemical composition. The inspection may take the form of checking a random number of items which will, statistically, guarantee the remainder or a detailed inspection of each item.

Issue of material to the production process is made against a materials requisition form. The requisition will indicate the materials and the quantities required and to which job their cost is to be charged. Rules should be laid down as to whom may authorise the withdrawal of stores as this is an important element in proper stock control. The information on the materials requisition form will, after the issue of the materials, be transferred to the stores records and the bin cards, and the costing department informed of the amount withdrawn.

As materials are withdrawn from stock for the production process the level of stock held declines. One of the storekeeper's most important tasks is to see that there is always sufficient stock available to meet production's needs. Minimum stock levels which need to be held are normally established by ascertaining the length of time it normally takes to replenish the stocks – this is commonly referred to as 'lead time'. Once materials requisitions take the balance on the stores records below this figure, stock should be reordered automatically. As an extra safety device the reorder level may also be indicated on the bin holding stock by a white line painted on the inside – when the white line is exposed it is time to reorder. Alternatively, 'lead time' stock may be kept in a sealed container and when the seal is broken it is time to reorder.

Other factors which may influence the level of stocks held include the cost of storage, the likelihood of deterioration or obsolescence, anticipated price movements, and the economies of buying in bulk. In practice the reorder level will be determined by discussions between the production, finance, and purchasing functions within the organisation.

In theory the balance shown in the stores records and the bin card should agree with the level of stock held in the bin. To ensure that records are correct and the loss from pilfering, deterioration, and waste is kept within acceptable limits a system of stocktaking must be introduced. Traditionally, an annual stocktaking, which corresponds to the organisation's financial year, is undertaken. Stores staff, together with external auditors, will physically check all items of stock, and agree a valuation which will appear in the organisation's annual accounts. An alternative to annual stocktaking is the perpetual inventory where a continuous process of stocktaking is introduced. The process is arranged so that each item of stock is checked at least once a year. Perpetual inventories have the advantage of minimising disruption in the day-to-day work of the stores and not requiring large amounts of labour over the short period of annual stocktaking.

Whatever system of stocktaking is adopted though, large discrepancies between the records and physical stock should be investigated. The records will also have to be adjusted for the discrepancy.

Our discussion of stock control has so far concentrated on the receipt and issue of materials and components to the production process. In practice, stock control is also responsible for the storage and safe keeping of other stocks of articles which the organisation owns. These would include work in progress, finished goods, and maintenance and repair items, and in some organisations office, canteen, and welfare items. The principles of stores control outlined above apply equally to these other stocks.

All organisations hold stocks of 'materials' against future demand and in many cases the cost of doing so is high. A good system of stores control may reduce this cost considerably by ensuring:

1. Stocks of each item are not too high or too low.

2. Poor stores layout does not result in excessive lighting and heating bills, or deterioration of stock, for example through rusting or breakages.

3. Pilferage is kept to a minimum.

Distribution

It is the responsibility of the distribution function to ensure that goods get to the right place at the right time, in the correct quantity and condition, and at the lowest cost commensurate with adequate service to the customer. In practice a compromise is always necessary – few firms can afford the luxury of a 'Rolls-Royce' distribution service. In order to minimise costs the distribution manager will be considering the following points.

What level of finished stock should be maintained?
Remember, distribution is responsible for getting the goods to the customer at the right time. Where goods are made to a customer's order the level of finished goods held will be low. Finished goods will be inspected for quality and soon after transported to the customer. A more difficult situation arises where goods are not produced to a firm order but for stock. Here the level of finished stock held will be based on what has been found necessary in the past, adjusted as required by the current sales forecast.

Stock levels are often a source of conflict between the production and marketing department. The marketing department, with its emphasis on serving the customer would wish to see stock levels sufficiently high to satisfy all customer requirements as and when they arise. Yet a large investment in stock is expensive, and the production department would prefer lower stock levels even if customer's requirements cannot be met immediately and some sales are lost.

How shall we transport goods to the customer?
There of course many modes of transport – air, sea, rail, road, canal – all with their own particular advantages. Thus sea is cheaper than air but takes longer. The decision taken will depend on a large number of factors including the nature of the goods to be transported (weight, fragility, perishability), the importance of the market, the level of service given by competitors, as well as cost.

Where, as in many cases, distribution is by road the manufacturer also has the option of owning or hiring transport. Often there is no clear-cut answer because the level of orders in a certain area justifies the use of company transport, but in other areas does not. The distribution manager will also have to consider whether are any special factors which preclude the use of outside carriers (fragility or perishability) or whether the image of the firm will be impaired by not having its own transport fleet to deliver goods. It is also worth remembering that the delivery man is often the only contact the customer has with the seller apart from members of the marketing department.

Often the decision is to own and run a transport fleet which is slightly smaller than necessary. This has the advantage of ensuring that the fleet is used to the full. Outside contractors will then be employed for the work which is surplus to capacity. Transport costs can be considerably reduced by careful routeing and scheduling of deliveries. Lorries should never leave the factory premises half loaded. Empty return journeys may also be avoided by collecting deliveries of materials or components to be used in the production process.

Advisory activities

Work study

'Work study' is a term which covers a number of techniques designed to improve the efficiency of the organisation and help in the control of costs. We will consider the two main techniques, method study and work measurement.

Method study is concerned with how the work is carried out. It looks at existing procedures with a view to improving them. In essence it answers the question, 'Is there a better way of doing this job?' Work measurement, on the other hand, questions how long a job should take. By scientific methods it determines what time should be allowed for a task and thereby provides an important element in labour cost control. Work measurement follows logically on from method study, for it is only after we have established the best method of doing a job that we can calculate how long it should take. We will consider method study first.

Method study
The procedure has six stages namely: select; record; examine; develop; install; maintain.

1. Select the job to be studied.   The request for an investigation will normally come from management within the production department who perceive problems such as:
● bad-quality work;
● high labour turnover and absenteeism or accident rates;
● production bottlenecks or under-utilised machinery;
● excessive overtime.

Once a job has been selected and authority has been obtained for its investigation the most important task before moving on to the next stage is to inform all those who will be affected by the study. Explaining the reasons for the study prior to its commencement will prevent misunderstanding and increase the likelihood of worker co-operation. However, it would be unwise to conduct method study in parts of the factory where there are bad labour relations.

2. Record the present method. A detailed analysis of present methods is necessary before we can move on to seeing what improvements are possible or desirable. The investigator will record details of the existing system under the headings of purpose, method, sequence, place, and person.

3. Examine the existing method; and

4. Develop the new improved method. The existing method which we have now investigated forms the basis for our search for new improved methods. In fact as we chart the existing method we find ourselves quite naturally questioning what we see, but during this stage we carefully question all that we have recorded. Each of the aspects we previously recorded we now challenge, ask for alternatives, and finally decide what action is to be taken. Figure 12.3 shows one particular form that is often used for this purpose. It is important that this stage is done systematically and that all alternatives are considered, however impractical they seem at first. For example, few people uninitiated in method would think of questioning why a particular activity is done at all, or if it can be eliminated. Yet this has proved to be one of the most effective ways of improving methods.

Eventually, out of the critical examination will come the ideas for the improved method. These will be discussed with management in the

Present facts		Alternatives	Decision
What is done	Why?	What else?	What should be done
How it is done	Why that way?	How else?	How it should be done
When it is done	Why then?	When else?	When it should be done
Where it is done	Why there?	Where else?	Where it should be done
Who does it	Why him?	Who else?	Who should do it

Fig. 12.3 Critical examination sheet

department concerned. Perhaps after these discussions ideas have to be amended or even dropped, but the work study officer must be satisfied that the criticisms are sound, for even managers are known to dislike and resist change!

At this stage it is also necessary to draw up a formal report which will outline:

- the changes recommended;
- the cost of those changes;
- the savings which will result;
- the time needed to institute the changes.

The report is presented to the management who instigated the investigation and once their approval is obtained we move to the next stage.

5. Installation of the improved method. Work study personnel must pay particular attention to two aspects of installation. First they must persuade everyone concerned of the need for change. A successful installation needs the co-operation of all staff. Secondly the installation will involve considerable planning. Liaison with the purchasing department to buy any new plant, equipment, or materials required, with the personnel department for the training or retraining of employees, with the maintenance department for installing or repositioning plant, and with production planning for the issue of new production orders.

6. Maintain the new method. The introduction of the new method will not be without its difficulties, but it would be wrong for work study personnel to consider changes immediately. It will take some time before all employees are fully conversant with the new method and reach the expected level of productivity. Indeed, work study personnel will be monitoring the new system for several months after it has been introduced to see that planned savings are achieved in practice, or whether any refinements are possible, but also – and very important – to guard against unauthorised change by operatives. Perhaps these changes are improvements, in which case they should be officially integrated into the new system, but it is all too easy for operatives to slip back into old ways or into new but bad habits.

Resistance to change

Men and women are creatures of habit – all of us are guilty of resisting change at some time or another in both our personal and professional lives. This is so even when, to the unbiased observer, it seems that the proposed changes will benefit us. Thus most of us would agree if asked that technological change – greater automation, the use of computers or word-processors for example, were necessary. Yet what we are seemingly unable to accept is that our personal situation should be disturbed in any way by these changes. The main reasons for resisting change are listed below:

- *possible loss of job or transfer to another job;*
- *skills become redundant;*
- *reduction in status or pay;*
- *social groups at work may be broken up;*
- *worries about establishing new friends or learning a new job;*
- *dislocation of social life by new working arrangements.*

As we can see, the question uppermost in most people's minds is, 'how is this going to affect me?'

Yet it is imperative that management reduce the level of resistance. Investments in new technology or new methods will not yield the expected benefits without the co-operation of the workforce.

Much of the answer lies in the degree of trust that has been developed by the management with the unions and the workforce over a period of many years – is the organisation one which 'cares for' and 'plays fair' by its employees?

However, the degree of resistance may be reduced if the principles below are followed:

1. *A proper manpower plan is developed, identifying new skills which will be required and offering retraining to those who may be displaced by the change. Reduction in the workforce should be planned in advance so that natural wastage and voluntary redundancy reduce the necessity for compulsory redundancy.*

2. *Do not keep the planned changes secret, the organisational grapevine can do more harm than the truth by exaggerating the scale and effects of the change. Tell people what their position will be, let them get used to the idea and give them time to plan their future.*

3. *Change is more acceptable if people participate in the making of those plans which affect their working lives rather than having it imposed upon them.*

4. *Change is more acceptable where work/social groups are not disturbed.*

5. *Employees who suffer financially should be compensated, e.g. removal and selling expenses where a house move is required, guaranteeing previous income for a period when moving to a lower-paid job, or generous redundancy payments.*

6. *Where possible introduce the changes slowly so that they are accepted and understood by those that are affected.*

Work measurement
Work measurement seeks to establish how long a particular job should take. It is necessary that this calculation be made so that we do not either over- or underestimate the total amount of work which we can carry out in any period of time. Overestimating the amount of work we can do means we fail to deliver on time and lose the goodwill of our customers, while an underestimation means that men and machines which could be earning money are lying idle.

There are several techniques by which we can measure work and establish a reasonable time for the job. The best known of these is 'time study', sometimes termed 'stop-watch studies'. By this method an operative is studied working at his normal job over an extended period of time. Each operation carried out is timed and retimed so as to arrive at a basic time for the job which represents the normal rate of working. It is not unknown for the subject of the study to deviate from his normal work methods in an attempt to make the job look more complicated and obtain a larger time allowance for that job. For this reason it is necessary that method study has previously established the correct method for the job and we now require the operative to conform to that method.

Time studies are made on a number of workers undertaking the same activity, and it is not unusual to find that the observed times vary considerably as each worker has his own pace of work. So as to establish a basic time for the job we therefore have to rate each worker in terms of the effort which he has expended. A scale is established from 0 to 100 with 0 representing zero activity and 100 representing the normal worker. We may then, for example, rate a slow worker at 80 and a fast worker at 120. Our next step is to adjust the observed time by the rating we have allocated to the worker:

$$\text{Basic time} = \text{Observed time} \times \frac{\text{Rating}}{100}$$

Let us for example assume that we have studied two workers over the same operation. Worker A took four minutes to complete the activity and was rated at 120, while worker B took six minutes and was rated at 80. Our basic time for worker A is

$$4 \times \frac{120}{100} = 4.8 \text{ minutes}$$

and for worker B

$$6 \times \frac{80}{100} = 4.8 \text{ minutes}$$

If our rating of worker effort is correct the adjustment to observed time will result in a very similar basic time in each case.

A description of work measurement so far has assumed that it is necessary to time study each job individually to establish the basic time. However, over a period a large number of different jobs will be timed and that information stored. Now many jobs will have certain activities or operations in common, and it is possible to obtain much of the information we need more quickly and cheaply from our records.

The basic time that we have calculated assumes that the worker can carry on working at the same speed all day. This is not so. All workers will relax their efforts from time to time, perhaps to talk to the supervisor, their workmates, to visit the toilet, to light a cigarette, and so on. To the basic time already calculated we add relaxation allowance. This may be as little as 10 per cent, or for highly fatiguing work over 100 per cent of the basic time. The resulting figure is known as the standard time for the job. It is defined as 'the rate of output achieved by a qualified worker naturally without over-exertion provided he adheres to the specific method and applies himself to his work'.

Standard times are used in a variety of ways throughout the organisation. Within the production department it is used to establish a reasonable workload for men and machines in the forthcoming period. Standard times can be used to monitor the times of individual workers. The personnel department will use standard times in determining future manpower requirements and in establishing incentive schemes. The accounting function will use standard times in the preparation of budgets, against which actual performance can be compared.

Quality control

Quality control is the system by which management ensures that goods produced conform to a predetermined standard.

Greater emphasis than ever before is placed upon quality control. The advent of the discerning consumer and the growing competition among manufacturers has had a widespread impact. Certain industries, food and drugs, are required to maintain high standards of quality by law. Others, concerned with assembling a product from a large number of components (e.g. the car industry) demand that less than 1 per cent of any component used be defective. This near-perfect reliability of individual components is required to guarantee the operation of the finished product.

As our definition implies, there are two parts to any quality-control system. First, the establishing of standards which we require the production process to conform to, and secondly, a method of inspection to see that this standard is adhered to.

What quality do we require our products to conform to? To the laymen quality implies some degree of excellence, yet this is not always required by the consumer. For example if we asked our average driver what standards of quality he required for his family car it would be unusual for him to demand the standard of a Rolls-Royce. Pressed further he would probably say it should be capable of cruising at 70 miles an hour, not consume too much petrol, and not be too expensive to repair and maintain. It is these factors that the manufacturer is interested in. To him quality may be defined as the product being fit for the purpose of the average consumer.

The question of quality is critical to the manufacturer, higher quality means higher costs and all too often we find that people are unwilling to pay the extra price associated with quality. This can be seen from Figure 12.4.

As we raise the quality of our product the manufacturing cost increases. Up to point C the selling value (i.e. the price we can charge) increases more rapidly. However, increase in quality beyond point C will raise manufacturing cost more rapidly than sales value and profitability therefore declines. Thus our manufacturer will seek to establish quality standards at point C because at this point the gap between his costs of production and sales revenue is largest.

Once quality standards have been decided upon, a system of inspection is developed. This system may be used in two particular ways. First, as a means of controlling the production process. Let us

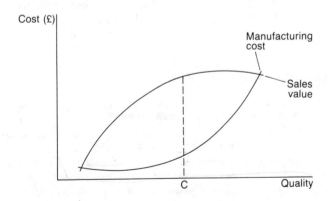

C = the point of maximum benefit to the manufacturer

Fig. 12.4 A comparison of manufacturing cost and sales value at different quality levels

take for example a company which has to achieve certain standards of accuracy in the dimensions of the product it is producing. Variations are bound to occur. The quality of material used may differ, one machine may have more play on it than another, even operatives may have an 'off' day. But by examining work at each production stage regularly we can ensure that standards are maintained.

Records of failures in quality should be kept so that over a period of time we should be able to spot consistencies in quality failures – establish the cause whether it may be men, machines, or materials, and take action to remedy the problem – perhaps retrain the men, introduce more rigorous maintenance schedules for machines, or change our material supplier. As we can see, inspection not only serves the immediate need of controlling the quality of the production process but also a longer-term aim of improving the process.

Although process control will uncover many failures in quality the vast majority of organisations still sample the finished product further to ensure its reliability. This is termed 'acceptance sampling' (and although we are referring here to the sample of a finished product it is relevant to the inspection of raw material and work in progress).

The procedure for acceptance sampling is that a random sample of the product is taken and subjected to a thorough inspection. The size of the sample may only be a small proportion of the total batch, but has been precisely calculated so that if the number of defects are below a certain level we can confidently predict that 95 per cent of the remainder will also be to the required standard. The sample size and degree of reliability required may very well have been previously agreed by the producer with the purchaser. Where the number of defects is outside the acceptable range the whole batch will be rejected or an individual inspection of each item undertaken. The great advantage of acceptance sampling is that we can confidently predict the reliability of our product at a reasonable cost.

Examination questions

1. Outline the circumstances in which (a) job production, (b) batch production, (c) flow production, would be an appropriate method of manufacture.

2. Define specialisation simplification and standardisation. What is the practical importance of these terms to the producer and consumer?

3. What are the respective product and production characteristics that are associated with each of the three basic manufacturing systems in use today?

4. Outline the activities involved in production. What is the role of each?

5. Describe and explain the role of production planning and control within a medium-sized manufacturing concern.

6. Quality control has been described as adding additional cost to a product without adding value or benefit to the purchaser. Do you agree?

7. Your company proposes to extend its manufacturing operations but is unable to do so on its present site. Write a report to the directors explaining the factors which should influence their choice of alternative sites.

8. What factors affect the planned quality of a product? How is quality maintained?

9. Briefly explain the importance of the purchasing function to (a) a manufacturer, (b) a retailer. What factors will a successful purchasing policy be concerned with?

10. The Works Manager of Comlon Ltd, a small manufacturing concern, is responsible for all aspects of the production function within the company. So that he may concentrate more on the manufacturing process it has been decided to relieve him of some of his duties.

    Select two specialist activities which are normally carried out as part of the production function and explain the benefits that Comlon can expect to gain having appointed staff to these positions.

11. What are the objectives of work measurement and method study. Outline the steps taken in each of these procedures.

12. Why is a system of stock control necessary for efficient production? Outline a system of stock control which you believe to be effective for a manufacturing concern.

13. What is the importance of maintenance to a manufacturing firm? How should it be organised?

Financial management
Chapter 13

The history of the accounting function goes back many hundreds of years. The art of bookkeeping – that is, the recording of financial transactions, can be traced back to the early fourteenth century. It was not until the nineteenth century though, that accountancy emerged as a profession. The Industrial Revolution and the growth of large-scale enterprise was fertile ground for the embryo accounting profession. Shareholders, not involved in the day-to-day running of an enterprise in which they had invested their money, required the managers of these companies to account for the use of their money. But in many cases misuse of investor's money still occurred. This eventually led to legislation requiring companies to submit to an annual independent audit of their records by a professionally qualified accountant. At the turn of the century the typical accountant in business was employed to:

- establish a sound system of bookkeeping;
- establish a system of internal check (audit);
    prepare the final accounts (profit and loss account, balance sheet).

This remained very much the role of the accountant in business until after the Second World War. Gradually though, accountants came to realise that the details of financial transactions which were so carefully recorded by bookkeepers could also be used to monitor the progress of the organisation against a predetermined objective – often termed 'control accountancy'. Later still accountants developed other techniques which enabled business to evaluate alternative uses of capital, or determine whether a project should or should not be undertaken. This was termed 'decision accounting'.

In business today the financial accountant's work corresponds broadly to the traditional role of accountancy with its emphasis on bookkeeping, auditing, and the presentation of financial results. An accountant who is involved in control accountancy or decision accountancy, on the other hand, is normally called a management accountant. The work of the financial and management accountant is shown in Fig. 13.1.

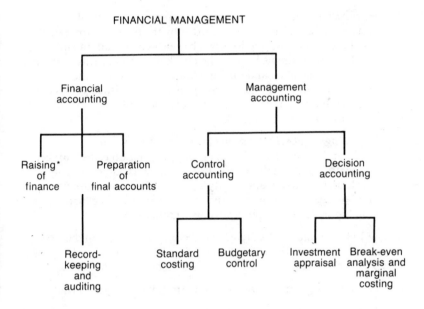

*See Chapter 18.

Fig. 13.1 Work typically undertaken within the finance function

Financial accounting

Bookkeeping and internal audit

The recording of all transactions entered into by an organisation lies at the heart of the accounting process. Details of sales, purchases, and expenses are required so that bills may be paid on time, debts can be collected, and the values of assets recorded. The same information may be used in the control of business activities through standard costing and budgetary control techniques. Lastly it is by relating expenditure to income that we calculate the profit or loss for the period.

Internal auditing of the bookkeeping system is undertaken to test the efficiency of that system. Internal audit seeks to ensure that transactions are processed quickly and cheaply, that a high level of accuracy is maintained, and lastly fraud, theft, or other irregularities are minimised. Characteristically, checks undertaken will fall into one of the following categories.

1. *Analysis of the accounting system.* This has the aim of improving efficiency through revision of procedures and training of staff. Additionally, such analysis will seek to ensure that the system is proof against fraud or theft on the part of staff operating the system.

2. *Verification of records.* It is obviously impossible to verify the accuracy of all transactions recorded by the business. Instead a small number of transactions will be selected at random and checked for accuracy. Should the check reveal inaccuracies further investigation will be undertaken. Additionally, where the business holds stocks of raw material, components, or finished goods the balance shown in the accounts may also be verified by means of a physical check of those stocks.

3. *Psychological checks.* Certain checks may be instituted so as to create an environment whereby misappropriation is discouraged by the possibility of discovery. For example irregular or spot checks may be made upon petty cash holdings, National Insurance and postage stamps. Alternatively, staff may be compelled to take annual holidays or accept transfers to other jobs.

The 1948 Companies Act requires all companies registered in Britain to present an annual report to shareholders and other interested parties (such as debenture holders). This report must contain the following:

1. A statement of profit or loss arising from the past year's trading.

2. A balance sheet as at the year end.

3. A director's report giving details of dividends, directors, director's shareholdings, employees, and total remuneration, together with charitable and political contributions.

4. An auditor's report affirming that the final accounts give a 'true and fair view of the state of affairs of the company' at the end of the financial year.

It is also normal, though not required by law, for the annual report to contain a chairman's statement on the company's activities during the past year and its prospects for the future.

The balance sheet

The balance sheet can be likened to a photograph. It provides a picture of a firm's financial position at a given point in time. It is constructed from the bookkeeping records of the business and shows how the company obtained the finance necessary for its operations and how that finance was utilised. Traditionally, balance sheets were presented in a two-column format showing liabilities (or sources of finance) on the left-hand side, and assets (applications of finance) on the right-hand side. The balance sheet in Fig. 13.2 uses that format and shows the subheadings commonly used.

Balance sheet

Liabilities	*Assets*
Shareholders' funds	Fixed assets
Loan capital	
Current liabilities	Current assets

Fig. 13.2 Layout of a balance sheet in traditional form

By convention, liabilities are shown in order of permanence to the business. Thus shareholders' funds – which provide the permanent capital of the business – are listed first. Shareholders' funds consist of ordinary and preference share capital together with reserves of undistributed or retained profits. Our second heading on the liabilities side of the balance sheet – loan capital – refers to money lent to the business for long-term financing. Examples would include debentures, mortgages, and bank loans.

Current liabilities are short-term borrowings which will normally be repaid within a year, and will include creditors – that is, amounts owing to suppliers of goods and services – and also bank overdrafts.

Moving to the right-hand side of our balance sheet we see that the money raised is invested in either fixed or current assets. Fixed assets refer to items that the company has acquired for use (rather than sale) in its business. Land and buildings, plant and machinery, and vehicles are examples of fixed assets.

Current assets consists of stocks, debtors – that is, amounts owed to the business by customers – and cash owned by the business. They are sometimes referred to as short-term or circulating assets due to the fact that they constantly change as the firm conducts its business.

There is no legal requirement as to how the business presents its final accounts. While the format adopted above has the advantage of grouping assets and liabilities together the modern trend is to present the information in tabular form as in Fig. 13.3 so as to highlight the long-term financing of the business together with the net assets.

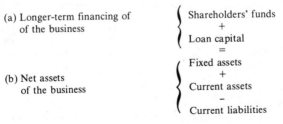

Fig. 13.3 Presentation of balance sheet in vertical form

In reality the only difference with this presentation is that current liabilities, instead of being included with the other sources of finance, are deducted from current assets. This has the advantage of showing the extent to which the business can meet its short-term liabilities from short-term assets without recourse to borrowing or sales of other assets.

Figure 13.4 shows the balance sheet of an imaginary company, Condor PLC, as at 31 December, 1984 in the columnar fashion described above. Comparative figures for the previous year, as is the normal practice, are also shown. Explanatory notes on the balance sheet (and the profit and loss account) would again be included in the annual report. Most of the terminology used in the balance sheet of Condor PLC should be familiar, but it is necessary to explain the following items:

1. Minority interests. Many public companies quoted on the Stock Exchange are groups of businesses which have been formed by merger

Condor P.L.C. Balance Sheet as at 31 December 1984

	1984 (£'000)		1983 (£'000)	
Capital employed				
Ordinary share capital		4,000		2,500
Reserves		15,792		13,248
Shareholders' funds		19,782		15,748
Secured bank loan	2,050		2,050	
Minority interests	591	2,641	591	2,641
		22,423		18,389
Employment of capital				
Fixed assets (less depreciation)		9,239		6,817
Subsidiary companies		5,429		5,429
		14,668		12,246
Current assets				
Stock	8,833		6,639	
Debtors	4,492		4,806	
Cash	1,830	15,155	816	12,261
		29,823		24,507
less *Current liabilities*				
Creditors	6,284		4,061	
Bank overdraft	123		532	
Taxation	825		1,388	
Proposed dividend	168	7,400	137	6,118
		22,423		18,389

John Smith
Arthur Jones   Directors

Fig. 13.4 Illustration of a typical company's published balance sheet

and take-over activity. Sometimes, not all shareholders are willing to trade their investment in the original business for a stake in the newly combined group. It is then necessary to show what amount of the subsidiaries' assets belong to shareholders outside the company. Thus the value of the subsidiary companies' assets in Condor PLC's balance sheet is shown as £5,429,000 of which £591,000 belongs to 'outsider' shareholders.

2. Depreciation. At the end of 1984 fixed assets in Condor PLC were valued at £8,239,000 after deducting depreciation. Depreciation is deducted so that the balance sheet gives a 'true and fair' view of the affairs of the business. If an asset through use, age, or obsolescence is now only worth, shall we say, 40 per cent of what it originally cost that fact must be shown in the balance sheet. Similarly, if an asset is used during in any financial period to earn profits and through use suffers a diminution in value, that reduction in value is an expense which should be set off against revenue in determining the true profit of the period.

3. Taxation and proposed dividend. Although neither of these items are liabilities arising from Condor's trading activities, both will need paying during the forthcoming year and in consequence are grouped with current liabilities.

The profit and loss account

In order to calculate the profit earned by a business all expenses which have been incurred in earning the sales revenue of that period must be charged against that revenue. The profit and loss account is divided into three sections (see Fig. 13.5). First, the trading account in which

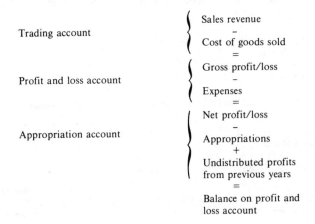

Fig. 13.5 The sections of the profit and loss account

gross profit is calculated by deducting the cost of goods sold (labour, raw materials, and other production costs) from sales revenue. In the central section which is termed the profit and loss account, the net profit is arrived at by deducting all business expenses for that period from the gross period. This is the figure which is normally quoted in the financial press. The final section, the appropriation account, shows the way in which the profit is used – how much is to go in paying corporation tax, what dividends are to be paid this year, leaving the residue to be added to the retained profits in previous years. In practice much of the detailed information contained in the profit and loss account could be useful to competitors and consequently companies are not required to show full details. The profit and loss account of Condor PLC (see Fig. 13.6) shows the details which have to be published by law.

Condor PLC Profit and Loss Account for the year ended 31 December 1984

	1984 (£'000)	1983 (£'000)
Turnover	53,000	42,300
Net profit	3,527	3,312
Taxation	825	1,032
Profit after tax	2,702	2,280
Dividends	168	137
Retained profits	2,534	2,143

Notes:

1. Depreciation for the year to 31 December 1984 was £1,531,000.

2. Director's emoluments. The renumeration of the highest paid director was £68,000 and that of the Chairman £40,000. The number of other directors in each range of remuneration was as follows:

	1984	1983
Nil–£15,000	4	4
£15,000–£20,000	—	1
£20,000–£25,000	2	1
£25,000–£30,000	2	2

3. Emoluments to employees earning in excess of £30,000 were as follows:

	1984	1983
£30,000–£35,000	2	—
£35,000–£40,000	1	2

4. Interest paid on loans

	1984	1983
Loans repayable over more than five years	£311,000	£327,000
Short-term borrowing	31,000	98,000

Fig. 13.6 Illustration of a typical company's published profit and loss account

Who uses the annual report?

Although the annual report is by no means the only source of information on a business which is available to interested parties it is the most easily obtainable, and is therefore the normal starting-point for research into any company. The annual report will provide information on:

1. *Profitability*: e.g. the trend of profits, adequacy of profits in relation to capital employed, are profits sufficient to finance further growth?

2. *Solvency:* can the business pay its debts when they fall due, is the working capital sufficient, does the business have the financial resource to survive an unforeseen crisis?

3. *Finance:* who provides the finance for the business, is the relationship between the long- and short-term sources of finance correct, is the gearing ratio correct, can the business issue more shares?

4. *Security:* what assets are available to satisfy creditors if debts are not met, is the ordinary share dividend safe, how far do profits have to fall before debenture interest cannot be paid?

Shareholders
Existing shareholders automatically receive a copy of the annual report, and potential shareholders may also obtain a copy by writing to the company at its registered office. Both groups will be interested in the trends of company profits (many companies now provide summaries of the past five or ten years' financial results as part of the report) and future prospects of the business. Apart from comments made in the press, the annual report is often the only source of information that small investors receive on the company they have invested in.

Employees and unions
Employees, like shareholders, have a vested interest in the success of the business and the annual report is one method of passing information to them. Many large companies produce an annual report especially for employees. Here the emphasis is on presenting information in a way which can be easily understood by the employees. Figure 13.7 shows an alternative way in which the information in the profit and loss account of Condor PLC could be presented to employees.

Employees and their representatives will be interested in how much profit has been made – this after all may be used as a tool in the annual wage negotiations, and the company's plans for the future with its implications for employment.

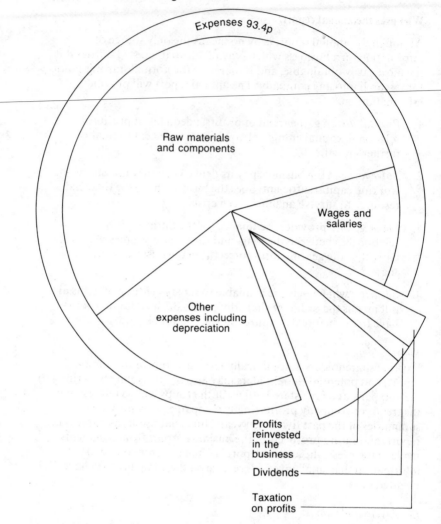

Fig. 13.7 Condor PLC – results at a glance: how each £1 of sales revenue was spent

Customers and creditors
Both groups are interested in the soundness of the business with whom they are contracting. Customers wish to ensure that the company has the financial resources and stability to carry out the contracts and provide the necessary after-sales service. Suppliers will examine the report and accounts to see if the business is creditworthy, and is able to pay its debts as they become due.

Bankers
Bankers will normally demand far more detailed information on company affairs than is provided in the annual report. In particular, they are interested in the security available for their loan, and how the business will repay the loan and interest.

The interpretation of final accounts

A ratio expresses the relationship between two figures. Ratios are often used by people in assessing a business's financial performance and position. Key ratios for the present year will be calculated and compared with similar ratios from previous years, other companies, or the company's own planned performance. By this method significant aspects of company performance are highlighted. The ratios most generally used relate to capital structure, profitability, and liquidity.

Capital structure
In Chapter 18 (p. 335) it is pointed out that the method of raising long-term capital would affect the degree of risk associated with investing in that firm. Where there is a high level of external borrowing with a fixed interest charge, there is a greater risk of profits being insufficient to pay either that interest charge or dividends. The degree of risk is measured by a gearing ratio:

Fixed interest capital : ordinary share capital

A company which makes little use of fixed interest capital in relation to ordinary share capital is said to be 'low geared'. Conversely, a high-geared company obtains a far greater proportion of its total funds in the form of fixed interest capital.

Profitability
Profitability is the yardstick by which business performance is most often judged. But the fact that one business's profits are twice that of another says little about the management efficiency in the use of resources. Profitability and performance are therefore assessed by comparing the profitability against the resources which were used to obtain those profits. This ratio is termed the 'return on capital employed' and is calculated thus:

$$\frac{\text{Net profit before tax}}{\text{Capital employed}} \times 100$$

where capital employed is total assets *less* current liabilities. Being expressed as a percentage the ratio can easily be used for purposes of comparison, and answers investors' questions such as, 'Is the management making good use of the firm's resources?', and 'Could I obtain a better return by investing elsewhere?'

The return on capital employed may be subdivided into two further ratios by comparing net profits and capital employed, in turn, against sales. The first, the net profit percentage, is measured as follows:

$$\frac{\text{Net profit before tax}}{\text{Sales}} \times 100$$

It is a measure of management's efficiency in keeping costs down.

Secondly, asset turnover measures how effectively capital or assets are used to generate sales. It is measured as follows:

$$\frac{\text{Sales}}{\text{Capital employed}}$$

A return on capital employed of 15 per cent may be earned in many different ways. A company may have a profit margin of 5 per cent, but turn its capital over (and earn the profit margin) three times during that period. Alternatively, the same return of 15 per cent could be obtained by turning assets once, but having a net profit of 15 per cent, or an asset turnover ratio of 2 and a 7½ per cent profit margin.

The nature of the relationship between profit margin and asset turnover is often determined by the industry in which the firm works. Heavy engineering industries, being capital intensive and with contracts often taking months if not years to complete, have a low asset turnover ratio but a high net profit percentage. Conversely, a supermarket will work on a very low profit margin but aim to turn its assets over very many times during the year.

Liquidity and solvency

There are many recorded cases of businesses trading profitably and yet because of a shortage of funds being forced to curtail their activities if not go into liquidation. Therefore, the management of working capital is of as much importance as profitability to shareholders, employees, and all the other interested parties.

By 'working capital' we are referring to those assets which may be rapidly converted into cash and used to pay the debts of the business. Working capital is also used to acquire the labour, materials, power, and other items needed before the fixed assets can operate, and to finance the business's sales activities. In balance sheet terms working capital is shown as the difference between current assets and current liabilities. For Condor PLC working capital was £7,755,000 in 1984 and £6,143,000 in 1983.

When working capital is inadequate the following difficulties may occur:

1. An inability to take advantage of favourable terms for settling indebtedness (e.g. discounts for prompt payment).

2. An inability to pay debts when they become due, with a consequent loss of goodwill and creditworthiness.

3. Stocks may be withheld by suppliers until payment is made in cash, thus damaging production schedules.

4. The business may be forced to purchase the goods that it needs in small and uneconomic quantities.

5. The firm may be forced to sell at reduced prices or to give excessive discounts so as to obtain funds quickly.

The best test of a business's ability to pay its debts when they become due is to be found in a cash budget. Unfortunately this information is not available outside the company and we are therefore forced to use information from the published accounts. One measure which is commonly used is the 'current ratio'. This examines the relationship between short-term assets and liabilities. It is often termed the 2:1 ratio, indicating the margin of safety which is generally accepted as being necessary to meet the uneven flow of receipts and payments. The current ratio is calculated as follows:

$$\frac{\text{Current assets}}{\text{Current liabilities}}$$

Although a ratio of 2:1 is normally recommended a marked degree of difference is found between industries. Heavy engineering, for example, tends to have a higher than average current ratio because of the large amount of capital tied up in raw materials and work in progress. However, our supermarket (which trades mainly for cash) can operate on an exceptionally low current ratio.

Two other ratios also tend to be widely used. The stock turnover ratio:

$$\frac{\text{Sales}}{\text{Stock}}$$

indicates the speed with which the company turns over its stock. A fall in the stock turnover ratio may be caused by a fall in sales – raising questions regarding marketing policy. Alternatively, an increase in the level of stocks held raises questions regarding stock control and purchasing policy.

The debtor turnover ratio, which shows the average number of days customers take to pay their bills measures the efficiency of the company's credit control system. Obviously the faster debts are collected the better. It is calculated as follows:

$$\frac{Sales}{Debtors} \times 365$$

There may, of course be perfectly adequate reasons for changes in these ratios. A decline in the stock turnover ratio may be due to a stocking-up process prior to an expansion in sales. Changes in the debtor turnover ratio may reflect a different management policy on credit trading. What is important with these ratios is that they focus attention on issues vital to the company's survival and profitability.

Interfirm comparison

The value of ratio analysis lies in its comparison with information of a similar kind. Traditionally, the comparison has been made with data from the same organisation for previous years. Yet even greater benefit can be obtained if comparison is made against the performance of other firms in the same industry.

Demand for such information has led a number of trade associations to develop schemes facilitating interfirm comparison. Individual companies within the industry supply information on their performance to the trade association on the understanding that it should be treated in strict confidence, and will only be revealed to other members in the form of industry averages.

A similar scheme, the Centre for Interfirm Comparison, was also established by the British Institute of Management in 1959. This seeks to cover those industries whose trade associations do not run an interfirm comparison scheme. Details of industry averages are again supplied, together with the range of performance. Comments on the strengths and weaknesses of the particular firm are also made.

Both trade associations and the Centre for Interfirm Comparison lay down rules for a common presentation of accounts and also specify methods by which assets should be valued or depreciated, thus ensuring comparability of performance.

Funds flow analysis

In addition to the balance sheet and the profit and loss account which are required by law, firms have also included in their annual report a 'funds statement'. In Britain this is often called the 'sources and applications of fund statement'. The statement aims to explain what sources of funds have become available during the past year, and how these funds have been utilised.

The technique for constructing a funds flow statement is relatively simple. A comparison is made of the business's balance sheet at two different dates, and the differences noted. Thus if examination reveals that creditors have increased during the period, it means that they are financing more of the business than previously, and represent a source of funds. Conversely, if the value of fixed assets has increased, the increased investment represents an application or disposition of funds. The rules for constructing a funds statement are summarised as follows:

- profits from trading are sources of funds;
- increases in liabilities are sources of funds;
- decreases in assets are sources of funds;
- losses on trading are disposition of funds;
- increases in assets are disposition of funds;
- decreases in liabilities are disposition of funds.

Figure 13.8 shows the sources and application of funds statement for Condor PLC which is based upon the final accounts for 31 December 1983 and 1984. It has been designed so as to explain the differences in the cash balance at the beginning and the end of the period. There is, however, no one standard format for such statements. The presentation may be adapted to explain why in a year of successful

Condor PLC Sources and Application of Funds for the year ended 31 December 1984

	£'000	£'000	£'000	£'000
Opening cash position				816
Sources of funds				
Ordinary share capital		1,500		
Net profit	3,527			
Add back depreciation*	1,531			
		5,058		
Debtors	314			
Creditors	2,223			
		2,537		
			9,095	
Disposition of funds				
Purchase of fixed assets		3,953		
Stock	2,194			
Bank overdraft	765			
Tax paid	1,032			
Dividend paid	137			
		4,128		
			8,071	
Excess of sources over applications				1,024
Closing cash position				1,830

*Depreciation, which has been charged as an expense in the profit and loss account, does not result in a flow of funds out of the business.

Fig. 13.8 Illustration of a typical company's published funds flow statement

trading, the business is suffering a cash crisis, or alternatively to explain the changes in working capital. In this way a funds flow statement fills an important information gap for management, investors, and other interested parties.

Management accounting

So far we have concerned ourselves with financial accounting, the main aim of which is to record all transactions of the organisation and at the end of the year summarise the results of trading in the profit and loss account and balance sheet. We have also seen how ratio analysis and funds flow statements can be used further to explain the performance and results of the business. But while such information is useful to management in the control of their operations it suffers from two defects. First the information is not always readily available. Traditionally, the final accounts are only drawn up at the end of the financial year. While some firms do produce these statements half-yearly and quarter-yearly, information for control purposes is needed very much more frequently. Secondly the information presented in the final accounts is of little use at the operational level of the business. Management needs cost information for product pricing, to ensure departments do not overspend, and to control the labour and material used in production.

Management accounting seeks to fill this gap and provide managers with the information they need to manage effectively. But, of course, let us be clear that cost information alone in insufficient for decision-making purposes. The manager will also draw upon his knowledge of the firm's environment – economic, political, technical, and social, and also the organisation's strengths and weaknesses. Indeed, often the manager may ignore cost considerations and make his decision upon other grounds; for example employee morale or customer goodwill.

Control accounting

Budgetary control
Budgetary control is undoubtedly the most widely used management accounting technique. On a personal level we are all familiar with the idea of budgeting – we have to plan our student grant or wage packet so that we do not run short of funds before next pay-day. On a national level the Chancellor of the Exchequer estimates government revenue and expenditure, and presents his proposals to Parliament in the form of a budget.

A company budget is much the same; it represents an attempt by the business to predict future income and expenses together with their effect upon profitability and the balance sheet. Equally importantly though, budgeting is seen as a means of ensuring that:

- future activities are planned;
- future activities are co-ordinated;
- future activities are managed effectively.

Budgeting is part of the overall planning process within the firm (see Fig. 13.9). Senior management will have considered a variety of strategies, and eventually decided the long-term or corporate objectives of the organisation. These objectives could be expressed, for example, in terms of profitability, sales revenue, new product development, or growth. However, it should be noted that corporate planning is a continuous process, not an activity to be undertaken, say, once every five years. Corporate objectives may very well be redefined as either environmental or organisational factors change.

Budgets are normally prepared on an annual basis and cover all aspects of the firm's activities. The process of drawing up a budget will start well before the year to which it will relate. Managers in conjunction with their supervisors will establish objectives for

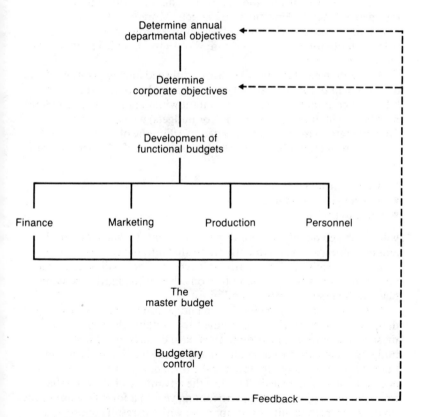

Fig. 13.9 Simplified budgeting process

themselves and their departments. It is essential that managers are involved in this process, otherwise objectives may be rejected as unrealistic. Such objectives must, of course, be consistent with the overall strategy of the organisation and also flexible enough to accommodate unforeseen changes in corporate objectives.

Additionally, these departmental objectives must also be consistent with those established by other managers. For example, it would be nonsensical for the sales department of an engineering firm to budget for a sales volume greater than production capacity. In practice we will find that there is one factor – the 'limiting factor' – which shapes or determines all other budgets. Often the limiting factor is sales, with the firm being unable to sell as much as it can produce. The production budget in this case would be based on what the marketing department believe they can sell.

The establishing of departmental objectives is considered to be one of the most important facets of the budgetary process. Managers are forced to sit back and systematically plan their operations for the next financial year. Co-ordination of effort is enhanced through the interdependence of departmental budgets. Moreover, the involvement of managers in the budget process not only establishes their responsibility for achieving the agreed objective but also provides the motivation.

Once departmental objectives are established and agreed the development of functional budgets can begin. In conjunction with the budget accountant – a senior accountant with the firm – departmental managers will draw up statements (or budgets) which quantify (in financial terms) the resources needed to attain the objectives.

Thus production objectives which were previously defined in terms of

- what to produce;
- how much to produce;
- when to produce.

will be broken down into monthly requirements for men, materials, and machines, and subsequently translated into the cost we expect to incur under each head. Similarly, sales cost budgets will detail, on a month-to-month basis, expenditure on advertising, market research, new product development, or administration.

At this stage responsibility for the budget process passes from the departmental managers to the budget accountant who develops the master budget for submission to the board of directors. Master budgets, which are based on information drawn from the functional budgets, are normally presented in the form of a profit and loss account and balance sheet. This has the advantage of showing the financial projections for the forthcoming year in a form familiar to the board and which facilitates comparison with the results of previous years. Should the budgeted results be deemed unacceptable the functional budgets will be referred back to the departmental managers for adjustment. This process will continue until the master budget is accepted by the directors.

Our focus must now turn from the creation of the budget to the budget as a means of control. The annual budget is divided into shorter control periods normally based on the calendar month or a period of a few weeks. Shortly after the end of each control period managers will receive a statement comparing actual results with budgeted figures.

Presentation of the information is important. Attempts should be made to highlight significant differences between actual and planned results (what constitutes a 'significant difference' will have been established previously – perhaps ±10 per cent from budget). A common method used is shown in Fig. 13.10. Alternatively, actual

Production Department

| | Period 3 | | | | Year to date | | | |
| | Budget | Actual | Variance | | Budget | Actual | Variance | |
Item	£	£	£	%	£	£	£	%
Labour	33,000	36,000	+ 3,000	9	99,000	95,000	– 4,000	4
Materials	50,000	45,000	– 5,000	10	155,000	140,000	– 15,000	10

Fig. 13.10 Extract from a budgetary control statement

costs may be shown as a percentage variation from budgeted costs on a graph (see Fig. 13.11). The dotted lines indicate percentage levels of variations which are considered significant and should be investigated.

However, while care must be taken with the presentation of budgetary information this does not guarantee effective control. Managers should be required by their superiors to investigate and report upon all significant variations from budget. The report to the superior will be in two parts. First an explanation of why the variances have occurred, and secondly what action is being taken regarding those variances over which the manager has some control. As a result of these investigations and reports departmental and organisational objectives may also be questioned, and if necessary revised.

Standard costing
Standard costing, like budgeting control, aims to provide a basis for the control of costs. However, where budgetary control creates targets for the various departments within the organisation, standard costing

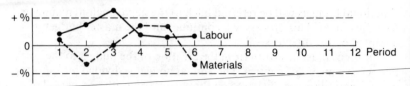

Fig. 13.11 The graphical presentation of budgetary variances

seeks to establish a check on each process or operation within an individual department. Standard costing is therefore a very much more detailed system of control.

To establish a system of standard costs an operation or process within a department will be broken down into its constituent parts. Each of these will be allocated a cost based upon certain clearly defined assumptions. For example, where materials are used the expected or standard cost for materials will be calculated by establishing:

- the amount of material used;
- any allowance for wastage;
- cost per unit of material.

In the same manner a standard labour cost will be based upon the (standard) time allowed for the job and wage rate for that class of labour. Standard costing thus establishes what the cost of an operation should be, rather than what it is expected to be.

As with budgetary control it is the comparison between actual and standard costs which forms the basis of control variances being investigated and where necessary acted upon.

Standard costing is widely used in industry, and because of its similarities with budgetary control is often incorporated into it.

Decision accounting

Break-even analysis
This is one of the most widely used decision-making techniques. Break-even analysis recognises that profit is a function of price, costs, and output. It allows managers to determine the effects of changes in these variables on overall profit.

Break-even analysis is based upon appreciating that costs may be either fixed or variable. Certain costs do not vary with the level of business activity. The rent and rates for the business premises have to be paid whether or not we actually produce anything. The same could also be said for debenture interest or management salaries. These costs are called 'fixed'. However, the point must be made that it is not true to say that fixed costs never alter. They will do, rents and rates will increase from year to year, and loan interest may be affected by changes in the interest rates, but they do not alter as a result of a change in the level of business activity.

Variable costs, on the other hand, are costs which change or vary with the level of the firm's activity. Thus if we increase output by 25 per cent we would expect exenditure on the raw materials, power, and labour involved in the production process to also increase by 25 per cent.

There are also some costs which do not fit neatly into either of the categories 'fixed' or 'variable'. In Britain, for example, telephone bills comprise a fixed element which has to be paid regardless of usage, but also a variable element based on the number (and length) of calls made. While it is possible to divide our telephone bill into its fixed and variable components by observation, this is not possible in many other cases. There are, however, simple statistical methods which may be used for this purpose.

The importance of the distinction between fixed and variable costs can best be seen through a simple example illustrating the impact of fixed costs on overall profitability and profit per unit (see Table 13.1). We note that as output increases unit cost decreases. The reason for this is that fixed costs are divided between units of production. When output is 500 units, each unit has to bear 1/500 of the fixed cost – that is, £8 per unit, but when we reach a production level of 1,500 units each unit bears only 1/1500 of that cost – £2.67 per unit. Variable cost per unit remains constant throughout this range of business activity at £6 per unit.

Table 13.1   Profitability at different levels of output

Units of output		500 costs £	1,000 costs £	1,500 costs £
Labour £3 per unit		1,500	3,000	4,500
Materials £2 per unit		1,000	2,000	3,000
Power £1 per unit		500	1,000	1,500
Total variable cost		3,000	4,000	9,000
Rent and rates	1,000			
Administration	2,000			
Loan interest	1,000			
Total fixed cost		4,000	4,000	4,000
Total cost		7,000	10,000	13,000
Revenue £15 per unit		7,500	15,000	22,500
Profit		500	5,000	9,500
Cost per unit		£14	£10	£8.67
Profit per unit		£1	£5	£6.33

Fixed and variable costs can easily be presented graphically, and when combined with information on sales revenue form the basis of what is known as the 'break-even chart' (see Fig. 13.12).

On the graph variable cost is shown as an upward-sloping line starting from the origin of the graph, since at zero activity variable costs will be nil. On top of the variable cost we have fixed costs giving us a line for total costs. The line for total cost lies above but parallel to the line for variable cost, reflecting the fact that fixed costs do not vary with output. To these two lines we may now add a third – sales revenue. Once again the line starts from the origin of the graph, for when sales are nil so is sales income; and afterwards rises proportionately to volume.

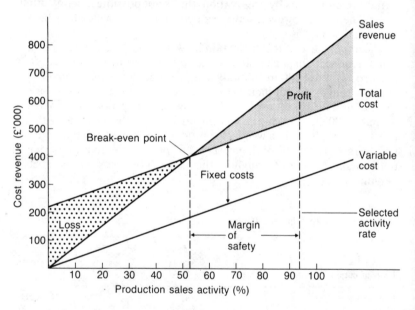

Fig. 13.12 The break-even chart

It is now possible to read off from the chart total costs and income for any level of activity. The break-even point on the chart indicates the level of activity where neither profits or losses are made, where total costs and total income are the same. The break-even point is of importance to the firm because it indicates the minimum level of production and sales needed to ensure the survival of the firm in the long run. While sales may occasionally drop below this level, and the firm survive, on balance the business must operate above this point. The margin of safety shows the amount by which sales would have to fall from the selected activity rate before we reach a loss-making situation.

The break-even chart can be used to answer the following types of question (which readers may try and answer for themselves):

- What is the profit or loss at activity levels of 30, 50, or 80 per cent?
- At what level of activity would we incur a loss of £100,000 or a profit of £200,000?
- What profit/loss do we make when sales revenue is £250,000, £350,000, or £450,000?
- What would be the effect on the break-even point and margin of safety if fixed costs were increased by £100,000?
- What would be the effect on the break-even point and margin of safety if sales prices were reduced by 10 per cent?

In short, break-even analysis is useful to management in making decisions relating to output levels, fixed/variable cost structure, or fixing selling prices.

Break-even analysis can be developed further into another decision-making tool for management termed 'marginal costing'. However, a consideration of this technique is outside the scope of this chapter.

Investment appraisal
Break-even analysis and marginal costing are short-term decision-making techniques. We now turn our attention to techniques suitable for the evaluation of long-term proposals. The importance of these decisions should not be underemphasised. First the supply of long-term funds available to the business is limited – acceptance of one project may mean the rejection of several others. Secondly, once funds have been committed to a project they cannot easily be withdrawn. The business has to live with and suffer the consequences of that decision – for better or worse!

The aim, therefore, of investment appraisal (or capital budgeting as it is sometimes called) is to ensure that funds are allocated correctly. The criterion which is normally used is profitability – the rate of return on capital employed in that project.

But not all projects can be assessed in strictly financial terms. New sports facilities and staff canteen are hard to justify financially – there is no obvious return on the investment. Yet many firms, believing that there is a definite, though unquantifiable, benefit in terms of employee motivation and loyalty to the business, continue to invest large sums in such projects. Similarly the erection of a new office block will show no obvious return in the profit and loss account. Yet improvements in administrative efficiency, and their effect on customer goodwill (in addition to the possible need to expand the administrative unit in future) may prove to be a very cogent argument for the building of the office block.

However, our concern here is with those projects which can be assessed by normal commercial criteria. There are many methods in investment appraisal used by business organisations. We will briefly consider three – pay-back, return on investment, and the present value method (discounted cash flow).

One of the most widely used methods of making investment decisions is the 'pay-back' method. This method does not take account of the overall profitability of the project but seeks to discover how long it is before the project pays for itself. The popularity of the pay-back method stems from two factors. First, most companies have limited financial resources, the shorter the pay-back period the sooner those funds can be reinvested in another project. Secondly, the shorter the pay-back period the shorter the risk to shareholders funds through, for example, unforeseen changes in the business environment.

Table 13.2 gives information on two potential investments, both requiring the same capital expenditure and having a similar life but with very different cash flows. On the basis of the pay-back period we would favour project A as it takes just three years to repay the initial investment compared with over four years on Project B.

Table 13.2   The comparison of two projects by means of the payback period

	Project A		**Project B**
Required investment	£20,000		£20,000
Estimated cash flow	£		£
Year 1	6,000		2,000
Year 2	6,000		5,000
Year 3	8,000	pay-back	6,000
Year 4	6,000	period	6,000
Year 5	2,000		10,000
Year 6	2,000		7,000
Estimated total cash flow	30,000		36,000

The major criticism of the pay-back period method of appraising projects is that it favours projects showing a quick return on capital and ignores those projects where the greatest return is made in later years. In project B profits do not reach their maximum until year 5, and should we consider the projects over their total life span the decision (to adopt project A) could very well be changed.

The return on investment method takes account of this criticism by comparing cash flow with investment. The average annual cash flow for projects A and B is £5,000 and £6,000 respectively. Assuming the investment has no residual value at the end of year 6, the average investment for both projects is £10,000. The return on investment is therefore:

$$\frac{\text{Average annual cash flow}}{\text{Average investment}} + 100$$

Project A:

$$\frac{5,000}{10,000} + 100 = 50 \text{ per cent}$$

Project B:

$$\frac{6,000}{10,000} + 100 = 60 \text{ per cent}$$

Our decision on changing the criteria would be to undertake project B rather than project A.

Return on investment has the advantage of emphasising the importance of profitability in any investment decision. Its drawback is that it fails to distinguish between the value of £1 of profits in each of the years of the project.

The present value, or discounted cash flow method of appraising capital projects has become increasingly popular over recent years. This stems from the fact that it encompasses the most important features of pay-back and return on investment, namely the timing of cash flows and overall profitability.

This method of evaluating projects is based on the fact that the timing of cash inflows affects their values. Consider which you would rather have, £1,000 today or in a year's time. The answer is £1,000 today because it is possible to invest it so that in a year's time it is worth considerably more than the initial £1,000. Using the same principle we can also answer the question, 'How much is next year's £1,000 worth today?' by calculating how much we should have to invest now to produce £1,000 in a year's time. For example, if we can invest the money at 10 per cent per annum we would need £909.10, while at 20 per cent per annum we would need £833.30. Put another way, we can say that the *present value* of £1,000 in a year's time is £909.10 when discounted at 10 per cent and £833.30 when discounted at 20 per cent.

In order to evaluate capital projects the principle of present values is extended so that we consider how much we have to invest now to yield a given sum in three, four, five, or more years from now. Let us see how this works in practice by considering our two projects, A and B again (Tables 13.2 and 13.3). The assumption made in comparing projects A and B is that money can be invested to earn a rate of interest of 10 per cent. The discount factor shows the amount which would have to be invested now at 10 per cent to yield £1 at the end of years 1 to 6. By multiplying the estimated cash flow for each year by the

Table 13.3 The comparison of two projects using discounted cash flow

	Project A			Project B		
	Cash flow (£)	Discount factor (10%)	Present value (£)	Cash flow (£)	Discount factor (10%)	Present value (£)
Year 1	6,000	0.9091	5,454.6	2,000	0.9091	1,818.2
Year 2	6,000	0.8264	4,958.4	5,000	0.8264	4,132.0
Year 3	8,000	0.7513	6,010.4	6,000	0.7513	4,507.8
Year 4	6,000	0.6830	4,098.0	6,000	0.6830	4,098.0
Year 5	2,000	0.6209	1,241.8	10,000	0.6209	6,209.0
Year 6	2,000	0.5645	1,129.0	7,000	0.5645	3,951.5
Total	30,000		22,892.2	36,000		24,716.5

appropriate discount factor we arrive at the present value of that cash flow. By converting all cash flows to present values and totalling the results we can see that the present value of project B is greater and should therefore be chosen.

By means of these and other techniques the accountant is able to provide management with information on which to base investment decisions. Yet the calculations made by the accountant are only as good as the information on which they are made. In estimating cash inflows and outflows the accountant is drawing upon the knowledge and expertise of many other members of the organisations. During this process many assumptions will have to be made regarding the firm's environment – the future level of economic activity, demand for products marketed, the degree of competition, changes in technology or products, and so forth. Assumptions will also be made on other factors internal to the firm, for example the expertise we have available, or the availability of men, materials, machinery and money. The accountant should therefore qualify his conclusions by drawing to the attention of management the quality of information on which the calculations are made.

Examination questions

1. Outline the work of the financial function within a medium-sized engineering company, explaining how it aids the overall efficiency of the business.

2. Explain the functions and responsibilities of financial management.

3. In what ways would either (a) the production department, or (b) the marketing department benefit from the services of the financial function.

4. Why do many firms employ management accountants? How does their role differ from traditional accountants? *(PSC 1976)*

5. What is budgetary control? How does it aid planning, co-ordination, and control within the organisation?

6. What are the objectives of each of the financial documents contained in the company's annual report?

7. Explain briefly the following terms: shareholders funds; working capital; net profit; auditing; gearing.

8. Select from accounting ratios which are commonly used in business, and explain their method of calculation and importance in the control of business operations.

9. Explain how *either* budgetary control *or* break-even analysis can be used by management.

Personnel

Chapter 14

The success of any organisation depends upon the efforts of its employees, employees who differ in their abilities, aspirations, and emotions. Employees, therefore, are more unpredictable and uncontrollable than any other input into the production process. The result is that special attention has to be paid to this particular input.

Personnel management, in so far as it deals with people within the organisation, is the responsibility of all managers and supervisors, yet many have little or no expertise in this area. The function therefore of the personnel department is to aid other managers and supervisors in their dealing with people, ensuring that most effective use is made of this valuable resource. The work of the personnel function is shown in Fig. 14.1. We will discuss each of these items in turn.

Manpower planning

Both the cost and difficulty of obtaining the right kind of labour have convinced management that labour is a resource for which careful planning is required. The function of manpower planning is to ensure that the organisation is not prevented from achieving its objectives because the correct mix of human resources is unavailable. The process involves considering our present manpower resources, our future requirements, and identifying those courses of action necessary to ensure that our future requirements are met. Figure 14.2 shows this process in detail, and makes the point that manpower planning is part of a wider plan – often termed 'corporate strategy' – involving the whole organisation and determining the organisation's long-term objectives.

In order to produce a strategy for an organisation it is necessary to consider:

1. *The environment in which the organisation operates.* The environment – economic, social, political, and technological – is constantly changing and provides threats and opportunities for any organisation. Some changes may have little effect upon the organisation, whereas others will have serious implications.

2. *The external position of the organisation* – its strengths and weaknesses, for example the ability to raise new finance, to develop new goods and services, or fight off competition. Out of this analysis will be developed a corporate strategy indicating what products are going to be made and what markets served, including the timing and sequence of major steps.

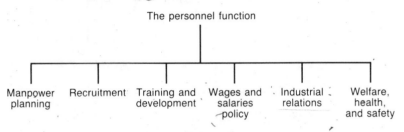

Fig. 14.1 Work undertaken within a typical personnel function

The organisation's future manpower requirements will stem directly from the corporate strategy. Discussions will take place with all departments to discover what their future manpower requirements will be, having regard to that corporate strategy. To avoid problems such as 'empire-building' such estimates should always by backed up by supporting evidence. It may also be possible to use other techniques to determine future requirements. For example if six salesmen generate £3 m. worth of sales revenue, a projected 50 per cent increase in sales revenue will require another three salesmen. However, such techniques should be used with care, economies of scale or diminishing returns may effect the relationship between salesmen and sales revenue. By these methods a picture of the organisation's future requirements in terms of employee numbers, qualifications, and experience is drawn up. This often termed the demand forecast.

The basis for the supply forecast – that is, the labour that will be available to meet the demand forecast is the current workforce. From personal statistical information held within the personnel department it is possible to predict for example:

- How many people will retire in the next few years.
- What percentage of new employees will remain with the firm.
- What percentage of other employees (by skill) will find other jobs.
- How many new managers and supervisors will we train.

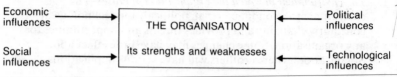

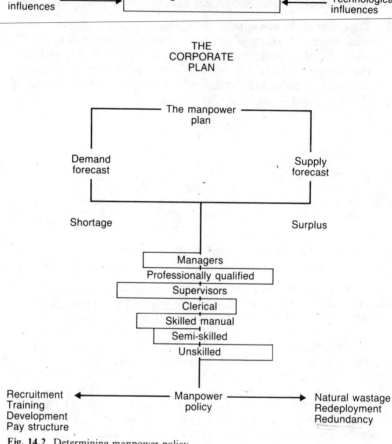

Fig. 14.2 Determining manpower policy

Projecting this information forward a number of years it is possible to make broad statements about the size of the workforce in different departments, their qualifications, and experience. These forecasts are of course very tentative – they assume past experience on labour movements is a reasonable method of predicting future changes in the workforce. More importantly the forecast also assumes that external forces do not change, yet the expansion or closure of other firms in the area (to give but one example) will very probably affect the supply forecast.

By comparing the supply and demand forecast for individual departments and skills within those departments it is possible to predict where the shortages and surpluses are likely to occur. The manpower plan is then drawn up so as to ensure that the predicted shortages and surpluses do not in fact occur, but that rather – through policies of recruitment, training, redeployment and redundancy – the manpower requirements of the organisation are met with the minimum of cost to the company and friction among employees.

Recruitment

Traditionally, recruitment lies at the heart of the personnel department's work. Except in extreme circumstances the organisation depends upon a continuous flow of new employees to replace those lost through death, retirement, resignation, or dismissal. Figure 14.3 illustrates the process by which a vacancy is filled. Once a vacancy has been notified to the personnel department the immediate task is to undertake what is termed job analysis in order to draw up two other documents, namely the job description and job specification.

Fig. 14.3 The recruitment process

Job analysis is the method by which all facts relating to a job are identified and recorded. With manual jobs the information will normally be obtained (if it is not already on file) by direct observation of the job. Where the task is more complex, techniques used may include an interview with the job-holder, the job-holder maintaining a diary of tasks undertaken in a given period or filling in a questionnaire. The information so obtained is then used to write up a job description outlining the content of the job. Items mentioned would include:

- *Basic details:* the title and grade of the job, the department concerned.
- *Job summary:* outlining the purpose of the job, identifying main tasks, secondary and occasional roles, the standards to be maintained. Information on the social and work environment.
- *Responsibilities:* clarifying the position in the organisation structure. Identifying subordinates for whom the job holder will be

responsible, and those to whom he himself will be responsible.
- *Conditions of employment:* salary, holidays, hours of work, pension schemes, welfare and social facilities, trade-union membership.
- *Training:* facilities for training to bring new employees up to standard. Attitude to/facilities for staff development.
- *Promotion:* opportunities for promotion, career structure within the organisation.

Once a comprehensive description for a job has been drawn up that information may be used in a number of ways. It may be adapted to form the basis of the recruitment advertisement, it may be used in wage and salary administration, measuring each job's level of difficulty and thereby deciding the salary to be paid. Job descriptions also tell us the skills, abilities, and knowledge we need to develop in training programmes. In the recruitment process job descriptions are used as the basis of the job specification. This identifies the qualities and qualifications of the person most likely to fill the job, and equally importantly fit into the organisation.

The format adopted for a job specification may vary widely. This reflects the specific requirements of different jobs. Thus in some occupations physical attributes may be important, while in others aptitudes for languages or dealing with people may be emphasised. Job specifications may also distinguish between what are considered to be essential and desirable features. Areas which are commonly covered include:

- *Physical:* age, health, and appearance.
- *Attainments:* academic education, professional qualifications, training.
- *Experience/Knowledge:* a general statement on the likely background of the successful candidate – the positions held, the knowledge gained.
- *Aptitudes:* mechanical, verbal, to work alone, ability to work under pressure, etc.
- *Domestic circumstances:* ability to move for the job, to spend time away from home, etc.

At the same time as the job analysis is being undertaken the personnel department is also considering how the vacancy should be filled. The two possibilities are to promote an existing employee or to bring in a new employee from outside.

Should the organisation have employees who have the necessary qualifications and experience there are distinct advantages from recruiting internally. Employees will be better motivated where the organisation has a policy of promotion from within. The fact that career paths exist within the organisation will tend to result in a lower labour turnover. A present employee is known to management and has proved himself in his present job. Promotion from within is quicker and cheaper. However, against these advantages should be set the fact that a new employee will bring with him different ideas and methods – 'the new broom' which may very well be beneficial to the organisation.

Where it is decided to recruit externally the sources normally considered will include:

1. Careers offices.

2. Private employment agencies for clerical and professional workers.

3. Professional bodies, employment registers.

4. Links with higher and further education institutions and schools.

5. National and local advertising.

The choice of the correct source is important because it is desired to attract as many potentially suitable candidates as possible.

Much of the advertisement itself can be drawn from the job description. Information on the job, its duties, qualifications, experience, salary, conditions of employment, and special requirements are all drawn from there. It remains to provide information on the organisation itself and the method of application.

While telephone applications may be asked for in unusual circumstances (perhaps the need for a replacement member of staff is urgent) the normal methods are letter of application or standard application form. A standard application form has the advantage that all candidates have to answer all the relevant questions, to a standard format which is convenient for comparison and administration. Letters of application, may, however, be used for senior positions because an application form does not provide sufficient room for all information

Once applications have been received the process of short-listing commences. Although critical to the selection process this task is sometimes entrusted to junior office staff! The filtering process is best conducted by reference to attributes identified in the job specification. Normally applicants are divided into three categories, suitable, not suitable, and marginal. It is with this last category that most care has to be taken. A rigid interpretation of the job specification may exclude one or more excellent candidates.

When the initial screening has finished unsuccessful candidates should be informed of the result as soon as possible. Candidates being called for interview should be sent interview details and their references taken up.

The final selection process seeks to establish, first will the candidate perform the job satisfactorily, and secondly whether he will fit into the organisation structure. The methods by which the candidate can be selected are numerous. Quite apart from the information contained in the application form and references there are a whole host of tests – aptitude, personality, and IQ being three of the more important ones

which may be used. Consideration of these tests is, however, outside
the scope of this book. We turn instead to the one common element in
all final selection processes – the interview.

It would be wise for the interviewers to prepare themselves for the
interview. The preparatory work which has to be undertaken includes
making oneself conversant with the candidate's background,
determining what questions should be put to each candidate, and in the
case of a panel of interviewers, who should put those questions. There
are several interview plans which seek to aid the interviewer; with all
plans, however, the real benefit lies in forcing the interview to prepare
himself prior to the inverview and systematically consider all points
raised in the job specification.

The interview itself will normally begin with a few opening remarks
and questions designed to put the candidates at their ease. Thereafter
questions put are designed to explain or amplify points made in the
application form. The role of the interviewer is to listen and evaluate.
Anything which prevents this – such as the interviewer talking too
much himself, or only half listening as he takes copious notes – may
result in a poor selection being made.

Care should be taken to see that questions asked are open-ended –
that is, cannot be answered merely by 'yes' or 'no'. The use of words
such as 'why', and 'how' often enables the interviewer to determine the
reasons behind the candidate's actions and his methods of overcoming
difficulties.

The interviewer will normally end with the candidate being asked
whether they still wish to be considered for the vacancy, and if they
have any questions they wish to ask. If selection is not being made
immediately after the interview has taken place, candidates should be
informed when they may expect to hear the result.

The necessity for a professional approach to recruitment and
selection cannot be overemphasised. The future of the organisation
depends upon the ability of managers, with the help of the personnel
department, to select the right candidates.

Wages and salaries policy

Wages and salaries are an important element in the total cost of many
organisations. Service industries including local government and the
Health Service can find that 75 per cent of their expenditure is on
labour. Wages and salary policy therefore has as its aim the attracting
and retaining of the right-quality staff at a cost that can be afforded by
the organisation.

It is customary to divide a consideration of this topic into two: first
remuneration for hourly paid workers, secondly remuneration for
clerical, professional, and managerial staff. However, the distinction

between the two groups has caused bad feeling in the past – best epitomised by 'them and us' attitudes of one group to another. For this reason and in an attempt to improve labour morale many progressive firms (encouraged by the Government) have given staff status and its associated benefits (pension schemes, better sickness and holiday arrangements) to all staff.

Wages and salary policy is intimately linked with motivation. The assumption of the earlier management writers, for example Taylor and Gilbreth, was that man was essentially passive, if not negative in his attitude to work. The results of this assumption were that his output could be increased by a properly designed system of incentive payments. Since that time other writers, for example Hertzberg and Maslow, have emphasised that money, although important in encouraging workers to greater effort, is only one factor in the 'motivation mix'. Other factors include:

1. *Security of employment* – many of the restrictive labour practices seen in British industry have their roots in the fear of unemployment.

2. *Comparative income* – the absolute level of income earned is often less important than how it compares with that received by workers in similar occupations. Consider how jealously wage differentials are guarded!

3. *Status* – where an occupation is valued highly by other workers, management, and society generally, entrants will be attracted even if financial rewards are not great.

4. *Group acceptance* – man is a 'social' animal working within a group, and being accepted by that group is highly important. Individuals may sublimate their own interests to obtain group acceptance.

The degree of job satisfaction is not only affected by the factors mentioned above, there are many others. For example the fact that the work is interesting and challenging, the knowledge that there are promotion opportunities and a sense of achievement. The recognition of these factors affecting motivation has led to a consideration of other techniques of motivating employees. The problem faced by employers is that because people's physiological and emotional make-ups differ the factors that motivate them also differ. Some employees will emphasise the need for social relations, others status, security of employment, and so on. Some will obviously emphasise the importance of money while the vast majority would place it high on the list. In the absence of other universal motivating factors money still remains the most obvious if not the most effective factor in the motivation mix.

But exactly how much money should we pay the secretary, the accountant, the production worker, or his supervisor? In practice the remuneration reflects both external and internal considerations. External considerations are those items affecting the level of remuneration which are outside the control of the organisation. For example a nationally negotiated wage settlement, the rates paid by competitors for similar skills, the level of unemployment in the area, or the employees' opportunities of obtaining another job. The primary internal consideration is to devise a system of payments which reflects the value of the job to the organisation. An important secondary consideration is to see that the wages/salary structure accords with the employees' views of fairness and justice. The method used is job evaluation.

For job evaluation to be undertaken information has to be available on the precise content of each job. In many cases such information is already available in the form of a job description – if not it is obtained in the manner described previously. The job description is then considered by a panel of trained evaluators who consider each element of the job in turn and allocate a numerical value to it according to its complexity. To help them in their task they may have available a senior member of staff from the department whose jobs are under consideration. Once evaluation has been completed the values of all the different elements are summed, and our secretary, accountant, production worker, or supervisor, and indeed all other workers will find themselves allocated into certain salary bands.

Although the numerical value on which the salary grading is based gives a semblance of objectivity, job evaluation is not a particularly scientific or objective way of calculating wages and salaries. Factors which are thought important and therefore emphasised by management may be entirely different to those considered important by the employee. Moreover, employees are apt to forget that it is the job and not themselves that are being evaluated. For these reasons it is important that trade unions or other worker representatives are involved throughout the process.

The personnel department not only has to consider what it is going to pay each worker, decisions also have to be taken on how to pay the worker. We will consider three major remuneration systems – flat rate, incentive, and measured day-work – in turn.

1. Flat-rate schemes. This provides for a basic wage to be paid where a previously agreed amount of time has been worked – hourly, daily, per week, or month. Beyond this period overtime, often at an enhanced rate, may be paid. Higher-paid salary workers may sometimes receive time off work instead of overtime pay. In its purest form flat rates are extremely easy to administer and result in a minimum of worker misunderstanding.

This system is often adopted where remuneration cannot be related to output, perhaps because the employee cannot control the pace of work (e.g. maintenance man, typists, telephonists) or maybe because of the unwelcome side-effects of payment by results schemes (consider the effect of paying policemen by results!). Flat-rate payments are said to be an act of trust on the part of the employer in that he expects a 'fair day's work for a fair day's pay'. However, in an effort to see that trust is not relied upon too much, supervisors, often with certain sanctions at their disposal, allocate and control the work of the employee.

Flat rates are often modified by an employer to provide some form of incentive for the employee – to work harder or to remain with the organisation. For manual workers bonuses may be awarded for good time-keeping and long service; similarly, salaried workers may benefit from merit awards (where the worker's effort is assessed as above average by the employer) or age/experience-related pay scales. All workers may benefit from other indirect incentives such as profit-sharing or issues of shares.

2. Incentive schemes.   Such schemes are also known as payment by results or piece-work (arising from the days when the worker received so much per piece or product produced). The logic behind these schemes is that workers should be rewarded for individual effort and that if incentives are high enough it will encourage them to work harder. Normally such schemes work by establishing an output norm (let us say 75 units of production per hour) for the average conscientious worker without extra financial incentive. Basic wages are set at this level and should the worker produce more than 75 units per hour then he is rewarded by bonus payments. If, say, he produces 100 units per hour his wage may be up to one-third higher than the basic wage. The advantage of incentive schemes are:

1. If well designed it will result in an increase in productivity.

2. The work study undertaken prior to the introduction of the incentive scheme may itself yield savings in the more efficient use of labour and equipment.

3. The more intensive use of plant and equipment results in a lower fixed cost per unit of output.

4. Supervision costs are reduced as the employee is more motivated to undertaking hard work.

The disadvantages associated with such schemes are:

1. Schemes are often complicated and easily misunderstood by workers.

2. They are often the cause of discontent among different groups of worker's because:

(a) workers may believe another base rate is easier to achieve than their own;

(b) indirect workers upon whom the direct production workers rely do not benefit from the incentive scheme;

(c) production workers may very well end up earning more than their supervisors and other salaried staff.

3. Unofficial agreements are often made by the men to restrict output regardless of the incentive so as to reduce the likelihood of unemployment, group disunity, and tighter rates.

4. Workers, over a period of time, will come to rely on the incentive as part of their basic earnings – even though the opportunity for earning the bonus may not always be available.

5. The worker may tend to disregard quality and his own safety in an effort to earn the incentive payment.

To overcome some of the criticisms of individual incentive schemes some organisations have introduced group incentives. Again the principle is that in establishing a base in which bonus payments are made the organisation and the workers can benefit from higher productivity. The group involved can be small or large, it may even cover the whole organisation. The bonus paid to the group may be split in proportion to basic pay, or alternatively, equally. Such schemes are advantageous because:

1. People naturally like working in groups.

2. It fosters a team spirit.

3. It includes indirect workers.

4. In their keenness to prevent bottlenecks and to achieve the incentive employees are more likely to adopt a flexible attitude to moving jobs.

Group incentive schemes do, however, also have problems. In particular the size of the group if too large may prevent the necessary team spirit developing, nor may the individual worker see how his efforts contribute towards the attaining of the bonus. The development of team spirit may also be hampered where labour turnover is high or where there are wide variations of ability within the group.

3. Measured day-work. This system seeks to bridge the gap between flat-rate and incentive schemes. The employer and employee agree a level of output, which the employee believes (and past experience shows) he can maintain. The employer agrees to pay the employee for this level of output regardless of short-term variations in productivity, while the employee is on trust to achieve the target agreed.

The advantages of measured day-work are:

1. Workers are able to predict and budget upon a stable wage.

2. The employer is able to predict productivity more accurately and therefore output and cost per unit.

3. As the employer is employing at the 'high rate' regardless of the level of output he will strive to reduce delays/breakdowns to a minimum, thus enhancing the efficiency of the production system.

Disadvantages of measured day-work are:

1. Differentials in wages are highlighted – which may cause industrial unrest.

2. How to control/discipline those who consistently fail to achieve their previously agreed target.

Education and training

Traditionally the attitude of the Government to education and training of workers has been that this was the responsibility of industry and commerce. While large firms have both the facilities and expertise to train their employees, the sole contribution of many small- and medium-sized organisations was to encourage the new worker to learn his job by watching the more experienced worker.

This haphazard nature of training was sufficient while the level and differentiation of skills was low, but during the twentieth century an increasing imbalance between the demand for trained labour and its supply has been noted. These bottlenecks in labour supply have prevented the UK industry from adopting new and improved technology, and expanding production in times of rising demand (thereby causing inflation and imports to flood into the country). It has also produced an élite of industrial workers who are able to demand extremely high wages, and resentment among those workers whose skilled jobs did not yield the same level of pay.

By the 1960s it had become apparent that government intervention was necessary and in 1964 Parliament passed the Industrial Training Act. This sought to ensure an adequate supply of properly trained manpower, an improvement in the quality and efficiency of training programmes, and the sharing of training costs between all firms in an industry through the auspices of Industrial Training Boards. Since 1964 the Government has played an important if changing role in industrial training. A summary of this role can be found under the work of the Department of Employment on p. 282.

While the interest of the Government in industrial training was on the effects of manpower shortages on the working of the economy, industry's interest arose because labour had become both scarce and expensive. Training had the primary objective of ensuring that employees had the skills and knowledge necessary to carry out their duties, to raise productivity, and to use new production techniques. Training also had the advantage that workers needed less supervision and provided the vehicle by which new supervisors and managers were developed. Improved quality of the finished product also reduced the number of the claims made by disappointed customers.

An effective system of training will cover the whole organisation from top to bottom. While inefficiencies in labour skills on the shop floor may be more obvious, the lack of necessary skills on the part of supervisors, clerical, executive, and managerial staff will have exactly the same adverse impact on the organisation. Moreover, there is no reason for assuming that there is a lesser need for training at these levels. The following approach to training (see Fig. 14.4) can be applied to any level of the organisation.

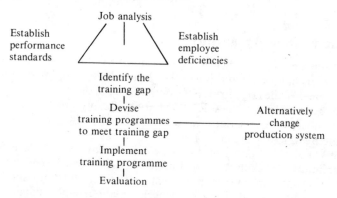

Fig. 14.4 Determining the training programme

Initial identification of a training need lies very much in the hands of departmental managers and supervisors who will inform the personnel department. Their first task is to establish that the need for training does actually exist. This falls naturally into two parts: first through job analysis identifying the performance requirements of that position (this may already be available having been prepared for recruitment and selection), and secondly establishing the existing skills, knowledge, and aptitudes and those which new employees bring to the job. The comparison of these two elements will then reveal the nature and extent of the training gap.

The presumption normally made, having identified the training gap, is that a training programme should be devised to remedy the deficiency. This may well be so, but does not automatically follow.

Thus redeployment of existing workers and recruitment of new employees with the right qualities could be considered. It is also open to the organisation to adapt the system (equipment and procedures) to suit the worker. Which of these methods is adopted will depend upon cost and feasibility.

The organisation may, having considered the options, decide to embark upon a training programme. The first stage in designing the training programme will be to identify precisely those skills and aptitudes that need to be developed. Decisions must also be taken on whom to train and whether that training is best conducted on or off the job. The training scheme is then drawn up and implemented. Finally the success of the training programme has to be evaluated. This may be done by checking to see whether the required performance standards are now being achieved. Alternatively the benefits accruing from the training in terms of higher performance standards may be compared with the cost of providing that training. If the benefits outweigh the costs the training programme has been to the advantage of the organisation.

Forms of training

Induction
The cost of recruitment is high and research shows that a high proportion of new employees leave within six months of joining the organisation. The reason for this high turnover is thought to be the difficulty the new entrant (especially the school-leaver) faces in understanding and adapting to the organisation, and more specifically his job within the organisation.

Most entrants will know little about the organisation which they have joined – it is all new (and very confusing). Induction training therefore tries to provide some of the background information, for example the company's history, its objectives, the organisation structure, the products made, and the markets supplied. Tours of the factory and offices may highlight the points made.

Information on the job to be undertaken clearly begins with a tour of the department and introduction to those members with whom the new employee will have to work or to whom he is responsible. It is also worth while explaining the work of the department and how the employee's efforts contribute to this. Departmental rules will also be explained. With manual jobs induction will also cover familiarisation with any machinery which has to be used.

Obviously the amount of information which the new employee has to absorb is vast. Indeed, trying to tell the employee everything about the organisation may have precisely the opposite effect to that intended. The secret of successful induction training lies in identifying what is essential for the employee to know and presenting it to him in a way he can understand.

Apprentice

Traditionally, apprentices have picked up their skills in a haphazard fashion through watching the time-served craftsman. There was little attempt at systematic training. In most trades now, though, the situation has changed, with a blend of academic and practical training designed to ensure that skills are learned. Systematic training has also had the effect of reducing the length of the apprenticeship in many cases.

Operative

Training of operatives is usually carried out by the organisation itself. In small organisations the training will normally be 'on the job', that is, undertaken in the normal work situation using the everyday tools and equipment. Such training is less costly than 'off the job'; it has the advantage of the worker becoming familiar with both the environment and the tools he will normally use. Large firms often have training centres away from the place of normal work. The training conducted in these centres is termed 'off the job' – as would training in a technical or higher education institution. It has the advantage of using specialist instructors, training in correct methods, away from the noise and pressure of the work environment.

Supervisor

All too often the person appointed supervisor has the necessary technical skills, but has not developed the interpersonal skills needed to motivate and control subordinates, and additionally to deal with senior management. Before undertaking any form of training though, it is important to identify their training needs in an attempt to adapt training to their particular requirements. Larger firms may very well run courses internally. However, the majority of firms are content to leave this training to the local technical or higher education institution where the supervisors can study for the National Examination Board's Certificate in Supervisory Studies.

Management development

This will normally be provided by means of courses run in the management departments of polytechnics and colleges of technology. There are many courses run, all of which lead to widely recognised qualifications. In some cases though a lack of discussion between the college, student, and employer results in courses being studied which meet neither the needs of the student nor his employer. Once more an analysis of training needs is vital to the success of the training programme.

As much of the training carried out within the organisation is 'on the job' and therefore under the control of the individual manager, it is difficult to divorce that line manager from some responsibility for training within his own department. However, the ultimate responsibility for training within the organisation rests with the personal department. Larger firms often appoint a training officer or manager having special responsibility for all aspects of training within the organisation. His duties would normally include:

1. Developing in conjunction with senior management an agreed training policy.

2. Consulting with all departments within the organisation and advising on training needs.

3. Developing and implementing in-company training programmes.

4. Liaising with colleges and polytechnics in the development of training programmes.

5. Advising on external courses available at colleges and polytechnics.

6. Maintaining training records.

Industrial relations

There are many potential sources of conflict between a worker and his employer, for example the worker wishes to sell his labour at the highest price possible while the employer wishes to engage labour at the least possible cost to himself. Other sources of conflict include the relativities that exist between different groups of workers, which groups of workers should be allowed to undertake certain duties, the nature of the work itself, the working conditions, and more generally, how much control workers should have over decisions which affect their working lives.

Yet at the same time both parties appreciate that it is in their common interest to work together in harmony. Without labour business cannot provide the products or services on which it relies for survival, and labour relies on business to provide employment and thereby the means to satisfy their demands for goods and services. Industrial relations is concerned with the way these two parties interact. More importantly it is concerned with the means by which disputes are avoided or overcome.

The parties to the industrial relations process are described below.

Trade unions

The Trade Unions and Labour Relations Act of 1974 defines a trade union as an 'organisation of workers whose principal purposes is the regulation of relations between workers and employers or employers associations'. There are over 400 trade unions representing in excess of 10 million working people in the UK. Traditionally, union members have held manual occupations; however, we have recently seen the rise of professional (or 'white-collar') unions as these groups too have seen the benefits of organised labour, as itemised below.

1. Improvements in remuneration, working conditions and status.

2. Protection against unfair practices and arbitrary management decisions.

3. Security of employment.

4. Involvement in the decision-making process at organisational and national levels.

5. The ability to take joint action.

More often than not the attitude of management to trade unions has been hostile. Management has seen trade unions as challenging and circumscribing its right to manage. Yet there are benefits which the organisation itself obtains from the organisation of labour. For example where management actions are likely to be questioned and have to be justified, decisions are taken more carefully. In particular, management is forced to consider the effect of its actions upon the workforce and its motivation. Moreover the trade union is the means by which information can be passed to the workforce, changes in wages and working conditions may be negotiated, and disputes settled. Trade unions tend to be classified in four ways, though the classification does tend to be somewhat arbitrary with few unions precisely fitting their classification.

Craft unions

These unions have as the basis for classification a common skill which may be used in many industries. Thus the Amalgamated Union of Engineering Workers (AUEW) seeks to represent all engineering workers wherever they are employed and whatever their engineering skills. Many of the craft unions have their origins among the medieval trade guilds, but most have changed considerably by either amalgamating with related crafts, or accepting workers with lower levels of skills. Consider again the case of the AUEW which started life as the Amalgamated Society of Engineers but now includes among its membership foundry and construction workers, draughtsmen, and labourers. Such unions tend to border upon our second category, that of industrial unions, and thereby provide a sharp reminder of the difficulties of classification!

Industrial unions

Industrial unions seek to recruit members within a specific industry whatever their grade or occupation. The National Union of

Mineworkers (NUM) and National Union of Railwaymen (NUR) are
normally cited as examples. Neither have been completely successful in
their aims. For example the National Association of Colliery Overmen,
Deputies, and Shot Firers (NACODS) and the Associated Society of
Locomotive Engineers and Firemen (ASLEF) recruit substantial
numbers in their respective industries. Although this form of union is
not popular in Britain many unions in the United States and West
Germany are organised in this way.

Occupational unions

As is implied by their name occupational unions, are those who seek to
recruit members who have a similar occupation often, but not always,
in the same industry. The National Association of Local Government
Officers (NALGO), for example, has members not only in local
authorities but also in the nationalised industries, and the health and
water services. The National Union of Teachers (NUT), the Union of
Shop, Distributive and Allied Workers (USDAW), and the National
Union of Public Employees (NUPE) are also often cited as examples of
occupational unions.

Most white-collar unions can be included in this classification. A
white-collar union can be defined as a union with its members working
in clerical, professional, or administrative occupations. While trade-
union membership generally has been declining in the last decade the
growth of white-collar unionism has been dramatic. White-collar
workers now account for approximately half of all union members.
There are several reasons for this growth. Previously white-collar
workers had believed themselves to be immune from the effects of a
recession. Recent attempts to cut back public expenditure in the UK
have increased the feeling of insecurity among these groups. White-
collar workers have also felt that their financial position has been
eroded compared to other groups of workers. They have looked to
unionisation and the growth of collective bargaining to remedy the
situation. With the growth of large and often impersonal organisations
white-collar workers have experienced a loss of status and control over
their working conditions. Through representation they seek once more
to be involved in that decision-making process.

General unions

These unions seek to unionise all other groups of workers which are
not covered by the above categories. Traditionally, these unions are
associated with unskilled workers in industries where other groups of
workers are already unionised, or those industries which either because
of recruitment difficulties or newness have no history of unionisation.
However, unions such as the Transport and General Workers Union
now organise both skilled and unskilled labour.

The Trades Union Congress

The TUC was formed in Manchester in 1868 with the aim of representing the interests of trade unions and their members. Today all major unions are affiliated to it and it can claim to represent over 10 million workers. It is an extremely powerful organisation. In the period 1971–74 it organised and led the very effective opposition to the Industrial Relations Act – opposition which was partly responsible for the fall of the Heath Government.

The TUC also enjoys considerable power through its relationship with the Government of the day. It is consulted on major issues, not only those relating to trade unions or industrial relations. For example the TUC makes representations to the Prime Minister or the Chancellor of the Exchequer each year prior to the budget. Members of the TUC also serve on most government committees or commissions.

A major function of the TUC is to represent the interests of its 10 million members. At its annual conference in September many resolutions are passed and these together form the economic and social policy promoted by the TUC General Council between congresses.

Other aims of the TUC include:

1. To give aid and assistance to workers in other parts of the world in their attempt to raise living standards.

2. To give aid and assistance to other organisations with similar objectives to themselves (e.g. the Labour Party or unions in other countries).

3. To help in settling disputes between (a) trade unions and employers (b) trade unions and their members; (c) trade unions themselves.

While the aims of the TUC are remarkably wide its power over the affiliated unions is limited. Each remains completely sovereign and implements or conforms to TUC resolutions as it thinks fit.

In very exceptional circumstances the General Council may exclude a union from membership of the TUC, but this power is rarely used.

Employers' associations

The national federations have a number of functions in the industrial relations sphere, they:

1. Ensure collective action on the part of their members with trade unions.

2. Negotiate with trade unions at a national level making: (a) procedural arrangements – e.g. the procedure for negotiating a

wage change or settling a dispute; and (b) substantive agreements on wages, working conditions, holidays, etc.

3. Provide information on industrial relations to their members.

However, the Donovan Commission on Trade Unions and Employers' Associations indicated that their functions were considerably wider. Some of the other more important functions identified were:

1. Provision of trade and technical information to members.

2. Representing and negotiating with Government and other bodies on behalf of their members.

3. Advice on and development of training schemes.

4. Provision of management consultancy services.

The concerted action of workers through trade unions brought a response from business in the form of employer associations, the employers' counterpart to the TUC being the Confederation of British Industry (CBI). Its objects are:

1. To represent industry's views and influence opinion on economic, political, social, and technical matters.

2. To encourage efficiency in British industry – where necessary providing services to that end.

However, unlike the TUC (and the CBI's counterparts in other countries) it has no specific function in the field of industrial relations – other than to draw up a general manpower policy to be put in effect by its members.

Towards better industrial relations

Although the popular press always equates a strike with poor industrial relations this is only the tip of the iceberg. A breakdown in industrial relations can manifest itself in far less dramatic (but no less costly or serious) ways by 'working to rule', refusing to co-operate with management, or even absenteeism and labour turnover.

The Trade Union and Labour Relations Act 1974 lays down a code of practice for maintaining good industrial relations. The code lays the primary responsibilities for good industrial relations on management. This involves establishing a policy for industrial relations covering:

1. The relationship between the organisation and trade unions. For example the organisation's attitude to unionisation, or what unions the organisation will recognise for bargaining purposes.

2. The establishment of collective bargaining and dispute-handling procedures.

3. The establishment of procedures for communication and consultation with the workforce including employee representation.

A consideration of point (1), that is, the relationship between the organisation and the trade union, is outside the scope of this book. Let us give our attention instead to the institutions designed to maintain and better industrial relations.

Collective bargaining

The fact that approximately three-quarters of the workers in the UK have their wages and working conditions established by some form of joint negotiation illustrates the importance of collective bargaining. Collective bargaining can be defined as the process by which workers through their trade union representatives negotiate changes in pay and working conditions with their employer or his representative.

The argument entered into by the parties falls broadly into two parts. Procedural clauses cover the methods by which the parties conduct their relationship. They will cover:

1. The composition and character of the negotiating body.

2. The matters which can be considered by the negotiating body.

3. The means by which:

   (a) bargaining is carried out;

   (b) disputes are settled;

   (c) information is passed to trade union members or their representatives.

Substantive clauses refer to the terms of employment established through the bargaining procedures outlined above. The items detailed below are by no means a complete list but are used to illustrate the scope of the substantive negotiations:

- Wages/salaries, incentive payments, overtime pay.
- Working hours, shift working, place of work.
- Holidays, layoff and redundancy provisions, pensions.

The precise nature of the agreement covering each industry, firm, or group of workers will have evolved over a number of years. Normally the agreement is reviewed annually, but it is unlikely that the parties will wish to renegotiate the whole agreement. In practice the annual negotiations will revolve around remuneration, working hours, and holidays with other clauses being negotiated as and when the parties feel necessary. Moreover the freedom of the parties to negotiate may be curtailed by legislation. Thus for most of the period between 1964 and 1979 free collective bargaining over wages was limited by government-backed policies of pay restraint.

Within the UK collective bargaining takes place at two different levels. First as a product of the inter-war years, we have a system of bargaining and negotiating procedure at national levels. At the time such national agreements were beneficial to both parties, providing workers with minimum wages and working conditions and the advantage of protecting employers from price competition arising out of other employers paying lower wages.

While the system of national agreements continued after 1945, the advent of full employment created a situation where employers found difficulty in obtaining the labour they needed. The national agreement over wages and conditions of work rapidly became a minimum which could be improved upon by employees and their representatives in bargaining at a local level. Today many groups of workers still have their terms of employment determined nationally; however, in both the manufacturing and engineering industry local bargaining is now more important.

Not all workers have terms of employment determined by collective bargaining. Over 2.7 million workers are in fact covered by Wages Councils. These statutory bodies exist because the growth of unionism has been insufficient to protect the interests of the workers. Wages councils exist in the hairdressing, catering, and retail sectors where: (a) the large numbers working in small independent establishments; and (b) the large proportion of women (who tend to be more apathetic towards trade unionism) make unionism difficult to establish.

Wages Councils consist of equal numbers of worker and employer representatives together with three independent members (one of whom is elected chairperson). The proposals of the Wages Council on wages and all other conditions of employment become the subject of a wages regulation order and thereafter are the minimum which may be applied in that industry. To ensure that the new terms of employment are enforced in all establishments affected by the order employers are required to display the proposals so workers may read them. Additionally the Wages Inspectorate has the power to check on any firm's records and may prosecute where the proposals have not been effected.

Under the Employment Protection Act (1975) a procedure exists whereby a statutory determination of terms of employment may be phased out in favour of free collective bargaining. Initially a Joint Industrial Council is formed in place of the Wages Council. The structure and the function of the Joint Industrial Council is precisely the same as that of the Wages Council with one exception – there are no independent members. Once the Secretary of State for Employment believes that free collective bargaining is working properly he may then abolish the Joint Industrial Council.

Joint consultation

Often termed 'worker participation in management', this idea of consulting workers and allowing them to participate in the decision-making process within the firm is not new. It dates back to the Whitley Committee of 1916 which suggested that, quite apart from the negotiating arrangements which should be established at a national level, works councils or joint production committees should be created. These would provide a platform for the discussion of those many other issues which are of common interest to the employee and employer alike. Today joint consultation is said to provide a two-way communication channel allowing:

1. Management to inform employees of the firm's progress, plans, and policy.

2. Workers to have a say in the decisions that affect them.

3. Suggestions to be made by workers for increasing productivity.

4. The development of a greater degree of understanding between the two parties.

The degree of consultation which takes place will vary enormously between countries and organisations. Thus in West Germany the law requires that:

1. Every company with over five employees to have a works council set up to resolve disputes within the firm.

2. Every company with over 100 employees to have an economic committee which meets to discuss any matters which may adversely affect worker interests, for example, mergers, changes in production, technology, or company structure. Work's councils have the responsibility of resolving conflicts occurring in the economic committee.

3. Where a company employs over 2,000 workers board-level representation for workers is provided for by the creation of a two-tier board. An upper supervisory board comprises of worker and shareholder representatives (five each) and an independent member agreed by both. The lower board is made of management representatives.

In Britain consultation is by no means so far advanced. Experiments with worker directors have been tried – for example on the group boards of the British Steel Corporation. Moreover, worker co-operatives illustrate a very complete form of worker participation in management. But when the Bullock Committee of Enquiry on Industrial Democracy (1978) proposed a system of board representation for workers very similar to that in West Germany, the adverse reaction from both management and unions resulted in the proposals being quietly shelved by the Government.

More success has been achieved in Britain through 'semi-autonomous work groups' which allow a large element of discretion and employee responsibility on items such as:

- Allocation of tasks between group members.
- Ordering of materials.
- Supervision.
- Quality control.

Those who support joint consultation argue that:

1. It makes greater use of the large body of knowledge and skills existing among the organisation's workers.

2. The more people involved in the decision-making process the better the decision.

3. It generates greater worker interest in the organisation.

4. It improves industrial relations.

5. It is morally right that workers should be involved because they have contributed to the prosperity of the organisation and, moreover, it is their livelihood.

Joint consultation has its fair share of problems. There are for example many management decisions where the employee will have little or nothing to contribute. Joint consultation is time-consuming (some would even say time-wasting). Many employees show little interest in participating, while trade-unionists are worried that their bargaining position with the organisation may be eroded by non-union representatives negotiating matters which they believe to be the proper subject of collective bargaining.

The role of the State in industrial relations

Traditionally the State has played a passive role in industrial relations, believing that free collective bargaining is the best means to settle disputes. Increasingly though, the Government has seen fit to intervene by:

1. Legislation to protect certain groups of people – handicapped, women, ethnic minorities, low paid.

2. Legislation providing ground rules for the conduct of industrial relations – often restrictive upon trade-union activity.

3. Providing institutions to arbitrate between the conflicting interests where the dispute becomes intractable:

(a) The Advisory Conciliation and Arbitration Service (ACAS), which is an independent but state-financed service. There are three aspects to its work: (i) conciliation – bringing the disputants together; (ii) mediation – providing grounds for settlement; (iii) arbitration – help in providing an independent mediator to settle the dispute.

(b) The Central Arbitration Committee set up under the Employment Protection Act (1975). It deals with trade-union recognition problems, disclosure of information to trade unions for bargaining purposes, equal pay, and references on arbitration from ACAS.

(c) Industrial tribunals. These deal with a majority of cases arising out of employment legislation. The cases relate to unfair dismissal, discrimination, equal pay, safety. Although the decisions of the tribunals are legally binding, unlike a normal court their proceedings are less formal and legal representation is not required.

Welfare, health, and safety

Dangers are bound to exist in an industrial environment and each year many workers are either killed or maimed in accidents at work. Today greater emphasis than ever before is being placed on an employee's health and safety in an attempt to reduce these injuries. A majority of workers in the UK are covered by either the Factories Act (1961) or the Offices, Shops, and Railway Premises Act (1963). These Acts lay down for the workers covered:

1. Minimum working conditions, e.g. lighting, heating, ventilation, sanitation, and overcrowding.

2. Safety requirements, e.g. the guarding of machinery with moving parts, maximum loads for lifting machinery, fire precautions.

3. Welfare provisions, e.g. washing and cloakroom facilities, first-aid facilities.

4. Women and young persons (under 18), e.g. limitations on night and shift work, overtime and maximum hours worked.

The Health and Safety at Work Act (1974) further provides that:

1. The organisation must have a written safety policy indicating not only what that policy is but how it is to be implemented, e.g. training and supervision on health and safety matters.

2. Employers must not charge for safety equipment or clothing.

3. Safety representatives forming a committee are to be appointed by trade unions. They are entitled to demand information on accidents, to inspect new premises, and make recommendations to the employer on safety matters.

Legislation relating to health and safety is enforced by the Employment Medical Advisory Service and the Factory Inspectorate who are entitled to enter and inspect any premises. Where breaches occur an inspector is entitled to issue an Improvement or Prohibition Notice. An Improvement Notice requires the offending organisation to remedy the situation within a given time. Alternatively, where the inspector believes the breach imposes a continuous danger upon employees and may result in injury a Prohibition Notice forbidding that activity (until the breach is remedied) may be issued.

Sanctions may also be imposed on persons responsible for the breach of Health and Safety Regulations. Crown Courts may fine such persons up to £1,000 in addition to a maximum of two years' imprisonment.

Breaches of Health and Safety Regulations, however, have far wider consequences than outlined above. Industrial injuries may result in the dislocation of work schedules, legal claims for compensation, and bad publicity. For these reasons many firms employ a specialist safety officer within the personnel department. His duties will encompass:

1. Inspecting all parts of the organisation to ensure that all health, safety, and welfare requirements are complied with.

2. Ensuring that all employees are well versed in safety procedures through lectures, training, and advertisements.

3. Responsibility for advising on the health and safety aspects of office and factory layout, new machinery, and new working methods.

4. Maintaining records of all accidents within the organisation, investigating their cause and taking preventive measures.

5. Liaising with the Health and Safety Inspectorate, fire service, etc. to minimise the likelihood of accidents and/or their severity.

Examination questions

1. You are responsible for appointing a replacement for your company's chief accountant who retires in six months' time. Outline the procedures you would follow until an offer is made to the successful candidate.

2. Put forward the arguments for promoting within or recruiting outside. *(PSC 1973)*

3. In what ways can the personnel department be particularly useful in the marketing department?

4. Outline the work of a personnel department. Answer with particular reference to the creation of personnel policy. *(PSC 1978)*

5. How far is it true to say the role of the personnel function is to maintain good industrial relations?

6. What are the major points to be considered in formulating a manpower plan?

7. Discuss the relative merits and demerits of two different wages and salary payment schemes with reference to workers, management, and the performance of tasks.

8. The best way to encourage employees to work harder is to pay them more. Discuss.

9. Outline the importance of education and training to industry and commerce.

10. Name and describe four types of trade union giving examples of each. What is the role of the TUC?

11. What are the functions of a trade union? How do they attempt to fulfil these functions?

12. Outline the structure of the trade union movement in your own country. What is the role in relation to wage bargaining? *(PSC 1979)*

13. Outline the role of collective bargaining and joint consultation in maintaining good industrial relations.

14. The terms: job satisfaction, job evaluation, job analysis, and job specification are all used in personnel work. Explain the meaning of each term and its importance to the organisation.

Services to business

Part IV

The role of the State

Chapter 15

The twentieth century has seen a dramatic expansion in the role of the State in Britain. Throughout the nineteenth century the doctrine of *laissez-faire* with its emphasis on individualism and self-help served to limit the extent to which the Government intervened in the workings of the economy. Certainly, the Government provided a stable framework for industry and commerce through the provision of non-commercial services such as law and order, defence, and foreign relations, but little more.

Today the State is involved in almost every aspect of our lives, and the distinction between business and government has become increasingly blurred. In part this involvement has arisen through the Government's desire to achieve certain macro-economic objectives such as stable prices, a high level of employment, economic growth, and a satisfactory balance of payments. But governments have also come under increasing pressure from the electorate, firstly to develop and expand social services thus providing a 'safety net' for the less fortunate members of society, and secondly to prevent the abuse of power and position by large business units.

The Government

Her Majesty's Government comprises those ministers who are responsible for the administration of national affairs.

The Prime Minister is appointed by the Monarch, as are all other ministers, though in the latter cases the appointments are made upon the recommendation of the Prime Minister.

The majority of ministers, and in particular senior ministers, are drawn from the House of Commons. Yet the Government must also be adequately represented in the House of Lords to defend and justify its actions there. The Lord Chancellor is always a member of the House of

Lords while in recent years the position of Foreign Secretary has also been held by a peer (Lord Carrington).

The term 'Prime Minister', meaning head of the Government was first used during the eighteenth century. The power of the Prime Minister stems from being able to command the support of a majority of the members sitting in the House of Commons, and the ability to appoint and dismiss departmental ministers. The Prime Minister is also First Lord of the Treasury, but leaves day-to-day running of the department to the Chancellor of the Exchequer. By convention the Prime Minister will sit in the House of Commons.

Parliament

Parliament is the supreme legislative authority in the UK and comprises three elements – the Monarch, the House of Lords and the House of Commons. The House of Lords consists of Lords Spiritual, that is, the Archbishops of Canterbury and York, together with twenty-four senior bishops of the Church of England, and Lords Temporal. The Lords Temporal comprise hereditary and life peers and the Lords of Appeal (Law Lords) who assist the House in its judicial duties.

The House of Commons consists of elected representatives, commonly termed Members of Parliament (MPs). General elections are held periodically, at least every five years, to determine who should represent each constituency. Each elector (broadly any adult over the age of 18) is given one vote which he may cast for the person (or party) of his choice. Electors are not forced to vote, but past experience suggests approximately 75 per cent will, in fact, do so. Candidates for election are normally drawn from one of the major political parties, and although they are not formally recognised in law the majority of successful candidates will be members of one of these parties. The leader of the party which wins the most seats or has the support of a majority of the members in the House of Commons will traditionally be appointed Prime Minister, and form the Government of the day. Approximately 100 members of the ruling party, drawn from both Houses, will receive ministerial appointments. However, real political power is vested in the lower house – the House of Commons.

Although the House of Lords and the House of Commons are constituted on very different principles, as constituent parts of Parliament their functions are the same. First, to pass laws. Draft laws (or bills as they are commonly called) must be passed – that is, agreed to – by each House. In practice, the right of the Lords to reject bills passed by the House of Commons is limited to approximately thirteen months.

Parliament must also authorise the collection of taxes – the means by which the Government carries out its policies. The power of the House of Lords to delay a tax bill is, of necessity, limited to one month.

Finally, Parliament exercises a measure of control over the

Government by scrutinising government policy and its administration. By means of parliamentary debates, question time, or references to the Parliamentary Commissioner (Ombudsman) the Government has to explain and justify its actions to Parliament and thereby indirectly the electorate.

As head of the Government the Prime Minister has many responsibilities. These include informing the Monarch of government business, representing the Government in the Commons and the UK internationally. The Prime Minister also presides over the Cabinet, exercises general supervision over all government departments, and acts as mediator where interdepartmental disputes occur.

Ministers responsible for government departments are known as secretary of state, minister, or may have some special title such as Chancellor of the Exchequer. The majority of these post-holders will be members of the Cabinet. There are also some ministers who have the status of departmental ministers yet have no department. For example the traditional offices of Lord President of the Council, Lord Privy Seal, and Chancellor of the Duchy of Lancaster have few departmental duties and are therefore available for any special tasks which the Prime Minister may see fit to give them. Thus at the present time the Lord President of the Council has responsibility for the administration of the Civil Service Department.

Departmental ministers are aided in the discharge of their duties by junior ministers – referred to as parliamentary under-secretary of state or alternatively, where their senior is not a secretary of state, as parliamentary secretary. Junior ministers may be given responsibilitity for specific aspects of their department's work, or otherwise aid the senior minister by taking part in debates, answering parliamentary questions, and relieving him of some of the routine work associated with his office.

The origins of the Cabinet stretch back into the seventeenth century when the Sovereign would seek the advice of trusted senior ministers outside the formal meetings of the Privy Council. Although the central role of the Monarch in politics was curtailed in the eighteenth and nineteenth centuries the practice of the Head of Government – now the Prime Minister – of taking the advice of senior colleagues continued. Today senior ministers, whether or not they hold departmental responsibility, may be selected by the Prime Minister to become a member of the Cabinet.

The functions of the Cabinet now are to determine policy, to control the Government (of which it is itself a part), and to co-ordinate the activities of government departments.

The Privy Council

Until the eighteenth century the Monarch held real power of government. The Privy Council was made up of men personally chosen by the King and on whom he felt he could rely for sound advice and faithful service. Together, the Sovereign in Council with his advisers, that is, the Privy Council, was the most important source of executive power in the State.

Gradually, as the political power of the King diminished the importance of the Privy Council declined. Many of its powers were assumed by the Cabinet and its activities taken over by government departments. The Privy Council's position today is largely formal.

There are between 300 and 350 members of the Privy Council at any one time. They are appointed for life and have the privilege of being able to add PC after their names. Members fall into one of two broad groups. Firstly all members of the current Cabinet will be sworn to the Council when first assuming office, and since Privy Councillors are appointed for life it follows that all former cabinet ministers will retain their membership of the Privy Council. Secondly, the Queen on the recommendation of the Prime Minister may appoint others, primarily as an honour for service in some branch of public affairs. Included in this category will be members of the Royal Family, the Church, the Judiciary, the Diplomatic Service, together with important citizens of the Commonwealth (e.g. the President or Prime Minister of some Commonwealth country).

The whole Privy Council meets only upon the death of the Sovereign or when the Sovereign announces his or her intention to marry. In practice the work of the Privy Council is conducted by a handful of members (three constitute a quorum) normally presided over by the Monarch. These members are responsible for advising the Sovereign to approve Orders in Council and issue royal proclamations (the most important constitutionally being the summoning or dissolving of Parliament).

The Privy Council has a number of other functions which are carried out by means of committees independent of the Sovereign in Council. Committees of the Privy Council will for example hear appeals from medical disciplinary tribunals, ecclesiastical courts, and a small number of Commonwealth courts.

During parliamentary sittings the Cabinet will meet for several hours once or twice a week. Its meetings are private and the discussions confidential. Members of the Cabinet are required by their oaths as Privy Councillors not to reveal its proceedings – though this has not prevented several ministers publishing diaries giving an unofficial account of the Cabinet's deliberations. Records of Cabinet proceedings, and other state papers only become available to members of the general public some thirty years after the event.

To economise on the use of Cabinet time only the most important issues are discussed in detail and most work is dealt with through a committee system. There are, at the present time, four standing committees – home and social affairs, defence, overseas policy, and economic strategy. Other committees may be created to deal with issues as they arise and will comprise of the ministers primarily concerned (they need not necessarily be members of the Cabinet). These committees consider items in detail and make reports to the Cabinet including recommendations for action.

In taking office all government ministers accept 'ministerial responsibility'. By this we mean that firstly, ministers bear a collective responsibility for the policies and actions of the Government and secondly, an individual responsibility for their department's work.

Through the doctrine of collective responsibility individual ministers are required to support government decisions and ensure that their department's policy is consistent with those decisions. Should a minister feel unable to support his colleagues he would be expected to resign. In exceptional circumstances, however, as in the 1975 referendum on the continued UK membership of the EEC (Common Market), ministers are allowed to campaign and vote against certain aspects of government policy without resigning their office.

Individual responsibility requires a minister to be answerable to Parliament for all the decisions and actions within his department. This responsibility extends even to decisions and actions for which he was not personally responsible. He cannot, for example, hide behind the authority of the Cabinet or claim that the matter was dealt with by Civil Servants without being referred to him. If the matter is sufficiently serious the minister may be required to resign. Indeed, it is not unknown for a minister to be 'sacrificed' by his colleagues to placate public opinion and reduce criticism of the Government as a whole.

Ministerial responsibility, both collective and individual, is an effective way of ensuring that the activities of Government are controlled by Parliament and that hasty or arbitrary decisions are prevented.

Government departments

Government departments are the primary means by which government policy is effected. These departments vary considerably in the work they undertake. Certain departments, for example Education and Health, are directly responsible for the provision of a specific service throughout the UK, some such as the ministries for Wales, Scotland, and Northern Ireland co-ordinate a wide range of activities within their area, while finally others – the Treasury and Cabinet office are prime examples – act as co-ordinators of government policy.

The Treasury

The Treasury is unique among goverment departments. In the first place its head, the First Lord of the Treasury, is the Prime Minister – though day-to-day control of its activities is vested in the Chancellor of the Exchequer. Secondly the Treasury in its role as regulator of economic activity controls the spending plans of all other departments. These departments must seek Treasury approval before engaging in any activity which will incur the expenditure of money. Equally important, no plans for departmental expenditure may be submitted to the Cabinet for approval until the Treasury has had the opportunity to study and criticise them. Finally, the Treasury supervises the work of two other government departments – the Boards of Inland Revenue and Customs and Excise. The work of the Treasury can be divided into one of four categories as given under the headings below.

Economic forecasting

Under the Industry Act of 1975 the Government is required to produce and make public two forecasts on the economy's short- and medium-term prospects. The first of these is presented to Parliament along with the Chancellor's budget speech, while the second in November allows Parliament to evaluate the effectiveness of government monetary and fiscal policy. There are numerous other forecasts which are not made but which allow the Chancellor to monitor the workings of the economy more closely.

Control of the economy

Treasury forecasts form the basis on which governments decide whether existing monetary and fiscal policy will achieve those broad economic objectives (e.g. low inflation) which they have set themselves. Where, as is often the case, deviations from plan are identified the policy measures introduced to put the economy back on course are again based on the work of the Treasury. Each policy proposal, together with information on the UK and world economies, will be fed into the Treasury computer, and the results evaluated for compatibility with government objectives.

Control of the public sector

Arising out of its role in determining monetary and fiscal policy the Treasury is also responsible for controlling the overall level of public expenditure and the PSBR. This brings the Treasury into direct contact with other government departments, local authorities, and nationalised industries. In each case spending plans have to be considered against the background of the Government's economic strategy. On many occasions spending plans need modification. Usually the Treasury will expect to gain acceptance of its policy, and for the organisation concerned to use its expertise to curtail or reshape its plans. However, in the last resort the Treasury may, through the Cabinet, seek to force its policy upon the errant organisation.

External affairs
The Treasury, acting on many occasions through the Bank of England, is responsible for Britain's international monetary policy. In the first place the Treasury is responsible for introducing any corrective measures which are needed to regulate the balance of payments (though its freedom of action is considerably circumscribed by Britain's membership of GATT and the EEC). Secondly the Treasury must ensure that exchange-rate fluctuations do not harm international trade, and intervene (to stabilise exchange rates) where fluctuations do not reflect underlying market trends. Finally the Treasury plays a central role in the development of policy towards, and the representation of, British interests on international bodies such as the IMF, the World Bank, and the Common Market.

The Department of Education and Science

The growth and development of education in Britain during the nineteenth and twentieth centuries is a response to the changing needs of society. Although education in the country predates the Industrial Revolution by many centuries the vast majority of people had little or no education. It was not until 1856 that the Government felt a need to create two separate departments, Education and Science, with the twin aims of developing a comprehensive and national education system and producing the scientifically and technologically trained workers so badly needed by industry. These departments were eventually merged to form the Department of Education and Science.

Today, the aims of the combined department remain broadly the same. The education service seeks to identify and develop fully the ability of all children, young people, and adults. The range of opportunities for academic, vocational, and leisure education now available are greater than ever before. Children are required to undergo full-time education between the age of 5 and 16 – the school-leaving age having been raised twice since 1944. Many new subjects, business and secretarial studies, the social sciences, and computer studies have been introduced into the curriculum. Increasingly, young people are remaining at school beyond the age of 16 to take advantage of these opportunities, often obtaining extra qualifications which improve their job prospects or qualify them for entry into higher education.

Considerable expansion has taken place in higher education since 1945. Approximately 7 per cent of all 18-year-olds enter higher education. Twenty-eight new universities have been established. A major contribution to the work of higher education has also been made by the creation of polytechnics who provide a wide range of courses at all levels, though there is a concentration on degree and other advanced work. The proportion of broadly vocational courses is much higher in polytechnics than in universities. In England and Wales there are now thirty polytechnics, while in Scotland there are fourteen central institutions undertaking similar work but administered by the Scottish Office.

The majority of courses at university and a substantial number of those at polytechnics (particularly at degree level) are full time. The Open University is a non-residential university providing part-time courses, normally leading to degrees. Students study in their own homes through a combination of television and radio broadcasts, supplemented by correspondence texts and other recommended reading. Although it is the policy to allow students to enrol regardless of academic qualifications its degrees have the same standing as those from any other university.

Over 25 per cent of all other school-leavers receive some form of post-school vocational education in further education establishments. Technical colleges, colleges of further education, and colleges of technology provide a wide range of courses reflecting particularly the needs of local industry. Industrial training boards, created by the Industrial Training Act 1964 made an important contribution to the work of this sector by persuading employers to invest in the training of their staff, and encouraging the growth of part-time day and block release courses at local colleges.

Traditionally, adult education has been concerned with non-vocational courses for those over 18. While it is true that such courses develop and encourage leisure pursuits, many courses such as learning a foreign language or computer appreciation have a vocational element. Another important element of adult education work is remedial, allowing people to make up for lost opportunities at school. The adult literacy campaign and programmes to help members of minority ethnic groups are just two examples of such remedial work.

To discharge its duties the Department of Education and Science works closely with local authorities to whom responsibility for the provision of all non-university education is delegated. Grants are made by central government towards the cost of providing this service. In the case of university education the department works through the University Grants Committee who will determine the distribution of funds allocated to the university sector. Finally, to encourage educational research the department has created five research councils, Science and Engineering, Natural Environment, Medical, Agricultural, and Social Science, to whom it allocates funds and who are responsible for its distribution.

As long ago as 1856 the Government acknowledged the importance of education by creating the Departments of Education and Science. Its importance has not diminished today, educational expenditure amounting to 6 per cent of GDP or 11 per cent of all public expenditure. To the individual, education provides the key to greater employment opportunities, increased earning power and the possibility of more interesting and satisfactory jobs. It allows people to learn new skills to replace those no longer required by industry and commerce. For industry, a steady stream of skilled employees from schools, colleges, and universities is required to fill manpower requirements. A more highly educated workforce allows for greater division of labour and specialisation which in turn leads to greater efficiency, economy, sales, and profits. Finally, it is only a short step from this to recognise that the attainment of macro-economic objectives such as a satisfactory balance of payments, high levels of employment, and economic growth are aided through the provision of a well-educated, highly trained workforce.

The Department of the Environment

This department is responsible for administering and co-ordinating government policy on a wide range of topics. These include regional planning, housing, and environmental protection. Many of its responsibilities are delegated to other bodies. The department provides the major link between central and local government.

Planning
Responsibility for regional and local planning is delegated to local authorities in the belief that the needs of a particular area are more likely to be correctly identified by people living in that area. County planning authorities are required to develop and submit to the Secretary of State for approval 'structure' plans. These are broad, long-term plans for the development and use of land, and the improvement of the physical environment in a particular area. Structure plans are used by district planning authorities as the basis for local plans on the allocation of land to housing, factory, and commercial development – or indeed any other use. Local plans must always be consistent with structure plans.

Housing
Local authorities are also involved in the implementation of the Government's housing policy. Building regulations designed to ensure that houses are both structurally sound and habitable are enforced by local government. Programmes for slum clearance and redevelopment or alternatively the modernisation and conversion of substandard houses are carried out by the local authorities. They are responsible for ensuring that the supply of housing within their area is sufficient, building and maintaining council housing where necessary. The Housing Act 1980 also established the right of any public sector tenant of three years' standing to purchase the freehold of their house from the local authority owner.

Environmental protection

The UK is one of the leading countries in environmental protection. In advanced economies pollution (land, air, sea, noise, and radioactive) is a constant hazard. Several government departments are involved in its control. The Secretary of State at the Department of Environment has a co-ordinating role, taking advice from an independent standing Royal Commission on Environmental Pollution. Government measures to combat land, air, and noise pollution are delegated to local authorities while the regional water authorities ensure that there are adequate arrangements for the disposal and treatment of sewage.

The department is also actively involved in the conservation of buildings having special architectural or historical interest, and the countryside. Lists of buildings of special interest are compiled by the department, and it is against the law to demolish or alter the character of any listed building without consent from the local planning authority. These planning authorities also have power to protect trees and woodlands from destruction by means of tree preservation orders. In England and Wales the Countryside Commission has been made responsible for (a) measures to conserve and enhance areas of natural beauty, and (b) the development of recreational facilities therein. The commission may recommend to the appropriate minister areas to be designated 'national parks' or 'of outstanding natural beauty'. Once confirmed, the owners of land in these areas are subject to extra controls designed to secure public access and preserve the area's beauty.

The Department of Employment

The Secretary of State for Employment is responsible for all aspects of manpower policy. The department's work falls into three broad categories: that of aiding the unemployed, protecting those in employment, and improving industrial relations.

Aiding the unemployed

Both Government and society deplore the waste of human resources and the human problems arising from unemployment. The Government has introduced a number of special measures designed to alleviate unemployment. Attempts to provide the long-term unemployed adult with work experience have been channelled through the Community Programme Scheme. The scheme is sponsored by industry and central and local government and undertakes projects which are of benefit to the community at large. There is special emphasis on areas of high unemployment.

Young people suffer most in a recession, for when employers reduce their workforce, those that are made redundant are either relatively new to the business or have little experience to offer. Young people form the most substantial part of both groups. Equally, young people find it particularly difficult to obtain employment during a recession because of their lack of experience. Through the Young Workers' Scheme employers are encouraged to employ young workers by means of a subsidy of £15 per week for a young worker who is paid less than £40 per week. The subsidy is reduced to £7.50 for those earning between £40 and £45 per week. The subsidy is paid for a year. The department also seeks to provide additional opportunities for the unemployed by means of 'job sharing'. Employers who split one full-time into two part-time jobs (thus reducing the number of unemployed) will be given a grant to cover their extra costs and provide some incentive.

Indirectly the Job Release Scheme also seeks to aid the young unemployed. Under the scheme older workers are encouraged to retire early (they receive a weekly allowance until in receipt of their state pension) and release their jobs for younger workers. It is estimated that industry will replace between two-thirds and four-fifths of those workers who retire early.

Further aid to the unemployed in the UK is provided by the Department of Employment through the Manpower Services Commission (MSC). The MSC comprises of a chairman and nine members appointed by the Secretary of State to advise him on manpower policy issues. The commission is aided in its task by a network of district manpower committees on which employers, employees, and other local interests are represented. The activities of MSC are almost wholly financed out of public funds.

The MSC's main function is to help people select, train, obtain, and retain jobs. As a natural concomitant of this function it assists employers to obtain employees. These duties are carried out by the MSC's Employment Service and Training Division.

The MSC's Employment Service operates a network of job centres and employment centres throughout the UK. These deal with all occupations other than professional, scientific, technical, and managerial for which a specialist branch of the MSC Professional and Executive Recruitment (PER) is responsible. Employers may (they are not required to do so by law) inform the job centre or employment offices of any vacancies they have. In 1981 approximately 1.5 million people were placed in employment through its services.

Professional and Executive Recruitment also operates through a national network of offices providing a comprehensive recruitment service. While the service is free to job seekers, employers are charged a fee for the service obtained.

The MSC Employment Service also runs a network of employment rehabilitation centres providing facilities for those who have been injured or are handicapped to regain working fitness. Disablement resettlement officers advise employers about the employment of disabled people (by law firms employing over twenty people are required to provide employment for registered disabled people). The MSC also makes annual awards to firms in recognition of their positive policy in the employment of disabled people.

The prime responsibility for employee training rests with industry and commerce. A number of statutory industrial training boards exist to promote training within their own particular industry. In addition many firms will employ a training officer who is required to identify and devise courses to meet their training needs. The role of the MSC Training Division is to ensure that such training as is undertaken by industry and commerce becomes part of a comprehensive strategy to improve the supply of trained labour within the economy. The Training Division have complemented industry's efforts by means of its own Training Opportunities and Youth Training Schemes.

The Training Opportunities Scheme provides people aged 19 or over with the chance to acquire new skills – particularly important where their original training is no longer relevant to the needs of industry. Training may be carried out in the division's own skill centres, where the emphasis is on engineering, construction, and automative trades courses, or in local colleges and employers' establishments where training in commercial, management, and technician skills is provided. Trainees are paid a weekly allowance by the Department of Employment, the amount varying with their personal circumstances.

The Youth Training Scheme is part of the Government's New Training Initiative designed to provide all young people under the age of 18 not in full-time education with an integrated programme of work experience, education, and training. In particular, the scheme will allow participants to gain practical experience and competence in a range of skills which are designed to increase their employability.

The scheme will be carried out in one of three ways. Mode A is employer based. The employer, who is termed the managing agent, is responsible for designing, managing, and delivering all aspects of the scheme. The managing agent will receive an allowance (at present £1,850 p.a.) for each young person employed or unemployed on their scheme. Modes B_1 and B_2 both have the MSC itself acting as managing agent and being responsible for arranging those parts of the scheme not provided by the sponsor personally. Mode B_1 refers to places provided by sponsors of community projects, training workshops and information technology centres, while mode B_2 places are provided through a network of linked schemes in colleges of further education and employers' premises.

Labour legislation

Britain has a long history of providing legislation designed to protect the interest of workers. Today all employees must be given written information on their terms and conditions of employment. Employees with over two years' service are entitled to lump sum payments upon redundancy. A system of industrial tribunals has been created to determine disputes between employee and employer, including unfair dismissal, discrimination, equal pay for women, and safety. In certain industries, where the structure prevents fair and free negotiation of collective agreements, legislation exists to determine minimum wages, conditions of work, and holiday pay. The department's Wages Inspectorate ensures that the provisions of these agreements are adhered to. About 2.7 million workers are subject to Wages Council agreements.

A duty is placed upon employers both at civil and criminal law to take care of their employees and provide a safe system of working. The principal act – the Health and Safety at Work Act 1974 – established the Health and Safety Commission which is responsible to the Secretary of State at the Department of Employment for developing policies, codes of practice, and proposals for further legislation designed to improve the workings of the Act. The Act also established the Health and Safety Executive, which through the Factory Inspectorate visits and advises upon activities in an extremely wide range of establishments. Inspectorates also exist for agriculture, mines and quarries. Inspectors appointed by local authorities but working under the guidance of the Health and Safety Executive are responsible for enforcing legislation in shops and offices.

Also reporting to the Health and Safety Executive are the Employment Medical Advisory Service and the Research and Laboratories Services Division. Both are concerned with reducing the number of potential hazards faced by employees.

Improving industrial relations
Industrial relations in Britain are essentially voluntary, being based upon free negotiation by employers and employees without state interference. Increasingly though, legislation is being used to provide ground rules for the conduct of industrial relations. Thus the 1980 Employment Act allows the Government to make funds available to promote the use of secret union ballots and to produce codes of practice promoting good industrial relations. The Act limited lawful picketing and secondary action on the part of trade-unionists, and gave the individual greater protection regarding the closed shop.

The Government, through the Department of Employment, has also established independent bodies to aid the negotiating process. The Advisory, Conciliation, and Arbitration Service (ACAS) is concerned with bringing disputants together, establishing grounds for settlement of the dispute, or providing an independent mediator to settle the dispute. Its services are available to both public and private sectors; ACAS conciliates in over 2,000 cases each year and provides arbitration in a further 300–400 disputes.

The Central Arbitration Committee was created by the Employment Protection Act 1975 as an independent body arbitrating on disputes submitted to it by ACAS. It deals with trade union recognition problems, the disclosure of information to trade unions for bargaining purposes, equal pay claims, and compliance with fair wages resolutions (relating to wages and conditions of employment to be implemented by government contractors).

The Department of Transport

An extensive and efficient system of transport is essential in any advanced economy. The Department of Transport which is headed by a Secretary of State is responsible for developing and implementing government policy regarding the transport system.

The department is responsible for all motorways and trunk roads throughout Britain, and allocates funds for their construction, maintenance, and improvement (non-trunk roads are the responsibility of the relevant county council). Research into the problems of road construction and safety is financed jointly by the Departments of Transport and the Environment and is conducted by the Transport and Road Research Laboratory.

Although Britain's accident record is better than most, the department is continually seeking ways of improving road safety. A comprehensive system of legislation already exists covering items such as speed limits, drink/driving limits, the wearing of safety belts for car drivers and crash helmets for motor-cyclists. Strict legislation regulates the design for cars and the testing of their mechanical condition once three years old. Heavy goods vehicles are tested annually at Department of Transport Testing Stations while the drivers of such vehicles are limited in the hours they may work and required to take minimum rest periods.

The Department of Transport is responsible for the nationalised transport industries – civil aviation, rail and bus, and also the shipping industry. The department appoints members to the boards of the nationalised transport industries – British Rail, British Airways, and the National Bus Company and represents them in Parliament, and internationally. Its general policy is one of minimum intervention in their affairs. A major aim of the Government regarding the nationalised transport industries has been to encourage competition, the development of new types of services, and greater efficiency, while at the same time maintaining the high standards of safety the public have come to expect. The Government has, for example, removed many of the restrictions on long-distance coach services and has encouraged competition between public and private sector operators. The result has been an increase in long-distance coach services and passengers carried together with a reduction in fares.

The long-term aim of the Government is to reach a situation where parts of these industries may be returned to the private sector (the National Freight Corporation and the British Transport Docks Board) have already been 'privatised').

The Department of Trade and Industry

This department has been formed by bringing together most of the functions previously exercised by the separate Departments of Trade and Industry. The activities of the department are co-ordinated by the Secretary of State for Trade and Industry to whom three other ministers of state and two under-secretaries report. The departments responsible are extremely broad ranging but fall roughly into one of four categories, namely: corporate and consumer affairs; technological advance; trade; and industry.

Trade
The department has a special responsibility for ensuring that British trade policy is adequately respresented abroad. It takes a leading role in the activities of international organisations such as GATT, the IMF, the OECD, and the EEC. Generally the UK retains few restrictions upon international trade (other than the Common External Tariff imposed by all members of the EEC) and is anxious to encourage the progressive elimination of barriers to trade throughout the world.

The department also provides assistance to exporters through the services of the British Overseas Trade Board (BOTB). The help given may be in the forms enumerated below.

1. Financial   Towards the cost of: (a) exhibiting at overseas trade fairs; (b) market research abroad; (c) visiting or breaking into an export market.

2. Information   (a) On export opportunities in over 200 overseas markets; (b) detailed guidance on selling particular goods and services overseas; (c) on overseas companies – their activities and potential as an agent.

3. Advice   (a) From the board's ten regional offices; (b) at seminars and conferences held throughout the country through BOTB publications (e.g. *Hints to Exporters,* booklets providing basic data and advice on individual countries).

Additional help to exporters is provided by the Export Credits Guarantee Department (ECGD) of the Department of Trade and Industry. The ECGD encourages exports by providing exporters with insurance cover against the particular risks of overseas trade. The main risks covered are the insolvency or protracted default of the purchaser, government action preventing the exporter receiving payment, import restrictions, and civil disturbance in the buyer's country. Cover under an ECGD policy is limited to 90 per cent of the loss arising from buyer risks and 95 per cent from political risks; ECGD insurance business is operated upon commercial lines and no cost is incurred by the taxpayer. The department provides insurance cover for approximately 33 per cent of UK export trade. The ECGD is also responsible for administering, through the commercial banks, the scheme by which exporters have access to finance at preferential rates of interest for export credit.

Industry
The department is responsible for government policy to industry, excluding those aspects of employment and manpower policy which are dealt with by the Department of Employment. In general terms the department's policy is to provide an environment conducive to industrial expansion. To this end the department is anxious to reduce the level of state ownership and the level of subsidy to the public sector. The proceeds of asset sales between 1979 and 1984 have brought in nearly £1,900 m., while those for 1984 and 1985 are expected to yield approximately £5,500 m. Public sector industries have been encouraged to find ways of providing services more efficiently, and also financing their capital requirements from internal sources. The department has also encouraged private sector participation in public work.

The department is also responsible for distributing government aid to specific industries and regions throughout the country. In recent years aerospace, steel, shipbuilding, and the motor industry have been major recipients of government aid. A system of incentives has been introduced by the department to encourage industrial development in those areas where unemployment is persistently higher than the national average. In conjunction with the Treasury a system of taxes and tax allowances has been devised to promote investment in new and improved capital throughout industry generally.

A separate division of the Department of Trade and Industry has been created to devise policy and provide a service to small firms. Small Firms Centres exist throughout the country providing an information and counselling service for small businesses. Government measures – there are over 100 in existence at present – are designed to improve the flow of finance to the sector, provide a more favourable tax regime, and reduce the administrative burden on small firms caused by 'oppressive legislation' and requests by government departments for statistical information.

Corporate and consumer affairs.
General supervision of business activity is undertaken by the department. Policy has been developed to check the growth of monopolies, mergers, restrictive trade and anti-competitive practices. The Secretary of State, by the use of statutory orders, has the power to remedy any abuse caused by a monopoly situation, prevent any merger which is deemed to be against the public interest from taking place, or ensure that firms do not indulge in anti-competitive practices.

Consumer protection also falls within the ambit of the department. Responsibility for the continuous monitoring of consumer affairs has been delegated to the Director General of Fair Trading who has power to deal with practices affecting the consumers' interests and also the persistent offender of consumer rights. The Director General is responsible for advising the Secretary of State where amendments to consumer protection legislation are required.

The Secretary of State is also required to supervise company law, consumer safety, trading standards, insurance companies, the Patent Office, and the Insolvency Service.

Technological advance
Each year the Department of Trade and Industry invests heavily in research and development with the aim of ensuring the rapid assimilation and exploitation of new technology by British industry. The department finances numerous research establishments. In addition a series of 'requirement boards' provides industry with research support through grants of contracts where projects are judged to be in the national interest and would not proceed without aid. The National Research Development Corporation (NRDC) is a public corporation responsible to the Secretary of State for the commercial exploitation of inventions developed by universities and other research establishments, and providing industry with the finance for innovation. The NRDC has been merged with the National Enterprise Board to form the British Technology Group.

The department has recognised the importance of developments in microelectronics for the future of industry. It has instituted a campaign to promote the awareness and use of the new technology through the Microprocessor Applications Project and the Microelectronics Industry Support Programme.

The Welsh, Scottish, and Northern Ireland Offices

These offices have wide administrative autonomy for affairs in their area. Each plays a major role in the planning and economic development of their region, including the provision of selective financial assistance to industry. The offices provide the major link between central government and local authorities in their area. They are responsible for the implementation of government policy in respect of health and social services, education, town and country planning, housing, and transport. Like other government departments these offices work through a wide range of public bodies to discharge their duties. Further examples of the work of government departments are given in Table 15.1.

Table 15.1 Other major government departments

Department	Major responsibilities	Associated agencies
Ministry of Agriculture, Fisheries, and Food	Policies for agriculture, horticulture, forestry and fisheries, food quality and supply. Water resources and sewerage (with Dept. of the Environment)	Intervention Board for Agricultural Produce (support to farmers under the Common Agricultural Policy), Agricultural Development and Advisory Service, Farm Animal Welfare Council. Forestry Commission. Regional Water Authorities
Energy	Policies for energy supply and conservation. The development of new energy sources. Relationships with the nationalised 'energy' industries, International collaboration on energy questions	Advisory Council on Energy Conservation, Energy Technology Support. Atomic Energy Authority, British National Oil Corporation, British Gas Corporation, Central Electricity Generating Board, Area Electricity Boards, National Coal Board, International Energy Agency
Foreign and Commonwealth	All aspects of overseas relationships, foreign policy, international negotiations. The protection of British interests – property and persons abroad. Aid to and co-operation with developing countries	Embassies and consulates. Overseas Development Administration
Health and Social Security	The social security system, the National Health Service, local authority social services, public health and hygiene. Treatment of offenders under 17 (shared with Home Office)	Regional and District Health Authorities, Health Education, local authority social service departments
Home Office	The maintenance of law and order, police service, courts and prisons, Civil Defence, regulation of firearms, dangerous drugs, gaming and lotteries, immigration and nationality questions, race relations, sex discrimination. Broadcasting	Metropolitan and provincial police forces, Probation Office, British Broadcasting Corporation, Independent Broadcasting Authority

Quasi non-governmental organisations

One prominent characteristic of central government in the UK is the extent to which it delegates its responsibilities to other bodies. There are of course exceptions to this – defence, taxation, and social security are the most important examples – but the majority of other government departments discharge their duties through non-departmental public bodies. These bodies, which are often collectively described as 'quangos' or quasi non-governmental organisations, are controlled by people appointed by the minister concerned and are responsible to him for the discharge of a specific duty such as the running of the Post Office, the Housing Corporation, the Gaming Board, or the Council for Small Industries in Rural Areas. The Bank of England is probably the most important and powerful quango. Estimates of the number of public bodies through which the Government works vary, some being as high as 3,000. In 1979 the Government instituted a review of these bodies as a result of which over 400 are being abolished. Since that time though, government departments have created other quangos to aid them in the discharge of their duties.

Quangos fall into one of three categories – executive bodies, advisory bodies, or tribunals. Executive bodies such as the National Health Service, the MSC, British Airways or the BOTB provide services to the public or industry, employ staff, and spend money on their own account.

Advisory bodies undertake research or collect information, thus giving ministers facts and informed opinion on which to base a decision. For example the Secretary of State for Education and Science discharges its duties in respect of research on the advice of the Advisory Board for the Research Councils, while the Secretary of State for Energy takes advice from the independent Advisory Council on Energy Conservation.

Although ministers may be required to consult an advisory board, the majority are created at the discretion of a departmental minister and arise out of his need for advice. Membership of the body varies according to the work involved, but will normally reflect the diversity of public opinion on the subject concerned. It represents an attempt on the part of the minister to involve key interests in the making (and in some cases the implementation) of government policy.

Where important issues are involved the Government may appoint a Royal Commission which will consider and make recommendations on a specific matter. The members of the commission, who are chosen for their experience and expertise, take written and oral evidence from all interested parties before submitting their recommendations. The Government may implement their proposals wholly, in part, or alternatively they may decide to shelve the report and take no further action.

Administrative tribunals, although outside the court system, exercise a judicial function. Many owe their existence to the large amount of social legislation (and its complexity) introduced in the last fifty years. Compared with courts, tribunals have an extremely limited judicial function. This function, their constitution and procedures are detailed in the legislation which created them. Tribunals may determine disputes between private citizens, for example rent or industrial tribunals, or alternatively may arbitrate in disputes between a government department and private citizen, for example social security.

In principle there is no reason why the courts should not have dealt with the work undertaken by administrative tribunals – in practice it is doubted whether they would have been able to cope with the volume of cases. Moreover, when compared with the courts they have several important advantages:

1. Members of the tribunals are experts in the work of the tribunal to which they are appointed.

2. Tribunal proceedings are less costly – for example lawyers are not involved and tribunal members only receive out-of-pocket expenses.

3. Tribunal proceedings are less formal and do not have strict rules of procedure which may confuse or intimidate a complainant.

Local government

Local government is a further, and very important, example of the way in which central government delegates the implementation of policy to other bodies. An extremely wide range of public services are provided through the democratically elected councils which represent local communities. The provision of services on a local rather than national basis is beneficial for the following reasons.
1. It would be impossible for any central organisation to deal efficiently with public services distributed to a population of 156 million living in an area of over 94,000 square miles.
2. It is a means by which the public exercises control over local affairs, prevents excessive central power, and, if necessary, expresses its disaffection towards central government policy.

Local government structure in England and Wales was established by the Local Government Act 1972. The reformed system which came into effect in April 1974 is shown in Fig. 15.1.

In England and Wales there are two tiers of local government organisation. County authorities are responsible for providing services which either require planning and administration over a wide area or need the support of substantial resources. District authorities administer those services best provided on a local basis. A major distinction, however, is drawn between 'normal' county areas and six heavily populated areas – West Midlands, Greater Manchester, Merseyside, South Yorkshire, West Yorkshire, and Tyne and Wear –

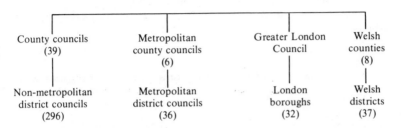

Fig. 15.1 Local government structure in England and Wales

which were given the title of metropolitan counties. These undertake a more limited range of services than the 'normal' county area. Because of their size of population metropolitan district councils take over responsibility for some large-scale services normally allocated to county authorities.

The local government system in Wales is very much the same as that of non-metropolitan county councils in England.

Local government in London was reorganised in 1965 and is administered by the Greater London Council which like the county councils has responsibility for large-scale services. Thirty-two borough councils administer services at a more local level.

The range of services provided by local authorities is remarkably wide. They can be classified according to the tier of local government responsible for administering them (see Table 15.2) or according to function – protective, environmental, personal, and recreational.

Protective services

Police
Police forces are controlled by the police committee of the 'county' authority. The committee which is made up of two thirds councillors and one-third magistrates is responsible for appointing the chief constable and maintaining an efficient police force for its area. Responsibility for the efficiency of the police service is shared with the Home Secretary who is concerned with the organisation and operation of each police force. Reports on the organisation and operation of the local police service will be made to the Home Secretary by inspectors of constabulary who periodically visit and inspect each force.

Fire
'County' authorities are required by law to maintain a fire service of sufficient strength for all normal requirements. The Home Secretary or the Secretary of State for Scotland have a responsibility to ensure that the operational efficiency of each brigade is high and may make

Table 15.2 Distribution of local authority functions under the London Government
Act 1963, and the Local Government Act 1972

Authority	Responsibility
England	
(1) London	
— Greater London Council	Strategic planning, transport aspects of housing (e.g. slum clearance)
— Inner London Education Authority	Education in Inner London
— London boroughs	Housing, personal social services, environmental health, education (outside Inner London), leisure services
(2) Metropolitan areas	
— Counties	Strategic planning, transport, police, fire services
— Districts	Local planning, housing, personal and social services, environmental health, education, leisure services
(3) Non-metropolitan areas	
— Counties	Strategic planning, education, personal and social services, transport, police, fire services, consumer protection
— Districts	Local planning, housing, environmental health, leisure services
(4) Wales	
— Counties	Strategic planning, education, personal and social services, transport, police, fire services, consumer protection
— Districts	Local planning, housing, environmental health, leisure services

regulations on a wide variety of issues including appointments,
discipline, training, and equipment.

Through the local fire brigade the 'county' authorities are also
concerned with fire prevention. Legislation requires that most
buildings used by the public should be inspected to ensure that
adequate fire precautions and safety facilities exist. Where the fire
authorities are satisfied a fire certificate is issued.

Consumer protection
Originally, trading standards officers were appointed to check on local
trading organisations and ensure that the consumer was not given
short measure. They were empowered to make test purchases, enter
premises, and when necessary take legal proceedings against offenders.

Today their work encompasses other trading practices including credit facilities and false or misleading descriptions of goods and services.

Local authorities also appoint inspectors to enforce regulations relating to the purity, storage, labelling, and fitness for consumption of food or drugs. Such inspectors have similar powers to trading standards officers.

Many local authorities have set up consumer advice centres providing advice to the consumer on possible claims against the provider of goods and services. In some areas local authorities rely on voluntary organisations, such as the Citizens' Advice Bureau to provide this service.

Environmental services

Environmental health

With the exception of refuse disposal which is undertaken at 'county' level the broad range of responsibilities which constitute environmental health are undertaken by district councils. These include:

1. Building regulations – enforcement of regulations relating to the construction of buildings including access, insulation, and drainage.

2. Control of nuisances – unfenced mines, quarries, and waste tips; insanitary buildings, offensive trades (e.g. glue-making).

3. Control of disease – activities to prevent the outbreak or spread of infectious disease, e.g. control of vermin, provision of public toilets.

4. Pollution – clean air, noise abatement, refuse collection, poisonous waste disposal, street cleansing.

Roads and transport

All public roads other than motorways and trunk roads are the responsibility of local authorities, normally the 'county' authority. However, local authorities may also act as agents for central government in the construction, maintenance, and lighting of trunk roads and motorways. Traffic management – responsibility for speed limits, traffic lights, one-way traffic regulations, pedestrian crossings, and so forth – is also undertaken by the 'county' authority. These authorities also have a statutory duty to promote road safety and accident prevention.

County councils are responsible for co-ordinating the provision of transport in their area and are required to submit five-year local transport programmes to central government. They may also provide public transport services or assist its operation through the payment of grants.

Planning

'County' authorities are required to develop, and submit to the Department of the Environment for approval, 'structure plans'. These outline in broad terms the strategy of the local authority in relation to proposed roads and the allocation of land for parks and recreational facilities, public buildings, including schools, housing, and commercial purposes. Local plans developed by 'district' authorities are based upon the structure plan and show how that plan is to be implemented within their area.

Local authorities are responsible for the implementation of these plans. All proposed changes in land use have to be notified to the local authority and planning permission obtained. Planning applications will be judged on many factors, but the most important will be consistency with the local and structure plan.

Personal services

Education

All education other than university is provided and administered by the local authorities. The education service is the local authorities' single most costly item. The 1944 Education Act requires the local authorities to provide adequate primary and secondary education for all children in their area. Grants are made by central government towards the provision of this service.

Local education authorities are also responsible for providing a wide range of full- and part-time courses in polytechnics and further and higher education colleges. The authority also administer the provision of grants to those students entering higher education.

Community education is yet another responsibility of local government. People may wish to remedy deficiencies in their formal schooling (e.g. literacy), or they may wish to improve job prospects by learning new skills. Alternatively, they may merely wish to occupy their leisure time in a constructive manner by taking up some new interest (e.g. woodwork, needlecraft, yoga).

Careers

The Employment and Training Act 1973 requires all local authorities to provide vocational advice and guidance for all young people attending, or having just left, educational establishments in their area. Local authorities appoint careers officers who visit schools and colleges and advise on job prospects, and the opportunities available in further and higher education.

Personal social services

Responsibility for these services rests with district councils in metropolitan areas, and the county council in non-metropolitan areas. Their services are directed towards the more vulnerable groups in society – the elderly, the disabled, young families with social problems, children from deprived backgrounds, the handicapped, the mentally ill, or young offenders. Social welfare facilities available include residential homes, foster care, training centres, help in the home, in addition to general advice or guidance.

Today the emphasis is on community rather than residential care and the range of 'in home' facilities provided by the local authority has been considerably extended. A great deal of additional care is given to these groups by the community itself through families, self-help groups, and voluntary organisations.

Housing

District councils are responsible for ensuring that the supply of housing in their area is adequate. At present local authorities provide approximately 30 per cent of all housing accommodation. New house construction, and the modernisation of existing stock is achieved by raising loans on the open market and central government grants. These grants are also used to subsidise the rents of council houses. The Housing Act 1980 gives council-house tenants, who have occupied that property for three years, the statutory right to buy the house at a discount (the level of discount is determined by their length of occupation).

Housing authorities are also responsible for distributing housing improvement grants in accordance with government policy – for example, converting houses into flats, installing running water or loft insulation. They are also responsible for processing claims and distributing rent allowances to tenants on low incomes living in privately (as opposed to council) rented property.

Recreational

All local authorities are involved in the provision of recreational or leisure facilities in their area. A wide range of facilities are available in all areas, including lakes, parks, playing-fields, golf-courses, tennis-courts, swimming-baths, and sports centres. In some areas schools' sports facilities (which must be provided by law) are used by the community outside school hours. Local authorities also seek to provide a range of cultural and other entertainments. These include art galleries, museums, and theatres, the promotion of local groups, drama, arts and crafts, or music festivals, agricultural and flower shows.

Examination questions

1. Select *two* government departments of your choice, outline their work, and explain how it affects business.

2. Outline the work of central government agencies for employment and training.

3. Select a government department and describe how its work assists commerce.

4. Explain why the Treasury is sometimes termed 'the Department of Departments'.

5. A distinctive feature of central government in Britain is the extent to which it delegates implementation of policy to other bodies. Explain this statement by reference to the work of two government departments.

6. Outline the pattern of local government organisations in England and Wales. What functions and services are carried out by the local authority in whose area you reside?

7. Explain the term quasi non-governmental organisations. Illustrate your answer by referring to the work of three such bodies.

8. Explain the present structure of local government in Britain. What are the major duties and responsibilities of the local authorities?

Insurance
Chapter 16

Risk is a part of everyday life. Everyone and everything is subjected to some form of risk. Of course the degree of risk varies. Some people are more at risk than others – the fisherman for example has a far more hazardous job than the office worker. The old and defenceless are more likely to be attacked and robbed than the physically fit. Equally, certain types of goods, for example fragile or perishable, run a greater risk of damage or deterioration than most.

Some of these risks we accept. After all the consequences may not be serious. Equally we may be ignorant of our danger, or it may be impossible to avoid the risk. But just as there are many risks we accept, there are many we avoid by taking precautions. The precautions may be as simple as looking both ways when we cross the road, or engaging the safety harness on entering a car. A firm may take precautions to lessen the danger of over-reliance on one product by a policy of diversification. Yet another precaution taken by both individuals and firms is insurance.

The basis of insurance is that in return for a small premium financial loss is borne, not by the individual to whom the misfortune occurs, but by an insurance fund created from the premiums of the whole insured community. To be fair on all participants the premium paid must reflect the risk of a claim being made, and also the likely size of any claim. A motorist with a bad driving record should obviously pay more than one who has never had an accident. In the same way, other things being equal, the premium required to insure a Rolls-Royce will be greater than for a Mini.

It is easy to underestimate the importance of insurance today. Yet many families within the UK will have insurance covering their house, its contents, and their car. A substantial number will save for the future with an insurance policy. The firm, too, will need to insure its premises, and their contents. It may also wish to insure itself against liability for injury to its employees, or third parties, against loss of profits, or any of many other eventualities.

To all these individuals and firms insurance removes the worry of misfortune causing financial disaster. Insurance imparts a confidence in the future without which many new business ventures would never start. But insurance benefits society in other ways. For example:

1. It aids the more efficient use of capital by releasing funds for investment which would otherwise be kept on one side to guard against unforeseen eventualities.

2. The accumulated insurance fund is an important source of finance for both industry and government.

3. The UK balance of payments benefits considerably from the export earnings of the insurance industry.

4. Costs of accidents and injury which would otherwise be borne by society through the social services will in many cases be met by insurance (e.g. car accidents).

5. By their advice and actions insurance companies play a positive part in the reduction of loss. Bad drivers are encouraged to mend their ways through higher premiums. Similarly, firms with bad accident records. Advice may be given on ways to avoid or minimise the extent of loss. Thus firms may be encouraged to install burglar- or fire-alarm systems.

The principles of insurance

Underlying the contract of insurance are four basic principles. These are insurable interest, good faith, indemnity, and proximate cause. They are part of every insurance contract whether or not explicitly stated in the agreement and can only be varied by a clear statement of that fact in the policy.

Insurable interest

Before a legally binding contract of insurance can be formed the insured must show that he has an insurable interest. It is the insurable interest which distinguishes the insurance contract from gambling – an agreement which is unenforceable in English law. An insurable interest exists where there is:

(a) an object of insurance – person, property or liability which is capable of being insured; and

(b) a recognised interest in the subject-matter of the insurance so that the insured suffers loss by its death, damage, destruction, by the creation of a liability or loss of a right.

Let us consider a few examples. A creditor may insure the life of his debtor, for if the debtor dies the creditor stands to lose the loan. But the policy could only be for the amount of the loan. It is common to find partners insuring the lives of their co-partners as the co-partner's death or incapacity may cause the firm financial loss. By common law a husband and wife have an unlimited insurable interest in each other, but this does not extend to other members of the family. A man may insure the lives of his children or his parents only if there is some particular financial loss which may come as a result of their death.

An insurable interest in property will obviously arise where it is owned by the insurer. Where there is joint ownership though, insurable interest is limited to the value of the individual share. Ownership is not the only basis for an insurable interest in property. People holding property as agent for the owner may be liable for its loss or damage and thus have an insurable interest. A similar situation arises where you use property (e.g. a motor car) with the agreement of the owner.

A person may also insure himself against the civil consequences of a criminal act. For example the injuries which an employee may suffer as a breach of health and safety regulations, or where another road user suffers as a result of negligent driving by the insured. Equally, an insurable interest exists where a right or financial interest of the insured is capable of being disturbed. Thus a businessman may insure against embezzlement by employees and customer bad debts.

Good faith

Insurance contracts are said to be *uberrimae fidei* – that is, 'of the utmost good faith', whereas for the vast majority of other contracts the common law principle *caveat emptor* – 'let the buyer beware' applies. In ordinary commercial contracts each party is expected to use his skill and judgement to decide whether the agreement is one into which he really wishes to enter. Thus your co-contractor is not obliged to point out all the defects in the car you are buying (but he must answer any questions put to him truthfully and not fraudulently conceal the defects). If you make a bad bargain the law provides no remedy!

Insurance contracts are different though in the sense that one party (the insured) has all the knowledge relevant to the agreement. The other party (the insurer) relies upon the insured to reveal all facts, whether or not the information is specifically requested, which would influence the decision or the premium to be charged. This responsibility rests heavily on the insured and should he fail to discharge it the insurance policy is of no effect. In the event of a claim the insurer has no obligation to make any payment whatsoever.

The duty to disclose all material facts exists until the contract has been entered into. At common law you are not required to inform the insurer of any change in the material facts. Many policies, especially motor and personal accident, do, however, insert a clause requiring such changes to be reported to the insurer.

Indemnity

The aim of insurance is to place the insured party in the same position after the loss to that which he was in before the loss. The insured is not allowed to make a profit out of misfortune, his claim is limited to the loss he has suffered. The insured could therefore not expect to receive the price of a new carpet when the one destroyed was five years old. A deduction will be made for wear and tear.

The extent of the indemnity may be futher reduced where the insurance policy is based upon the assumption that the sum insured represents the full value of the property. Many householders inadvertently under-insure the contents of their house. If the house contents are under-insured by, say 20 per cent then any claim for partial loss will also be reduced by 20 per cent.

Mention must also be made of two further points allied to the principle of indemnity, namely:

1. *Subrogation* – once the insurer has indemnified the insured for any loss he has suffered, he is entitled to exercise any rights or remedies available to the insured. Where a motorist has his car damaged by the negligent driving of another person he may claim and receive compensation from his insurers. Through subrogation of rights the insurers may then proceed to recover the amount of the indemnity from the negligent motorist or his insurers. Similarly where stolen goods, which formed the basis of an insurance claim, are later recovered they are the property of the insurers.

2. *Contribution* – this allows an insurer to require other insurers to share in the cost of meeting an insurance claim. The right arises where there are two or more insurance policies which cover the same claim. Such a situation may occur where an item like binoculars are included on the 'all risks' section of house contents insurance, yet also be insured under a motor insurance policy when carried in the owner's car. If the binoculars are stolen from the car the insurance company, from whom an indemnity is sought, may claim a contribution from the other.

Proximate cause

It is essential to discover the cause of a loss to determine whether or not the insurer is required to give an indemnity under an insurance policy held by the insured. The policy will clearly cover some 'perils', a personal accident policy will clearly cover a pedestrian injured or killed by a car, a fidelity guarantee will cover theft by dishonest employees. But some perils are in fact uninsured. Should our pedestrian have in fact tried to commit suicide any claim under the personal accident policy would fail.

Difficulties really arise though where there are a number of causes which together have produced the loss upon which the insurance claim is based. Some of these causes may be insured perils, others uninsured. The rule of law then is to find the 'proximate' or most immediate cause of the loss. The insurer will then not be liable unless the proximate cause was an insured peril. Let us consider the situation where a fire leaves a wall standing in a dangerous state. A few days later a high wind causes the wall to collapse and damage some other property. Is the owner of the wall entitled to obtain an indemnity for that damage under a fire policy, or is the high wind the immediate cause? In similar circumstances (*Gaskarth* v. *Law Union* 1876) it was held that the fire was only a remote cause of the damage, a new intervening event – the high wind – was the proximate cause.

Classes of insurance

There are in fact several ways of classifying the various categories of insurance. We will adopt the traditional classification of marine, life, fire, and accident considering each in turn.

Marine insurance

This is believed to be the oldest form of insurance. Mediterranean traders are known to have used insurance as early as 1000 BC. In the UK though, the earliest signs of development did not occur until the fifteenth century. But the growth of the insurance industry was rapid, and London soon became the major centre for marine insurance throughout the world.

Today marine insurance falls into one of three categories:

1. *Hull* – this refers not only to the hull itself but also all fixtures and fittings including machinery. The policy covers all dangers of the sea except collision. It is now customary for an additional clause to be added to the hull policy covering collision damage.

2. *Cargo* – this refers to the goods carried by the ship. It is normally issued for the period of the voyage, or more precisely from the moment it leaves the warehouse to be loaded on to the ship in the exporting country until it is received into another warehouse in the importing country. An alternative to the voyage policy is the floating policy where lump-sum insurance far in excess of the value of an individual cargo is taken out. The value of any cargoes carried are declared to the insurers who deduct this from the lump-sum insurance. This continues until the lump sum is exhausted. It

has the advantage of reducing the time-consuming and expensive procedure of issuing individual policies for each cargo.

3. *Freight* – the owner may insure against the loss of freight (transportation) earnings.

The potential liability arising from marine insurance is so great that normally the risk is spread among many underwriters.

Life assurance

While all other forms of insurance are intended to indemnify the insured against financial loss in the event of an unforeseen occurrence, with life assurance the event (e.g. death) must occur at some time. Such contracts are normally long term for a period of ten years or more, with a level premium being paid each year. In Britain the premiums normally qualify for tax relief. (In his 1984 budget the Chancellor of the Exchequer abolished tax relief on policies taken out after 5th April 1984.) There are a vast number of policies which are available, but the majority come within the following categories.

1. *Term assurance* – this is the cheapest form of assurance available. It guarantees a sum of money if, but only if, the assured die within the specified period. It may be used by a businessman preparing to take a business trip to provide his dependants (in the event of his death) with a lump sum, or to cover a loan (e.g. an outstanding mortage on the house).

2. *Whole of life assurance* – as the name implies these policies provide cover throughout the life of the assured. On death a fixed sum is payable to the assured's dependants or into his estate. If such a policy is taken out while the assured is relatively young a substantial sum assured is obtained for a relatively small monthly payment.

3. *Endowment assurance* – is by far the most popular class of assurance. It provides for a sum to be paid either upon the death of the assured or upon expiry of a fixed terms of years. It has the advantage of providing for dependants in the event of death, yet benefiting the assured should he survive the term of the policy by providing him with a lump sum.

Both endowment and whole of life assurances may be 'with profits' or 'without profits' policies. The standard contract available guarantees the assured a fixed sum on death, or alternatively in the case of endowment assurance on expiry of a specified period of time. For an extra premium this may be converted into a 'with profits' policy which entitles the assured to share in profits made by the life assurance fund. There is no guarantee that such profits will materialise (they are called bonuses by the insurance industry), but in practice policy-holders are seldom, if ever, disappointed. Where bonuses are 'paid' they are added to the value of the assured policy and inflate the sum to be received on death or policy maturity.

Industrial life assurance

Endowment and whole of life assurances are also provided by industrial life offices – the biggest and best known being the Prudential. The origin of industrial life assurance goes back to the years of the Industrial Revolution. Few working-class people could afford the annual premium for life assurance. Yet the desire to provide for one's dependants, or at least ensure a decent burial for themselves was there. To meet this demand policies were created upon terms which would appeal to these classes. The premiums which were paid weekly by the policy-holder to a collector who called at his home – 'the man from the Pru' – were for small amounts. The sum assured was correspondingly small. Today these offices not only transact whole of life and endowment assurance but many other forms of insurance as well. In many cases the premiums are still collected weekly at the policy-holder's house. The collector often has the power to issue cover notes for motor insurance and settle small claims.

---

4. *Annuities* – these are not truly contracts of life assurance. In return for a lump sum the assurer agrees to pay the annuitant a sum of money – the annuity for the rest of his life. An annuity may be 'deferred' in which case the payments will not start now but at some agreed future date.

Fire assurance

The scope of basic or standard fire policy is extremely limited. It will compensate where property has been burnt in the course of a fire which was accidentally started. It does not, however, normally cover a situation where the proximate cause was lightning, earthquake, explosion, or riot. These, and many other perils may be added to the fire policy for an additional premium.

Fire policies are becoming increasingly linked with other forms of accident insurance (e.g. burglary, public liability) in what is commonly termed a combined policy. One particular policy which is often linked in this way by businessmen is for consequential loss. This policy seeks to compensate firms for the disruption of their business. Dependent upon the precise terms agreed it can compensate for loss of net profits, fixed costs payable during the period of disruption and any extra expenses necessarily incurred to put the firm back upon a business footing (e.g. temporary accommodation).

Accident insurance

This is very much a mixed bag of insurance policies which have very little in common except the fact that they all developed considerably later than marine, life, and fire insurance. For the most part they are products of the nineteenth century. We will confine our attention to fidelity guarantee, employer's liability, public liability, credit, motor, and engineering insurances.

1. Fidelity guarantee.   This policy exists in several forms. In its commercial form it seeks to protect an employer from the dishonest acts of his employees. Local government, too, may take out such policies in respect of specific officials. The guarantee in this case not only covers loss through dishonesty, but also through mistakes made by the persons guaranteed.

2. Employer's liability.   During the nineteenth century the attitude of society towards industrial accidents and injuries was callous in the extreme. In accepting the work it was said, the employee accepted the risks which went with the job. By law if he was injured by a fellow employee, or if he had in some way contributed to his own injuries he had no claim against his employer. Today these restrictions on an employee's right to compensation for an industrial accident no longer exist. Employer's liability protects the employer against claims made by his employees for injuries suffered at work. The policy may also cover the legal expenses incurred in dealing with the claim – these may be extremely heavy where court hearings are involved. By reason of the Employer's Liability (Compulsory Insurance) Act 1969 an employer is now required by law to obtain this insurance cover.

3. Public liability.   This provides compensation to the insured in respect of claims made by members of the public. Claims may be made against the negligent pedestrian or cyclist who causes a road accident, against the firm or householder whose property in some way injures third parties (e.g. the collapse of a wall, falling slates, etc.), against businesses for the sale of faulty products or the provision of a substandard service, and even against sportsmen.
    A public liability clause is often included in a policy covering the building and contents of a house.

4. Credit insurance.   This is often called 'bad debts' policies and protects the firm against default by customers who have obtained goods on credit terms. By far the greatest risk of default on debts occurs in the export trade though, and it is the Government through the ECGD which provides protection for the exporter.

5. Motor insurance. It is an offence to use any motor vehicle without having basic insurance cover which indemnifies the motorist for death or injury of third parties arising out of the use of that vehicle. It is more common for motorists to obtain cover extending the indemnity to the property of the third party, and to loss or damage of the motor vehicle caused be fire or theft. Such policies are often termed 'third party, fire and theft'. The broadest form of insurance cover available is known as 'comprehensive' and among the more important clauses included is an indemnity for accidental damage to the insured vehicle.

6. Engineering insurance. This is not required by law. The law does, however, require many types of plant to be inspected by a competent engineer. That service is often undertaken by specialist engineering insurance companies. As their name implies these firms also provide insurance covering damage to plant and surrounding property, third-party liability and consequential loss.

The insurance market

The bulk of insurance in the UK is conducted through three insurance organisations – mutual companies, profit-making companies, and Lloyds underwriters.

Mutual companies

Such companies have no shareholders. The policy-holders are the owners of the organisation. They share in the profits of the organisation, but less well realised is that they may be required to make good any losses. Although many specialise in life assurance they are free to deal with other clauses of insurance if they wish. Many profit-making insurance companies today are drawn from the ranks of mutual companies. Some still retain the word 'mutual' in their title.

Profit-making companies

These have shareholders who as owners of the firm are entitled to the profits made after the deduction of expenses. Policy-holders are not required to contribute to losses made by the company, nor do shareholders have any liability normally beyond the amount they have paid for their shares. Should the company run into financial difficulties it may have to go into liquidation.

Lloyd's underwriters

Lloyd's underwriters derive their name from the coffee-shop run by
Edward Lloyd in the late seventeenth century where they first used to
meet to transact their business. Today, Lloyd's is a corporation which
was created by Act of Parliament in 1871. Lloyd's provides the
facilities wherein underwriters carry on their business. Lloyd's itself
does not transact insurance and incurs no liability on the contracts
entered into by its members.

To be accepted as a member of Lloyd's an individual must find six
existing members to support his application, and satisfy stringent
financial and other conditions. The majority of members will form
themselves into syndicates (these vary greatly in size) and specialise in
one particular type of insurance. Each syndicate will appoint one of its
members as underwriting agent, and it is he who acts on behalf of the
syndicate and arranges business. Technically Lloyd's underwriters are
sole traders in business on their own behalf, even though they may be
members of a syndicate. They are therefore personally liable for all
risks underwritten, and may be made bankrupt if they are unable to
meet the claims arising from the underwriting. Should any member be
unable to meet his commitments the policy-holder may be
compensated from the 'Central Fund' created out of the contributions
made by all members of Lloyd's.

Members of Lloyd's do not transact directly with the public, but deal
only through a recognised broker. The business of 'underwriting'
actually occurs when a broker acting on behalf of client prepares a
brief statement of the risks to be covered and invites underwriting
agents to accept a proportion of the liability (for an agreed premium).
The underwriting agent on accepting the risk will sign the name of his
syndicate, detailing the premium and proportion of liability accepted
below the statement of risks. The syndicate is only liable for the
proportion of the risk it has opted to underwrite. Later a policy will be
prepared for the policy-holder from the information on this slip of
paper.

Brokers and agents

Insurance brokers and insurance agents are the middlemen of the
insurance industry acting as a link between the client requiring
insurance and the organisation providing it. In strict terms neither is
necessary (the exception being, of course, should you wish to deal with
a Lloyd's underwriting syndicate), most large insurance companies
having branches throughout the country. However, in practice, the
majority of insurance business is channelled through these
intermediaries.

Insurance intermediaries are only allowed to call themselves brokers
when they have satisfied the Insurance Brokers Registration Council

that they have the necessary combination of qualifications and business experience to give the public impartial advice on all classes and aspects of insurance. Transacting insurance business is the full-time occupation of the insurance broker. He has contacts with many insurance companies – the larger firms with Lloyd's underwriters as well. He receives his remuneration by way of commission from those companies with whom his clients take out insurance. The broker is expected to use his skill and judgement to get the best possible deal for his client.

The broker is expected to abide by the Insurance Brokers Registration Council's code of conduct, which is designed to control the selling activities and techniques of the broker. The code consists of a statement on acts or ommissions to act which are considered unprofessional. A broker may be removed from the register if he fails to achieve the council's required standards. Additionally, as the broker holds himself out to be an expert he may also be liable in law (professional negligence) should be fail to achieve the standard which could be expected of the average member of his profession.

Insurance agents are not normally engaged in insurance as a full-time occupation. Their appointment as agents arises out of their position to introduce new business to the insurance company. Thus a garage proprietor may have an agency with several companies specialising in motor insurance, or the bank manager and solicitor with insurers dealing with life assurance or pension plans. Like the insurance broker the agent receives commission from the insurance company for his services. The activities of these insurance agents, and there are many, are not governed by the Insurance Brokers (Registration) Act, nor are they expected to show the skill and judgement expected of a broker. Indeed in a majority of cases they are not expected to give advice, their role is to introduce the client to the insurer. It is the insurer through a full-time member of staff termed 'inspector of agents' (normally abbreviated to 'inspector') who will give the expert advice and attention required by the client.

Examination questions

1. On what principles does the existing world pattern of insurance operate? Refer in your answer to practical examples.   *(PSC 1980)*

2. Briefly outline the types of insurance which would particularly interest the following business organisations:

    (a) a sole proprietor owning a single corner shop;

    (b) a public limited company operating an international passenger airline fleet;

    (c) a medium-sized manufacturing company producing garden and agricultural chemicals and fertilisers.   *(PSC 1980)*

3. Which types of insurance is a medium-sized manufacturing company of electrical consumer goods likely to be interested in? For each type of insurance you mention, fully explain the various risks covered.   *(PSC 1979)*

4. Describe the work of the following people involved in insurance: (a) underwriter; (b) broker; (c) agent.   *(PSC 1977, 1981)*

5. What is the purpose of insurance and how does it benefit business and society?

Banking

Chapter 17

The origins of our commercial banking system today go back to the activities of goldsmiths in the seventeenth century. Goldsmiths who worked with and traded in gold found other people, particularly merchants, wishing to deposit their holdings of gold with them for safe keeping. The goldsmith would give the depositor a receipt for the gold received, which could be used to redeem the gold (though it was very seldom the same gold) by the holder of that receipt. Over a period of time merchants took to the habit of paying debts with these receipts rather than gold – it was after all far more convenient and safer.

Soon the goldsmiths came to realise that the gold which was lying idle in their vaults could be put to better use – that is, lent out at suitable rates of interest to merchants and other groups wishing to finance business operations. But the loan was made, not in gold (though a request for gold would have been met), but by means of promissory notes which were indistinguishable from the receipts issued against the custody of gold. Later goldsmiths came to realise that only a small proportion of these promissory notes were likely to be presented for payment in gold at any one time. The total amount of gold in their vaults could therefore finance lending on a far greater scale than hitherto considered – the system hinging on the public's confidence in the goldsmith's (or banker's) ability to pay.

Today the basic function of the commercial banking system remains much the same – the borrowing of money from current account or deposit account holders and the making of loans, or 'advances' as they are sometimes termed, to industry and commerce.

But in other ways the banking system has changed dramatically. Commercial banks no longer have the right to issue (promissory) notes, they have developed many other services for the benefit of their customers, there are other private financial institutions who play an important role in the provision of finance, while the Bank of England carefully monitors and controls the activities of the whole sector.

In this chapter we shall consider the role of the principal financial institutions – that is, the commercial and merchant banks, the discount houses, and the Bank of England. We turn our attention first to commercial banks.

Commercial banks

By far the greater proportion of commercial banking business in the UK today is carried out by members of the Bankers' Clearing House – Barclays, Lloyds, Midland, National Westminster, National and Commercial, and the Bank of Scotland. The Bankers' Clearing House is the system by which the banks settle whatever claims they have against each other. These claims arise out of the cheques drawn by the banks' customers on their various branches throughout the country and which are payable to the customers of another bank. Interbank indebtedness is not settled by transfers in cash but through the accounts that all banks hold at the Bank of England. Certain commercial banks, for example the Co-operative Bank, some Scottish banks, and the British branches of overseas banks, are not 'clearing banks'. These will employ a member of the Bankers' Clearing House to act as their agent.

The functions of a commercial bank

The receipt, safe-keeping, transfer, and encashment of money
Money may be placed with a bank either on a deposit or current account. The larger amount of funds placed with banks are in deposit accounts. These are interest-paying accounts, where one normally puts money that is not going to be needed for some time. For that reason they are sometimes termed 'savings' accounts. Although banks may demand notice before withdrawal from a deposit account, this requirement is normally waived.

Traditionally, deposits on current account made up the bulk of the funds deposited with a banker. However, today people are financially more aware of the loss they incur keeping large sums of money on current account and now tend to place their surplus funds into an interest-bearing account. Current accounts though, are far more useful than deposit accounts because apart from the receipt and safe-keeping of money the facilities detailed below are also available:

1. The use of a cheque-book. The vast majority of payments are made this way.

2. Standing orders. Instructions to bankers to make a periodic payment from your account direct to the account of another person or organisation until such time as you countermand payment. Many people use standing orders (or bankers' orders as they are sometimes called) to make the monthly payment of mortgage interest to their building society or rates to the local authority.

3. Credit transfers.   Used by individuals to pay a sum of money (which could not be determined in advance) direct to the current account of the creditor, for example the quarterly gas bill. Businesses often use credit transfers to pay the salaries of their employees, debiting their own account by means of a single cheque.

4. Bankers' cards.   These may be either a credit or a guarantee card. Where an individual holds a credit card goods may be purchased without immediate payment. Instead the shopkeeper records details of the transaction and the credit card on an invoice which the customer signs. At the end of the day the shopkeeper will pay the invoice into his bank with the rest of his takings – the total amount being credited to his account. At the end of the month the shopkeeper's customer receives a statement from the bank itemising his credit transactions for the last month and requiring payment.

A guarantee card does not allow the holder to obtain goods on credit, but makes payment by cheque more acceptable to the shopkeeper. By noting the guarantee card number on the back of the cheque, and comparing the signature on card and cheque for similarity, a shopkeeper is guaranteed payment of any cheque up to £50 where the drawer of that cheque defaults.

5. Cash withdrawal.   Stocks of coins and notes are kept on hand at all branches and may be drawn as needed (subject to current account balance!) by customers. Many branch banks have also installed automatic cash dispensers to enable customers to withdraw cash outside banking hours.

6. Night-safe and safe-keeping facilities.   Cash takings received by traders outside banking hours may be deposited in the bank's night-safe in a sealed leather container (wallet). The following morning bank cashiers in the presence of the customer will check the amount deposited. Banks are also used as repositories of valuables. Thus the bank may hold bearer bonds, share certificates, or other valuable documents on behalf of the business or individual customer. Equally the items deposited may be jewellery or precious metals. These items, which are held under lock and key at all times, will only be released to the order of the customer.

7. Customer references.   While a banker is under a duty of secrecy not to reveal any details of his customer's account he is often called upon to vouch for the reliability of that customer. Thus a trader who is unsure of the financial standing of one with whom he trades may approach his own bank and request that an 'opinion' be obtained. His bank will then approach the other person's bankers who will provide information of a very general nature. The banker must in no circumstances disclose the balance on his customer's account.

Loans and overdrafts
By far the most important function of the bank is the granting of loans and overdrafts to current-account holders. Let us consider the case of a manufacturing business borrowing money from the bank to buy better plant and machinery. The economy benefits through the immediate increase in economic activity and reduction in unemployment and additionally, in the longer term, from the growth in productive potential. The lending creates extra work and profits for the firm making the plant and machinery while our manufacturing business itself will become more profitable through the use of more efficient machinery. Lastly, customers benefit through lower prices and often better-designed and made products.

When a customer obtains a bank loan a separate account is opened and debited with the amount of the loan. The customer's current account is then credited with that amount. Interest will be charged on the full amount of the loan regardless of the state of the customer's current account. Since the bank has agreed to lend the money for a specific length of time it cannot call in its loan unless the borrower defaults on one of the terms of agreement.

Where the bank agrees to make overdraft facilities available, the customer is allowed to overdraw his current account up to the agreed amount. Interest is calculated daily on the overdrawn balance of the account. The borrowing must be regarded as temporary as the bank reserves the right to demand payment of the outstanding amount at any time. In practice though, the bank would only do this if it believed the borrower to be in financial difficulties and that the situation could only worsen by continuing to lend the money.

Ancillary activities
As commercial businesses seeking to earn a profit for their shareholders, banks have been quick to identify other activities which do not conflict with their two primary functions. Today banks aim to provide a complete range of financial services for their customers, these include those given below.

1. Foreign business. The growth of world trade has encouraged banks to play a more active role. The bank can provide information for the would-be exporter on overseas markets, tariffs, documentation required, and exchange rates. Banks have invested heavily in the technology necessary to transfer money speedily between financial centres as well as providing the travellers' cheques and foreign currency so necessary for business trips.

2. Investment advice and management.   Bank managers often provide advice to their customers on stocks and shares. They may also purchase, hold, or sell shares on their customer's behalf. Several go further, Barclays Bank for instance has one subsidiary Barclays Bank Trust Company which undertakes investment portfolio management, and another, Barclays Unicorn, which manages a number of unit trusts. Barclays Bank Trust Company also provides a new issue service to companies wishing to raise capital.

3. Executor and trustee services.   Banks will act as executors to wills, obtaining probate and distributing the estate. They will also act as trustees to estates – holding and managing property for the benefit of others. A trust is often used by the well-to-do to ensure that their wealth is used in a particular way after their death.

4. Insurance and taxation services.   Until recently insurance services were limited to advice on life assurance and personal pension plans; now many are providing a far broader service, for example Barclays Insurance Service.

Banks and credit creation

Do banks actually create money? The answer is yes, and is based upon the fact, which seventeenth-century goldsmith-bankers discovered, that not all depositors demand or withdraw their money at the same time. Obviously the banker has to keep a certain proportion of his assets in cash to meet demands for cash, but the rest may be invested in some way to earn him money. Consider the case where a banker discovers over time that prudence dictates he should keep 10 per cent of deposits in cash. Let us also assume that the banker has received a deposit of £100 cash from a member of the public. His balance-sheet is shown in Fig. 17.1. Now, our banker knows that depositors are only likely to demand 10 per cent of their deposits in cash. His £100 cash will therefore support liabilities not of £100 but £1,000. Taking advantage of this, his balance sheet would be as shown in Fig. 17.2.

	£	
Assets		The deposit of £100 with the bank is a
Cash	<u>100</u>	liability, since it is a debt owed to the
		customer. The cash which is now held by
Liabilities		the bank is an asset which may be used to
Deposit	<u>100</u>	repay the liability.

Fig. 17.1 Balance sheet XYZ Bank

	£	£
Assets		
Cash	100	
Advances	900	1,000
Liabilities		
Deposit	100	
Deposit (loans)	900	1,000

Fig. 17.2 Balance sheet XYZ Bank

The bank acquires extra liabilities by agreeing to lend customers £900. This amount is credited to their loan accounts. But the bank also has claims against these borrowers for the repayment of their loans and this appears as an asset in the balance-sheet.

But what would happen if our initial depositor decided to withdraw not £10 but £50 in cash? The remaining £50 cash would not be sufficient to support bank advances of £900. Assuming that our banker still made the maximum loans possible what would his balance-sheet look like? Try filling in the missing figures in Fig. 17.3.

In practice to avoid the obvious loss of goodwill caused by the curtailment or recalling of loans bankers normally have a second line of defence, 'liquid assets' – that is, assets which may be quickly converted into cash. For many years banks were required to maintain an 8 per cent cash ratio and a 30 per cent liquidity ratio (this includes the 8 per cent cash ratio). Today, these requirements are no longer in force. Commercial banks are required to hold $\frac{1}{2}$ per cent of their deposits in non-interest-bearing accounts at the Bank of England, but that is all. At the present time though, banks are maintaining a liquidity, or near cash, ratio of approximately 20 per cent.

The structure of assets that a bank maintains is a compromise between profitability and liquidity. This is because the more liquid the asset the lower its yield. Consider, the yield of cash is zero, on bank

	£	£
Assets		
Cash		
Advances	____	____
Liabilities		
Deposit		
Deposit (loans)	____	____

Fig. 17.3 Balance-sheet XYZ Bank

advances 12–15 per cent. As Fig. 17.4 indicates, advances constitute
the greatest (and most profitable) part of the bank's asset portfolio.

Liquid assets comprise cash, bills, and market loans. Cash is held
either in the till to meet the daily requirements of customers or at the
Bank of England. Bank of England balances are used to settle
interbank indebtedness and can, for practical purposes, be treated the
same as cash in the till.

Bills discounted are relatively liquid assets, the majority maturing
within two months of purchase. They are normally obtained from the
discount houses, and fall into one of two categories – trade or Treasury
bills. Trade bills were a popular method of financing overseas trade,
and formed the greater proportion of discounted bills held by the
banks until the First World War. Today the majority holding is of
Treasury bills, that is, bills issued by the British Government to finance
current expenditure.

In recent years the workings of the old-established discount market
have been overshadowed by the growth of 'parallel' or 'secondary'
money markets. Secondary money markets now deal with a greater
amount of short-term funds than the discount markets. Bank holdings
of market loans, varying between 15 and 20 per cent of their total
assets, reflect the growing importance of the secondary market. The
most well established of the secondary markets is 'money on call or at

Fig. 17.4 The relative importance of different assets in a bank's balance sheet

short notice'. These are surplus funds which the bank lent primarily to the discount houses but also to other financial institutions in the City, subject to the proviso that it is returned on the day on which the demand for payment is made. This is the most liquid of the banks' investments but carries only a low rate of interest.

A second market deals with sterling certificates of deposit (CDs). These acknowledge the fact that a sum of money has been deposited with the bank issuing the negotiable instrument (CD), and that this principal plus interest will be repaid upon a stated date.

The London Money Market

The London Money Market is part of the total capital market in the UK which facilitates the movement of money between lender and borrower. It specialises in the provision of short and medium-term finance. The Money Market comprises the commercial and merchant banks active in the City of London together with the discount houses and the Bank of England.

There is in fact no actual market-place. It is in the relationship between the interested institutions and the act of negotiating the raising or investment of capital that the market can be said to exist.

The commercial banks provide most of the funds for investment, often for very short periods of time and always at low rates of interest. The biggest individual borrower is the UK Government which finances current expenditure by the issue of Treasury bills. However, in total, private sector borrowing by discount houses and firms is greater than that of the public sector.

In practice the period for which banks borrow these funds may range up to five years. It is a useful method of financing longer-term borrowing and yet because they are so easily sold in the market provide additional valuable liquidity.

A third market is the sterling interbank market. This consists of the majority of banks – commercial, merchant, British, or overseas acting in the UK. Its members deposit surplus funds with one another for periods ranging up to five years. For banks accepting the deposit it provides valuable cash funds which can be used to cover cash withdrawals by customers.

Fourthly, the currency movements of central banks, multinational corporations, and private individuals (especially from oil-producing states) form the basis of the Euro-currency market. Euro-currencies can be defined as funds denominated in a different currency to the currency of that country where they are deposited. For example dollars held by a Japanese multinational may be deposited with a London bank. These funds then become available for lending by that bank on the Euro-currency market for periods normally not exceeding three months.

Finally, two smaller markets also exist based upon finance houses (hire-purchase specialists) and local authorities raising money for up to a year.

All assets discussed so far are easily converted into cash, or mature within one year, and are therefore termed 'liquid'. We now turn our attention to those assets of the bank which are relatively illiquid – investments and advances. These are often termed 'risk assets' reflecting the risk of losing money if the banker were forced to sell investments before maturity, or a customer defaulted on an advance.

Investments held by a commercial bank are normally bought on the open market. The vast majority are government securities with up to ten years to run until maturity. These yield a higher return than Treasury bills. Banks will ensure they carry a balanced portfolio of investments so that at any time some are near to maturity and will provide a steady stream of cash. By far the largest proportion of bank assets though are loans and overdrafts in customers – perhaps as high as 70 per cent of total assets. These are the most profitable of the banks' assets earning a return of 1 to 4 per cent above their base lending rate. The precise rate reflects the length of the loan, the creditworthiness of the customer, and the security offered.

Merchant banks

The origins of merchant banks go back several hundred years to a time when they were merchants who specialised in overseas trade. Their knowledge and experience of overseas markets quickly drew them into the work of providing finance for international trade and accepting bills of exchange. While this is still an important part of the business of merchant banks, they have successfully diversified their activities into several other areas.

Acceptances

One major problem which has always existed in international trade has been finance. Briefly the exporter wants his money as soon as he ships the goods to the importers, while the importer cannot afford to pay until he has received and sold the goods. The method used to surmount this problem was the bill of exchange. When our exporter was ready to ship the goods a bill of exchange (as shown in Fig. 17.5) was drawn up. This would be sent to the importer together with documents verifying that the goods had been shipped. On receiving the bill our importer acknowledged his liability by signing it across its face. The bill was

```
                          Exporter's Address
                          1 Jan 1984

    £5,000


    At 90 days after date pay to the order of
    'Exporter' or his order £5,000, for value
    received.

                          (Signed) Exporter

    To Importer
        Importer's address
```

Fig. 17.5 A commercial bill of exchange

then returned to the exporter who could hold the bill to maturity, or more usually discounted the bill (i.e. sold it to another person). But potential buyers of the bill were often deterred by the fact that they knew neither the exporter nor the importer.

A bill of exchange may be defined as 'an unconditional order' in writing addressed by one person (the exporter) to another (the importer) to pay on demand or at some fixed or determinable future time, a sum certain in money to, or to the order of, a specified person or bearer.

To discount the bill our exporter had to find someone who would, for a consideration, personally guarantee that the bill would be paid if the importer defaulted. This was the role of the bank who, by placing its name on the reverse of the bill, was said to have endorsed or 'accepted' the bill. By accepting the bill the merchant bank does not provide the exporter with any funds, it merely enables the bill to be discounted. Bills carrying the name of a well-known merchant bank, a member of the Accepting Houses Committee (e.g. Barings, Rothschild, Schroder Wagg, Hambros – there are sixteen members in all), are eligible for discount at the best rates by the commercial banks and the discount houses. However, before a merchant bank will commit its name to any bill the creditworthiness of the importer is ascertained.

As an extension of their work in overseas trade merchant banks have also become foreign exchange dealers and important members of the London Gold Market. Some will also help with export and import documentation. Additionally, through their knowledge and experience of short-term financial markets, they have become active in the secondary money markets – giving advice and buying and selling securities on behalf of their clients, as well as being involved in the factoring of company debts.

New issues

Merchant banks who undertake work connected with the issue of shares or stock are members of the Issuing Houses Committee. In recent years though, their monopoly of new issue work has been challenged and broken by other financial institutions, particularly commercial banks.

The basic function of an issuing house is to help find finance for those companies wishing to expand, but the merchant bank is also prepared to, and in normal circumstances will, undertake the administrative work concerned with an issue of stocks or shares. Thus it will prepare the prospectus or other documents required for the issue, arrange the underwriting, handle the applications, determine the allocation of shares where the issue is oversubscribed, and arrange for a Stock Exchange listing. Additionally, it has the connections to place shares with institutional investors such as pension funds or insurance companies.

For the smaller, relatively unknown company wishing to issue shares for the first time the help of a merchant bank is invaluable. It is the act of the bank in allowing its name (and therefore its reputation) to be associated with the issue that ensures success. Sometimes the issuing house will take over the whole issue itself and resell to the public.

Issuing houses offer a similar service to that described above to foreign firms and governments wishing to raise capital in London. The importance of these overseas customers, especially multinationals, has encouraged merchant banks to develop and extend their traditional links with banks in other countries, participating in the development of multinational banking consortia, and to set up offices in other major financial centres around the world.

Advice

The relationship between merchant bank and client built up during the share issue often continues after the event. Sometimes the bank will maintain the company's statutory registers on members, directors, director's interests, mortgages, and charges. They will help their client make best use of his assets by advising on finance, organisation, and management. But it is with the number of firms seeking to obtain the benefits of economies of scale, reduced competition, greater competitive strength, and enhanced status through mergers and take-over bids that they have become well known. As adviser to the firm wishing to expand through merger or take-over their work involves identifying those businesses which fit the requirements of their client. They will estimate the value of these businesses to their client, and therefore the price to offer per share. More generally they will consider what defensive arguments may be raised against the take-over bid and how best to counter these. In the same way, the advisers to the firm defending itself against an unwelcome take-over bid will be devising the best tactics and presentation of information against the merger.

Many merchant banks have also developed large investment advisory services for clients. By far the greatest number of these clients are institutional investors such as pension funds, local authorities, investment and unit trusts. Some banks have gone further and now offer a complete investment management service, taking over the day-to-day running of the investment portfolio, buying and selling securities as they think fit.

The discount houses

The discount market consists of financial institutions who are involved in the purchase, or sale of, commercial and Treasury bills. The work of the discount house is central to this process. There are, in fact, twelve discount houses.

The function of the discount house is to borrow funds (which are not being used by their owners) for short periods and make these funds available to government and business for longer periods. The commercial banks are the major source of funds to the discount houses – providing over 90 per cent of all funds in use at any one time.

These funds are used in two ways. First, the funds are used to purchase Treasury bills which are made available for weekly tender by the Government. The discount houses tender for these bills in competition with one another, and other bidders. The price tendered is lower than the maturity value of the bill (i.e. it is discounted – hence the name 'discount houses'), and establishes the market rate of interest.

Today the discount houses undertake to purchase whatever bills are left after the allocation to other bidders. In return they receive a slightly more advantageous discount rate, and the right to turn to the Bank of England (as lender of last resort) for help should they run short of funds.

Attempts by governments to reduce their dependence on short-term borrowing, and the consequent reduction in Treasury bills available has forced the discount houses to find other homes for their short-term funds. Treasury bills now account for approximately 10 per cent of their assets, the remainder being split in roughly equal proportions between commercial bills of exchange and short-term investments on the secondary money markets (see p. 318).

The willingness of the discount houses to purchase commercial bills of exchange depends upon their quality. In this respect the work of the acceptance houses is important. Bills accepted by these houses obtain the best discount rates in the market. Where a bill has not been endorsed by the acceptance house it will only be marketable if the credit standing of the importer responsible for payment of the bill upon maturity is well known, and then only at a substantially higher rate of discount.

Discount houses do not always hold the bills to maturity. Often they are parcelled together on the basis of maturity dates and rediscounted to the commercial banks. The commercial banks' objective being to build up a portfolio of bills with a proportion maturing each day.

Although the discount house policy of 'borrowing short, lending long' seems a certain recipe for disaster it is not often that the market is left short of funds. While commercial banks may be left short of funds at the end of a day's trading and have to demand repayment of 'money on call and short notice' from the discount houses, this is normally offset by another bank having a surplus which it is willing to lend out. In practice it is more likely that discount houses will be left short of funds as part of government policy to influence short-term interest rates than for any other reason. Yet, even where the discount houses have insufficient funds they are always able to borrow from the Bank of England as lender of last resort. But whenever possible they try to avoid this remedy for the rates of interest charged by the bank are high, and they normally lose on the transaction.

In most other countries there is no comparable institution to the discount houses. Banks lend direct to the Government. But while some would argue that the discount houses are superfluous and that the cost of short-term borrowing could be reduced through their demise, both the commercial banks and the Bank of England have argued for their retention. To the commercial banks it is a means of maintaining money in an extremely liquid form, but at the same time earning interest. To the Bank of England it provides a mechanism for exercising control over short-term interest rates. Finally, through its agreement to absorb whatever portion of the weekly lender of Treasury bills is left unsold, the Government is certain that its short-term borrowing requirements will be met.

The Bank of England

The Bank of England was founded by Act of Parliament in 1694, and was nationalised in 1946 because of its importance to the Government in the implementation of monetary policy – a position it had held for almost 200 years. Its position is that of a state bank, more often termed 'central bank', epitomising the position of such a bank at the hub of the system of banking and other financial institutions in market economies.

A central bank differs from a commercial bank firstly because it does not operate for profit, rather it is operated by the Government in (what it perceives to be) the national interest. A central bank will normally have no private customers – the Bank of England has a few, dating back to the days before nationalisation, but will open no new accounts for private individuals or organisations. Such a bank provides a lead to the commercial banks. It establishes rules of good conduct and ensures that they are adhered to. Finally, it is the institution through which monetary control is exercised.

Functions of the Bank of England

Note issue

The Bank Charter Act 1844 removed private banks' right of note issue. This applied where new banks were established or where two or more existing banks amalgamated. By 1929 the Bank of England had emerged as the sole note-issuing authority in England and Wales. The Bank Charter Act did not apply to Scotland and Ireland, and a number of these banks still issue their own notes. At one time note issue was limited by the amount of gold the Bank of England held. This is not so today, only a small fraction is covered by gold holdings, the rest – the fiduciary issues – is backed by the issue of government securities.

Banker to the Government

It was first through the many accounts which eighteenth- and nineteenth-century governments held at the Bank of England that its role as central bank developed. Today as the government banker it still maintains the most important accounts. It arranges financial assistance through the issue of Treasury bills or Ways and Means advances should the account become overdrawn. Government borrowing, long and short term, is arranged by the bank, and administrative arrangements relating to the keeping of stockholders' registers, the payment of interest, and redemption of stock are also entrusted to it. Finally the bank gives advice to the Government. Working closely with the Treasury the bank examines and forecasts changes in economic indicators, and gives advice on whatever changes in monetary policy or control that it thinks necessary.

The bankers' bank

Commercial banks use the Bank of England in a similar manner to a business using its bank account. The commercial banks maintain large deposits of cash at the bank – a minimum of ½ per cent of their eligible liabilities, and also special deposits (i.e. assets which the Bank of England has demanded to reduce the banks' liquidity and which are not available for use). The former are used to set off any interbank liabilities which arise as a result of the day's trading. The Bank of England is also in a position of influence *vis-a-vis* the commercial banks – so much so that even informal requests, say to reduce lending or concentrate lending in certain sectors, are a powerful lever.

External affairs
Movements of international currencies for investment or trading purposes may cause considerable fluctuations in the value of sterling. Where the Bank of England believes that fluctuations do not reflect underlying market trends, it may intervene to stabilise the exchange rate by buying or selling sterling. The Bank of England, on the instructions of the Treasury, is also empowered to control the movement of sterling into other currencies. This is normally effected through issuing instructions to the commercial banks. Today few restrictions exist on the transfer of currencies, but as recently as 1978, restrictions on sterling/foreign currency transactions were in force. (Many developing countries use exchange controls as a means of limiting imports and avoiding balance-of-payments difficulties.)

The Bank of England liaises closely with other central banks and international monetary institutions, with the aim of ensuring greater stability in the international monetary system. Many of these countries or organisations hold their sterling balances in accounts at the Bank of England.

Monetary policy
By far the most important function of the bank though, is its role in implementing the monetary policy of the Government. It is the Government's wish to control the level of economic activity within the economy so as to attain objectives such as a high and stable level of employment, stable prices, satisfactory economic growth and balance of payments. The Government has a number of weapons at its disposal: fiscal policy, incomes policy, and monetary policy. We will consider here the techniques which the Bank of England may use to implement monetary policy.

In practice there are two main ways in which the Bank of England can affect the economy through monetary policy. The first is by controlling the supply of money. We have already seen that the commercial banking sector has the ability to create money – an ability that is dependent upon the amount of money customers deposit with them. Therefore, the central bank may, by affecting their cash (and other liquid assets), enhance or impair their ability to increase money supply. The second method of control is also designed to affect the quantity of money, but this time through the operation of interest rates, which is believed to affect borrowers' willingness to borrow.

1. The cash ratio. Since 1981 all banks with eligible liabilities of more than £10 m. are required to hold ½ per cent of those liabilities in cash with the bank. These balances are non-interest earning and therefore provide a source of revenue to the bank. Commercial banks often maintain higher balances though, to cover interbank indebtedness.

Prior to 1981 the Bank of England influenced bank lending through the wider base of liquid assets. Commercial banks were required to hold 12½ per cent of their liabilities in eligible reserve assets. Broadly, these were the more liquid of banks' assets such as cash, money on call or at short notice, or Treasury and commercial bills. These requirements were discontinued simply because they were considered ineffective – commercial banks will always maintain a proportion (often in excess of 12½ per cent) of their assets in relatively liquid assets merely as a matter of prudence.

2. Open market operations.   The Bank of England is active in the money market, buying and selling securities each day. Its actions are designed to offset the large and often unpredictable flows of funds between the public sector and the banking system – fluctuations which, if unchecked, would leave the banking system alternatively short or with a surplus of liquid assets. The bank can therefore affect the liquidity of the commercial banks by its actions in buying or selling securities. Should the bank in accordance with government policy wish to restrict bank credit, it may increase its sales of securities to the private sector. Payments to the Bank of England for these securities will reduce the level of deposits held by the commercial banks, causing them to restrict their loans and advances.

The bank may also affect the liquidity of the clearing banks by funding – the process of converting short-term into longer-term securities. Treasury bills and other government stocks with less than a year to run to maturity, form part of the stock of liquid assets held by the commercial banks. Should the Bank of England issue fewer Treasury bills (and even perhaps purchase them on the open market) and in their place issue long-term government stock, the structure of the commercial banks' assets is changed. Liquid assets have been replaced by investments. To maintain their ratio of liquid to total assets the banks will reduce advances.

3. Lender of last resort.   But not only do open-market operations by the central bank lead to a reduction in lending by commercial banks, they may also be used to engineer an increase in interest rates. Open-market operations work by affecting the commercial banks' balances at the Bank of England. In an effort to restore these balances, the banks will demand repayment of their 'money on call and short notice' from the discount houses. It is the discount houses which are now starved of funds, and they must turn to the Bank of England as 'lender of last resort', for help. They will offer to sell the bank some of their Treasury, local authority, or commercial bills, stating their price. If the price is consistent with the monetary policy which it wishes to pursue, the bank will purchase the bills. But if the bank wishes to see, say, an increase in the short-term rate of interest, it may refuse the bills, leaving the discount houses to make further offers at lower prices (i.e. discount them at a higher rate of interest). Now the discount houses rely on a small difference between the rate at which they borrow and discount bills to make a profit. The raising of interest rates by the Bank of England has eliminated that profit margin. The discount houses will restore that margin by raising the rate at which they will purchase bills in the market.

Conversely, when the bank wants the rate of interest to fall, it will increase the price at which it is prepared to purchase bills from the discount market.

4. Directives and special deposits. It has already been noted that the Bank of England has considerable moral influence over the whole banking sector. This can, for example, be seen in the directives which the bank issues to the clearing banks. Such directives will normally require the banks to limit lending generally, but perhaps also restrict certain groups even further (e.g. property dealers) or exempt others (e.g. exporters). These instructions on how the commercial banks are expected to help aid economic objectives, do not carry the force of law, yet have never been openly disobeyed even though bank profits will often be adversely affected.

However, to require the commercial banks to comply with too many directives would probably weaken the moral authority of the Bank of England. For that reason the bank introduced a system of special deposits by which commercial banks are required to deposit a specific proportion of their liquid assets in a special account at the Bank of England. Interest is paid upon these deposits, but they do not form part of the commercial banks' holdings of liquid assets.

Examination questions

1. What are the sectors of the English banking system? How are they linked?
    (PSC 1980)

2. Outline the major functions of each of the following, clearly illustrating their distinguishing characteristics: (a) commercial banks; (b) merchant banks; (c) central bank.
    (PSC 1977)

3. (a) Is it a sign of a healthy economy when businesses overdraw their current accounts?

    (b) How do (i) the customers of businesses, (ii) the banks themselves, benefit by the banks making loans to businesses?
    (PSC 1983)

4. Does the asset structure of a commercial bank provide an adequate picture of its activities?

5. What services do commercial and merchant banks offer to industry regarding the provision of capital?

6. What role does a commercial bank play in encouraging industrial and economic growth?
(PSC 1980)

7. Explain the role and functions of the Bank of England. How may it influence monetary conditions within the economy?

8. Confusion is often caused by the following terms: (a) discount houses; (b) acceptance houses; (c) issuing houses. Explain clearly and concisely the role and importance of each to the economy.

Sources of finance

Chapter 18

Capital is needed by all organisations to finance their business operations. In many organisations capital is required even before business commences. Money has to be invested in fixed assets – land, buildings, machinery, and vehicles. Once business has commenced money is needed for working capital – raw materials, finished stock, and debtors. Employees have to be paid, as do the rent, rates, lighting, and heating bills. Moreover, as a going concern the organisation may require extra capital – to cover a temporary cash-flow crisis, to purchase new improved machinery, or simply to expand.

Sources of finance are usually classified by time into long, medium, and short term. Long-term finance is defined as money raised for a period in excess of five years, medium-term any period from one to five years, and short-term as borrowing of less than one year. Long-term capital should be used to finance the permanent needs of the business – that is, its normal investment in fixed assets. Medium- and short-term sources will be used to finance its investment in current assets. The distinction has a practical importance. Permanent needs should never be financed from short-term sources of funds, for the business may find difficulty in renewing that resource at the end of the loan period. Similarly, with long-term capital costing more than short-term we must be sure that any expansion of operations is permanent before exchanging short- for long-term finance.

Not all potential sources of finance are external to the firm. Often the best sources of capital are to be found hidden in the business's own balance-sheet. Let us consider fixed assets. Land and buildings may be surplus to requirements. We may own land which we have never developed. Alternatively, we may be producing in five locations when two would do. By employing a policy of simplification we may reduce the product range, thus releasing land and buildings, plant and machinery. Perhaps we may question why we purchase plant and machinery at all when we can lease these assets? Similarly, investments in other companies may be realised rather than raising capital from expensive external sources. Yet again current assets provide a potential source of funds through better inventory or credit control. Finally, consider the business's dividend policy. Shareholders may be prepared to accept lower dividends now in return for the promise of increased capital growth and dividends in future years. Undistributed or 'ploughed-back' profits have traditionally provided the bulk of funds needed for expansion.

Long-term sources of finance

Ordinary shares

The holders of these shares are the ultimate risk-takers. It is only after all expenses have been paid and other classes of shareholder have received their due that ordinary shareholders are entitled to their share in the profit. The amount which they receive will vary from year to year, reflecting the changes in the company's fortunes. They may even, in bad years, receive nothing at all. Similarly, should the business be put into liquidation, ordinary shareholders will not receive repayment of their investment until all other creditors have been paid in full. In many cases, where the business has been trading unsuccessfully for a number of years they will receive little or nothing. Where, however, the business is successful ordinary, or equity shareholders as they are sometimes called, stand to benefit most from high profits and the appreciation in the value of the company.

As owners of the business, ordinary shareholders control its activities. They have the right to attend and vote on all resolutions made at the annual and other general meetings. They appoint directors to act for them, and should they disagree with the director's policy or actions they may terminate that appointment.

Preference shares

Holders of these shares receive priority over ordinary shareholders in two respects. First they are entitled to a fixed rate of dividend each year before the ordinary shareholders may participate in profits, and secondly they are normally entitled to priority of repayment of capital should the business be wound up. However, although preference shareholders are members of the company they do not normally participate in the control of the business, but receive only those rights accorded to them in the Articles of Association.

Preference shares may be cumulative, participating, or redeemable. Cumulative preference shares carry the right to have arrears of dividend paid to them before ordinary shareholders receive a dividend. All preference shares are cumulative unless stated otherwise.

Participating preference shares are entitled to receive a fixed dividend together with some further addition should the dividend to ordinary shareholders exceed a certain percentage. For example, the preference shareholders' fixed rate of dividend may be 10 per cent, but where the ordinary share dividend exceeds 20 per cent they may be entitled to receive 1 per cent extra for each additional 2 per cent received by the equity shareholders. Where a company issues redeemable preference shares it gives itself the right to repurchase those shares on or after a specified date. This is the only form of non-permanent share capital which exists.

Debentures

A debenture is a document issued by a company acknowledging a debt. Normally the debenture holder will receive a fixed rate of interest on the loan and will be given a security for that loan. The security may be by way of a fixed charge over land and buildings, plant and machinery, or a floating charge over working capital. Debentures receiving the security of charge on company assets are termed 'mortgage debentures'. Debentures issued without security are termed 'naked' or 'simple'. The debenture deed will also give details of when the loan has to be repaid and the rights of the holder should the company default on payment of interest or repayment of capital.

From the debenture-holder's point of view debentures are attractive because their loan is secure and their interest guaranteed even when the company makes little or no profit. To the company the advantages are that the debenture holders are not members of the company and therefore cannot take part in the management of the company, the rate of interest payable is generally lower than that paid to preference shareholders due to the greater degree of security of capital, and such capital may be redeemed out of future profits. Finally, inflation reduces the real burden of paying debt interest and repaying capital.

However, an issue of debentures is not advantageous in all circumstances. Debenture interest must be paid whether or not the company makes a profit. Default on either interest or capital payments may allow the shareholders to appoint a receiver, thus removing control of the company from the shareholders. Again a charge on the assets of the company reduces the ability of the company to use those assets as it thinks fit.

In recent years some companies have been issuing convertible debentures or loan stock. Often this is unsecured but gives the holder the right to exchange his stock for ordinary shares at some specified date in the future. This conversion is often allowed at advantageous prices so as to reduce company reliance on fixed-interest loans.

Mortgages

Most of us are familiar with the term 'mortgage', as it is the recognised method by which many people purchase their houses, but mortgages are also an important source of finance for the industrial and commercial sector. Mortgages may be granted to businesses wishing to purchase land and buildings by institutional investors such as pension funds, insurance companies, and investment trusts who use the property as security for their loan. Businesses may obtain a loan of up to two-thirds of the purchase price of the property which may be repayable over twenty or twenty-five years.

The distinction between a mortgage and a debenture lies in the fact that a mortgage is a debt owed to a single lender, a debenture is a loan obtained from a number of people or organisations.

Sales and lease back

Businesses owning property may raise money by selling that property – normally to an institutional investor and at the same time negotiating to lease that property back at an agreed rental (subject to periodic revision) for time spans of up to 100 years. The purchaser will wish to ensure that the vendor has a good profit record, and that in the event of default on the lease it will be reasonably easy to obtain alternative lessees.

Sale and lease back has the advantage of releasing funds locked up within the business for other purposes while guaranteeing long-term occupation of the premises. However, the company loses an asset which is likely to appreciate in value over time, which would provide security for loans, and the loss of which substantially increases the level of fixed costs which have to be paid by the business.

Methods of issuing shares and debentures

When a firm wishes to raise new capital by the issue of shares or debentures it has a number of options open to it: (a) issue by prospectus; (b) rights issue; (c) offer by tender; (d) offer for sale; placings.

Although the method of issuing shares may differ, most firms, including large ones, find it beneficial to obtain the help of intermediaries such as issuing houses, merchant banks, and specialist departments of clearing banks. These will advise on the benefits of the different methods and on the timing and pricing of a share issue. For smaller firms the appointment of such an intermediary is a necessity in order to gain the interest and confidence of the investor.

Issue by prospectus

Shares are offered directly to the public by the company at a stated price. This is probably the most well-known form of share issue as the prospectus will appear in several newspapers. The prospectus contains information on:

(a) company activities past, present, and future;

(b) directors, management, and staff;

(c) the company's financial record, profits, dividends, prospects for the future.

The prospectus also invites potential shareholders to apply for shares as prescribed therein.

The cost of raising money by this method is high. For an established business it is unlikely to be less than 5 per cent, while for a smaller, unknown business it will almost certainly be substantially higher, perhaps as much as 15 per cent of the capital raised.

A significant proportion of the extra costs incurred by the smaller company arises from the higher cost of underwriting the issue. Underwriting is the process by which issuing houses agree to guarantee that all shares offered for sale are in fact sold. In the event of the investing public subscribing for, say, only 60 per cent of the shares offered, the issuing house will purchase the remaining 40 per cent. The company is thus assured of the success of the issue.

Rights issues

Many of the costs associated with issues by prospectus can be avoided by selling extra shares to existing shareholders. New shares are offered to shareholders in proportion to their present holding, often at a price which is less than that currently quoted on the Stock Exchange. Thus a company may offer existing shareholders two new shares for every five already held at a price of 80p per share when the market value of the shares already issued is 90p. The shareholder has the option of taking up the offer himself, or alternatively selling his 'rights' on the Stock Exchange to third parties.

Issues by tender

The procedure followed is similar to where shares are issued by prospectus with one important exception. Investors are invited to subscribe for shares at a price above a specified minimum and investors who wish to hold these shares may be willing to pay significantly more than this. The price at which shares are finally sold will be the highest possible commensurate with selling all shares.

Tenders are often used when market conditions are uncertain, or where there is no share already quoted on the Stock Exchange which can be used to establish a reasonable price. Although the company is unsure of the exact amount of capital (above the minimum) it will raise, this uncertainty is offset by the potential premium it can obtain if the issue is successful.

Offer for sale

By this method a company, probably medium-sized and making its first issue of shares to the public, will sell the share issue to an issuing house. It will then offer the shares to the public at a price higher than that which it paid for them, thus covering its expenses. The offer for sale by the issuing house will, as with an issue by prospectus, give full details on the business – its history, financial record, current position, and future prospects.

Placings

A private placing of shares will be used where the size of the company and the capital required are insufficient for a Stock Exchange quotation. An issuing house will approach investment trusts, insurance companies, and pension funds who it believes will be interested in holding shares in this type of business. A high rate of return (and therefore a low purchase price) will be required by these institutional investors to offset the lack of marketability and the high degree of risk of the investments.

A public placing of shares is used where less than £350,000 is being raised, but the company requires a Stock Exchange quotation. The procedure by which shares are sold is similar to a private placing with the exception that 25 per cent of the share issue must be made available to the general public through the facilities of the Stock Exchange, and the placing must be advertised nationally thus helping to create a market for the shares.

Capital gearing

As we have seen, long-term needs of a company can be satisfied in a number of ways – perhaps by an issue of ordinary shares or preference shares, alternatively by the issue of debentures. Gearing indicates the relationship that exists between ordinary share capital and other forms of long-term finance (fixed-interest capital). The company will be described as high geared when it has a high proportion of fixed-interest capital compared to ordinary share capital, and conversely as low geared when there is little fixed as opposed to equity capital. Gearing is normally expressed as a ratio:

Fixed-interest capital : ordinary share capital

The effect of gearing upon a company is shown in Table 18.1.
Companies A and B have raised the same amount of long-term finance
but have different capital structures. Company A is low geared having
a ratio of 1:9 (£100:£900) whereas company B which makes for greater
use of debentures is said to be high geared with a ratio of 9:1.

Table 18.1 The impact of gearing upon profitability

	Company A (£'000	Company B (£'000)
Ordinary shares	900	100
Debentures (10%)	100	900
Total long-term finance	1,000	1,000
Situation 1		
Profit	100	100
Debenture interest	10	90
Residue available to equity shareholders	90	10
As a % return on ordinary share capital	$10\%(\frac{90}{900})$	$10\%(\frac{10}{100})$
Situation 2		
Profit increases by 10%		
Profit	110	110
Debenture interest	10	90
Residue available to equity shareholders	100	20
As a % return on capital	11%	20%
Situation 3		
But what would happen if profits decline by 10%?		
Profit	90	90
Debenture interest		
Residue available to equity shareholders		
As a % return on capital		

In situation 1 where both companies make £100,000 profit, ordinary
shareholders receive a return of 10 per cent on their capital after
payment of the debenture interest. But in situation 2 where the profits
of both businesses have increased by £10,000, shareholders in company
A which is low geared receive a return of 11 per cent while in company
B the return has doubled from 10 to 20 per cent. The increase in profits
in the high-geared company has benefited the ordinary shareholders
far more than in company A.

The logic of high gearing then is that if we can borrow fixed-interest
capital and earn a return in excess of the interest charge this will go to
the ordinary shareholders. Moreover the higher the gearing the fewer

the shareholders to spread the excess among, and the more dramatic will be the increase in the return on ordinary shareholders. A subsidiary benefit of high gearing will be that it enables the business to increase its long-term finance without reducing the shareholders' control of the company.

While high gearing benefits the ordinary shareholders in prosperous times, a fall in profits will have an equally dramatic effect on their return. Readers may like to consider what would happen in situation 3 if profits declined by 10 per cent from those in situation 1. There is a real risk that in one year profits may be insufficient to pay the interest on debentures and preference shares. The prudent company will therefore allow itself a margin of safety for fluctuations in profit, and it is recommended that profits should normally cover fixed-interest charges at least three times.

The Euro-currency market

Quite apart from the national market for business finance there exists an international market in Euro-currencies. Euro-currencies are deposits of funds with European banks in a currency other than that of the host country. For example a UK company exporting to the United States may invest the dollars it receives in France or West Germany.

The origin of the market lies in the high rates of interest offered in Europe compared with the United States after the Second World War and the chronic United States balance of payments deficit which greatly increased the availability of the dollar internationally.

As the major currency available is the United States dollar the market is often referred to as the 'Euro-dollar market'; it would, however, be more correct to refer to it as the 'Euro-currency market'.

Euro-currencies have traditionally been used as a source of short-term finance for international trade. More recently though, government and local government agencies have used the market to cover their short-term indebtedness.

It is also possible to borrow longer term from the Euro-currency market in a manner similar to issuing a debenture. Such loans are termed 'Euro-bonds'.

Medium-term sources of finance

Hire-purchase

By this method a firm may obtain assets which are needed in the business immediately, but spreads the cost of payment over a period of up to five years. Normally a down payment of between 20 and 35 per cent of the cost of the asset is required with the remainder, together with interest on the loan, being repaid monthly.

The major attraction of hire-purchase is that no form of security is required for the loan. Instead the asset remains the property of the hire-purchase company until the final payment is made. Moreover, once the finance has been arranged it is impossible to alter the terms of the agreement and the hirer is protected from changes in interest rates.

However, while the cost of hire-purchase facilities will vary from firm to firm it will often be twice that of overdraft facilities. For that reason it is popular with small firms who, without security, are often unable to obtain finance from other sources.

Leasing

It is possible to lease most forms of plant and equipment today. Examples include computers, office machinery, aircraft, dental equipment, and commercial vehicles. In many ways leasing is similar to hire-purchase – the business has the use of an asset which it does not own and has to make regular payments to the lessor under the agreement. The most fundamental distinction between the two is that under a leasing agreement the asset never becomes the property of the business hiring it.

The lessor, who may be the manufacturer, a finance house, a merchant or commercial bank, normally divides the agreement into primary and secondary periods. The lessee is not allowed to repudiate the agreement during the primary period without penalty, for it is during this period that the lessor expects to recover his investment. Thereafter, during the secondary period, the lessee may rent the asset at will and may repudiate at any time without penalty. The rental charged is nominal during this secondary period.

Among the more important advantages claimed for leasing are the following:

1. There is no demand on existing cash resources, nor are other assets tied up as security for the loan.

2. The rental may be paid from income generated by the use of the asset.

3. It is particularly beneficial where assets may become obsolescent rapidly.

4. The lease is a fixed contract, the facility cannot be withdrawn or its terms altered because of changes in the economic climate.

Bank loans

Traditionally, banks have preferred to lend short term; more recently though they have extended their operations into medium- and long-term finance. An agreement is entered into between the bank and its customer whereby a specified sum of money is borrowed for a stipulated period up to a maximum of ten years at a cost of 2–4 per cent above market rates of interest. The agreement will also cover other points such as security, repayment of the loan, and penalties for failing to adhere to the terms of the agreement.

In 1981 the Government introduced a loan guarantee scheme which is designed to encourage banks to provide extra finance for small firms. The scheme is likely to benefit new enterprises lacking security for loans. Under its provisions the Department of Industry will guarantee loans of up to £75,000 made for periods of between two and seven years. The Department of Industry charges the borrower 3 per cent of the guaranteed amount for this service. In the event of the borrower failing to repay the loan the Department of Industry will reimburse the bank.

Venture capital

Cash-rich firms and financial institutions are always looking for new and profitable ways to invest their money. Often the focus of their attention is the young, successful business whose development is being stunted by an inability to raise extra capital. In return for an equity (ordinary share) stake in the business the venture capitalist will provide the finance necessary for development until such time (perhaps five or ten years) as the company can be floated on the stock market. More importantly the venture capitalist can provide that valuable management expertise which may not exist within the business.

Apple, the personal computer manufacturer, is a perfect example of venture capital at work. In 1976 Steven Jobs and Stephen Worsnick aged 21 and 26 respectively were building personal computers in a garage. An investment of equity funds and the introduction of marketing expertise by a venture capitalist resulted in Apple expanding sufficiently to 'go public' in 1980. The owners of the business immediately became multimillionaires.

Of course, not all investments by venture capitalists are so wildly successful. American experience suggests 20 per cent of investments are highly profitable, 20 per cent fail, and the remainder at least break even and probably yield a reasonable return on the investment.

Short-term sources of finance

Bank overdrafts

This is by far the best known and most popular source of short-term funds. Although commercial banks have moved into the medium- and long-term finance markets they still regard themselves primarily as short-term lenders financing borrowing for purposes such as seasonal trade; finance for a specific contract, or to cover the non-payment of a debt.

In deciding whether to grant an advance the bank manager will consider many factors including:

1. The proposition – its viability. How much money will be required? How will the advance be repaid?

2. The borrower – what degree of ability and experience does the borrower have? How much of his own money is the borrower investing in the proposition?

3. Security – in the event of the proposition failing how will the bank recoup its advance?

Technically an overdraft is an agreement by which the customer may draw cheques on his current account to a stipulated limit. Interest is charged daily on the outstanding amount, and the bank will normally require some form of security from the business. Where the business has no assets to offer as security, the owners may be required to give a personal guarantee that the debt will be repaid.

The temporary nature of the overdraft facility is emphasised by the fact that the bank manager may require the overdraft to be repaid on demand. In practice this rarely happens, and although bank advances are normally only made for six months they are often continually renewed by the customer thus providing an almost permanent source of funds.

Factoring and invoice discounting

Delayed payment by customers is often disastrous for small- and medium-sized firms. Poor cash flow will inevitably hinder growth and may in extreme cases force the business into liquidation. Yet it is precisely these firms which, lacking industrial muscle, are likely to find debtors taking an extended period of credit. Factoring and invoice discounting remedy this problem by advancing cash against debtors, thereby turning a credit sale into a cash sale.

Factors actually purchase the book debts, take over administration of the sales ledger, and assume the risk of non-payment. The factor also assumes responsibility for collecting the debts and deals directly with debtor customers.

The benefits of factoring lie in:

1. Providing immediate cash in return for debts thus aiding liquidity.

2. The fact that factoring is not borrowing and therefore does not affect the ability of the business to borrow.

3.   The clerical and administrative savings arising from the factor taking over debt collection.

4.   The reduction in the risk of bad debts.

With invoice discounting the business again sells its debts, but this time is responsible for collecting those debts on behalf of the specialist financier and also for bearing the loss arising from bad debts. Up to 75 per cent of the value of the invoices will be paid immediately, the remainder when the debts are paid.

Invoice discounting, like factoring, has the advantage of providing immediate cash, and not affecting the borrowing potential of the business. It also has the advantage of not revealing to the customer that book debts have been discounted – historically a sign of imminent bankruptcy.

Factoring and invoice discounting provide an important source of immediate funds to many medium-sized firms; however, the cost which is 1–3 per cent of turnover is significantly higher than interest on bank advances.

Specialist institutions

While medium-sized and large firms with good profit records and prospects have little difficulty in raising the funds they need, it has long been recognised that smaller firms may experience difficulties in raising the finance needed to expand operations. While some small firms rely on short- or medium-term sources of finance, especially bank advances or hire-purchase simply through ignorance of other sources, there are some sources which are just not available – the business may be too small to raise money by means of a share issue, or it may not have the assets needed to pledge as security for a loan. Alternatively the cost of finance reflecting risk and administrative expenses may be too high.

Recognising the importance of small firms to the economy the Government and the financial institutions have created a number of bodies designed to bridge the funds gap experienced by this sector of industry.

Finance for industry

Finance for Industry (FFI) is an amalgamation of Finance Corporation for Industry (FCI) and Industrial and Commercial Finance Corporation (ICFC). It is owned and financed by the Bank of England together with the English and Scottish clearing banks.

The Finance Corporation for Industry provides long-term loans for the medium-sized or larger firm where the market is unwilling to provide the funds because of the high degree of risk attached to the investment. Major investments have been made in the mining, steel, and textile industries. More recently funds have been channelled into investments designed to reduce reliance on imported goods.

The Industrial and Commercial Finance Corporation is more concerned with the small firms sector, providing long-term funds – equity or loan capital where it was not readily available from other sources. It also provides a management advisory service for small firms. Also coming under the ICFC umbrella is Technical Development Capital (TDC) which is concerned with the commercial development of technologically based companies, and Estate Duties Investment Trust (EDITH) which seeks to prevent capital transfer tax payable on the debt of an owner of a business causing a break-up of that firm.

Equity capital for industry

Equity Capital for Industry is financed by city institutions (pension funds, insurance companies, and investment trusts are the main contributories) and seeks to aid those businesses whose existing long-term borrowings prevent them raising more loan or equity capital through the normal channels. The funds provided are in the form of an equity stake in the business, and ECI may also require management changes as a prerequisite of support.

Government aid

1. Assisted areas

Regions which have, in the past, suffered higher than average unemployment may benefit from government loans under Section 7 of the 1972 Industry Act. Much of Scotland, Wales, the north-east and the south-west of England are covered by these provisions. Loans will only be granted if:

1. Finance is unobtainable from other sources.

2. They will create new employment or safeguard existing employment.

Loans may also be obtainable for certain areas from government agencies such as: the Highlands and Islands Development Board; the Northern Ireland Finance Corporation; the Council for Small Industries in Rural Areas (CoSIRA); the Scottish Development Agency; the Welsh Development Agency.

Industry aid

The Department of Industry may provide financial assistance under Section 8 of the Industry Act 1972 to specific industries where it is shown that the investment would benefit the British economy. Approximately £250 m. has been granted under these provisions to industries such as textiles, papermaking, clothing and electronic components.

Tax incentives

For many years the Government has encouraged investment through a series of tax allowances. Such allowances may be set against business profits thereby reducing tax liability. Thus the cost of plant and machinery may be set against profits in the year of purchase. Similar allowances are granted in respect of industrial buildings and the extra investment in stock caused by inflation.

There are also special tax advantages to be obtained from starting your business in one of the new Enterprise Zones (e.g. Newcastle upon Tyne, Salford, Speke, Dudley, Corby, Belfast, Wakefield, Hartlepool, Isle of Dogs, Clydebank, and Swansea Valley). These include:

(a) the cost of purchasing any new building can be set against profits in the year of purchase;

(b) complete exemption from local authority rates;

(c) complete exemption from development land tax.

To encourage private investors to finance new small businesses the Government under the Business Start Up Scheme will allow the investor to offset his investment against his highest rate of tax. The maximum investment allowed is £10,000. For example, if an investor pays tax at 60 per cent and invests the maximum of £10,000 allowed in any one year, the Inland Revenue will repay £6,000.

The Stock Exchange

Our discussion so far has concentrated on the primary markets for funds – that is, the specialist institutions who provide finance – long, medium, or short term for business. There is also, however, for long-term funds, a secondary market – a market for existing stocks and shares which aids the transfer of securities between investors. This is termed the Stock Exchange.

In the UK the major centre is the London Stock Exchange. There are also a number of provincial exchanges dealing in stocks and shares of companies generating local rather than national interest. The functions of these Stock Exchanges are to:

1. Provide a market for stocks and shares. Without this market neither the public nor financial institutions would so readily provide finance due to the difficulty of realising their investment.

2. Aid the issue of new securities by granting companies a Stock Exchange quotation.

3. Provide a means of valuing securities.

4. Provide protection for investors by:

   (a) vetting those companies seeking to obtain a Stock Exchange quotation;

   (b) requiring full information to be given to investors by quoted companies;

   (c) providing compensation to any investor who has suffered loss through a broker failing to meet his obligations;

   (d) establishing rules of conduct for members of the Stock Exchange and quoted companies, e.g. the City Code on Take-overs and Mergers.

Stock Exchange procedure

The Stock Exchange is not an open market on which private individuals can transact their business personally, instead the work is carried out by its members – stockbrokers and stockjobbers. Stockbrokers act as agents for investors wishing to buy or sell securities, charging a commission for their service. They are the only members of the Stock Exchange who are allowed to deal directly with the public. Their work also includes giving advice on investments. Many issue a monthly or quarterly newsletter with their recommendations.

Stockjobbers are dealers in stocks and shares acting in rather the same way as wholesalers in the distributive trades. Jobbers tend to specialise in certain groups of stocks, for example gilt-edged (government stock), shipping, textiles, plantations, and earn their living by selling shares for more than they paid for them. They are only allowed to deal with other members of the Stock Exchange.

Let us now consider a typical transaction to see how the Stock Exchange works. Our investor Mr Average instructs his broker to sell 250 British Petroleum (BP) shares 'at best' – that is, the highest price possible. Mr Average may in fact not know a broker and give these instructions instead to his bank, his accountant, or his solicitor – the result is the same with these intermediaries transmitting the instructions to a broker and often sharing his commission.

The broker will then approach jobbers specialising in 'oils' – there are always two and for the more important shares several more – and ask him/them to give a price for BP. At this stage a broker does not reveal whether he wishes to buy or sell and the jobber replies by giving two prices – the lower being what he is prepared to purchase at, and the higher what he will sell for. The difference is known as the 'jobbers turn' or profit, and the more uncertain the market is the wider the margin will be. Keen prices in the market are guaranteed because jobbers are competing against one another for the broker's business, and because they have to quote both buying and selling prices.

Prices quoted by the jobber reflect the supply of and the demand for each individual share. Should the jobber receive a greater preponderance of orders to sell rather than buy BP shares he will adjust his prices downwards. He aims to strike a price at which orders to buy and sell BP broadly match one another. In doing so he ensures that he is not left with too many (or too few) BP shares on his hands. But the adjustments made to the prices of the shares by the jobber do not always reflect buying and selling orders. Sometimes he may feel that there is no good reason why BP shares should be unpopular and will maintain the present price despite a number of orders to sell. In doing so he reduces the temporary fluctuation in price which may occur due to the lumpiness of transactions, but lays himself open to loss if he has read the market feeling incorrectly.

The broker will return to the jobber offering the best terms, confirming that the prices quoted still hold and then reveal that he wishes to sell BP stock. For small transactions the jobber is required to adhere to the prices quoted. If, however, the order is so large that it could depress or raise the price of that share the jobber is not bound to honour those prices.

Once details of the transaction have been agreed the parties note the particulars. Unless the transaction relates to central or local government stock when the settlement is made the following day, all transactions are for 'the account'. The Stock Exchange year is divided into twenty-four account periods, twenty of two weeks and four, around the major bank holidays, of three weeks. Settlement day for company securities is the second Tuesday following the end of the account. On this day all moneys have to be paid and shares handed over.

Traded options
Option dealing is a form of speculation. An option gives the right to buy or sell shares at current prices during the next three months. Should a speculator believe that the share price of BP is going to rise from its present level of 350 he will purchase a call option. This gives him the right to purchase BP at 350 (the striking price) during the next three months. If the price of BP rises, let us say to 400, our speculator will exercise his option to buy at 350 and will then sell these shares in the market at current prices thus realising his profit.

Conversely, should our speculator feel that BP is overpriced he will obtain 'put' option allowing him to sell BP shares at the striking price of 350 in the next three months. Assuming the share price does in fact fall he will exercise his option to sell at 350, purchasing the shares he needs in the market at the lower price.

We have assumed so far that the price of BP moves in line with the speculator's expectations. That is, of course, not always the case. Should the share price move against the speculator he will abandon the option.

Factors affecting the price of shares

The prices at which shares are traded are published each day by the Stock Exchange, extracts of which will be reproduced in the daily papers. Each day you will find that the prices of many shares quoted will have moved. Normally the movement is marginal – perhaps 1 or 2p, but sometimes the variation is more dramatic. Underlying these changes in price is investor confidence which will be based on the factors enumerated below.

1. Primary
Those relating to the firm or industry. Investors follow with great interest the fortunes of each company – after all their money is at stake! The publishing of the interim and annual financial results provides shareholders with periodic information on which to evaluate their investment. But in reality the flow of information on which investors make their judgements is continuous, for example:

- news of an important contract;
- the development of a new product;
- the possibility of a take-over bid;
- increased competition for the firm or the industry;
- the closing of factories or depots;
- the resignation of senior personnel or directors;
- poor labour relations;

may all affect share prices.

2. Secondary
The economic and political environment of business. Business does not exist in a vacuum, and the investor should not ignore the environment within which the firm operates. It is impossible though, to identify all sources of information which may affect the investor's judgement – the following illustrate the diversity of information available:

- indices on inflation, unemployment, economic activity, balance of payments, consumer spending (especially where trends are discernible);

- surveys by the CBI, stockbrokers, universities or other government institutions;
- the value of sterling;
- the United States economy;
- legislation affecting business, e.g. consumer protection or industrial safety;
- international relations;
- political instability in other countries;
- statements by government officials or other heads of state;
- press comment.

Examination questions

1. What are the major sources of finance available to a multinational company?
   (PSC 1981)

2. Critically examine the sources of finance available to a medium-sized engineering company. *(PSC 1977)*

3. A small private limited company wishes to extend its operations. How may it raise the necessary finance? What difficulties could it face?

4. (a) Distinguish between the terms: (i) ordinary share; (ii) preference share; (iii) debenture. 6 marks

   (b) Your business wishes to acquire a computer and has a choice of: (i) immediate payment; (ii) hire-purchase; (iii) leasing. Which would you choose, and why? 10 marks.

5. Comlon a large manufacturing company wishes to extend its business. What sources of finance should it consider and what factors should be taken into account in deciding which sources to use?

6. How is the operation of the Stock Exchange linked to the activities of a public limited company and of central government? *(PSC 1978)*

7. What are the functions of the Stock Exchange? *(PSC 1979)*

8. Explain the work of the Stock Exchange indicating its importance to industry and government.

9. Describe the work performed on the Stock Exchange by jobbers and brokers. How does the Stock Exchange aid the growth of the economy?

10. In what ways do commercial banks assist in the financing of industry and trade?

11. Your employer, a manufacturing company, is undertaking two extra projects:

    (a) to develop a new factory in a depressed area;

    (b) a special order which will be completed in two years.

    Both will involve an extra investment in machines, material, and labour. What sources of finance could you recommend for each of these projects? *(PSC 1982)*

Consultancy,
non-profit-making,
and export services

Chapter 19

Consultancy

Management consultants

As business and its environment become more complex, an ever-increasing burden is placed upon the management of the organisation. Add to this the extent to which many companies in recent years have pruned their workforce (at all levels) and it can be seen that the existing management is ill placed to deal with any problem or project which diverts them from the task of carrying out their routine duties.

Management consultants are independent organisations or individuals who, in return for a fee, will give advice on any problem – or set of problems – which are of concern to the client firm's management. In investigating any problem the consultant will draw upon his wide experience of industry. He is likely to be graduate, probably with a professional qualification as well, and will have had line responsibility and experience in several companies. But the consultant's greatest strength is his accumulated experience as an adviser to companies. While each situation encountered is unique in terms of environment, organisation structure, and personnel, the basic problem is often one which the consultant has met before. He is therefore able to draw upon this reservoir of knowledge in advising his clients.

Management consultants will be used when:

1. The business does not have sufficient managerial time or talent to deal with the problem.

2. Where there is not a permanent need within the firm for the particular skill and expertise required.

3. Where the firm is unable to take a sufficiently detached and analytical view of the problem.

The use of management consultants is now widely accepted in the UK – and indeed most other advanced economies. They are used not only by industry and commerce but also by central and local government and other state agencies. The range of services offered by consultants has grown considerably over the years and now includes:

1. *Policy and planning.* Establishing corporate objectives, medium- and long-term planning, organisation structure and communications problems, control procedures. Advice on expansion – mergers and take-overs.

2. *Marketing function.* Product evaluation, promotional policy, channels of distribution, marketing research.

3. *Financial function.* Advice on financial structure and the raising of capital, profitability, control of working capital, asset utilisation, costing and budgetary control, investment analysis.

4. *Personnel function.* Selection, training, and development schemes, welfare, health, and safety policies; management succession; motivation and wage-payment schemes; industrial relations.

5. *Production function.* Factory location and layout, production planning and control, materials control, quality control, organisation and methods studies.

6. *Management techniques.* Operational research, network analysis, value analysis, simulation techniques, computer applications, systems development.

Advertising agencies

The modern advertising agency has its origins in the work of the nineteenth-century space brokers. These brokers acted as intermediaries between the advertisers and the newspaper and periodical owners. They would purchase large blocks of space in a newspaper or magazine and break it down into smaller lots which would then be sold to the individual advertiser.

For their service to the media owner they received a commission. Thus, should a broker purchase £1,000 worth of advertising space in a newspaper he would be invoiced for £850 (the common rate of commission being 15 per cent), but would sell that space to his clients for £1,000.

Media owners found the service of the space broker very much to their advantage. Administratively, it was easier for the media owner to deal with and obtain his money from a limited number of brokers, rather than the very large numbers of individuals who advertised in his publication. Moreover, the risk of not filling advertising space was borne by the space broker not the media owner.

Indeed it was this last factor which caused space brokers to break from their traditional activities, and move towards the work of the advertising agency as we know it today. Very simply, space brokers saw that it would be much simpler to sell their advertising space if they could show how it should be used. Artists and writers were employed to create advertisements for their clients.

Today's advertising agency still buys space for its clients' advertisements, receiving a commission from the media owner concerned, and still employs artists and writers to produce advertisements. But many agencies offer a far broader range of services. The typical full service agency will undertake all work involved with a large advertising campaign – the planning and buying of media space, together with the creation, production, and testing of the advertisement, as well as marketing research, public relations, sales promotion and new product development. Many of these full service agencies are well-known names such as J. Walter Thompson or Saatchi and Saatchi.

In advertising parlance a clients' business is called an account. Each account held by the advertising agency will be supervised by an account executive. He is the linchpin in the relationship between advertiser and agency, acting as liaison between the two – representing the agency to the client, and translating the client's requirements into action. The account executive must be very much an all-rounder, having experience in all aspects of advertising. He must also be an able co-ordinator and motivator – capable of drawing together those disparate skills needed to service the account, and motivating all those working for him to produce their best work.

In broad terms there will be three groups of people working with the account executive (see Fig. 19.1). The creative team, consisting of copy-writers, artists, typographers, script-writers and film producers, are responsible for developing and producing advertisements. The marketing and market research team are responsible for any research which may be undertaken to identify the target population and their attitudes towards the client's products. As a result of these investigations the client may be advised to alter the product or package in some way, undertake some form of sales promotion other than advertising, or modify their approach to public relations. The team may also carry out advertisement testing.

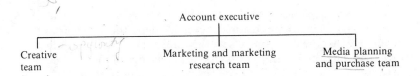

Fig. 19.1 Co-ordination function of the account executive

The aim of the media planning and research team is to identify the appropriate media for the advertisement, and advise on items such as size, length, or timing of advertisements. Having obtained agreement from the advertiser, space or time will then be negotiated with the media owners.

In recent years the traditional agency structure described above has been undermined by a large number of businesses also describing themselves as advertising agencies, but offering a limited specialist service. These agencies have developed through being able to offer a specific service or range of services more expertly and cheaper than the full service agency. Services offered in this way include:

1. Creative agencies – sometimes known as 'hot shops' they specialise in creativity – for example, promoting new products or inventing new product names.

2. Product development agencies – dealing with the whole process of new product development up to and including the commercial launch.

3. Media agencies – specialising in the purchase of time or space from the media owners.

4. Industrial agencies – specialising in the advertisement of industrial rather than consumer products. Their work often involves the production of sales catalogues and literature. They will also negotiate space in specialist magazines and journals.

5. Sales promotion agencies – willing to create and administer competitions, gift coupons, free samples, special offers for other products (e.g. £25 off your holiday), or any of the many other schemes devised to promote sales.

Market research companies

The roots of the independent market research organisation are to be found in the work of the early advertising agencies. Within these agencies market research was used as a tool for establishing the effectiveness of an advertising campaign. Even today many advertising agencies include a market research service as part of their range of activities.

Many large organisations find it possible to carry out their own market research work by creating a specialist department. This has the advantage that the department's workers are not only experts in their own field, but also develop considerable knowledge of the organisation's products. The department is also able to monitor continuously the organisation's markets and the performance of their products.

But large organisations are only able to afford the luxury of their own market research department because its high cost is spread over many products and units of sales. The option of a market research department is not available to medium-sized or small firms. Specialist market research organisations have therefore developed to provide this service.

The function of the commercial market research organisation is to provide its client with information on:

1. The structure of the market – its size, location, organisation, consumers, etc.

2. The acceptability of products – consumer requirements, the popularity of specific products (including competitors), the effect of advertising on acceptability, etc.

3. Channels of distribution – information on the effectiveness of various distribution systems with the aim of:

   (a) reducing the risks to which the client is exposed; and

   (b) identifying and highlighting new market opportunities.

These functions are achieved by planning, implementing, and interpreting market research investigations on behalf of the client. In carrying out these investigations a wide range of statistical and psychological techniques may be used. The procedure for such an investigation is described in Chapter 11 (p. 179).

Many market research organisations provide a complete service and are willing to undertake any kind of market research investigation. There are others, though, who specialise in one aspect of market research work, for example concentrating on consumer as opposed to, say, industrial market research. Alternatively, the organisation may specialise in market research investigations into certain industries (the Nielson Company, for example, provides specialist information on the food and drug industries), or certain research techniques, for example audience surveys or opinion polls.

Non-profit-making services

Chambers of commerce

Chambers of commerce, or chambers of commerce and industry as some (e.g. London, Birmingham) are called, exist in most important commercial centres throughout the U.K. They are voluntary associations of people prominent in local business – industry, commerce, and the professions.

The first chamber of commerce in this country is that of Glasgow which dates back to 1783, while the most important – the London Chamber of Commerce and Industry (LCCI) was established in 1881.

Although chambers of commerce operate individually their activities are linked through membership of the Association of British Chambers of Commerce. This organisation acts as spokesman for the interests of chambers throughout the country, making representations to the Government, and representing chambers on various government bodies.

The work of the chambers of commerce is twofold. In the first place they make representations to central and local government or other bodies on matters of interest to their members. For example during its centenary year the LCCI took up the following issues on behalf of its members (there were many more):

- economic policy, public finance, and taxation policy;
- the structure of local government finance and the level of rates;
- the adequacy of roads, airports, and public transport in London and the south-east of England;
- aid and incentives for small firms.
- further and higher education fees for overseas students;
- unitary tax system in the USA;
- the £1 coin.

Other chambers throughout the country will be making representations on a similarly diverse range of issues.

The second broad area of work chambers of commerce are involved in is the provision of services to the business community. One important aspect of this work is aid and advice on exporting. Information can be provided on openings for trade in overseas countries, the appointment of foreign agents and distributors, international trade procedures and requirements, customs regulations, and legal restrictions. British chambers of commerce arrange overseas trade missions and exhibitions, and will also provide help and advice to overseas trade missions visiting this country. Through British chambers abroad and links with overseas chambers they are also able to provide up-to-date information on conditions in many overseas markets.

The larger chambers of commerce also aid exporters by the issue of 'export of commercial samples' carnets. These allow samples of goods to be imported temporarily into overseas countries without paying duties or going through normal customs formalities. These chambers will also issue certificates of origin, analysis, or quality in respect of goods for export.

At home, chambers of commerce, through their libraries and research facilities, can provide members with information on current legislation, be it employee rights, health and safety, consumer, restrictive practices, food and drug regulations, or many others. Chambers may provide business training courses for executives, many of which are concerned with aspects of exporting, though courses in modern business skills are also run. Many chambers will provide translator and secretarial services. Commercial disputes may also be settled through their arbitration services.

Finally, mention must be made of two chamber of commerce services available nationally. First, through the LCCI's Commercial Education Scheme, examinations are conducted in all commercial subjects, also for the Private Secretary's Diploma and Certificate and the Junior Secretary's Certificate. Courses leading to these examinations and qualifications are provided by many colleges throughout the UK and abroad. Secondly, in conjunction with chambers of commerce in Birmingham, Cardiff, and Merseyside, the LCCI has established a registry of business names *The LCCI Business Registry* which is intended to supersede the *Registry of Business Names* previously controlled by the Department of Trade. Registration is intended to show proprietorship of the business name, reduce the risk of confusion caused by companies having similar names, and 'warn off' a new business which searches the *Register* before setting up in business with a similar name.

Chambers of trade

Chambers of commerce tend to be found in our larger towns and cities, but most towns boast a chamber of trade. Its members are drawn from shopkeepers and traders in the locality. The services of chambers of commerce and trade overlap to some extent. Both seek to establish agreement among their members on matters of common interest and to act as spokesmen on these matters. The distinguishing feature of chambers of trade is that they concentrate almost exclusively on matters of local interest and lack the national and international dimensions of chambers of commerce. Chambers of trade would be concerned with matters such as parking facilities, shop hours, delivery regulations, or the impact of a new road on business in the town.

Trade associations

Although firms in the same industry, trade, or service are often in fierce competition with one another there are many matters in which they have a common interest and where co-operation and joint action are mutually beneficial. Trade associations, such as the Society of Motor Manufacturers and Traders, the Machine Tool Traders Association, or the Advertising Association, are the organisations created by these firms to protect and promote their common interests. Some, like the National Federation of Building Trades Employers, began as employers' associations. These, although initially established to negotiate wages and conditions of work on behalf of all firms in the industry, now offer a far broader service to their members.

Trade associations exist in most sectors of industry and commerce.

Their principal functions are to decide, through meetings and conferences, policy on the many issues which affect their members' interests, and to represent that policy in discussions with the Government and other bodies.

Many trade associations provide a significant range of ancillary activities. Research is often undertaken on new materials or processes. This, and other information on the trade or industry will be made available through journals or magazines published by the trade association. Information on new and better materials, processes, and management practice may also be made available through information exchange bureaux financed and staffed by the association.

On the marketing side trade directories may be published while advertising, export production, and publicity campaigns designed to promote industry's products or image may be undertaken. Many trade associations will give advice to their members on export opportunities or procedures and have available confidential information on potential export or overseas agents.

Many trade associations are themselves members of the Confederation of British Industry, commonly referred to as the CBI. Its primary function is to represent the views of all industrialists (rather than the sectional interests of the individual trade association) to the Government and thereby influence government policy. It is very much part of the tripartite system of consultation established in British politics between the TUC representing the trade unions, the CBI representing business, and the Government. The CBI representatives sit on government bodies, submit evidence to many government enquiries or commissions, and are regularly consulted by government departments on matters affecting industry and commerce.

The CBI provides an advisory service for its members, providing information and advice on a wide range of topics such as legislation, trade statistics, export markets, methods of exporting, and finding overseas agents. It has also established a number of permanent offices abroad.

Export services

For many companies exporting is a step into the unknown. There are so many differences between home and overseas trading. In the first place language, culture, and tastes are often very different. The exporter may very well have to adapt his product to satisfy these tastes. Alternatively, product changes may be necessary to conform with local regulations relating to the sale of the product (e.g. product safety).

Quite apart from these differences in the market, many problems are caused by export documentation and procedure. Although several attempts have been made to reduce and simplify export documentation the would-be exporter is still required to fill in numerous forms. The

importing country will require various forms to be completed in order
to satisfy import regulations, exchange controls, and import duties.
Inevitably the number and content of these forms varies between
countries. Documentation relating to transport (e.g. shipping) and
insurance also tends to be more complex.

Finally the exporter may encounter financial difficulties. Banks may
be less willing to finance export than home trade because of the greater
risk of loss. Developing countries may be less stable politically or
economically. It is more difficult to pursue a claim (and more
expensive) against an importer through foreign courts. Moreover, an
unforeseen fluctuation in the exchange rates may turn the exporter's
profit into a loss.

Large firms are able to cope with many of these difficulties. The
volume of overseas trade undertaken is often sufficient to justify a
specialist function within the firm. Small firms though, unable to
afford this luxury, rely heavily on external aid and advice.

Reflecting the importance of overseas trade to the UK economy,
many such sources of help exist. They fall into one of three categories,
namely governmental, commercial, or non-profit-making. The role of
the latter, non-profit-making, organisations such as chambers of
commerce or trade associations has already been noted in this chapter.
We turn our attention now to the aid provided by government and
commercial organisations.

Governmental

Valuable assistance is given to the exporter through the BOTB and the
ECGD. The BOTB is able to provide advice on a large number of
specific markets together with information on the prospects for
particular goods and services in each of these markets. The BOTB's
export intelligence service also distributes on a daily basis trade
information obtained from Diplomatic Service commercial posts in
approximately 200 overseas centres. Moreover, should such
information be insufficient for the exporter's purposes the BOTB will
give advice on, and financial assistance for, additional market
research.

The BOTB also helps promote British exports by organising
overseas trade fairs, exhibitions, and in-store promotions. Financial
assistance is given to British firms bringing potential importers of their
goods to this country. Similarly, financial help may also be given for
group visits to overseas markets where the visit is sponsored by a trade
association or chamber of commerce. Finally the *Board* in conjunction
with the Central Office of Information and the BBC External Services
operate an export publicity service. Through radio, television and press
releases it aims to publicise the success stories of British Industry.
While the major purpose of the project is to publicise British industry

as a whole, individual firms often benefit from the world-wide publicity.

Since 1921 ECGD has provided credit, insurance, and finance for exports. The basic credit insurance policy, the comprehensive short term guarantee, covers exporters against the risk of loss for periods of up to six months. The policy-holder is required to insure all his export turnover so that the risk of default is spread as widely as possible thereby reducing premiums. In recent years though, due to economic and political instability in developing countries, the ECGD has been forced to modify the policy in respect of some markets by imposing a surcharge or modifying the conditions of cover.

A number of variations on the basic policy exist. The policy, which covers default of the purchaser, government action preventing payment, import restrictions, and civil disturbance in the buyer's country may be extended to cover currency fluctuations, periods in excess of six months, and specific guarantees for large capital projects. Similarly, where an exporter holds goods abroad as stock in trade the ECGD is prepared to insure him against government confiscation of those goods, regulations preventing the re-export of these goods, or the risk of war between the UK and the overseas government.

The ECGD also provides a guarantee against loss of earnings for those firms providing a service to overseas clients, bonds to overseas clients (stating that the exporter will comply with the conditions of the contract – or the buyer will receive compensation), and cover where members of a consortia, participating in overseas contracts, suffer loss as a result of the insolvency of one of their number.

As an insurance agency the ECGD does not itself provide funds for exporters. The ECGD is, however, prepared to give the exporter's bank a guarantee. In the event of the exporter being unable to repay his bank loan (due to the failure of the overseas buyer to pay him as agreed) the ECGD will make good the bank's loss. The bank having received this assurance is willing to finance the exporter's business at favourable rates of interest.

An exporter wishing to obtain these benefits first calculates the maximum amount of export finance that he will need at any one time and then applies to the ECGD for a guarantee to be given to his banker for this amount. Should the department agree to the application it issues a facility letter to the exporter's bank outlining the terms and conditions of the guarantee. At the same time the exporter is required to pay a premium for this service and also to sign a 'recourse agreement' with ECGD. This allows the department to claim from the exporter any sums which it has to pay out under guarantee. The exporter in turn makes a claim against the ECGD under his separate comprehensive short-term insurance policy.

An exporter also has the option of arranging 'buyer credit finance'. This has the advantage of enabling the importer to settle with the exporter on cash terms. These loans carry extremely favourable rates of interest for the importer. Buyer credit finance is often used in large capital contracts undertaken by a consortium of UK firms. Once the principle of buyer credit has been agreed by the consortium and importer a financial institution ready to finance the borrowing has to be found. Most commercial banks are willing to participate in these schemes. The exporter and prospective lender will then approach the ECGD in order to negotiate a 'buyer credit guarantee'. This guarantee will cover the whole of the loan made by the financier and ensures that he will receive payment should the importer default on payments of interest or repayments of capital.

Commercial

Goods may be exported direct or through the services of an intermediary. Where the product being sold is in one of the specialist fields of engineering, where the firm's export business is sizeable, or the exporter has considerable experience of selling overseas selling direct to an importer may prove advantageous. However, in most cases the task of selling directly to an overseas customer is extremely difficult and can create many problems. The small or inexperienced exporter is well advised to turn to one of the many intermediaries in the export trade.

Buying houses

The origins of many buying houses are to be found in the activities of the great trading companies of the British Empire. For very many years these companies have been involved in the export of local produce and the import of those consumer and capital products not manufactured locally. Today it is cheaper and easier for local business to use the buying houses' long-established international connections to find and purchase whatever imports are required than to establish their own network of overseas contacts.

Buying houses are agents for their overseas principals, acting on their instructions and solely in their interests. Their work may be limited to confirming an order which has already been provisionally arranged through other intermediaries. For this reason buying houses are sometimes also known as 'confirming houses'. In confirming the order the buying house guarantees the exporter payment for the goods supplied, paying for them on the due date and recouping their expenditure from the importer.

Where the buying house receives an order from the importer which stipulates the business from which the goods are to be obtained it is termed a 'closed indent'. An 'open indent' specifies the goods to be obtained but leaves the choice of supplier to the buying house. In this case they will discuss contract terms and obtain quotations from several manufacturers before placing an order.

Once an order has been placed the buying house will arrange for the packing and freighting of the goods, and undertake the necessary documentation. For their services to the importer buying houses are paid a commission which is calculated on the value of goods purchased.

Quite separate from their business as agents for overseas firms, buying houses often act as hosts for visiting buyers from overseas countries. Large retail organisations (departmental stores in particular) maintain teams of buyers who visit many countries in search of new, quality goods. Such buyers visit the UK regularly. Details of their visits and the buying houses where they are based are available from the BOTB's Export Intelligence Service, trade journals and the British Export Houses Association's monthly bulletin.

Export houses
In its widest sense the term 'export house' encompasses many of the intermediaries engaged in promoting international trade including buying houses, buying agents, and confirming houses. More strictly the term refers to a situation where the house acts as manager for a manufacturer's export business, or purchases on its own behalf.

An export management agency acts as a UK firm's export department. The agency is responsible for familiarising itself with the exporter's product range, conducting market research to identify suitable outlets, entering into contracts on their principal's behalf, and dealing with all aspects of export administration.

Many export management agencies will also act as export factors. In this role they pay the manufacturer for the goods as soon as they are shipped, obtaining settlement at a later date from the overseas customers. This is primarily a financial service to the exporter not a form of insurance. The export management agency is not a party to the contract and may (depending upon the terms of the contract) have recourse to the exporter should the buyer fail to make payment to the agency. However in return for an extra fee or commission the agent may guarantee the exporter against bad debts. In these circumstances he is termed a *del credere* agent and the extra payment he receives is termed the *del credere* commission.

Export merchants, unlike management agencies, operate on their own behalf. The merchant purchases goods from the exporter on his own behalf as principal, and then resells them at a profit to an overseas client. The merchant thus takes the risk of not finding a customer, or not making a profit on the transaction. The merchant at the same time as purchasing the goods may also negotiate a 'sole distributorship' agreement giving him exclusive rights to sell this product in specified markets overseas. The merchant may then appoint distributors to act for him in different localities or alternatively undertake distribution himself.

Overseas agents
These are intermediaries who undertake, in return for a payment, to
represent an exporter in an overseas market. Great care should be
taken before appointing such an agent – a wrong decision may result in
few export orders, a damaged reputation, and much wasted time and
money. The exporter must ensure that the prospective agent:

- is not representing a competitor;
- has experience in promoting the right group of products;
- has the ability (finance staff and other resources) to take on
  additional commitments;
- has a good reputation within the business community;
- is able to supply satisfactory credit and trade references;
- shows an enthusiasm for the exporter's business.

Exporters looking for an overseas agent to represent their business
may obtain help from various sources. The BOTB, with the help of
British embassies, provides an Agency Finding Service. The large
commercial banks maintain lists of suitable agents. They will also
provide information on the prospective agent's financial standing and
arrange introductions where required. Chambers of commerce,
through their connections with overseas chambers, provide a similar
service to that of the BOTB and the banks. They will also advise on the
form and terms of agreement which should be entered into with an
overseas agent.

It is important that the terms of the agreement are clearly
understood by both exporter and agent. Once an agent is appointed his
position is protected by law. Dismissal will be difficult and costly. A
typical agreement will contain terms relating to the area in which he is
the exporter's representative, whether he is the sole or exclusive
representative in that area, the products covered by the contract, what
sales promotion he is required to undertake, how he is to be paid, the
date the agreement starts and ends, reasons for terminating the
agreement, and provision for arbitration in the case of a dispute.

Shipping and freight forwarding agents
Where a manufacturer conducts his own export business, either
personally or through an agent, much of the detailed work associated
with overseas trade can be avoided by using shipping and freight
forwarding agents. Shipping agents perform the more limited service,
dealing with the transportation of goods from port to port. Freight
forwarding agents, on the other hand, undertake to convey goods from
the manufacturer's to the agents or importer's premises overseas. In
doing so they will:

1. Advise on the best form of transport, having regard for the nature
   of the goods, their destination, the time factor, the costs involved,
   and the buyer's wishes.

2. Advise on packing, labelling, and export documentation to conform with the requirements of the carriers and regulations of the importing country.

3. Arrange freight space, warehousing, customs clearance, and co-ordinate all transporation.

4. Offer the benefits of special (low) freight rates through the grouping of numerous exporter's products into one large consignment.

5. Provide container facilities, especially for traffic between the UK and Europe.

Shipping and freight forwarding agents advise on and arrange transportation for a very large proportion of UK exports.

Banks

Almost inevitably exporting makes extra demands on a firm's financial resources. Generally both delivery of the goods and payment for them take longer. However, in accordance with Bank of England instructions, banks in the UK will give priority to providing finance for those firms engaged in exporting. This finance can be provided in a number of ways.

Many businesses will already have an overdraft facility with their bank. It is extremely easy to extend this facility to provide the extra funds required for exporting. For a small premium the ECGD will guarantee that it will reimburse the exporter's bank should the importer default on payment. Drawing on existing bank overdraft facilities provides much of the finance for 'open-account' transactions (nearly three-quarters of UK exports are paid for by this method). Under an open-account transaction goods, together with all necessary documents, are sent to the buyer. He, in return, agrees to pay the amount owing within a specified period – normally not more than six months. The method is particularly appropriate where there are regular two-way dealings between the firms with say, a UK firm exporting goods to a firm in Hong Kong and importing goods from the same business.

The use of the open-account method of payment is based upon trust in the integrity of the importer – often established over many years' trading. There are, however, many situations where the degree of trust between the two parties is insufficient to warrant using this method of payment. Historically, the most important alternative has been the bill of exchange (see Ch. 17, p. 319). Here the banking system aids the exporter in two very different ways.

First, the exporter may utilise his bank's international connections by sending a bill of exchange for the value of the exports to the importer through the banking system. The UK bank will pass the bill of exchange, plus all relevant documents, to its overseas branch (or bank which acts for it). This bank – termed the collecting bank – presents the bill to the importer for him to sign and acknowledge liability. The documents are then released to the overseas buyer. This procedure gives the exporter greater control over his goods, and also means that the importer does not have to pay for the goods before delivery.

Secondly, banks are also willing to either purchase bills of exchange from the exporter holding them to maturity, or alternatively advance moneys against the security of the bill.

Finally, banks may also aid the exporter by means of a documentary letter of credit – a method by which the exporter receives payment. It consists of a promise by a banker that bills of exchange drawn upon the bank will be honoured, provided the exporter has complied with the terms of the credit. It has the advantage of replacing the name of the little-known importer on the bill of exchange for that of a well-known bank. The exporter is thus able to discount the bill more easily and at a finer rate of interest.

The letter of credit is established by the overseas buyer instructing a bank in his own or the exporter's country to accept a bill of exchange (alternatively the letter of credit could stipulate immediate payment for the goods) against the deposit of documents relating to the goods being exported. By selecting a reputable bank the exporter is guaranteed payment, and the importer is confident that the export documents needed for transfer of title have been completed satisfactorily and delivered to the bank.

Letters of credit are normally irrevocable. By this we mean that once the exporter has agreed or complied with the terms of the letter of credit they cannot be cancelled or altered without the exporter's agreement.

Even greater security of payment can be obtained by the exporter should the irrevocable letter of credit be 'confirmed' by the UK bank through whom the credit is advised. Provided then that the exporter has conformed to the terms of the letter of credit the exporter will receive payment from the confirming bank who in turn look to the overseas bank for payment. The exporter is not liable to reimburse the confirming bank in the case of default on payment by the overseas buyer or his bank.

Examination questions

1. Chambers of commerce, trade associations and the CBI are all concerned with the promotion of trade. Outline the work of *two* of them.

2. What are chambers of commerce? How do they differ from employer's associations? In what ways are they useful to business people?

3. A company manufacturing electrical consumer products wishes to improve its marketing. How could market research companies and advertising agencies help?

4. Outline the services offered to the business community by management consultants.

5. Outline the major functions and the relationships which exist between the business community and two of the following: advertising agencies; market research companies; management consultants. *(PSC 1978, 1981)*

6. Selecting examples from your own country, explain how the process of exporting may be aided by both government and non-government bodies. *(PSC 1978)*

7. What factors discourage firms from exporting? How does the Government help overcome these difficulties?

8. Outline the work of the main organisations concerned with the selling and arrangement for the shipment of exports. *(PSC 1979)*

9. How may a country improve its export trade? Why is such trade important? *(PSC 1980)*

10. Your firm has decided to enter the export market for the first time. What difficulties does it face? Briefly outline what help and advice is available to it.

Index